Also by R. W. Apple Jr.

Apple's America
Apple's Europe

FAR FLUNG AND WELL FED

The Food Writing of

R. W. APPLE JR.

ST. MARTIN'S GRIFFIN
NEW YORK

www.stmartins.com

Book design by Phil Mazzone

The Library of Congress has cataloged the hardcover edition as follows:

Apple, R. W. (Raymond Walter).
    Far flung and well fed : the food writing of R. W. Apple Jr. / R. W. Apple Jr.—1st ed.
        p. cm.
    ISBN 978-0-312-32577-0
    1. Gastronomy. 2. Food habits. 3. Cookery, International. 4. Dinners and dining. I. Title.
TX637.A65 2009
641'.013—dc22

                                                                                    2009016755

ISBN 978-0-312-65063-6 (trade paperback)

First St. Martin's Griffin Edition: December 2010

10   9   8   7   6   5   4   3   2   1

To the next generation—Catherine and Grant,
John and Charlotte, travelers all

CONTENTS

ACKNOWLEDGMENTS

Far Flung and Well Fed is most certainly a celebration of a life on the road aided and abetted by so many. Sadly, Johnny is not here to thank and acknowledge all the many good and generous souls who fed and inspired him over the years. A heartfelt thank-you to all the chefs, sous-chefs, sommeliers, waitstaff, cheese makers, winemakers, farmers and inspired ones whose years of hard work made for many a splendid meal described here in this book.

Elizabeth Beier of St. Martin's Press and Alex Ward of New York Times Books have been enthusiastic champions of this book. Many thanks for their unwavering support. My mother, brother and I are all deeply grateful.

A big thank-you to Corby Kummer for his eloquent foreword about Johnny's food writing and for his constant friendship.

In particular, we would like to thank *The New York Times*. Johnny loved being a reporter, and even more, he loved being a reporter for *The New York Times*.

Far Flung and Well Fed tells the story of a man with a boundless enthusiasm and curiosity. Yet it is also the story of my stepfather, Johnny, and his wife (and my mother), Betsey, and their adventures around the world. Johnny was lucky to have found a fellow traveler in Betsey. Her intelligence, wit and patience made a perfect foil for "the Big Boy," as we called him. Johnny greatly appreciated her acute observations and, most important for their travels, her timekeeping; she always managed to get him to the airport on time!

—Catherine Collins

EDITOR'S NOTE

For over 40 years, my stepfather, R. W. Apple Jr., reported for *The New York Times* on war, politics and culture in more than 100 countries. Universally known as Johnny, he lived a good deal of his adult working life on the road and traveled just as often for pleasure. He toted stacks of maps, Michelin guides, history books, a bottle of Tabasco and a pocket-size pepper grinder wherever he went. No matter where Johnny landed, whether Des Moines or Tehran, he knew where to head for a good meal, high or low. Only Johnny could have sourced the best *kafta* (meatballs) in Monrovia, or famously warned fellow reporters on President Clinton's trip to Uganda, "No prawns at this altitude!"

Johnny's interests were wide—history, music, art and architecture. But food, and later, writing about it, became his great passion. It allowed him to do what he relished most: to travel, learn, taste and report. He regarded a country's food as the story of its people, its culture and its history, without which one couldn't hope to understand or report on a place.

Far Flung and Well Fed is a collection of Johnny's food writing from around the world. The book is organized geographically by country and region and takes the reader on a gastronomic journey of the first order. With his reporter's eye, his gourmand's palate and his big

Midwestern heart, he takes us from the shores of the Chesapeake Bay to the elegant rooms of Taillevent in Paris to the food stalls in Singapore. But this is not a guidebook. Rather, it is a memoir of some lively and unforgettable adventures. While the reader will certainly be inspired to seek out restaurants that Johnny wrote about, or to track down some of the local produce he sampled, fair warning: Some restaurants may no longer exist and producers may have moved on to other ventures.

On a personal note, it has been an immense pleasure to work on this book. Johnny's writing is so vivid and his voice so distinct that reading hundreds of his food pieces brought back many memories. I remember one time Johnny took us—my brother and me—to Allard, a 1930s Left Bank bistro with hearty traditional fare. It was our first trip to France, and after several visits to two- and three-stars where we would squeal, "Ooh, that fish still has its head on it," or "Calves brains—that is gross," Johnny had had enough. "Right," he bellowed as we were ushered into Allard, "no more cheese pizzas." He then proceeded to order the Challans duck with olives. He blinked and the duck was gone. Since then, we've probably eaten at more Michelin-starred restaurants with him as "the kids" than we ever will as adults!

Yet it is the cozy dinners around his kitchen table in Georgetown that I miss the most. There, he would be at his most relaxed as he cooked up something inspired from his travels, told tales of the politicians, chefs, winemakers and artists whom he'd met along the way, described a painting that he'd detoured to see in a small museum or recounted a fascinating bit of history that he had just learned. And then, as the glow from the last trip waned, he would invariably start planning another trip, and the cycle would begin again. He opened a wider world for me with his infectious enthusiasm and curiosity, and I believe *Far Flung and Well Fed* will do the same for you.

—Catherine Collins
Dubai, 2009

FOREWORD

by Corby Kummer

For years and years there wasn't a food and travel writer alive who didn't want to be Johnny Apple and have his expense account and his wife, Betsey—preferably both. But what they didn't have, as this feast of a collection demonstrates on every page, was his style, gusto and encyclopedic field of reference. Not to mention his diligence.

It was a legendary expense account, yes. "A big number," he said to me one day, and then named it. I nearly fell off my chair, and I wasn't sitting down. But what use he put it to! Like what the French and the Chinese do with the pig, I'd say. Every trip, every meal got turned into a piece—often, several, for *The New York Times,* of course, and also for a range of other magazines he wrote for, in the kind of careful retreading a beginning freelancer works months to line up. Or an extremely experienced and successful—and driven—one.

And the productivity! Long before the day of the blogger who feels compelled to share every trivial thought and petty, undigested experience, Johnny filed constantly, on wars, on an unbroken string of presidential campaigns, on world-shaking and chaotic events in calm, magisterial Page One accounts so sweeping that editors made his name into a verb ("Let's Apple that"). He would meticulously plan his trips and come home and file stories seriatim, sitting down early each morning at the "piano," as he called the laptop keyboard.

Far Flung and Well Fed is a time capsule not only of the diners, crab houses and satay stalls that were open when Johnny and Betsey schlepped to every one of them, but of an era in journalism when one voice could guide you around the world as tastes changed (including his), being by turns your pontificating uncle, your chiding brother, your friend. And it is a guide to restaurants and food you'd like to eat made by people you'd like to meet, all written with a grandiose panache not even the *Times* could coin a word for.

This book is really Johnny's invitation to the world as he traveled it whenever the whim suited him, becoming as fascinated by the food and agricultural history of a place as he was by its cultural and political history. Send him a particularly sweet and juicy grapefruit, as a Georgetown neighbor did, and he'd be off to McAllen, the "heart of the Texas citrus industry," to find out what made it so good.

And this being Johnny, the neighbor was Ken Bentsen, nephew of a four-term senator named Lloyd Bentsen. Johnny made it his business to know everyone who ran the world, and wasn't coy about letting drop that a guest at one of his dinners had been, say, Paul Bocuse. When he went to see how Galatoire's and other iconic New Orleans restaurants were faring post-Katrina, he dined with a fellow Lucullan, Paul McIlhenny, heir to the makers of Tabasco sauce and one of several McIlhennys living on Avery Island, a few hours down the Gulf Coast. He had already stayed with his friend and feasted on the fare of Eula Mae Doré, the family cook and a regional legend. Of course, Doré put on the dog, dressing up the traditional Acadian chicken and sausage gumbo with andouille sausage and a goose McIlhenny had shot himself. Everybody put on the dog for Johnny.

But he also made it his business to know everyone who made good food. Plebeian fare available to all is much more abundant in this collection than put-on-the-dog meals available to Johnny and Betsey alone. On another trip along the Gulf Coast, he goes out of his way to find Bonin's, a Cajun butcher shop in New Iberia that is a favorite of McIlhenny's and Calvin Trillin's, and to note approvingly that the customers who line up for warm, spicy boudin squeeze the sausage filling out of the casing as they leave the store. While visiting Milwaukee, he drives an hour north to Sheboygan to visit Terry's Diner, "a no-frills establishment housed in a battered, concrete-brick building in a working-class neighborhood," for "smoky sausage and crusty semmel crumbling together in the mouth, condiments merging into a single slithery sharpness and buttery juices dribbling down the shirt." He might get advice on Philly cheesesteaks and Singaporean street food from colleagues he would be sure to credit (most unusual for a journalist), from food celebrities and from celebrity celebrities. He was, after all, a reporter, and something of a starstruck one at that. But he made the results accessible to everyone, noting and adding the contact information and hours he always, being a reporter, took down and filed along with his stories.

And, being one of the Last of the Lucullans, Johnny ate everything. A Singaporean street-food "feed," as he would call it, would be more like a morning binge as he hit one street vendor after another, interspersed with stops at a dim sum palace or two. Researching Cajun food for a comprehensive, for-the-ages piece, he remarks: "The day I went to Suire's I had already eaten a lot. I might say I had already eaten breakfast and brunch, but that would be a lie. In fact, Suire's was my third lunch of the day; there is so much good food in Acadiana that sometimes you have to extend yourself." Betsey, sensibly, wouldn't find her way to the feast any earlier than lunch (and would limit herself to one).

He was large in his appetites. "Fat," as he often called himself, though always dapper in the trademark picnic-check shirts that inspired a number of followers, including me as I write this, to say we're wearing our Johnny shirts whenever we put one on. He ate seriously and he liked rich.(He wrote approvingly and slyly about Curnonsky, "the self-styled Prince of Gastronomes," who suggested stewing a pound of morels with three ounces of butter and a quarter pint of thick cream and turning the result into puff pastry shells: "But, of course, he never met Jenny Craig.") His eating was pre-PC, pre–environmentally trigger sensitive, pre–obsessed with worker conditions, and pre-locavore—pre-"locavore" as even a word. But he was also an early and ardent champion of the artisan, utterly dedicated to who made your food and to putting a face to it before it was the fashion. His natural gregariousness put Johnny years ahead of the Slow Food times.

A theme running through *Apple's Europe* and *Apple's America*—the two previous passe-partout guides that with this make a triumvirate—is his love of characters and his ability to fall in fast love. In these pages he falls in love with food and then with the person who makes it, not always in that order. For instance, he meets Robert Stehling, maker of champion breakfasts ("Funny about breakfasts: You remember the best ones for a long time, always in geographical context") at Hominy Grill, in Charleston, and keeps going back for more of Stehling's food—biscuits and gravy, shad roe with scrambled eggs, meatloaf sandwich with green-tomato ketchup—and his story.

Once a food friend, always a friend. Johnny was a complete loyalist, to the food people he admired and also to his fellow political reporters. A fact far less noted than his expense account was that his generosity was just as big. Some people took his magnanimousness for grandiosity, pointing out that he had been everywhere, he knew everyone, he recognized young political and cooking talent before anyone else did and singlehandedly created careers, he was always right. (All true, to varying degrees.) But they failed to add that he was as quick to aggrandize others as himself. He threw a bearish arm around almost every new colleague and spent a good part of any conversation praising friends and protégés. The last time I saw him, a few weeks before he died, he spent a good part of our visit telling me how terrific his new editors at the *Times* were (and characteristically claimed credit for getting two of them hired).

Every page in *Far Flung and Well Fed* has some bit of information you should have known but didn't, showing the love of esoteric knowledge that almost matched Johnny's love of people. Those Sheboygan brats are pronounced the German way to rhyme with "pot," not "pat." Alewives are menhaden. Soft-shell crabs grow new exoskeletons and are best within four days of molting. References to classical authors and art and architecture pop up everywhere—a John Marin landscape in Maine, a Craftsman-style roadside restaurant. So are quotations from the best food writers or authoritative if esoteric books: C. Anne Wilson's *Book of Marmalade,* Jane Grigson on anything. So is his own field of reference. No one but Johnny could encounter *acarejes,* African-influenced fritters with a base of bean purée, ginger and dried shrimp, in a restaurant in the Bahia region of northeastern Brazil and write, "I wouldn't swear to it, because nobody's taste memory is that good, but I think I once ate something very similar in Benin, the long, narrow country just west of Nigeria that gave birth to voodoo."

And there's the sheer pleasure of his writing. I kept coming upon wish-I'd-thought-of-it descriptions like "glacier-white plates" and "tofu fresh as springwater," and wish-I'd-written-it sentences with musical rhythm like "Most of what is sold these days is nothing but sugar, sugar, sugar, but at its best, water ice has the unmistakable tang of fresh fruit, intensified." He stayed current, calling morel foragers "secretive souls who guard their happy hunting grounds as carefully as their PIN codes." He delighted in tossed-off turns of phrase like "deep-fried catfish, as crisp as tissue paper." You can just hear his knowing chortle when pointing out a cook's reply when he asks how she made a "smashing three-mushroom tart": "'With cèpes and other things,' she said with studied vagueness." Or describing as "twee"—a favorite word of his—a Devon tearoom in the village of Lustleigh that "looked as if it must be inhabited by dainty mice wearing pinafores." Or finding the object of a long New York City quest and declaring, "Real kosher corned beef isn't unobtainable after all."

Johnny's judgment was flawless, which is a critic's way of saying that when we ate the same thing we agreed. He described, for instance, Cowgirl Creamery's finest product as "rich, creamy, subtly tart, triumphantly cheesey cottage cheese that puts soupy commercial rivals to shame." But even when you've eaten nothing even vaguely like what he is describing, reading Johnny is like eating.

Yes, this culinary atlas was the result of a legendary expense account. But it will have a longer half-life than any other I can think of. It remains joyously current, and will have you mapping out road trips to discover, as I intend to, the regional American sweets he found.

Who could fail to *need* to taste the butterscotch sundae at Ted Drewes, the St. Louis birthplace of frozen custard, with butterscotch "the color of a lion's mane and the texture of satin, with the real roasted-sugar flavor usually found only in Scotland"? (I didn't share all of Johnny's appetites—that would be hard—but I certainly did for anything sweet, and we both had a dangerous craving for "tablet," the hard Scottish sweet he means.) Or you'll be plotting your way to Singapore for the world's best, and perhaps safest, street food. Or to that twee Lustleigh tearoom.

We won't see Johnny's like again, and not just because there won't be another Johnny. The system that allowed him to hone his craft and become pro, pundit and sage is being progressively dismantled; the world he wrote in—the one that made his adventures and, just as important, his expense account possible—is unlikely ever to exist again. So this collection is a tribute to both a nonpareil character and a specific moment in journalism.

And it is a tribute to a nonpareil marriage. Betsey, from whom Johnny would part on the telephone with "Love you to pieces" and whom he mentioned in every travel and food article he wrote ("like counting the Ninas," he said, meaning the hallowed Sunday *Times* game when looking at an Al Hirschfeld drawing), was his traveling partner and his spiritual home base. He reveled in her company and her reactions. "'Mmmmmm,' said Betsey, who was too busy slurping to compose one of her customary apothegms.'" About a cherry pie in Beulah, Mich.: "I have shivers down to my toes." She was a constant companion and a constant delight—and he loved her enthusiasm, because enthusiasm was the wellspring of his own love of people and place and food.

On our last visit, he told me that he had recently advised the *Times* food section to "Make room for enthusiasts. Make people want to call up and order what you're writing about, to go out and eat it." Johnny made you love learning and eating almost as much as he did, even if you could never learn or eat anywhere near as much as he did. He was always engaged, never indifferent. If we can't follow his and Betsey's every footstep—no one ever will—we can aim for that.

Food should taste like what it is.

—**Curnonsky**

INTRODUCTION
The Good Life: How Good *Is* It?

I really can't say when I decided what the good life might be, and I certainly never set out in pursuit of it. But as far back as I can remember, about 60 years or so, I knew I wanted to travel, which probably had a lot to do with my conviction that Akron, Ohio, where I was brought up, was not exactly the Athens of the flatlands. To travel where? To see and do what? The answers to those questions emerged more slowly.

My wanderlust, as it turned out, has been a lifelong companion. It led me to take up writing, a highly portable activity, as a vocation. In my younger years, journalism gave me an orchestra seat at some of the great events of my time and the opportunity to portray and try to explain them to a distant audience. More recently, it gave me the opportunity to circle the globe, writing about food and drink, travel and the arts, subjects dear to my heart that I had learned more about in my decades on the road, frankly, than in my sketchy university career.

For me, this has been the good life: the privilege of living on four continents and reporting from a hundred countries, knowing remarkable people like the Rev. Dr. Martin Luther King Jr. and Margaret Thatcher (as well as equally intriguing, if less earthshaking, figures like John Gielgud and Julia Child), covering ten presidential elections and a dozen wars and revolutions and witnessing momentous events like the tumultuous 1968 Democratic convention and the fall of the Berlin Wall. All those things, plus the chance to explore the great cities of the planet, to delve into the riches of the natural world, to hear the great singers and orchestras, to visit the great museums, to view from close range the great buildings of the present and the past and to eat and drink at the tables of the great chefs.

Obviously it hasn't been all Champagne and caviar. I have thrilled to Japanese moss gardens in the rain. I have been swept away by the incredible color and vitality of India. I adore the calm of the Cotswolds, where my wife and I have a cottage. But I could have done without the philistine tank towns I had to visit on the political beat and the winter nights in Moscow when my nose would freeze as I trudged from my flat to my car. I didn't much like the slogs through Vietnamese rice paddies with water up to my armpits, either, or a flight into Biafra on an elderly plane flown by a cowboy who refueled himself from a pint of whiskey. But, on balance, it has been a hell of a ride, and it isn't over yet.

I don't think I ever covered a story as important, wrenching and ultimately gratifying as the civil rights struggle in the American South, which changed the world forever. The protesters in Birmingham had to withstand assault by fire hoses and dogs, and their leader, Dr. King, was very nearly killed by a segregationist's bomb as he sat in the A. G. Gaston Motel. I happened to be there that night, and amid the chaos it never occurred to me that the black people of Birmingham and of the South in general stood on the brink of victory. I could never have imagined that on another night, 26 years later, I would stand in Prague as the Velvet Revolution neared a climax and listen to thousands of Czechs singing "We Shall Overcome," the swelling anthem of Dr. King's movement.

Often big stories landed me in the midst of, or within reach of, sites and sights of rare beauty. On my first trip back to Iran after having covered the revolution there, I persuaded my minder to let me travel to Isfahan to see its serenely elegant blue mosque, convincing him that I was a cultural journalist temporarily sidelined into less noble work (well, close enough). During a summit conference in Venice, security forces swept nearly all the boats from the Grand Canal, affording the privileged few of us who remained the chance to see that matchlessly exotic city almost as it must have looked two or three centuries ago. And during my days in East Africa, I had breakfast many mornings with a giraffe—my house adjoined a Nairobi game park, and he would crane his long neck into my garden.

There was a time, while the cold war raged, when I made quite a few reporting forays into then-forbidding places like Bulgaria and Romania, but I regularly managed to give myself a little R&R in Vienna. At the time the Hotel Imperial did not charge the moon for its sumptuous rooms, and I would put up for two or three days before plunging back into the people's paradises to the east. Herr Benes, the concierge, would always produce a ticket for *Fidelio* or *The Magic Flute.* Years later, when I took my wife, Betsey, to that most musical of cities at Christmastime, I had to reach a little higher for tickets to the famous New Year's concert at the Musikverein. Stymied everywhere I turned, I finally found a pair by lodging an appeal with the Austrian chancellor, Bruno Kreisky. He gave me his.

I have no musical talent myself (I was a boy soprano, and when my voice broke, that was it), nor have I ever longed to write poetry or fiction (I got about 50 pages into a novel once, which was enough to send me, reeling, back to journalism). But I aspired for a time to be an architect. Poking around the country on political duty over the years, I have stumbled upon many little-known gems, like Frank Lloyd Wright's Dana House, in Springfield, Illinois, and Louis Sullivan's National Farmers' Bank, in Owatonna, Minnesota. My army years paid dividends, too, allowing me to wander across Virginia on weekends, soaking up the genius of Thomas Jefferson, architect, in Charlottesville and elsewhere. One afternoon in Glasgow, traveling on a campaign bus with Prime Minister James Callaghan, I spotted a fascinating-looking building, asked the driver to stop and jumped off. The rest of that day's activities on the hustings went unreported. The building was the Glasgow School of Art, the masterpiece of Charles Rennie Mackintosh, of whom I had never heard. Wised up, I took out a life membership in the Mackintosh Society a few days later. Another passion, Romanesque architecture, took longer to develop, but great cathedrals like Autun, in Burgundy, and Durham, in northern England, with their massive arches and evocative sculpture, quickly leaped to the top of my private hit parade.

People constantly ask me, now that I write a lot about food, to name the best meal I ever ate. It's an impossible question to answer, and not only because I have eaten so many, on duty and off. How do you compare a luscious lobster roll in Maine with a plate of gossamer dim sum in Hong Kong with an array of *smørrebrød* in Copenhagen, all of which I wake up craving several times a year? I like quotidian food quite as much as haute cuisine; both are equally important to the good life, as long as they are good. Same with wine. A really well-made Sancerre (from Henri Bourgeois, perhaps) is as satisfying in its way, as much a part of the good life, as a well-aged Barbaresco from Angelo Gaja. But, 35 years later, I still remember the meal that first convinced me that the French were the world's master chefs (I remain convinced, although the Australians, with their magnificent raw materials and stunning ability to blend East and West, are giving the French a run for their money lately). It was in the little industrial city of Roanne, near Lyon, at Troisgros, which had two stars then, and has had three for decades now. The menu: thrush pâté, the now-famous scallop of salmon with sorrel sauce, a chunk of superlative Charolais beef with poached bone marrow, a gratin *forézien* (scalloped potatoes with a Ph.D.) and a chariot of desserts, including fresh and poached fruits, sorbets, ice creams, tarts and cakes. It came with lots and lots of wonderful Burgundy, white and red, and it left me in a state of pure bliss.

I ought to say how many thousands of happy, even exalting hours I have spent looking at pictures, especially by Carpaccio and Dürer and van Eyck, among the Old Masters, and by Matisse and Malevich and Pollock, among the new. And how important books have been to me—fiction when I was younger, mostly history and biography now. I can't imagine living the good life without piles of books beside my bed, on tables and chairs, on the floor, everywhere, although I am not yet as depraved as Isaac Foot, the English bibliophile who nearly drove his wife mad by piling books on their staircase.

What stitched my good life together for many years was the satisfaction that I was contributing my bit to the commonweal by doing work, as my friend and colleague Martin Nolan once described it, "of marginal social utility." But I am an old dog now, and I have come to see that the sine qua non of the good life is home and family. Many years ago, my wife's father gave her mother a copy of a sonnet, composed and finely printed by the great Belgian typographer Christophe Plantin, entitled *Le Bonheur de Ce Monde*—"Happiness in This World." It came eventually to our house, where it hangs to this day, celebrating food, wine and flowers, all things that mean a lot to both of us. My favorite phrases, however, are those that speak of the joys of *une maison commode, propre et belle*—"a roomy, clean and pretty house"—and *une femme fidèle*—"a loyal wife."

Those I have, in spades.

—*Washington, D.C., November 2005*

NORTH AND
SOUTH AMERICA

NORTHEAST / MID-ATLANTIC

The Glorious Summer of the Soft-Shell Crab

The sun was a blood-orange disk pinned to the horizon as Thomas Lee Walton eased his 24-foot Carolina Skiff into the creek and headed toward the Rappahannock River. An osprey was perched in a dead tree on the far shore. It was 6:05 a.m. We were going crabbing.

Our quarry was the Atlantic blue crab—*Callinectes sapidus* to marine biologists, which means "savory beautiful swimmer" in Latin. But not the run-of-the-mill fellows you boil up with plenty of Old Bay seasoning, then crack with a hammer before pulling out the sweet, delicate white meat. Mr. Walton fishes for "busters" or "peelers," which are crabs that have already begun to shed their shells, or are about to, before growing new ones.

"Watching them shed," Mr. Walton said with a tender reverence suprising in a rugged outdoorsman, "it's like they're reborn."

If you catch them at the right moment and pull them from the water, the process of growth stops and you have a soft-shell crab, one of summer's most prized treats, not only here on the rim of the Chesapeake Bay, but also, increasingly, in cities across the United States.

They seem to be on every menu in New York this summer, prepared in more or less the same way: You eat the whole thing, claws, legs and all, sautéed or grilled, maybe seasoned with a squeeze of lemon juice. Before you try one, it sounds decidedly dubious, like tripe or seaweed. But a single taste makes a convert.

Years ago, I served a soft-shell, grilled in my garden, to Paul Bocuse, who formed a wildly inflated view of my cooking skills as a result. Soft-shells can be deep-fried, too, which makes them crunchier, and good ol' boys like to stick them between two slices of white bread to make sandwiches. Me, I prefer my soft-shells sautéed, because I think the crust masks the flavor.

All crabs molt, up to 20 times during their lives; they must do so to grow. But the soft-shell form of the Dungeness crab on the Pacific Coast or the king crab in Alaska is seldom eaten, if ever, and Europeans use soft-shell crabs mostly for bait. In this as in so many things gastronomic, the Venetians are an exception. They consider Mediterranean shore crabs that have shed their carapaces, which they call *moleche*, a great delicacy.

Even here, where soft-shells have been savored for more than a century, putting them on gourmands' tables is a dicey proposition, requiring luck, hard physical labor and painstaking attention to detail, in roughly equal proportions. Nobody has found a way yet to farm crabs. Mr. Walton and his fellow watermen, as they call themselves, must catch peelers in wire-mesh traps, take them ashore, transfer them into shallow seawater tanks and check each one carefully every six hours around the clock, waiting for them to shed their shells.

The crabs, elusive and pugnacious, don't make it easy.

In William W. Warner's fine book about crabs, *Beautiful Swimmers* (Little, Brown, 1994), he quotes a splendid triple-negative aphorism he heard from a waterman on Maryland's Eastern Shore: "Ain't nobody knows nothing about crabs." Mr. Walton agrees, steeped though he is in crustacean legend and lore. "Catching crabs is mostly instinct," he said.

"Every time you think you've got them figured they change on you," he added, standing at the tiller of his boat, bronzed from a summer's work. "We try to outthink them, but they don't think. They just react to changes in the water, little changes in chemistry that we don't understand."

He put in a fresh wad of Red Man chewing tobacco and squinted into the sun, looking for the buoys that marked one of his lines of traps.

Mr. Walton's family has lived and worked on the water for generations—how many, he could not say. They moved to Urbanna from remote Tangier Island, out in the bay, after a terrible hurricane in 1933. They have been here ever since. He, his brothers, his uncle, his aunt and his son, Lee, are all crabbers, all true Tidewater folks who pronounce "about" not at all like the rest of us, but about halfway between uh-BOAT and uh-BOOT.

Jimmy Sneed is what the Walton family and their neighbors call a "come-here"—someone from somewhere else. But after almost a decade he has won their confidence, and they have taught him most of what they know about soft-shells, which is one reason his restaurant in Richmond, the Frog and the Redneck, may serve the most delectable soft-shells anywhere.

Bearded, ribald, shod day and night in one of his 14 pairs of Lucchese boots, Mr. Sneed is (and is not) the redneck in his restaurant's name. It comes from a moment of comic conflict more than a decade ago, when he was working for the French chef Jean-Louis Palladin, then the proprietor of Jean-Louis in Washington and now installed at Palladin in Manhattan.

As Mr. Sneed tells the story, Mr. Palladin was shouting at him, not for the first time, and Mr. Sneed snapped. "Shut up, you stupid frog," Mr. Sneed shouted back. Mr. Palladin whirled, glared, slammed his knife on the counter and demanded, "What did you call me?" When

Mr. Sneed repeated the epithet, Mr. Palladin yelled, "Then you must be a . . . a redneck!"

He isn't, of course, though he sometimes relishes the role; the son of a Veterans Administration administrator, he grew up in a dozen towns and cities, including Charleston, S.C., and Peekskill, N.Y. Of course, Mr. Sneed and Mr. Palladin became close friends. And of course, when Mr. Sneed decided to move to Richmond after five years of running a restaurant in Urbanna, he could not resist naming his new place in honor of his mentor.

Crab has become Mr. Sneed's metier. Every night of the year, he serves a rich, red pepper cream soup garnished with crab, as well as ethereal crab cakes, made of prime backfin lump crab meat, bound together with little more than a dab of mayonnaise and the chef's prayers. He serves them even when crab is so scarce, as it is right now, that he has to charge $32.50 for them to make a profit. When soft-shells are in season hereabouts, from May until mid-October, he serves them, as well.

Mr. Sneed buys mostly from Thomas Lee Walton, who saves the softest of soft-shells for him. These are the ones that have been culled from the tanks within a half-hour of molting. (The tanks are called "floats" by the watermen because in the early days of the industry they were slatted boxes floating in the creeks.)

The new crab shells begin to form at once, and because the watermen can't hover over the tanks, they get only a fraction of the soft-shells at the optimum moment. These are called "velvets" in the colorful terminology of the crabbers. Plump and bursting with salty-sweet flavor, they are also very fragile, so Mr. Sneed, his wife or his daughter drives to Urbanna every other day, a two-and-a-half-hour round trip, to fetch them at the source.

"Soft-shells are very important to us," Mr. Sneed told me in a rare outburst of understatement. "And you have to try for the premium raw materials, no matter how much trouble it is. Product is king."

A self-described culinary minimalist, Mr. Sneed cooks the crabs in the simplest way imaginable. He pulls them from the refrigerator, dusts them with Wondra flour, which is milled extra fine so that it doesn't clump, and slides them, shell side down, into a heavy cast-iron frying pan filled to a depth of a quarter of an inch with a 50-50 mix of canola oil and drawn butter. After 60 seconds, he turns them and cooks them 30 seconds on the other side.

"Careful," Mr. Sneed warned. "When soft-shells are really fresh, they're full of salty water, so they tend to pop and burn you."

And don't serve them with tartar sauce, not unless you want to make the nonredneck see red.

It took the watermen many years to make the discovery that put the soft-shell trade on a sound commercial footing. Finding a buster in a pot or along the shore is a relatively rare occurrence. They needed some means of forecasting when other crabs were about to molt, so they could take it ashore and wait for it to do its thing. Finally, some unstoried hero noticed that on the next-to-last section of the articulated swimming leg, the most translucent part of the crab, a white line that later turns pink, and finally an intense dark red, can be detected when a crab is about to shed its shell.

It can be detected, that is, by an experienced waterman like Mr. Walton. I could just barely make out the line at its cherry reddest, when the crab was an hour, maybe minutes, from molting, but the rest of the time I couldn't break the code, no matter how closely I looked.

The crabs with white lines, known for some reason as "greens," shed in two weeks; those with pink lines, sometimes called "ripe," will molt within a week; and the red liners, termed "rank," will need a day.

In fact, the telltale lines are the edges of new shells, or exoskeletons, forming inside old ones in anticipation of molting.

I marveled at Mr. Walton's skills. When we arrived at the traps, or pots, that he had set out along the northern shore of the Rappahannock estuary, he chugged up to the first, set the tiller so it kept the boat tracing a circle around the pot and put on an oilcloth apron and two pairs of gloves. Then, with practiced grace, he snagged the buoy with a boathook and pulled up the line attached to it, hand over hand, heaving the pot into the boat until it broke water.

The pot is a cube-shape contraption with three conical entrances, which crabs can swim into but not out of. In the first one were a half-dozen crabs, as well as a croaker and an alewife, as menhaden are called hereabouts. Mr. Walton undid the latch and dumped the catch onto a sorting table, then quickly pitched the fish and the hard-shells back into the water, closed the latch and lowered the pot.

Only five or six times all morning did he expend more than a passing glance in "reading" which crabs were peelers and which not. Most of the time, he instantly tossed the greens into one bushel basket at his feet, the ripes and ranks into another and the few busters into a blue plastic basin filled with river water so that they could continue to molt there. When he was unsure, he held the crab in question up to the sun, its claws a beautiful powder blue, studied it and pitched it in the appropriate direction.

On picking the right crabs on such slim evidence rests his livelihood. He makes few mistakes.

But if the crabs aren't there, no crabber can catch them. Mr. Walton pulled about 70 good peelers and busters from his first line of 50 traps, but from the second and third, he got only about 10, and then he quit for the day. August is never the best month for soft-shells. That comes each May, when he usually takes five or six bushels of crabs off his boat at day's end—about 1,000 to 2,000 crabs. The May catch is almost as big as those of all the other months put together.

At $1.50 each, the morning's work grossed about $120. But out of that Mr. Walton has to pay for gas and the upkeep of his boat, his pickup truck, his pots (which cost $12 each) and his two dozen shedding tanks, which look like shallow plastic bathtubs. No formula for instant riches.

Is the overall crab catch in the bay and its tributaries shrinking, as the harvests of striped bass and oysters did in recent years, with disastrous economic consequences? Many watermen, and Mr. Sneed, think it is, and they blame winter crabbing with dredges, which pull hibernating crabs from the mud, along with laws permitting crabbers in Virginia to keep female crabs carrying a spongelike mass of eggs.

Not so, said Mike Osterling, the top crab expert at the Virginia Institute of Marine Science at Gloucester Point, near Hampton.

"I've seen no records indicating a long-term decline in soft-shells," he said. "Soft-shell fishing has its good days and bad, like anything else. But more people are going into the soft-shell business every day, all the way from here to Texas, and that's no sign of a fishery in decline."

Tradition says that the Chesapeake produces the best soft-shells, and I'm a great respecter of food traditions. But the season lasts a little longer farther south because of the warmer water, and I've eaten some pretty good soft-shells taken by fisherman in Louisiana and North Carolina, mostly small operators like the watermen on the bay.

As for Mr. Walton, he sells all the velvets he has to Mr. Sneed, and those with a slightly firmer shell, called "shippers," he ships. Every so often, a refrigerated truck stops here, picks up trays of crabs covered with wet paper or eel-grass and heads north toward the big fish market at Jessup, Md., near Baltimore.

Sorted by size—whales are the biggest, spiders the smallest, with jumbos, primes, hotels and mediums in between—they go to a wholesaler named Louis Foehrkolb, whom Mr. Walton has never met. He keeps track of the shipments and sends Mr. Walton a check at month's end.

I asked whether he ever worries about being shortchanged.

"Nah," said Mr. Walton, whose smile is as roguish as ever at 52. "I figure if he stops sending me money, I'll stop sending him crabs."

—*Urbanna, Virginia, August 11, 1999*

• •

TEMPURA OF SOFT-SHELL CRABS
(Adapted from the Frog and the Redneck, Richmond)
Time: 20 minutes

8 cleaned soft-shell crabs
1 cup flour
1¼ cups water
¼ teaspoon baking soda

2 ice cubes
Peanut oil for deep frying
Sea salt to taste

1. Lay crabs back side down on a cutting board, and cut in half lengthwise, so that each half has a claw.
2. Stir about 1¼ cups water into the flour to make a smooth, thick batter. Add baking soda and ice cubes.
3. Pour enough oil into a deep pot to fill it halfway, and heat to 375 degrees. (To test, carefully sprinkle a drop or two of water into the pot. If the oil rumbles, it's not hot enough. If it crackles, it is.)
4. Dip crab pieces, four at a time, into batter, and immediately drop into hot oil. Stir after several seconds to separate the pieces, then cook until golden brown, 30 to 45 seconds. Drain on paper towels. Repeat with remaining crab pieces. Salt to taste, and serve immediately.

Yield: 4 servings

ROASTED RIPE TOMATO SALSA
(Adapted from Lucky Star in Virginia Beach, Va.)
Time: 1 hour, 20 minutes

10 plum tomatoes, halved lengthwise and cored
5 tablespoons olive oil
1 teaspoon herbes de Provence
Kosher salt and freshly ground pepper
3 ripe tomatoes, cored and diced large
3 shallots, peeled and julienned
1 yellow bell pepper, stemmed, seeded and diced medium
3 scallions, trimmed and sliced
1 teaspoon red wine vinegar

1. Heat the oven to 400 degrees. Place a large cast-iron skillet inside it and heat 15 to 20 minutes.

2. Place the plum tomatoes cut side up on a rack over a baking tray. Drizzle them with 1 tablespoon olive oil, then season with the herbes de Provence, and salt and pepper to taste.

3. In a large stainless-steel bowl, toss the diced tomatoes with 2 tablespoons olive oil, 1 teaspoon kosher salt and ½ teaspoon pepper. Spoon into the heated skillet. Place the sliced plum tomatoes in the oven as well. Roast 45 minutes, or until plum tomatoes appear to be drying and diced tomatoes have released their juices. Remove from the oven, and let cool.

4. Place a skillet over medium-high heat, add remaining 2 tablespoons olive oil, shallots, bell pepper and scallions, and sauté 2 to 3 minutes, or until softened. Transfer to a large bowl.

5. Cut cooled plum tomatoes into quarters and add to bowl along with diced tomatoes. Toss to combine. Season with vinegar, salt and pepper.

Yield: About 6 cups

SAUTEED SOFT-SHELL CRABS
(Adapted from the Frog and the Redneck, Richmond)
Time: 20 minutes

1 cup flour
Salt and pepper to taste
8 cleaned soft-shell crabs
¾ cup clarified butter
½ cup canola oil
3 tablespoons lemon juice
1 tablespoon chopped parsley

1. Heat a large cast-iron skillet over medium heat. Place flour on a plate, and season with salt and pepper. Dredge crabs in flour, shaking off excess. When the skillet is hot, add half the butter and canola oil to a depth of about ¼ inch. Add four crabs, back side down, being careful to avoid spattering. When they brown lightly, turn, and finish cooking on the other side, until cooked through, 3 to 5 minutes total, depending on the size of the crabs. Drain on paper towels, and repeat with remaining crabs, adding more butter or oil to pan if needed.

2. In a small bowl, stir together remaining clarified butter and lemon juice. Drizzle over crabs, sprinkle with parsley and serve immediately.

Yield: 4 servings

● ● ● ● ● ● ● ● ● ● ● ● ● ● ● ● ● ● ●

In Bawlmer, Hon, Crab Is King

Baltimore is a quirky kind of town," its former mayor Kurt Schmoke said not long ago. "Its heart is still working-class, even if the economic realities have changed. It is suspicious of anything elegant or stylish or pretentious. We have this world-famous educational institution, Johns Hopkins, in our midst, but it has never quite won the affection of ordinary Baltimoreans."

You can see that spirit in the refreshingly unpompous local politicians, including the two senators, a tough, wisecracking Polish-American, Barbara Mikulski, and a reserved, cerebral Greek-American, Paul Sarbanes, as well as William Donald Schaefer, a wacky former mayor and governor who once settled a bet by diving into the seal pool at the National Aquarium. You can see it in the city's sports heroes, gritty men like Frank Robinson, Johnny Unitas and Cal Ripken, who never blew their own horns.

And you can see it in the work of Baltimore's favorite-son moviemakers, John Waters, who celebrated beehive hairdos, and Barry Levinson, who fondly explored the world of siding salesmen. Both like to set their films in their hometown, in what the iconoclastic Mr. Waters calls "this gloriously decrepit, inexplicably charming city."

The standard form of greeting is "hon," a term of endearment commemorated by a faux-'50s restaurant called Cafe Hon in Hampden, up north near the main Hopkins campus and the national Lacrosse Hall of Fame.

Baltimore's eating habits are idiosyncratic, too. The city loves crabs, oysters and rockfish from Chesapeake Bay, which its poet laureate, H. L. Mencken, once described as "an immense protein factory." It prefers diners and taverns tucked into venerable row houses to newer, trendier spots. It shops in the city's old-fashioned covered markets, a half-dozen of them—the only places except the Ravens and the Orioles games where all of Baltimore comes together, blue-collar and blue-blooded, black and white, Greeks and Italians and Germans.

Crab is king. People here can't live without their crab soup, their crab cakes and especially their spicy steamed blue crabs, which they rip open, split in two, crack with a wooden mallet and prod with a knife, excavating every last bite of sweet snowy meat with all the fervor of an Egyptologist opening a pharaoh's tomb. In the winter months, when the big hard-shells—scientific name Callinectes sapidus, which means "savory beautiful swimmer"—are not available locally, the leading purveyors fly them in from ports in the South.

Unhappily, most visitors miss the best of Bawlmer eating. Taking the line of least resistance, they stop at the unfortunate mass feederies along the north side of the Inner Harbor, or at commercialized, gentrified crab houses like Obrycki's, or in Little Italy. Marty Katz, a Baltimore photographer and food critic, dismisses the copycat restaurants in that neighborhood as "our versions of Mamma Leone's."

My nominee for the single best crab dish in Baltimore, if not the Western Hemisphere, is the jumbo lump crab cake at Faidley's Seafood in the Lexington Market, which was founded in 1782 and refurbished only recently.

You eat it standing up, at a counter or at a table with no chairs. Nancy Faidley Devine, 67, makes every one herself, including those she ships by mail, and last Christmas week she shipped 2,800.

"Other people handle the stuff too much," she told me, "and it ruins the cake's texture," the same way that overworking sometimes toughens a pie crust.

In summer, Faidley's crabmeat comes from packinghouses in Wingate and Crisfield, Md., farther down the bay, and in winter it comes from Texas, Florida and North Carolina. Mrs. Devine won't use imported crabmeat—"Pretty," she said, "but no flavor"—and she won't use pasteurized crabmeat, because it has a flat, metallic taste.

She said she watches carefully to make sure the meat contains plenty of yellowish "mustard," or fat, which is as important to the flavor of a crab cake as marbling is to the flavor of a sirloin.

Faidley's sells a crab cake made from claw meat for $4.50 and one made from backfin for $7.95, as well as the jumbo lump cake at $12.95. Each is seasoned differently and each has its virtues, but the costliest one, about the size of a slightly flattened Major League baseball, deep-fried to a golden turn, with crisp little hills and dales all around, is well worth the premium.

Delicate, delicious, creamy and sweet, it may not quite be heaven, but by my reckoning it's a persuasive preview.

Mrs. Devine is canny about her recipe, except to say that it contains only a touch of Baltimore's ubiquitous Old Bay seasoning, which can impart a harsh taste, plus broken saltines for body, mayonnaise, several mustards and spices. Her husband, Bill, 71, a retired naval officer who never lost the habit of salty talk, said the secret would die with his wife. "I sleep with her," he added, "and she won't tell me."

It takes 20 minutes or so to drive to Dundalk, just east of the city line, where giant maritime cranes serve the docks, and the huge Sparrows Point mill spews out smoke and hot-rolled steel. The Costas Inn is there, a blue jeans and CAT hat tavern disguised as a crab house. Several of the Baltimore *feinschmeckers* I talked to said it serves the best steamed crabs in town, and it certainly impressed me.

You get the whole proletarian nine yards: Lots of good beer on draught, including amber-colored Pennsylvania-made Yuengling, from the nation's oldest brewery; stacks of paper towels (not napkins) to clean up with; tables covered with heavy butcher paper; the spice-slathered crabs dumped unceremoniously in front of you from plastic trays.

And what crabs! Crab houses here describe size in terms of price, and the ones my friend and I ordered were 44's, meaning they cost $44 a dozen. Huge brutes, heavy, full of luscious meat. Three each were plenty after a bowl of spicy Maryland crab soup, rich with vegetables. When we finished, our lips were stinging, our fingers were smeared with reddish gunk and a tumulus of shell and cartilage rose before each of us. Finger bowls were not provided.

Taverns, the prototypical Baltimore eating places, come in many varieties. Two of the best, in addition to Costas, are Duda's, a laid-back bar facing the water in Fells Point, which serves what may be the best hamburger in the city, a plump disk of meat grilled to moist, deep-red perfection, and Henninger's, a sweetheart of a back-street establishment in the same neighborhood, where I felt like a regular after two minutes.

Henninger's décor is eclectic, to say the least, featuring old black-and-white publicity photos of strippers alongside a tapestry portrait of John F. Kennedy, Robert F. Kennedy and Martin Luther King Jr. The food has ambition. When I stopped in, the menu included fried oysters on a bed of spinach with fennel and Pernod sauce, cooked by Jayne Vieth, and thin-sliced brisket of beef, deftly smoked by her husband, Kenny. The two of them own the little place.

Baltimore is a good breakfast town, too. Movie buffs should try the Hollywood Diner, a streamlined chrome beauty not far from the courthouse. This is where Boogie, Eddie, Fenwick and their friends, all of them afraid of growing up, hung out in the Barry Levinson classic, *Diner* (1982). Get there before 9 a.m. and you can have an egg and cheese on toast for only 99 cents.

If civilized talk and an unhurried session with the newspapers is your morning game, Baltimore provides City Cafe. The bagels are Manhattan-worthy, and the oatmeal is Ohio-worthy. Blue Moon, a hip cubbyhole all but impossible to get into on weekends, makes everything from scratch, including smoothies, cinnamon rolls and potato pancakes laced with bacon and green pepper. The scrapple is to die for: cut thin, fried crisp on the outside, molten on the inside. No easy thing to achieve, that.

In Helmand, Baltimore has the most unlikely of ethnic restaurants, an upmarket Afghan place, run by Qayum Karzai, brother of the Afghan head of state, no less. Its *kaddo* (sautéed pumpkin) and *choppan* (charcoaled rack of lamb) merit the raves they win from local critics year after year.

Attman's is something else again in the ethnic line, a deli in business since 1915 whose corned beef—a bit grainy, a bit sour, not too salty—deserves to be mentioned in the same breath with New York's best. You have to wait in a long line at lunchtime for Attman's bulging sandwiches, Dr. Brown's cream soda, half-sour dills and all-sour pickled onions. The 1100 block of Lombard Street is called "Corned Beef Row," but most of it is a wasteland now, except for Attman's and the slightly ersatz Lenny's, whose Kelly green paint job gives it away.

I wish I could wax as enthusiastic about Baltimore's famous pit beef. They serve it in joints on Route 40, the Pulaski Highway, a real boulevard of broken dreams, lined with cheap motels and shabby car lots. The beef is top round, dry-rubbed, grilled over charcoal, sliced thin, slapped into a kaiser roll and painted with horseradish.

My friend Calvin Trillin, down from New York, came along for a taste test. At Big Fat Daddy's, a sullen kid served us drab, dried-out mystery meat that reminded me of boarding school. We found the sandwich at Big Al's O.K., if not a tenth as enticing as the spiced beef sandwiches Chicago loves.

A busy port for more than 250 years, Baltimore has long had a sizable Greek population, which gathers at Samos, across from the Orthodox church on Oldham Street in East Baltimore. In this row-house neighborhood you see two of the other things that set the city apart: white marble steps called stoops and facades of Formstone, a cement-based falseface for porous brick.

Nick Georgalas presides in the kitchen at Samos. Tall, mustached, fierce-eyed, he looks like the partisan fighter that his father was, and he is one of those cooks who gives new life to culinary clichés. His grilled shrimp had too much dried oregano for me, but his *dolmades*, his souvlaki, his *tsatziki* and his grilled pita were worth much more than the modest prices asked.

The Black Olive in Fells Point, also Greek-owned, gets in trouble because its prices are high. Many people are reluctant to spend real money for Greek food (and Chinese food), which is a mistake. Owned by Stelios Spiliadis, whose brother runs Milos in New York, Black Olive

is built around a display of fish from far and wide, which are presented atop a bank of ice: red snapper from the Gulf of Mexico, turbot
from the North Sea, *daurade* from the Mediterranean, striped bass from
the Chesapeake (which Marylanders call "rockfish," supposedly because the best ones were once caught off the port of Rock Hall).

Simply grilled or pan-fried, dressed with a squirt of lemon and
a few drops of best extra virgin olive oil, the fish is fabulous. So are
the *mezes*, or starters, especially the chunky hummus and the olives,
which are house-marinated in *zaatar*, a Middle Eastern spice combination that includes sumac, crushed sesame seeds and a thymelike
regional herb from a woody bush.

You'll accuse me of stretching a point, but I would include the Wom-
en's Industrial Exchange in this roll call of ethnic eating in Baltimore.
Founded in 1880 as a means of helping needy gentlewomen earn an
income, it has been going strong ever since on the same corner of
North Charles Street, selling handmade craft articles in the front
room and handmade WASP food—plain, unadorned, old-fashioned,
superbly ordinary American food—in the back room.

Outside Greenwich and Locust Valley, there aren't many cheerlead-
ers these days for WASP food, but if a few more serious eaters would
try the industrial exchange (closed for renovation until late spring)
maybe that would change. How's this for lunch: a pile of the best
chicken salad you've ever tasted, a block of ruby-red tomato aspic and a
deviled egg, for a big $6.75? Add a cupcake—yes, a cupcake—or a
wedge of lemon meringue pie for $3.

Mencken fans will have noticed a few things missing. The old
grouch was a great drinker who called himself "omnibibulous" and
described the dry martini as "the only American invention as perfect
as a sonnet." He was a great eater, who termed crab à la Creole "the
most magnificent victual yet devised by mortal man." But much of
Mencken's Baltimore is gone, despite the city's predilection for the
tried and true.

The hometown beer, National Bohemian, the beloved Natty Boh, is brewed in North Carolina now. Other icons of the Teutonic culinary culture have vanished as well, including many of Mencken's favorite restaurants, like Miller Brothers, where my father took me as a lad to eat turtle soup; Schellhase's, where Mencken's Saturday Night Club met; and Haussner's, which was stuffed with paintings and sculptures that brought more than $10 million at auction when it closed down. You can still find a snickerdoodle cookie, but sour beef and dumplings, Baltimore's version of sauerbraten, is disappearing fast.

Depressing to report, Marconi's, a deliciously anachronistic French-Italian salon on Saratoga Street, has lost much of its charm, thanks to an aesthetically criminal remodeling ordered by its new owner, Peter Angelos, a strong-willed millionaire who also owns the Orioles. The handsome Venetian wallpaper is no more, an ugly acoustic ceiling has been installed and the floor has been overcleaned.

But the thick broiled lamb chops with electric-green mint jelly (a favorite of Mencken's and of my wife, Betsey) have survived, at least until now, as has the fudgy chocolate sundae so beloved by generations of well-bred Baltimoreans.

Bright new places have sprung up, of course. One of the first was Nancy Longo's Pierpoint, still the place to go for modern versions of traditional Baltimore dishes and innovative uses of prime Eastern Shore produce. Gotta try her smoked crab cakes. Much more recently, the Red Maple, a long, skinny room designed by someone just back from the Milan Furniture Fair, has mesmerized the city's noctambulist young. More a bar than a restaurant, it nevertheless serves classy Asian "tapas" like duck egg rolls and shrimp and tuna tartare.

But the undisputed prince and princess of Baltimore gastronomy at the moment are Tony Foreman and his wife, Cindy Wolf. A grape nut and a buddy of Robert Parker, the internationally influential critic, who lives not far from here, Mr. Foreman oversees the couple's two restaurants, Charleston, downtown, and Petit Louis Bistro in semisuburban Roland Park. Neither is Baltimore-specific; Petit Louis features dishes like choucroute garnie and cassoulet, in Paris-level versions, and Charleston's long menu owes as much to Maine, South Carolina and Louisiana as to Maryland.

"This is an in-between town," Mr. Foreman said over a bottle or two of fine Châteauneuf-du-Pape. "Not Southern, not Northern. People have a Northern edge and a Southern graciousness. They care. If they dig it, they let you know; if they don't, they let you know. That makes our job easier."

Ms. Wolf's crisp, light-as-air fried green tomatoes make a splendid foil for her crab and lobster hash. Her shrimp with grits, *tasso* and andouille takes you to New Orleans in an instant. Her lamb and pork and ultrafresh fish never disappoint. And the cheeses, a dozen or more every night, knowledgeably chosen and intelligently served, are enough to make any restaurateur proud.

Now why, you may be asking, especially if you grew up just after World War II, why has he written all this without a single word about Lady Baltimore cakes? Well, those delectably rich confections, whose layers are separated by fluffy, rosewater-scented white frosting studded with chopped raisins, orange peel, figs and pecans, have little or nothing to do with this city.

The name originated in *Lady Baltimore*, a 1906 novel by Owen Wister about a young man who walks into a tearoom in a Southern city, modeled on Charleston, S.C., to order a wedding cake. What he chooses is a Lady Baltimore cake, no doubt about that, but exactly why it is so named is unclear. Cecil Calvert, the second Lord Baltimore, founded Maryland, but history records no link between his wife and baked goods. Neither of them ever visited North America.

My mother used to make Lady Baltimore cakes for family festivities, and they are favorites of mine. I have never come across one in a restaurant here, but Eddie's of Roland Park, the city's premier fancy grocery, makes a dandy one on special order.

—*Baltimore, February 19, 2003*

In Hoagieland, They Accept No Substitutes

When the future Edward VII, then the Prince of Wales, visited this staid old city in 1860, he had a little trouble getting his bearings. During his stay, he reported later, "I met a very large and interesting family named Scrapple, and I discovered a rather delicious native food that they call 'biddle.'"

Almost a century and a half later, venerable families and idiosyncratic foods remain evocative parts of the Philadelphia scene, as familiar as the statue of William Penn atop City Hall and the exploits of Rocky on film. There are still oodles of Biddles around, and scrapple still adorns the breakfast menus of lowly diners and elegant hotels alike.

Some Philly Phoods remain resolutely local, like scrapple and water ice. Others, like cheesesteaks and hoagies, have spread across the country, though often in ersatz form. Here on their home turf, you and I can sample the genuine articles in their unpretentious, calorific, often sloppy splendor.

Italian-Americans from South Philadelphia and German-Americans who settled in and west of the city, misleadingly known as the Pennsylvania Dutch, have contributed the most to making Philadelphia a street-food showcase, a kind of Middle Atlantic Singapore.

But stop in some noontime at the 110-year-old Reading Terminal Market in Center City, where all the culinary streams flow together, or at Sarcone's Deli or Jim's Steaks, a few blocks to the south, and you will quickly realize that this food has won the hearts of Everyman and Everywoman—blacks and whites, locals and tourists, beefy working stiffs, primly dressed matrons, youngsters wearing the No. 3 of their hero, Allen Iverson of the 76'ers.

An astonishing number of old institutions survive. Bassetts ice cream, founded 1861, is the nation's oldest brand and one of its best. Pat's King of Steaks has been around since 1930. Esposito's has been in the meat business since 1911 and Termini Brothers in the pastry business since 1921.

Sadly, though, pepper pot soup, one of the grand Philadelphia gastronomic traditions, appears to be all but defunct. Although George Washington's chef at Valley Forge probably did not invent it, as myth maintains, it was for decades as integral a part of southeastern Pennsylvania life as Independence Hall and sculls on the Schuylkill.

Gone with the wind is the rousing cry of the street hawkers:

All hot! All hot!
Pepper pot! Pepper pot!
Makes backs strong.
Makes lives long.
All hot! Pepper pot!

Old Original Bookbinder's closed last year, depriving not only those who devoured the spicy soup at its tables, but also those (like me) who used to buy the brew in cans. The City Tavern still serves pepper pot, but it is made with salt pork and salt beef, not with tripe, as specified by the noted Philadelphia cook Sarah Gibson Rorer in her classic cookbook of 1886. For the authentic version, pepper pot lovers must now repair to the Swann Cafe at the Four Seasons Hotel, where it is served intermittently, October through January.

Philadelphia's greatest food export is the cheesesteak, which is built around beef sliced paper thin and sizzled very briefly on a griddle. Although not in the same food-as-fuel league as the hamburger, the hot dog and the pizza, it has made a national name for itself in the last quarter-century, and its hold on the city of its birth seems unshakable. Which raises an eschatological question: Why should pepper pot soup die out while the cheesesteak and its cousin, the hoagie, thrive?

"Philadelphia is subject to the same trends as the rest of the country," said Elaine Tait, the longtime food editor of *The Philadelphia Inquirer*, now retired. "We've stopped eating things like kidneys and liver and tripe. We're a snack food nation now, and the cheesesteak and hoagie are perfect—quick, inexpensive meals on a bun."

The Big Three of cheesesteaks, each championed with pugnacious intensity by a phalanx of ferocious partisans, are Jim's, Geno's and Pat's. Risking damage to my digestive system, to say nothing of my clothing, I returned to all three of them recently, in pursuit of gastronomic truth and beauty.

Pat's and Geno's, a pair of squat, unadorned, utilitarian structures, stand diagonally across from each other at the southern end of the Italian Market, where Ninth Street, Wharton Street and Passyunk Avenue cross. Neither has indoor seating. Each has one service window for sandwiches and another for drinks and fries. Each is rimmed by plastic tables and benches firmly bolted to concrete sidewalks and shielded from sun, rain and snow by flat metal roofs that project from the main building. Each is open 24 hours a day.

This is the drill: You stand in line, inching toward the window. When you get there, you speak your piece to the stone-faced counterman quickly, unless you want trouble from those behind you. If you say, "Whiz, with," as you should, your sandwich will come with grilled onions and Cheez Whiz, the unabashedly orange processed goo made by Kraft Foods; for this purpose, if few others, it is absolutely ideal. White American cheese and provolone are much less satisfactory options. "Without," meaning "hold the onions," sounds subversive to me.

Pat's, the oldest of the Big Three, claims to have originated the cheesesteak. It uses torpedo-shaped rolls from Vilotti's bakery; they are a bit firmer than the Amoroso bakery's rolls favored by most other cheesesteak emporia. A good thing, too, because so much meat and other stuff is jammed in that a flabby roll might fall apart.

When you pick up your Coke or iced tea or whatever at the drinks window, look down. There, buried in the sidewalk beneath your feet, is a red stone bearing a surprisingly reverent inscription: "On this spot stood Sylvester Stallone filming the great motion picture *Rocky*, Nov. 21, 1976."

Geno's steaks are almost self-effacing. The cheese dissolves into a runny sauce; the strips of beef are laid precisely on the roll, rather than in a tangle; and the onions are sparsely applied. But one thing is boldface: the owner's point of view. It's on display: "Joe Vento says, 'Let Us Never Forget 9/11 and Never, Never Forgive.'"

Jim's is something else again. Much closer to Center City, in the midst of the South Street tourist district, it draws far more cheesesteak neophytes. Its black-and-white faux–Art Deco interior makes a stab at décor. It has indoor tables, chairs and even toilets. Its grill men chop the steak into small pieces with a few quick blows from the edges of their spatulas.

The resulting sandwich is a near-perfect amalgam of juicy, greasy bits of beef and bland, gummy cheese—maybe not Philly Mignon, as proclaimed on one Web site, but irresistible. Both raw and grilled onions are offered; a mixture gives the sandwich a welcome bite. Jim's wins my blue ribbon, but then, what do I know? I'm not Italian and not from Philadelphia.

Cheesesteaks are only one of the lures of South Philadelphia, which is the heartland of the city's Italian-American community. The Ninth Street Market, with shops and stalls flanking the street for a dozen blocks, is a delightful anachronism—the oldest working outdoor market in the nation.

Claudio's cave of marvels, packed with olive oils, anchovies, tuna and balsamic vinegars, is entered through a curtain of hanging cheeses. Cannuli's butcher shop, whose floor is covered with sawdust, has a gargantuan oven that can, and regularly does, cook 16 boned and stuffed pigs at once.

Settlers from Naples, Sicily, Calabria and Abruzzo poured into

South Philadelphia in the 1880s and 1890s, and in the 1950s singers like Mario Lanza, Frankie Avalon, Fabian and Bobby Rydell sprang from these hard streets. But in the last quarter-century, more and more Italian-Americans have moved to the suburbs, notably those in New Jersey. Latin American and Asian immigrants have taken their place, and now Huong Lan, on Eighth Street, offers "Vietnamese hoagies," whatever those might be, along with *pho* and *bun bo Hue*.

According to those who have explored the murky recesses of local food history, hoagies owe their name to the Hog Island shipyard on the Delaware River. During the Depression, or so the story goes, construction workers there used to buy Italian sandwiches from a luncheonette operated by one Al DePalma, who called them "hoggies." Time changed the name to hoagies.

Hoagies are not fundamentally different from New York's heroes or Boston's grinders or Everytown's submarines. Call them what you like, but Philadelphia must eat more per capita than anyplace else, and in a city where almost everybody, including Wawa convenience stores, fills eight-inch-long bread rolls with cold cuts, South Philadelphia fills them better than anyone.

The bread is the key to quality. So who better to make a great hoagie than a great bakery? That would be Sarcone's, a fixture on Ninth Street, which a few years ago opened a tiny deli a few doors away. Its Old Fashioned Italian (Gourmet) hoagie is a minor masterpiece. A roll with a crunchy seeded crust and a soft, yet densely chewy, interior provides a solid base with plenty of absorptive power. Both are sorely needed after they pile on the prosciutto, *coppa*, spicy *sopressata*, provolone, oregano, tomatoes, onions, hot peppers, oil and vinegar.

A slug of Fernet-Branca (fittingly Italian) might help, too.

Ed Barranco, owner of the nearby Chef's Market, which serves Society Hill's carriage trade and catering clients across the city, pointed us toward Sarcone's, and since we liked it so much, we decided to take him up on another recommendation. We would be well advised, he said, to try the chicken cutlet, sharp provolone and broccoli rabe sandwich down at Tony Luke's.

"Good?" I asked him. "Good?" he replied, eyes shining. "Nah, it's more than good. It's Italian."

So we found the joint, tucked under an I-95 overpass, in south South Philadelphia. We ordered roast pork instead of chicken—I have a thing for Italian-style roast pork—and ate it in the company of weight lifters and truck drivers, several of whom left their rigs idling at the curb.

A canny combo it was, too: bitter, garlicky greens; pungent, smoky cheese; and tender, mild, juicy pork.

After heavy lifting like that, especially on a warm day, what you need is a Philadelphia-style Italian water ice, served in a little paper cup with a plastic spoon. It is less grainy than granita, more so than sorbet. It dissolves as you eat it, so you get food and drink at once. Most of what is sold these days is nothing but sugar, sugar, sugar, but at its best, water ice has the unmistakable tang of fresh fruit, intensified.

John's is the classic spot, a tiny stand that serves only four flavors—cherry, pineapple and lemon (all made from fresh whole fruit, not syrup), plus chocolate. The cherry tastes the way cherries taste in northern Michigan in high summer. In keeping with the times, Pop's, which started as a cart pushed by Filippo (Pop) Italiano in 1932, offers 15 flavors on most days.

My wife, Betsey, ordered lemon, and I ordered mango, both marvelous. But neither of us tore into ours with quite the exuberance of Rocky, a three-year-old in from Jersey with his mother for a day's grocery shopping in her old neighborhood. Rocky opted for root beer.

German-American food entered the Philadelphia mainstream long before the first Italians arrived here. Scrapple and pretzels have survived.

I have never quite understood the squeamishness that scrapple excites in a lot of people. True, the ingredients sound slightly revolting—"pork stock, pork, pork livers, pork skins, pork hearts, pork tongue," to quote part of one label. But sausage generates no such qualms, unless you consider the old admonition against watching the unappetizing manufacturing process.

No matter. Pennsylvanians, former Pennsylvanians and inhabitants of adjacent states like Delaware and New Jersey have eaten scrapple for centuries with no harmful effects. Philadelphia lawyers eat it. Benjamin Franklin supposedly ate it.

As the name implies, it is made from the scraps of pork left over after most of the pig has been turned into ham, bacon, pork roasts and pork chops. These scraps are cooked with spices (usually sage and pepper), cornmeal and sometimes buckwheat or whole wheat flour. The resulting loaf is cooled and cut into half-inch slices, which are fried in butter or shortening until they turn a crisp, ruddy brown on the outside. The inside remains soft and luscious.

Growing up in a Pennsylvania Dutch family in Ohio, I learned to eat scrapple with maple syrup, which made it seem to me like a combination of pancakes and sausage. In Philadelphia, it is sometimes served with ketchup, and in the Dutch country, where it is often still called *panhaas*, I have seen it topped with dark molasses.

Made by a company dating from 1895, Hatfield scrapple, more peppery and less intensely sage-flavored than some, is served at the luxurious Rittenhouse Hotel. The Silk City Diner features another local favorite, Habbersett, alongside huevos rancheros, bagels and grits, cooking it to an unusually golden hue. The inside is as creamy as an oyster.

But nothing topped the scrapple we were served at the nonpareil Down Home Diner in Reading Terminal, a bastion of Pennsylvania Dutch quality. The diner belongs to Jack McDavid, who comes from rural Virginia and is known for ferreting out prime ingredients. His scrapple is made by a small company called Godshall's, based in Telford, Pa. Pale, salty, moist and buttery, it appears to contain more spice, more meat and less filler, giving the end product an unusually rich texture.

Like scrapple, pretzels originated in Germany, where they are called *"Brezels."* This part of Pennsylvania produces tons of standard, hard-baked pretzels, but it also produces something special—soft pretzels, made of nothing more than flour, yeast (to make them rise), water, a little salt and a smidgen of brown sugar.

At the Fisher family's stand, the dough is mixed in an ancient Hobart machine. The pretzel bender, an elderly Amish lady in a gauzy white bonnet, rolls it out with her hands to the diameter of a little finger, then twists it into shape in one practiced motion. After baking, the pretzels are sprinkled with coarse salt and sold while still hot. A coat of melted butter is optional; a filigree of brown mustard is absolutely required. Without mustard, you'll look like an auslander.

The pretzels are incomparable—light, airy and tasty. Their leaden street-corner competition can't cut it, any more than an airline bagel can match one of Murray's.

Well, then. Scrapple for breakfast, a couple of pretzels for lunch. What's for dessert? The market has an answer for that, too, in the form of Bassetts ice cream. The company that makes it, established 140 years ago by a Quaker schoolteacher, is run today by his great-great-grandson. At its marble counter, you can order a cup, a cone or several pints, packed in dry ice for travel if need be.

Excavated from the tubs with an old-fashioned spade rather than a scoop, this is small-town, butterfat-laden, raid-the-fridge-at-midnight ice cream. A spoonful is as satisfying as a gallon. Of the 40-odd flavors, vanilla is the favorite (no surprise), but there are also hard-to-find, old-time treats like butter pecan, banana, rum raisin, peach and nut-laden pistachio.

Why not try two scoops, say double chocolate and cinnamon?

—Philadelphia, May 28, 2003

Bagging the Endangered Sandwich

When I first came to New York, at 17, I pestered the school friend I was visiting until he took me to Lindy's for corned beef and cheesecake. I figured that that was the closest an Ohio kid was likely to get to the fragrant, seductively shady world of Damon Runyon and Walter Winchell—"boxers, bookmakers, actors, agents, ticket brokers, radio guys, song writers, orchestra leaders, newspapermen and cops," as Runyon described them, "still sleep-groggy" as they gathered for breakfast at 1 p.m., "but shaved and talcumed and lacking only their java to make them ready for the day."

Lindy's has long since vanished from Broadway, along with Leo Lindemann, its creator, and Sky Masterson, Nathan Detroit and the other urban wayfarers in Runyon's cast of semimythic characters. Gone, too, are Phil Gluckstern's and Arnold Reuben's and Lou G. Siegel's, where serious *fressers* (overeaters) could count on finding corned beef with *taam*, the indispensable Jewish taste. They're all part of the Oh-So-Long-Ago, as Winchell called it, like Jack Dempsey and Jack Benny.

Now, newcomers to New York—not 17-year-olds, I guess, but 21- and 22-year-olds—angle for tables at Balthazar or Nobu. Pals initiate them to Krug instead of cream soda.

Corned beef is alive and well, of course. It shows up around the world, in one guise or another. But in New York, where once it was king, good kosher-style corned beef is as rare as nightingales' tongues.

You find plenty of corned beef in Dublin, as the centerpiece of corned beef and cabbage, the reliably nourishing standby of the frugal housewife, and in Boston, as an essential component of a New

England boiled dinner. You find it in corned beef hash, which has been a staple on American restaurant and club menus for decades.

My stepdaughter, Catherine Brown, found it in a jungle clearing on an Indonesian island—Brazilian corned beef, straight from a can with a cow on the label, heated over a kerosene stove, served with sweet potatoes.

All the other varieties, to tell the truth, pale in comparison with the moist, garlicky stuff Jewish immigrants brought with them to New York from central and eastern Europe. Yet, today you can spend yourself halfway to the poorhouse and give yourself heartburn (not to mention heartache) looking for the kind of corned beef sandwich that defined eating in Manhattan the way onion soup defined eating in Paris: steamed, thinly sliced meat stacked high on rye bread, slathered with spicy mustard, a half-sour pickle on the side.

Woody Allen gave Manhattan corned beef one last (or next-to-last) hurrah in *Broadway Danny Rose*, his 1984 film about a small-time Broadway agent, which included scenes shot in the Carnegie Delicatessen. But Jerry Seinfeld and his buddies, the quintessential pop-culture New Yorkers of the 1990s, hung out not in a deli but in a diner or outside a gussied-up soup kitchen.

Except for the Carnegie and the Stage, today's Broadway is mostly a glorified food court, packed with franchised joints of every description, serving hamburgers and bagels and pizzas and the like, many of them owned by a family of real estate operators, Murray, Dennis and Irving Riese.

There is also a Riese-owned restaurant called Lindy's on Broadway between 44th and 45th Streets, but any resemblance to the original is purely coincidental. The only authentically New York aspect of the place is the surliness of the service.

So where do you find the good stuff? Apprehensive about possible doubts—make that probable doubts—concerning the corned beef credentials of a man of Midwestern Lutheran origins, even if said Midwestern Lutheran has been dribbling deli mustard down his ever-expanding front for many decades, I sought the help of Tim Zagat, the guidebook publisher. A New Yorker in both palate and pedigree, he claims to have eaten corned beef regularly since puberty, including once a week at his Riverdale prep school.

Mr. Zagat's 1999 guide to New York restaurants reflects the declining role of the delicatessen, and hence corned beef, in New York gastronomy. Not one of the 50 establishments top-rated for food is a deli, although two are pizza parlors and one is a soup kitchen. Zagat's amateur critics ate in delis a lot (the Carnegie was the seventh-most-visited spot in the survey), but they must have suffered.

Throwing caution to the wind, Mr. Zagat and I decided to taste for ourselves. As a concession to age—neither of us is young anymore—we asked the countermen to give us thinner sandwiches than usual. Though obviously offended, they complied.

The sign outside the Stage Delicatessen (834 Seventh Avenue, between 53rd and 54th Streets), meant to take a poke at the Carnegie, betrays a certain defensiveness. "Why wait on line," it asks, "when you could be eating now?" In the heyday of Max Asnas, the founder, the Stage bragged about the quality of its food, not how quickly it could find you a table.

But the place still smells right (a little greasy, a little garlicky), waiters and customers still abuse each other in a good-natured way and the sandwiches are still named for celebrities (though it's a stretch to think of Fran Drescher and Richard Simmons, both creatures of television, as Broadway types). It still deals gently with Iowans who don't know which is the bagel and which the lox.

As for the corned beef, it's a comedown from the 1960s, when the Stage was listed in a book called *Great Restaurants of America*. The meat is too dry, too pink, too wan in flavor. If there is really a "secret recipe," as claimed, they must have forgotten to let the cook in on the secret.

Another big disappointment came at Katz's (205 East Houston Street at Ludlow Street), a 112-year-old institution that figured in *When Harry Met Sally*. There's nothing not to like about the terrazzo-and-Formica ambiance, with a cafeteria counter along one side and signs instructing you, as of yore, to "Send a Salami to Your Boy in the Army." You have to love the fact that they still use meal tickets (does anyone else?) and cut the corned beef by hand, with venerable knives sharpened down almost to nothing.

Katz's hot dogs, crisped on the grill, and its garlic-laden knoblewurst are both *vaut le voyage* downtown. But the corned beef sandwich is only O.K.—moist meat with a rough texture, but with a slightly musty flavor instead of the bright, pungent taste that you look for. The bread is rather bland, as well—a lot like supermarket rye, though I wince to say so.

The Second Avenue Deli (156 Second Avenue, at 10th Street) has the least authentic interior—a recent redesign by Adam Tihany, no less— but the most authentic everything else. This was the domain of Abe Lebewohl, a true Manhattan treasure, part social worker, part delica- tessen genius, who was gunned down in 1995 by an unknown villain who remains at large.

Here everything is kosher; even the cheesecake is made with tofu, to avoid transgressing the boundary between meat and dairy. Many other delis serve "kosher-style" food, which means that it looks and (they say) tastes the same, but is not prepared in strict compliance with Jewish dietary laws.

And here the corned beef, prepared in the basement, is the genuine article. "Juicier, richer, more zaftig," as my grease-spotted notes say. "A real knockout." Real kosher corned beef isn't unobtainable after all.

I think the question always asked by Abe Lebewohl's brother Jack or one of the other servers has something to do with it. "Lean or juicy?" they ask, before anyone has a chance to say "extra lean." Con- fronted with that choice, most people opt for juicy, which means they get enough fat, Jack Lebewohl says, to boost the flavor and make sure the sandwich doesn't get dry.

Another thing: People from Sweden walk in, sure, as three did just a few days before our recent visit, but this is still primarily a neighbor- hood spot. Some customers come in six or seven times a week, and on Friday, the locals pack the place. They know their corned beef; they make sure that Jack keeps things up to snuff.

The Carnegie (854 Seventh Avenue at 55th Street) is only a half-step behind, if that, despite the agonizingly corny names it gives to some of its sandwiches (e.g., "The Mouth That Roared," which is roast beef and Bermuda onion). And despite a less demanding clientele (big groups from Kansas City and Utah, on my last visit, but some from the Bronx, too). Sometimes the country boys exhibit unacceptable table manners; when he was running for the vice presidency, former Senator Lloyd M. Bentsen of Texas tried in vain to eat his bulging sandwich with a knife and fork.

Every week, the Carnegie corns 15,000 pounds of beef at a plant in Carlstadt, N.J., starting with well-marbled 8- to 12-pound briskets cut from the breast of the steer. Injected first with a saline-and-garlic solution enriched with allspice, thyme and mustard and coriander seed, the beef is then pickled for about a week in barrels filled with the same solution.

Some is sold to other restaurants, but about 10,000 pounds a week are cooked as needed in the Carnegie's damp, dungeonlike basement. The meat is boiled for two to two and a half hours in 35-gallon pots, then carried upstairs, where it is steamed and sliced to order, across the grain, of course, on razor-sharp rotary cutting machines. The blades are replaced once a month; the machines themselves, exhausted by constant use, are sent back for rebuilding every three months, said Sanford Levine, one of the Carnegie's co-owners.

Sandwiches are built on thin, seeded rye bread delivered four times a day from the Certified Bakery in Union City, N.J. More than a dozen ultrathin slices of beef go into the average sandwich, a few lean, a few fat. That's the way Leo Steiner, who first put the Carnegie on the map, liked it best.

"It should melt in your mouth," he confided to a reporter almost a decade ago. "I don't like to chew. Thinner, the flavor comes through."

Broadway and environs still have plenty of delicatessens, of a sort. There's the All-American Gourmet Deli, the Celebrity Deli, Roxy's (named after a defunct theater), the Crown Deli ("Featuring Colombo Yogurt") and the 55th Street Deli, a produce stand-cum-convenience-food shop. Downtown, I spotted delis touting waffles or salad bars.

These are the kinds of places that would happily sell a passing inno-
cent a corned beef and Swiss on toasted seven-grain.

It goes without saying that none of them, or their yuppified counterparts elsewhere, are authentic, thumb-in-your-soup, garlic-scented,
damn-the-cholesterol delis. That kind of place has mostly vanished
from midtown and the Lower East Side as the Broadway crowd has
thinned and the Jewish population has scattered to New Jersey and
Queens and Long Island, losing touch with its roots in the process.
We're talking heavy social anthropology here, but we're also talking
gastronomy.

"When we were all on the Lower East Side, every mom-and-pop
store cured its own," said Rabbi Arthur Herzberg, a professor of hu-
manities at New York University and a kosher food maven of considerable standing. "That was one thing. Now you get two-week-old
corned beef, supermarket corned beef and corned beef and cheese—
utter desecrations of Jewish soul food."

The genuine article is even harder to find elsewhere in the country. Some film people swear by Nate 'n Al's in Los Angeles, but in my
experience, kosher corned beef starts to fade once it wanders beyond
commuting range of Manhattan. (Zingerman's in Ann Arbor, Mich.,
is an honorable exception.)

Branches of New York nosheries have failed in Beverly Hills, New
Jersey, Boston and the Washington suburbs in recent years, and several decades before that, my friend Stanley Karnow, the Brooklyn-
born journalist and historian, lost his shirt, or at least a sleeve or two,
struggling to teach the long-suffering Hong Kong Chinese the finer
points of Jewish gastronomy.

Without a maven or two a day among its customers, any deli will
sooner or later lose the touch, exactly like a Thai restaurant in Afghanistan. And without real delis, there can be no real New York
corned beef—rich and warm and tender, slightly salty but also slightly
sweet, with just enough fat clinging to the meat to keep it moist. Ordering the stuff extra lean, the way some people do, is about as point-
less as drinking 3.2 beer.

—New York City, September 15, 1999

● ● ●

Correction: September 21, 1999, Tuesday

An article last Wednesday about a search for a good corned beef sandwich in New York City misidentified the delicatessen that has a sign
saying "Why wait on line when you could be eating now?" It is the
Ben Ash Delicatessen, on Seventh Avenue and 54th Street, not the
nearby Stage Delicatessen.

Enduringly Yankee, with
a Modern Twist

Not so long ago, lobsters and baked beans pretty well defined the parameters of Maine gastronomy—at least for "folk from away," as outsiders are called in the local lingo. The old reliables are still there: a traveler heading north along the coast from Kittery soon starts seeing signs advertising lobster pounds, and the B&M baked bean plant, a sentinel of Down East tradition, stands along Interstate 295 near downtown Portland.

But times have changed. In the last decade or so, Maine fishermen have begun harvesting a broader range of marine delicacies. Maine farmers have begun raising traditional breeds of pigs and sheep by old-fashioned methods. Despite a cranky climate, Maine market gardeners have found new ways to coax remarkably toothsome vegetables from the state's thin, rocky soil.

As the raw materials have improved, so have the restaurants. Home-grown chefs and newcomers from all over the country have evolved cooking styles with a strong sense of place, the beginnings of a regional, seasonal Maine haute cuisine. At the moment, says Corby Kummer, who reviews restaurants for *Boston* magazine, "Maine is where you find the food action in New England."

On a trip that my wife, Betsey, and I made late this spring, in impossibly beautiful weather, with blue sea and bluer sky vying for attention, four places stood out from the crowd. John Thorne was no doubt right when he said in his fine newsletter, *Simple Cooking*, that "the Maine temperament is enduringly Yankee in its sneaking delight in the mortification of the flesh for the good of the spirit." But for us, at least, there was only pure pleasure that week.

Clark Frasier, a Californian, and Mark Gaier, who grew up in Piqua, a small town in western Ohio, met in the kitchen of Stars, Jeremiah Tower's groundbreaking brasserie in San Francisco. They have turned an old post-and-beam farmhouse on a back road near Ogunquit into Arrows, an urbane restaurant surrounded by sumptuous flower and vegetable gardens, where they combine Maine-raised belon oysters, Maine scallops and Maine venison, among many other local products, with French, Italian and Chinese preparation techniques.

A Mainer through and through, Sam Hayward runs Fore Street, a perpetually packed restaurant near the Portland docks. Cooked without fuss in a wood-fired oven and on rotating spits in an open kitchen, unobtrusively served in an old warehouse, the food speaks in the laconic accent of his state. "Pork Loin," the menu announces. "Hanger Steak. Marinated Maine farm rabbit." There is an integrity to the man and his work as rock-ribbed as the Maine coast.

Farther north in Rockland, Melissa Kelly, a New Yorker who won plaudits by the bushel at the Old Chatham Sheepherding Company Inn in the Hudson Valley, is rapidly building a new following with Primo. In a Victorian farmhouse with kitchen gardens (and a couple of Gloucestershire Old Spot pigs) out back, she gives freer rein to lessons learned from her Italian-American mother than she did at Old Chatham, adding pancetta to a creamy pea and fiddlehead fern soup, and serving seared black sea bass on a bed of fennel and Sardinian couscous.

Tom Gutow, who comes from Walloon Lake, Mich., is not as well known yet as the others. The Castine Inn, which he has run since 1997, is tucked away on a peninsula that leads down toward the fishing port of Stonington, well off the tourist track. But Castine may be Maine's best-kept white-clapboard village (Mary McCarthy and Robert Lowell both had houses here), and Mr. Gutow shops and cooks with an unbridled passion. When he really gets going, he uses ingredients from as many as 30 regional producers in a single evening's dishes.

The single best thing we have eaten this year resulted from Mr. Gutow's skills as a produce scout and Mr. Hayward's steadfast refusal to paint any lily. When Mr. Gutow took us to meet Eliot Coleman and Barbara Damrosch at their remarkable Four Seasons Farm, one of his main suppliers, they gave us several small bags full of freshly pulled or picked vegetables, including some golf-ball-size baby turnips. We had reservations that night at Fore Street, so we took the turnips along and asked Mr. Hayward to cook them for us.

He steamed them, added salt, a knob of butter and a shower of chervil, and served them as a separate course so that they might shine on their own. Shine they did. We had found the Platonic ideal of turnips. That typical metallic sourness was there, but the cold Maine winter had intensified their sugars, adding a burst of sweetness.

They reminded me of one of my favorite dishes of the 1970s, the roast duck with turnips that André Allard served in his Left Bank bistro for a few weeks each spring. Only then, he explained, were the turnips right. Now I understand what he meant.

Before taking a closer look at the pioneers of the new Maine cuisine, let us take a fond glance at those who keep faithfully to the old ways.

I have been stopping for years at Bob's Clam Hut on Route 1, founded in 1956, around which Kittery's complex of outlet malls has since grown up. Bob's hasn't changed; it remains for me a kind of roadside seaside Nirvana. They convert hard-shell Quahog clams into buttery, blessedly unthickened chowder, and they fry soft-shell Ipswich clam bellies to golden crunchy perfection. These people are demons at the Frialator, changing the oil several times a day to ensure freshness. Their onion rings and lemonade are good, too. Stop in on your way to Bar Harbor or some more proletarian retreat this summer.

Route 1 is littered with diners and cafes. Moody's Diner in Waldoboro is the genuine old-fashioned article. John Thorne recommends the fried tripe with onions, a reminder that this remains a hardscrabble state, but we took the suggestion of Holly Billings, our cheery young waitress, and ordered four-berry pie. A slice of bliss appeared, still hot from the oven, juices of raspberries, strawberries, blackberries and blueberries oozing through tender (lard-based?) crust.

The Thomaston Café is a hybrid, embracing the traditional (haddock fishcakes and fluffy baking-powder pancakes), the innovative (wild mushroom hash) and the eclectic (cheese blintzes with blueberry sauce and black bean burritos). The filling in the divine coconut cream pie is creamy, not gluey, and the graham cracker crust is crunchy, not soggy. The names of suppliers are listed on the menu. Clearly a chef, no mere cook, is at work here; he is Herbert Peters, German-born, with 30 years in the trade.

With typical Yankee frugality, he charges extra for real Maine maple syrup.

No occasional visitor should dare to say who serves Maine's best lobster roll, that magical concoction of lobster and mayonnaise served on a toasted bun, unique to New England, which resembles two slices of bread hinged together. But my childhood friend Ethel Stansfield, a longtime resident of Wiscasset, says the best she has eaten are at Red's Eats, an idiosyncratic kiosk at the foot of the village's main street. Others agree. Red's is so small that it's portable; it was trucked over from Boothbay Harbor several decades back.

Waterman's Beach Lobster, just south of Rockland near Spruce Head, won a James Beard award last year. It is the quintessential Maine lobster shack, consisting of a small gray house, a deck with picnic tables, partly covered with an awning, and a jetty with traps and buoys stacked at the far end.

That's it, and that's enough. Sandy Manahan and Lorri Cousens, the sisters-in-law who run it, open only Thursday through Sunday, devoting the other three days to their children. Their menfolk catch the shellfish and deliver them daily; the women steam them in big pots. "Never, ever boil them, an inch of water, no more," Ms. Manahan told me. The result is sensationally sweet, supremely tender lobster, distinguished by its fine-grained texture.

A pair of one-pounders, with chips, coleslaw and soft drinks, cost us $28. The bay view toward fir-clad islets, a John Marin panorama in three dimensions, was free.

● ● ●

Both vegetable and flower gardens play parts in the allure of Arrows. An arbor covered with wisteria leads to the front door, and the main dining room, furnished in understated Craftsman style, looks out over trees outlined in tiny white lights, à la Tivoli, with pools of colorful blossoms beneath.

Thanks to cold frames and a greenhouse, the vegetable plots were already bursting with life in May: so much arugula, frisée, butter lettuce, red romaine, oak leaf and radicchio that Mr. Gaier said he couldn't use it all. Although it wasn't on the menu, we asked for a mixed salad. What arrived was fresh proof of the primacy of ingredients; it was subtle, sweet, crisp as spring, with each leaf sounding a distinctive note.

The kitchen whiffed once or twice, but it hit a half-dozen home runs, including delicious house-cured prosciutto, smoky sweetbreads, planked Atlantic salmon with ginger and an artful plate of contrasting tastes and textures: roasted scallops served with Burmese rice cakes and a tart Vietnamese salad with mint, basil and peppers. When Arrows opened in 1988, Mr. Frasier said, "supplies were scarce, and there was no really good seafood to be had, believe it or not." That problem has clearly been solved.

If Arrows has big-city aspirations (and big-city prices, with main courses about $40), Fore Street has a smaller-town feel (and smaller-town prices, with the most costly main dish at $26). It is Portland's crossroads, patronized by young and old, rich and not so rich, with a bustling bar and a glassed-in larder full of handsome produce like the tender aromatic young mizuna from New Leaf Farm in Durham that Mr. Hayward pairs to masterly effect with Jonah crabmeat and avocado.

This is unashamedly bold-tasting food. Mussels are cooked with garlic-almond butter, the almond bits adding both crunch and sweetness. The rabbit, a good-size beast, comes with strips of applewood-smoked bacon from a Vermont butcher. Wild mushrooms, some of them gathered by the restaurant's forager, Rick Tibbets, are roasted in the wood oven. I had deliciously meaty New Hampshire oyster mushrooms touched with veal broth; other seasons bring morels, chanterelles and pheasantbacks.

Fore Street's bracing stew of mussels, tuna, sablefish and salmon, flavored with fennel, tomatoes and more of that applewood bacon, is another product of the wood oven. Desserts are just as plain-spoken; as a lifelong foe of slimy rhubarb, I was thrilled by Mr. Hayward's chewy rhubarb crisp with a scoop of goat cheese ice cream.

You can eat plain or fancy at Ms. Kelly's Primo. The wood-fired pizza (including a white pie with Vidalia onions, roasted garlic and wilted arugula) is hard to resist. So don't. Order one to nibble while you decide whether to have "lobster pulled from its shell and served in a buttery nage of peas with their shoots," maybe, or Winterpoint oysters from the Damariscotta River estuary, deeply cupped, with a mineral finish and roasted with ramp butter.

Some of the fish swam in distant seas (Copper River salmon from Alaska, *daurade* from France), but Ms. Kelly is also a dab hand with lobster. In season she does an aristocratic lobster and asparagus salad with curry oil. But we made do, and then some, with humbler dishes: a crackling fritto misto of whitebait, Meyer lemon and baby artichokes with sorrel aioli; juicy rosemary-grilled lamb chops with gnocchi, peas and mint; and a bowl full of warm, utterly irresistible zeppole (round doughnuts) tossed in cinnamon and sugar.

We might have been in Sorrento.

Mr. Gutow's time in France with Michel Guérard and others shows in the delicacy and ambition of his cooking. A tiny starter of Penobscot Bay crabmeat with lavender mayonnaise and cardamom curry oil would have pleased the master with the way in which the flavors complemented rather than warred with one another. Steamed cherrystone clams with rice wine vinegar and sweet cicely, a seldom-used herb related to chervil, had an agreeably smoky taste.

A scallop from Blue Hill Bay, across the peninsula from Castine, rode to our table on a little raft of grilled leeks floating in a vividly, almost luridly, green chive broth. Sophisticated, labor intensive, not at all what one expects to find in a rural inn, it was flawlessly executed. So were minuscule rib chops from a just-weaned Cole Farm piglet. In the best French tradition, Mr. Gutow served a quartet of choice New England cheeses, notably York Hill Capriano, a goat cheese somewhat reminiscent of Parmigiano-Reggiano, which is also served at Craft in New York. It came with zinfandel honey.

The service, alas, was in the *Fawlty Towers* tradition. We waited 30 minutes for our starters and had to ask twice for bread. This is part of the risk in running a restaurant in so remote a spot. But Mr. Gutow and his wife, Amy, will eventually fix that, and meantime there are compensations like the gentle mural of the village that circles the dining room and the gorgeously orange-yolked eggs served at breakfast.

That, and the good Maine air. The longer I was in Castine, the more I thought of E. B. White, the *New Yorker* stalwart, who owned a saltwater farm in North Brooklin, not far from Castine. The breezes there, he once wrote, bear the "smell that takes man back to the very beginning of time, linking him to all that has gone before."

Maine's best-known purveyors of food ship fish and other fishy things. Rod Mitchell of Browne Trading Company in Portland sells not only cod from Casco Bay, haddock from the Gulf of Maine and sea urchins from inshore Maine waters, but also elvers from Spain and caviar from the Caspian Sea. Eric Ripert of Le Bernardin and Daniel Boulud of Daniel are customers.

One of his competitors is the improbable Ingrid Benis, who teaches American literature to Russian students in St. Petersburg in winter and prowls the docks of Stonington in summer, buying the best scallops, lobsters and peekytoe crab that she can find in these nutrient-rich waters. She ships them to 20 restaurants across the country, including Thomas Keller's French Laundry in the Napa Valley and Charlie Trotter's in Chicago.

Richard A. Penfold of Stonington Sea Products, an Englishman who learned his craft in the Shetland Islands, produces a superbly balanced smoked salmon in the Scottish style, neither as bland as the Norwegian product favored by the French nor as pungent as the typical Nova Scotia side, and a rich, glossy smoked haddock, known to the Scots as finnan haddie. (Cooked and flaked, it is the vital ingredient in a satisfying British breakfast and supper dish, the Arnold Bennett omelette.)

Mr. Penfold, who is 40, said he used both cherry and hickory wood in his ultramodern smoking plant, which opened in 2000. Although praised by critics and served by discriminating restaurateurs like Mr. Gutow, Stonington's products are only now starting to reach the general market.

Great Eastern Mussel Farms, based in Tenants Harbor, is the largest mussel processor in the country. On a blustery May afternoon, I pounded across Casco Bay in a flat-bottomed boat with Tollef Olson toward one of his rafts, anchored near Clapboard Island, off Portland. He grows mussels on ropes hanging from four rafts, selling the production of two of the rafts to Great Eastern and marketing the output of the others himself. Each of the rafts, which are 40-by-40 feet, yields 60,000 pounds a year, provided that predatory eider ducks can be kept at bay.

Farmed mussels grow faster than wild ones, explained Mr. Olson, a onetime diver. Domestic consumption has doubled from 40 million to 80 million pounds in five years, in part, I feel sure, because techniques have been developed to trim off the bivalves' wiry beards and get rid of the grit in their shells.

Big things are afoot ashore, too. Kelmscott Farm near Lincolnville, named after the English village where William Morris lived, and financed by Robert M. Metcalfe, one of the inventors of the Ethernet, breeds rare varieties like Cotswold sheep. It provided Ms. Kelly's Gloucestershire Old Spots.

But Maine affords nothing quite as special to the gastronomically minded tourist as Four Seasons Farm on Cape Rosier, south of Castine. Mr. Coleman and Ms. Damrosch, who are as fit and burnished by sun and wind as the things they grow, have found ways to raise vegetables all winter, beneath unheated polyester hoop houses. "Outside, the climate is Maine," Mr. Coleman said. "Inside, it's New Jersey. And under the covers over the seedlings, it's Georgia."

The fruit of these new techniques is sold to markets and restaurants close to Castine. But the farm's doctrines have spread across the land, through a television series and appearances at organic farming conferences. When Odessa Piper, the chef at the celebrated L'Etoile in Madison, Wis., had to cook at a New York gala before the growing season had begun in the upper Midwest, Mr. Coleman and Ms. Damrosch came through with vegetables—mâche, carrots, red-veined chard—whose vibrant flavors matched their good looks.

—Castine, Maine, July 10, 2002

SOUTH

Americana, Salted, Smoked and Sliced Thin

They have been curing hams in this tidy little community of 7,000 on the southern shore of the broad James River, only a few miles downstream from Jamestown and Williamsburg, for 200 years and more. Queen Victoria, it is said, was an avid consumer of the local delicacy.

Long ago the town was dotted with smokehouses. Every fall hogs were turned into the region's peanut fields, where they feasted on the stubble and the nuts left behind by inefficient harvesting methods. Come winter, the hogs were slaughtered. The hams were then salted, hardwood-smoked and hung up to age for a minimum of 180 days in the heat of summer, until they developed a mahogany color, a smoky aroma, a pungent flavor and a firm but never leathery texture.

Smithfield ham, granddaddy of all the dry-cured country hams produced in a half-dozen Southern states, bears about as much resemblance to your pink, watery, run-of-the-mill brine-cured ham as a horse chestnut does to a chestnut horse. It is much more like Yun-nan ham, for which it is often substituted in Chinese restaurants in New York, San Francisco and elsewhere.

I go way back with Smithfield ham. It was an abiding favorite of my father's, though he had no discernible connection with the South, and my mother gave him one for Easter or Christmas every year. He kept a special knife, long and flexible, for carving his treasures, and its use for anything else was strictly verboten.

You want ultrathin slices, he told me. Otherwise the flavor, concentrated by the ham's loss of 30 percent of its weight during aging, would be overwhelming, and the meat would be too chewy. The real family experts on this subject are my wife, Betsey, and her sister, Pie, who grew up in Richmond. In their household Smithfield ham was served either as a "side meat," a foil for something blander, perhaps chicken or turkey, or on beaten biscuits with drinks before dinner. More anon on the biscuits.

Some years ago Betsey brought a Virginia country ham—essentially a Smithfield-style ham made elsewhere in the state—on a trip to Scandinavia. We picnicked on sandwiches in Norway and Sweden and then, cruising on a friend's boat on the rainy Gulf of Finland, made a restorative split pea soup with the hock.

Smithfield wears its age well. St. Luke's Church, one of the country's oldest, built in rosy brick about 1632, stands east of town, and beautifully preserved Colonial and Victorian houses, some of them sheltered by magnificent magnolias, line streets near the Pagan River. But things have changed in two centuries. Peanuts aplenty still grow here in southeastern Virginia (Planters' headquarters is in nearby Suffolk), but hogs no longer forage in the peanut fields. Mechanical heating and refrigeration have made the changing seasons moot, and Smithfield hams are made all year.

State law still specifies that only hams "cured, treated, smoked and processed in the town of Smithfield" may be sold as genuine Smithfield hams. What that means in practice is that they must be produced in the factory of Smithfield Foods, which owns the only remaining smokehouse in town. Whatever the label says—Joyner, Luter, Amber,

Gwaltney or whatever—all Smithfield hams are made in that one plant from hogs that are raised to Smithfield Foods' specifications, here and in North Carolina.

Smithfield Foods is a behemoth formed by the combination of two old-line local companies, Smithfield Packing, controlled by the Luter family, and Gwaltney, as well as the subsequent acquisition of numerous smaller companies, including Krakus of Poland and American packers like Morrell and Cudahy. The nation's largest processor of pork, Smithfield ranked 256th among the American companies on the Fortune 500 list in 2004, with revenues of $7.9 billion.

To keep the Smithfield plant going, a total of some 50,000 hogs a day are slaughtered five days a week in three Smithfield Foods abattoirs, two here and one in North Carolina, according to Timothy A. Seely, Gwaltney's president. Each carcass yields two hams (one ham from each hind leg), which adds up to about 24 million hams a year. Of those, 92 percent are made by the vastly cheaper wet-cure processes and need not concern us here; the other 8 percent are country hams, produced by traditional methods. And of those, only 140,000, not even three days' worth of hogs, are real Smithfields.

Even with modern technology, it is a finicky process. How much salt? How long do you smoke? Lee Edwards, Smithfield Foods' ham master, told me: "You worry. I'm bald because it takes six months to find out whether you did things right."

John Egerton, an authority on the South's culinary traditions, grew up in Trigg County, Ky., which produces some of the country's best artisanal hams. Country ham, he wrote in *Southern Food* (Knopf, 1987), "is an ancient and inimitable treasure, the highest form of the Southern gastronomic art." Like many in the region, he fries quarter-inch slices of uncooked ham for breakfast, adding water or black coffee to the skillet to make red-eye gravy.

Today's Smithfield hams, Mr. Egerton argues, are imperfect because they "hang in artificially heated and cooled aging rooms, never experiencing the summer sweats" as in old-fashioned smokehouses.

I'm less particular than he, I guess, and Betsey and I regularly order either a whole cooked Smithfield ham—cooking your own, believe me, is a long, tedious, messy process—or packaged slices of cooked Smithfield ham, usually from Gwaltney. A favorite dish in our house is what used to be called crabmeat Norfolk: slices of Smithfield ham, arranged in individual ramekins (the kind often used for crème brûlée), topped with premium jumbo lump backfin crabmeat, dotted with butter and run under the broiler. Surf and turf, sweet with salty.

The beaten biscuits of Betsey's girlhood have all but vanished. Indeed, Mary Stuart Smith said as early as 1885 in her *Virginia Cookery-Book* that they were "sadly out of vogue" because of the labor involved in making them. The invention of a biscuit-making machine only slowed their decline. Now even the most heritage-conscious restaurants in southeastern Virginia serve ham with modern substitutes.

With its copious plantation breakfast, featuring eggs, grits, sausage, bacon and ham, the Old Chickahominy House, on the Williamsburg–Jamestown road, offers square, pitalike, baking-powder biscuit pockets. The Surrey House Restaurant, at Surry, fills small, buttered dinner rolls—three to a portion—with thinly sliced ham. Both use the superb country ham produced by S. Wallace Edwards & Sons Inc., also in Surry, which is slightly milder than Smithfield ham.

For a quick fix, we like to pair Virginia ham, either Smithfield or Edwards's, with the fluffy potato rolls widely sold in Maryland and Pennsylvania, or even the baking-powder biscuits that come chilled, ready for baking, in cardboard tubes.

Samuel W. Edwards III, the third-generation president of his family's firm, which has been in business for 79 years, said he tries "to take the best of what Mother Nature used to provide us with before refrigeration, and try to duplicate it all year." He finds the hybrid hogs of the sort Smithfield Foods uses too lean for his purposes, so he buys pork from Duroc and Berkshire hogs locally, in the Midwest or in Pennsylvania.

During a recent talk Mr. Edwards told me about a source in Lynchburg, Va., for the elusive beaten biscuits. The size of half-dollars, about three-quarters of an inch thick, they have the same jaw-breaking consistency as New England common crackers. A tin of 36 costs $12 on the Web at www.thefarmbasket.com. If I order some, Betsey promises, she will split them, butter them, heat them up a little and then slap slivers of ham between the halves. They will be a life-changing experience, she vows.

Smithfield Foods dominates its hometown. John B. Edwards, the editor of the *Smithfield Times*, the local weekly, told me, "They own everything around here that has anything to do with pigs."

Its scale is certainly enormous. I visited a cold room where hundreds of hams, coated with a mixture of 3 ounces of nitrite for each 100 pounds of meat, were stacked on wooden pallets, gradually yielding much of their moisture. Each pile bore a tag showing the date when it had been salted. One said, "1/21/05," and the hams in that pile, already well along, had tallowy fat. Hogarth would have felt completely at home.

The next stop is an intermediate step known as "equalizing," and then the hams go into a series of chambers in a smokehouse built largely of wood, "so it can expand and contract with the heat," as Lee Edwards, the ham master, explained. (Half the people in the area seem to be named Edwards, and they all insist that they're not related.) Fires are built from aged oak and green hickory in 55-gallon oil drums below, then topped with wet sawdust to keep them smoldering. The smoke rises through slats to the thousands of hams hanging above.

To get a glimpse of smaller-scale country-ham making, a visit to Darden's Country Store, deep in rural Isle of Wight County, south of Smithfield, seemed in order. When Betsey and I pulled up, the young woman minding the shop told us that Tommy Darden, the owner, was out on his tractor, feeding the cows. So we killed a few minutes poking around the place, decorated with mounted bucks' heads and a Virginia Tech banner, and inspecting the shelves, sparsely stocked with moon pies, tinned mackerel and big wheels of Wisconsin cheese.

Mr. Darden, a beefy man of sweet disposition, wearing a camouflage hunting cap and a Washington Redskins sweatshirt, told us that he makes about 750 hams a year in the little smokehouse across the road from the store, and sells every one of them to people who find their way to him through word of mouth. That saves him, he said, from the kind of regulatory headaches experienced by the big guys. (Smithfield Foods, from which he buys raw hams for curing, has run afoul of state and federal regulators because of its enormous manure lagoons, which critics say cause water pollution.)

"I started in the Future Farmers of America, and I do exactly what my father did," Mr. Darden said. "I salt for a day and a half per pound, I smoke over hickory and apple wood, I coat the hams with pepper and borax to deter bugs, which is washed off before I sell them, and I hang them right there in the shed, with no temperature or humidity controls at all. The older they get, the redder they get, the saltier they taste.

"I'm the last farmer in the county, I think, who's still doing it this way. It's a dying art, a dying something."

It's also a sideline for Mr. Darden, a kind of hobby for a man who cherishes agricultural tradition. He farms 600 acres (peanuts, cotton, soy and corn) and raises beef cattle in addition to making hams. By my lights it's worth it; his country ham has the subtlest flavor of any I've tasted, and I couldn't resist buying one, cooked and boned, for $92. Who knows when I'll get back to the wilds of Isle of Wight County?

—*Smithfield, Virginia, March 23, 2005*

Bourbons in the Cognac League

B orn in the backwoods traditions of the 18th century, bourbon has lost much of its kick in the last decades of the cosmopolitan 20th. To much of the country, it has seemed as up-to-date as a typewriter, as chic as a Studebaker.

Ask almost anyone. Dry is cool, he will tell you, and bourbon is sweet. Exotic is cool, and bourbon is familiar. See-through booze like vodka is cool, and bourbon is brown. Except in the southeastern quadrant of the country, bourbon has been shunned as the drink of the rube and the codger. Old Crow, Old Forester, Old Grand-Dad, Wild Turkey, Early Times—the very names seem calculated to turn off urban America, in its manic pursuit of the newest and the slickest.

But all that is changing.

Deluxe bourbons, richer and subtler in flavor than the run-of-the-mill product, with far less rasp in the back of the throat, have fueled a modest revival of interest in the Manhattan cocktail that parallels the recent vogue for the martini. Bourbon and branch water, that standby of Southern politicians, is slowly seeping back into style in the North. Most surprising, single-barrel and small-batch bourbons, as deluxe whiskeys are called, have joined Cognac and Armagnac in the after-dinner snifters of Americans, and are winning the plaudits of sophisticates in France and Britain.

Like the popularity of single-malt Scotches, which helped set American distillers onto this new and profitable road, the vogue for deluxe bourbons grew out of the realization that heavy drinking caused severe health problems and slaughter on the highways. Getting pickled (loaded, smashed, plastered—choose your adjective) wasn't funny anymore. As Gary and Mardee Haidin Regan tell the story in their *Book of Bourbon* (Chapters, 1995), people turned to "the good stuff," looking for drinks to linger over, not guzzle. The beneficiaries were wines, premium gins and vodkas, single malts and, finally, high-quality bourbon.

Still, overall domestic sales have dropped more than 50 percent in the last quarter-century, with per capita bourbon consumption in 1995, the last year for which the Distilled Spirits Council can supply figures, at 0.16 gallons, compared with 0.4 in 1969. (Sales abroad, on the other hand, are rising.) Ed O'Daniel, a spokesman for the Kentucky Distillers' Association, said that only nine companies account for Kentucky's entire bourbon output, compared with the hundreds of years ago. A shrinking market, the demand for huge capital investment and an emphasis on marketing have pushed the little guys out of a business once dominated by individualists.

But the new products have restored the buzz to a weary industry.

Blanton's, Knob Creek, Baker's, Basil Hayden's and Rock Hill Farms, priced at $30 a bottle and up, have taken their place in liquor stores and on bars in Chicago, New York, Washington, San Francisco and other big Yankee cities. In Kentucky, where all are made, acceptance has been slower; drinkers tend to stay with the brands they have knocked back all their lives.

Bourbon is as American as the saloon, and like those other patriotic tipples, Coca-Cola and Pepsi-Cola, a product of the South. Scottish and Irish settlers in Maryland and Pennsylvania brought a knowledge of distilling with them, set up stills well before the Revolution and staged a violent uprising against the young federal government in 1791, a protest against new taxes known as the Whisky Rebellion. Eventually, the distillers found their natural home in Kentucky, which had ample land suited to cultivating distillable grain, plentiful white oak for barrels and subsurface limestone in the area around Louisville.

That limestone confers many blessings: lush bluegrass paddocks that feed Kentucky's fabled, Derby-bound racehorses; the buttery limestone lettuce beloved of salad mavens and the pure, sweet spring water that goes into whisky. The local product subsequently took the name of Bourbon County, east of Lexington, where riverboats picked it up for distribution across the country (just as England's Stilton cheese is named for a stagecoach stop where farmers took their product for shipment to London).

By 1822, "ardent spirits," as Jefferson called them, were so popular that a visitor to the state defined a Kentucky breakfast as "three cocktails and a chaw of terbacker." That was the era of Dr. James C. Crow, a Scottish physician, who developed the sour-mash method of recycling part of each distilling run in the next.

At about the same time, unknown pioneers first charred barrels of new white oak for aging whiskey. Both techniques are used in making today's bourbons, which by federal law must be distilled at not more than 80 percent alcohol (160 proof) and must contain at least 51 percent corn (though most contain more, plus rye or wheat, in proportions ranging from 2 to 37 percent, and malted barley).

So what makes the new bourbons special? Some are older, which means they have spent more time in contact with the oak that tames some of their fire and gives them the tastes that connoisseurs love—vanilla, smokiness, caramel, with hints of peaches, cloves and honey. Some are stronger, cut with little water.

They offer the same sort of pleasure a good Cognac does, with their complex perfumes and their amalgams of fruit, sugar and spice flavors, begging to be rolled around the mouth. They are meant to be drunk slowly, perhaps with a good cigar. In their rustic quality, they resemble Armagnac, with the flavor of corn, not grapes.

But deluxe bourbons differ less from mass-produced brands like Jim Beam or I. W. Harper than single-malt Scotches differ from Dewar's or Cutty Sark. The Scotches are blends of one or more single malts with neutral spirits, but all the straight bourbons, whether standard or deluxe, are 100 percent bourbon.

Premium bourbons are shamelessly ballyhooed by the advertising and public-relations fraternities. A distiller may tout the special mashbill, or recipe, he uses for his premium brand, when in fact he uses much the same formula for both the cheapest and costliest products in his range. A lot of nonsense is put about on the subject of "secret" strains of yeast.

Labels fairly drip with hyperbole, as in this on Blanton's Single Barrel, a mahogany-hue product of the Ancient Age Distillery that started the whole deluxe craze in 1984: "We believe this is the finest bottle of whiskey ever produced."

Nonetheless, it is hard to argue with Nancy Lintner, vice president for marketing of Jim Beam Brands, which makes four small-batch bourbons, when she insists that "small-batch and single-barrel bourbons have a more refined taste, a unique taste that almost everyone who tries them recognizes immediately."

The first upscale bourbon to enter the market was Maker's Mark, produced at an old distillery in Loretto, Ky. Technically neither a single-barrel nor a small-batch whiskey, it is nonetheless carefully crafted (with a hand-dipped red seal on each bottle), and it is a bargain at about $16, half the price of the deluxe brands.

If you like your alcohol powerful, there is no better choice than Booker's, the only bourbon bottled straight from the barrel, uncut at about 125 or 126 proof and unfiltered, which leaves the flavor-bearing elements called congeners intact (in cold weather they can cause a bit of cloudiness).

Booker's was first produced by Jim Beam in 1987 as a Christmas gift for favored wholesalers and named for Booker Noe, a master distiller and a grandson of Jim Beam himself. It went public in 1989. This is a small-batch whiskey, which means that very little is produced, not that it is separately distilled in small batches. It is blended from barrels kept in the center of Beam's warehouses, where temperatures vary little, avoiding the rapid evaporation that Kentucky's summer heat produces in other parts of the sheds. Aged six to eight years, it has a bold, decidedly alcoholic flavor, with flashes of tobacco, wood and oranges in the background. Only about 6,000 cases are made each year, whereas some 3 million cases of Jim Beam, the market leader, are sold annually in the United States.

• • •

A mellower whiskey of great distinction, introduced in the last few years, is Woodford Reserve, produced along Glenn's Creek in Woodford County, Ky. Whiskey has been made on the site since 1812. This is Kentucky's sole pot-still whiskey, 20 years old, made in copper vessels in an old stone distillery. The flasklike bottle says Labrot & Graham, but the big Brown Forman combine of Louisville, which makes Old Forester and Early Times, owns this operation, too. None of this affects the smooth, nutmeggy flavor of 90.4-proof Woodford Reserve, or its notably long and supple finish. If Booker's barks, Woodford purrs. Both should be drunk neat, after dinner.

The favorite of Susan Reigler, the knowledgeable restaurant critic of the *Louisville Courier-Journal*, and of others who have tried it, is the jokily named, 20-year-old Pappy Van Winkle's Family Reserve. Available mainly in stores in Louisville and surrounding Jefferson County, this is the one to tuck into your suitcase if you find yourself there on business or vacation. Its aroma and taste murmur of raisins, spices and vanilla, and it has a thick, rich body. "Grand stuff, with so many layers of flavor it reminds me of old Bordeaux," Ms. Reigler says.

Abraham Lincoln, a teetotaler himself, was supposedly so impressed by the prowess of Gen. Ulysses S. Grant, his bourbon-loving commander, that he asked what Grant's brand was, so he could send some to his other, less aggressive commanders. History does not record the answer, but any of the single-barrel or small-batch bourbons would have done wonders for Burnside, McClellan and their mates.

—*Kentucky, September 17, 1997*

Where the Biscuits Meet the Gravy

One of the things that brightens the lives of itinerant scribblers like me is breakfast.

As it happens, I've spent a lot of time over the years in the American South, a region that has always specialized in big, bountiful breakfasts, at least partly because an energy-giving meal is better consumed in the morning than at midday in its steamy climate. In the South, culinary tradition was largely shaped in rural kitchens with access to a restricted range of ingredients, notably corn and pork, which, in the form of superb ham, bacon, sausage and grits, still grace regional breakfast tables. Starting from there, more prosperous Southerners devised elaborate hunt breakfasts and plantation breakfasts, with mint juleps and silver chafing dishes.

At a little place called the Hominy Grill in the not-yet-quite-fashionable Cannonborough neighborhood of Charleston, they serve boffo breakfasts of the traditional kind. These may well be the best breakfasts in the Carolinas, which means some of the best in America. This is a place whose breads are homemade, where instant grits and quick grits and machine-ground grits find no welcome. Fried eggs are gentled to perfection, with the yolks brilliantly glossy and just slightly set and none of those dry, disagreeably frazzled edges on the whites.

At the Hominy Grill, in other words, breakfast is no gastronomic stepchild. It is cooked as carefully as if it were a banquet.

Funny about breakfasts: You remember the best ones for a long time, always in geographical context. The feasts I've eaten recently at the Hominy Grill have taken a place in my mind alongside the noodle soup called *pho* that women in conical straw hats dispense in the streets of Saigon, the ricotta pancakes at Bill's in Sydney, Australia, and the gargantuan feeds, complete with blood sausage, that I used to put away in the English Lake District.

When I think of Iowa, I think of the softball-size cinnamon buns served in Amana, the utopian community in eastern Iowa. The Baltic countries, for me, mean brisk herring-and-salami eye-openers, and Wyoming means tinglingly fresh pan-fried trout with hash browns. Now breakfast at the Hominy Grill is bracketed with Charleston and its gentle ways.

All over the South, breakfast means grits, sometimes plain, sometimes with cheese mixed in and sometimes with grillades—thin, square-cut pieces of fried pork or veal. Here in the Low Country it can also mean shrimp and grits with lashings of black pepper, though the sweet little river shrimp—once sold door-to-door in Charleston by hawkers from the barrier islands calling out, "Swimpee, swimpee"—are mostly a thing of the past.

In early spring, breakfast at the Hominy Grill means the supreme delight of mahogany-dark, gamy-tasting shad roe, gently sautéed in butter and still a bit pink in the center, served with scrambled eggs.

But Robert Stehling, the grill's chef, is by no means tradition-bound. He modifies some of the old favorites, using country ham and mushrooms instead of crumbled sausage in the gravy ladled over biscuits and scattering sliced, uncooked scallions over all to provide a crisp, green contrast.

Why not stick strictly to the old formula? I asked him. "I had to make one nod to people's arteries," he replied. "We're right near the hospital."

Mr. Stehling invents, too, notably at brunch. His fried green tomato BLT, the tomatoes crunchy in bread-crumb jackets, is a big hit on weekends. So is an omelette of spinach, Cheddar cheese and chunks of bacon, which, though warm, somehow retains some of the freshness of a spinach salad.

As for his homemade meatloaf sandwich with green tomato ketchup, a condiment he developed while working in New York, I devoured it with an alacrity unbecoming in someone who gets paid to taste carefully.

Mr. Stehling, 36, is a big, bashful North Carolinian who owns the restaurant with his wife, Nunally Kersh, the producer of Spoleto Festival USA, Charleston's yearly spring bash of music, theater and dance (this year, May 26 through June 11). Mr. Stehling and Ms. Kersh, 34, an elfin, energetic woman, moved to Charleston in November 1996.

She had been working at the Lincoln Center Festival in New York; he had done stints in the kitchens of Arizona 206 (under Brendan Walsh), Sarabeth's, the Monkey Bar (under John Schenk) and Home. But he learned his most important lessons at the stove long before reaching New York, during six years at the side of Bill Neal, who made Crook's Corner, his restaurant in Chapel Hill, N.C., one of the incubators of modern Southern cooking. Mr. Stehling started as a dishwasher and left as executive chef.

In *Bill Neal's Southern Cooking* (University of North Carolina Press, 1985), Mr. Neal, who died in 1991, harks back to the antebellum South and argues that "the best legacy of that society is what still makes some of us Southerners: the architecture, the literature, the food, the continuity of man and nature that shapes our perceptions." I can't imagine Mr. Stehling saying or writing something like that—he never finished college, and he remains too much the country boy to use fancy words—but I am sure he believes it.

Mr. Stehling and Ms. Kersh took over a 19th-century barbershop that had been converted into a restaurant before they bought it. The *Charleston Post and Courier* had said it served "the worst food in town."

Stripping purple paint off the handsome old tongue-and-groove vertical paneling, the two of them painted it white and left other features intact, including a stamped tin ceiling, heart-pine flooring and three paddle fans. Brown butcher paper covers the tables at breakfast. The most incongruous items in the airy room are the pleasantest—oversize reproduction Windsor armchairs that afford a degree of comfort rare in restaurants.

The couple began with just breakfast and lunch, hoping to attract a neighborhood clientele; now they do "three squares a day" every weekday, Ms. Kersh said. But breakfast and brunch (on Saturdays and Sundays) remain firm favorites of locals and out-of-towners, to say nothing of Mr. Stehling, who told me that "breakfast in the South remains very traditional, perfect for what I always wanted to do, good plain food, made from scratch."

All kinds of people show up at the grill. One day I saw a Rolls-Royce parked outside, another day, three Harley-Davidsons. On Sundays, Ms. Kersh said, different folks turn up at different hours: at 8, the runners and the tennis players; then, around 10 or 10:30, "people who are mildly hungover," followed, around midday, by the churchgoers, including a fair number from the very posh Grace Episcopal, and finally, along about 2:15, "people showing real damage from the night before."

Like all good chefs, Mr. Stehling is fussy about ingredients. He uses grits ground on a stone wheel at the Old Mill in Guilford County, N.C., near where he grew up. His father still lives near there, and every time he comes for a visit, he throws a couple of hundred pounds into the trunk of his car. But not everything, Mr. Stehling said, is as he would like.

Eggs, for example. Mr. Stehling uses supermarket eggs, because he needs 60 dozen every weekend, and no one in this area keeps enough free-range chickens to produce that many. Sometimes, he said, the store-bought eggs are fine, but sometimes they are too old and have too much water content, which causes the yolks to break when the eggs are flipped in frying.

"Eggs are an art," he said.

At the Hominy Grill, unlike some refined eating places downtown, lard, not olive oil, is the shortening of choice. Collard greens are stewed, not wilted. And biscuits come from Mr. Stehling's hands, not a tin. He also makes granola from scratch, and banana bread and even sausage.

Ah, the sausage. Southern sausage tastes different, and Mr. Stehling's tastes very Southern—although it is not as fatty as he would like, because he can't find pork with a high enough fat content in these days of superlean hogs. Southern sausage usually comes in patties, not links, but the shape is not the main point. The seasoning is. Starting with Boston butts, a shoulder cut, Mr. Stehling grinds the meat with chili peppers and cracked black peppercorns, for pungency, and sage, for the essential, characteristic musky taste.

"Rubbed sage, dried sage," the chef emphasized. "Don't ever try it with fresh sage. The rubbed sage gives it its Southern drawl."

—*Charleston, South Carolina, April 26, 2000*

• •

MUSHROOM GRAVY
(Adapted from the Hominy Grill)
Time: 15 minutes

    8 ounces mushrooms
    3 tablespoons butter
    2 tablespoons all-purpose flour
    1 cup milk, more as needed
    Tabasco sauce
    Salt and freshly ground black pepper

1. Using a food processor, finely chop mushrooms; do not puree. In a large skillet over medium-low heat, melt butter, then add mushrooms. Saute until liquid released from mushrooms has evaporated and they begin to brown.
2. Reduce heat to low, add flour and stir constantly for 2 more minutes. Slowly add milk to mixture, stirring constantly. Allow mixture to thicken for a minute or two, then add more milk as needed to achieve the consistency of thick gravy. Season to taste with Tabasco sauce, salt and pepper.

Yield: About 2 cups

HIGH-RISE BISCUITS WITH MUSHROOM GRAVY AND SCALLIONS
(Adapted from the Hominy Grill)
Time: 30 minutes

  4 cups all-purpose flour, more for dusting
  2 tablespoons baking powder
  1 teaspoon salt
  2 teaspoons sugar
  4 tablespoons chilled butter
  2 ounces chilled vegetable shortening
  1 ounce chilled lard
  1½ cups milk
  mushroom gravy (see preceding recipe)
  3 tablespoons thinly sliced scallions, for garnish

1. Preheat oven to 425 degrees. In a large bowl, sift together the flour, baking powder, salt and sugar.
2. Using a pastry cutter or two knives held in scissors fashion, cut butter, shortening and lard into the flour until slightly crumbly. Add milk, and stir gently until mixture is cohesive.
3. Turn dough onto a lightly floured surface. Knead lightly (less than 10 strokes) and loosely shape into a ball. With floured hands, pat into a large disk about 1¼ inches thick. Using a floured 3-inch biscuit or cookie cutter, cut 12 biscuits. Place on a baking sheet about 2 inches apart.
4. Bake biscuits until golden brown, 10 to 12 minutes. To serve, place two biscuits on each of six plates. Top with mushroom gravy and scallions.

Yield: 12 biscuits

Ten-Gallon Grapefruit: Living Up to Texas Legend

One dispiriting winter night a year ago, when spring seemed an implausible prospect, our neighbor Ken Bentsen rang the doorbell.

"Have something for you," he announced in his laconic way, handing over a paper bag that felt as if it had cannonballs in it.

Some cannonballs. What we found, in fact, were several enormous grapefruits, each fatter than a slow-pitch softball, with crimson-tinged yellow skins. They were the biggest we had ever seen, and as we discovered when we cut into them at breakfast the next morning, the reddest and sweetest. Like blood oranges and Meyer lemons and Key limes, whose acquaintance we had happily made in earlier years, in Morocco, California and Florida, they were a spectacularly different breed of citrus. Forget spring; they brought summer sunshine flooding into our winterbound kitchen.

"Mm," said my wife, Betsey. "Mmmm," said I. "Mmmmmm," said Betsey, who was too busy slurping to compose one of her customary apothegms.

It was not hard to figure out where the big fellows had come from. Mr. Bentsen is a congressman from Houston, a nephew of the former senator and secretary of the treasury Lloyd M. Bentsen. The clan made a fortune in the Rio Grande Valley, along the Mexican border, in real estate and banking, cotton and citrus fruit.

I presumed (correctly, as it turned out) that the giant grapefruits had been specially selected for family and friends; they were the biggest of the crop. I knew perfectly well that supermarkets carried similar if smaller stock. What I wanted to know was: Why do Texas reds look and taste so different from ordinary grapefruit? Mr. Bentsen suggested that I head for McAllen, the heartland of the Texas citrus industry, and find out for myself.

So I did.

Before I came, I discovered I was not alone in my enthusiasm for Texas grapefruit. Over lunch at her restaurant Chez Panisse in Berkeley, Calif., Alice Waters, who usually reserves her encomiums for foods produced within close range of her kitchen, made an exception: "I'm in love with those things—in a big way," she said. Across the country in Manhattan, Alain Ducasse, another raw-material maven, has been serving an airy red-grapefruit soufflé.

The grapefruit in question, the Rio Red, is the offspring of nature and science, of natural mutation and painstaking work in the lab. It is a result of a century-long search, here and in Florida, for a frost-resistant and heavy-bearing tree that would yield fruit with flesh as juicy, as nearly seedless and as deeply ruby-hued as possible.

The red color comes from lycopene, one of a series of naturally occurring pigments called carotenoids, which also colors watermelon and tomatoes. In addition to making things look pretty, lycopene is said to reduce the risk of cancer, heart attacks and certain kinds of blindness; much of this research has been underwritten by Heinz, which has a vested interest, of course, in persuading people to consume more ketchup.

But how did the lycopene get into the grapefruits? And why only certain varieties? Good questions, but I had no luck in finding definitive answers, even from John V. Da Graca, the scholarly deputy director of Texas A&M's Citrus Center at Weslaco, a few miles east of McAllen.

"We know that it suddenly turned up in a few grapefruits on trees that had previously produced pale grapefruits," he said. "The first time that happened was in Florida, in 1907. It happened again, here in the valley, in 1929. These were sports, or natural mutations. Citrus, which has a rather fragile genetic structure, lends itself to mutations more easily than most fruits."

All grapefruits, which bear the whoop-de-do botanical name Citrus paradisi, stem from a natural cross between a sweet orange (Citrus sinensis) and a pomelo (Citrus grandis), an aromatic, low-acid fruit with many segments. Both parents are Southeast Asian, but the hybrid developed, scientists believe, on Barbados in the 18th century.

And why "grapefruit"? Because it grows in clusters like grapes, not for its flavor.

The first grapefruit grown on a large scale in the United States was the white-fleshed Duncan, which apparently predates the Civil War. From that came the Thompson and Foster varieties, both pink, and the Marsh, which is white. Specimens of all three were brought from Florida to form the basis of the commercial citrus industry in Texas. It flourished for a time as far north as the town of Orange, near the Louisiana border, but freezes in 1949, 1951, 1962, 1983 and 1989 wiped out millions of trees (and cleaned out not a few bank accounts).

"You lived through that, you'll never have to look up the dates," said Don Bentsen, Ken's uncle, as we drove west from McAllen to visit a citrus grove. "Killed the trees right down to the ground. Before that, we'd never really seen a tree-killing freeze in the valley. Hundred-year freezes, they called them, one a century. We had a whole bunch, fast. Bang! Bang! Bang!"

(Devastating freezes hit California and Florida from time to time, too. But there the groves are much more widely dispersed, so some escape damage.)

Very quickly, action shifted to the lab. A quest began for hardier red grapefruit varieties, and Richard A. Hensz, a Texas horticulturist, began irradiating seeds with thermal neutrons, or X-rays, at Brookhaven National Laboratories on Long Island in the hope of inducing further mutations. In 1965, he produced the Star Ruby, released to growers in 1970. It was pleasingly red, the color of a glass of claret held up to light.

But the Star Ruby tree proved to be unusually sensitive to damage from herbicides, and it bore fruit with disconcerting irregularity. Back to the drawing board went Dr. Hensz, and in 1976 he came up with the Rio Red, the paragon among red grapefruits, at least so far.

Released in 1984, it is now grown worldwide. Both varieties are now sold under the label Rio Star.

At least two things, growers told me, give Texas grapefruits their unusual sweetness. One is soil. Valley groves are laid out on the dead-flat alluvial bottomlands several miles north of the Rio Grande, an area of highly alkaline, very sandy loam. The soil in grapefruit-growing areas of Florida is similar, they said. The second big factor is weather. The valley has warm overnight temperatures and long, warm springs and autumns.

"Our trees flower in February and March," explained Paul Heller, vice president for field operations at Rio Queen Citrus Inc., as we walked through a grove. "By April the fruit is pea-sized, by May it's the size of a golf ball and in September or October we start harvesting, and that lasts until April or May. Sometimes you have two crops on the same tree at once. You take off only a little bit at a time; the tree is by far the best place to store the fruit."

Left uncultivated, grapefruit trees grow as high as 50 feet, but they are kept to 9 to 12 feet in the groves, planted in straight lines about two feet apart. In some of the biggest orchards, the rows stretch for miles, well beyond the eye's reach, merging to form a sea of grapefruit on dry land.

I had expected McAllen to be a one-horse town, but it turned out to be a peppy little burg of half a million, full of Mexicans come to spend the day shopping in its stores. Shaded by palm trees, which benefit as much as citrus from 330 days of sunshine a year, it also attracts tens of thousands of "winter Texans" each year, who flee the snow and ice of the upper Midwest.

Eventually, many of the visitors stay. That helped make the Mc-Allen metropolitan area, which includes Edinburg and Mission, the third-fastest growing in the nation in the last decade. (Only Laredo, Tex., 150 miles up the valley, and Las Vegas are growing faster.) Land that once grew grapefruit now sprouts tract houses.

Growth and the freezes are the main reasons for the decline in acreage devoted to citrus production here. Texas had 100,000 acres in citrus in the 1940's, compared with about 33,000 today, of which 23,000 or so are in grapefruit. The state ranks fourth in the United States in citrus output, after Florida, the dominant factor in the business, California and Arizona.

The appearance of Texas grapefruit can suffer from wind scarring, but that doesn't affect the taste, and TexaSweet Citrus Marketing Inc. earns its public-relations dollar by describing the blemishes as "tropical beauty marks" and ascribing them to "gentle Gulf breezes."

Texas still earns $50 million a year from citrus fruit, the bulk of it from grapefruit, according to Ray Prewett, executive vice president of the Texas Citrus Mutual, a trade association. Once there were 28 commercial packinghouses in the valley; now there are seven, but they are much bigger.

The biggest is Rio Queen's in Mission, a vast shed that has a processing line the length of two football fields. More than four million 40-pound boxes of citrus are packed there every year. Early in the season, until about Dec. 1, the fruit is held briefly in curtained-off bays where heat and ethylene gas help brighten its color. Later on, the weather will do that.

A million pieces of fruit a day pass through a series of clattering machines on the line. They are cleaned in the "car wash," where high-pressure jets spray them with a mild chlorine solution. Then the smaller grapefruits, plus the misshapen and badly bruised ones, are picked out by inspectors and sent to the juice plant. The money is in the fresh fruit, not in juice.

The fruit has a matte finish when picked; a light coat of wax, dried in an oven, makes it shine. Next the grapefruits are weighed, one by one, by electronic load cells as they pass by. A computer translates weight into size, automatically sorts the fruit and keeps a record of what it has done. The biggest are called 18's because it takes that many to fill a standard box; the smallest are 56's. All are hand-packed, about two boxes a minute.

The Martin family, who came here from Missouri 30 years ago, are the uncrowned kings of Texas citrus. They own 3,500 acres of their own, farm 1,000 more for other people and process the production of dozens of smaller growers, who maintain plots as small as 10 or 20 acres.

One of the most innovative growers is Dennis Holbrook, a rebel against what he terms "the pharmaceutical conception of agriculture." Unlike any other, his company, South Texas Organics, produces red grapefruit without pesticides, herbicides or chemical fertilizers. He became an organic farmer, he said, partly to please his wife, who was worried about the chemicals in the food that their children were eating.

"I figured it was worth a try," he continued, "because I was trapped in a vicious cycle anyway—more irrigation, leaching more nutrients from the soil, which meant more fertilizer, which meant more weeds and more herbicides. When you finished, you had almost a sterile medium, with very little organic matter in the soil, and you had no choice but to keep the cycle going.

"The big freeze of 1983 let me hop off the merry-go-round."

Now Mr. Holbrook uses naturally mined sulfur to help fight scale and rust mites. To minimize weeds, he plants cover crops like hay grazer, which has the additional benefit, he said, of creating a habitat for beneficial insects that eat less desirable ones. He makes his own compost from manure and poultry litter. And he has gradually scaled back from 10 irrigations a year to 4 or 5 as his trees have gradually developed much deeper root systems.

It costs 20 to 25 percent more, Mr. Holbrook estimated, to farm citrus organically, mainly because of labor costs for weed control. But his grapefruit and other products command prices 10 to 25 percent higher, from clients like Kroger, and the Whole Foods chain, based in Austin.

He is just as threatened as conventional growers, however, by the brown citrus aphid, which carries the lethal virus tristeza. It killed 30 million trees in Argentina and Brazil, reached Florida in 1995 and the Yucatán last year. Trees planted on sour-orange rootstock that originated in Brazil, like those in Texas, are most vulnerable, but so far the aphid has not reached the valley.

—*McAllen, Texas, March 7, 2001*

It Takes More Than Crayfish
to Make a Cajun Wiggle

Here in the land of drive-through daiquiri joints and truck-stop casinos, you often eat better in grocery stores, butcher shops and cafes than you do in restaurants. There are exceptions, of course, but in Acadiana, as a rule, the more rudimentary the surroundings, the more genuine the grub.

Bare bulbs, in other words, are what you look for, not recessed lighting, paper napkins, not linen.

Another thing: the best Cajun cooking isn't blisteringly hot, contrary to popular belief. It's not about incinerating fish and meat. The guardians of regional tradition produce rich, slowly simmered soups and stews, more boldly flavored than most American food, yes, but not one-dimensional.

Take Suire's Grocery, three miles south of here, on the edge of the rice country. The name rhymes with "beer," the décor runs to soft-drink coolers and Formica tables and the menu lists some weird combos like crawfish fettuccine. But the crowds don't come to Kaplan for that. Hunters out for duck and speckle-bellied goose stop in for the fabulous turtle sauce picante, which few cooks bother with anymore, or luscious, old-fashioned shrimp and egg stew, or deep-fried catfish, as crisp as tissue paper.

It can take up to four hours to cook the turtle meat until it's tender enough, one of the Suire daughters told me, but it's worth it. Served without ceremony in a plastic-foam box, bathed in a glistening, peppery, reddish-brown gravy, the turtle tastes like chicken dark meat but better, with the smoky, untamed tang of the bayou.

Cajun food is poor people's food. Many of the ingredients are there for the taking, like turtles and alligators, game birds and shrimp and crabs, and many of the others are cheap, like oysters and cane syrup. Tomatoes and okra and mirliton (a kind of gourd or squash) are easily grown; pigs, easily raised in the backyard, yield matchless sausages like andouille and boudin, *tasso* ham and *gratons* (fried pork skins).

The first Cajuns had no choice but to make do. Thousands of settlers were driven from the colony of Acadie in eastern Canada in the 1750s because they refused to swear an oath of allegiance to King George II after the British wrested control from the French. Over the next 50 years, 3,000 to 5,000 of them found their way to southwestern Louisiana. Some came directly from Canada; others went to France before coming here.

Broussards and Robichauds were among them, and Broussards and Robichauds are prominent in Acadiana today. Isolated from New Orleans and the rest of the outside world until Huey P. Long began building bridges in the 1930s and Uncle Sam began drafting their sons in the 1940s, the Cajuns clung doggedly to their own patois, a linguistic gumbo of modern French, 17th-century French (*maringouin* rather than *moustique* for "mosquito," for instance, and *catin*, which means "harlot" in modern French, for "doll"), African languages (gris-gris for a hex or spell) and invented expressions (*tac-tac* for "popcorn" and *gru* for "grits").

"For 200 years we've been an island of French culture in the middle of English-speaking America," said David Greely, a fiddler in a top Cajun dance band, Steve Riley and the Mamou Playboys. "We're hardheaded."

They guard their food traditions just as zealously as their linguistic traditions. Recalling her childhood in the town of St. Martinville, Marcelle Bienvenu, an authority on Cajun food, wrote a decade ago: "I can't remember a day that tables were not filled with tureens of gumbo or stew, platters of baked chicken or variously prepared seafood, bowls of garden vegetables and baskets of French bread and biscuits. I walked through my childhood believing everyone enjoyed the pleasure of preparing and consuming jambalaya, crawfish bisque and stewed okra. Food and its preparation were at the center of our lives." But even here, Ms. Bienvenu said recently at her bright, snug cottage near Bayou Teche, "it's a battle" to keep the younger generations conscious of their heritage. Her nieces and nephews, she said, "were ready to settle for fast food—cheeseburgers with their boyfriends and girlfriends." She added, with a satisfied smile: "I taught them otherwise. Now they make gumbo."

The day I went to Suire's I had already eaten a lot. I might say I had already eaten breakfast and brunch, but that would be a lie. In fact, Suire's was my third lunch of the day; there is so much good food in Acadiana that sometimes you have to extend yourself. Arnold Goodman, a famous lawyer in London, a man of formidable forensic skill and gargantuan appetite, was known as Two-Dinners Goodman; I guess I'll be known in the future as Three-Lunches Apple.

Well, so be it. I had company—my wife, Betsey, and two of our Washington neighbors, Jurek Martin, a longtime foreign correspondent for the *Financial Times* and a sumo aficionado, and his wife, Kathleen Newland, an expert on refugees, whose parents live in Lafayette, La., the Cajun capital. She is a home cook of note and one of those infuriating people who eat like a horse and stay as lean as a greyhound.

We started in New Iberia—not in semi-bustling downtown New Iberia, but on the more utilitarian side of town, which has a lot of boarded-up and burnt-out buildings. We started with boudin, a khaki-colored link sausage filled with a mixture of rice, ground pork (mostly the less attractive parts of the pig) and spices (including plenty of cayenne and a fair amount of garlic).

Cajun boudin bears no resemblance at all to French boudin, which is either a blood sausage (*boudin noir*) or a mild sausage of veal or chicken (*boudin blanc*). It has more in common with Pennsylvania Dutch scrapple; that, however, is bound with cornmeal rather than rice, flavored primarily with sage rather than pepper, and sliced, then fried, not boiled or steamed whole.

Billboards on every highway in Acadiana promote the boudin at this gas station or that grocery store. They are as common as kudzu. But we headed for Bonin's, a butcher shop that has no need of billboards; it is the favorite of not only Calvin Trillin, the *New Yorker* writer, and James Edmunds, a certified New Iberia chowhound, but also Paul McIlhenny, the chief executive of the company that makes Tabasco sauce.

Others prefer the Best Stop Supermarket in Scott, which makes boudin with more liver and less heat, as well as chewy, pungent, cherry-red *tasso*; or Boudin King in Jennings; or Hebert's in Abbeville.

Our rendezvous, housed in the simplest of white frame buildings, is the domain of Waldo Bonin, known as Nook, and his wife, Delores. It stands a few blocks from Shadows-on-the-Teche, the plantation where Bunk Johnson, the great cornet man, worked as a gardener. An out-of-date calendar hangs on the wall, and the glass-front meat cases are filled only with soft drinks.

Nook, a tall, bald man with a trim little white mustache, does the selling. He smiles a lot and talks as little as possible. Delores, small and voluble, with a wonderfully mellifluous voice, makes 300 pounds of boudin and 100 pounds of even spicier head cheese every Friday. It goes on sale Friday afternoon, and it is usually gone by midday Saturday. There is none to be had from Sunday through Thursday.

"We do everything the way they did it 50 or 100 years ago," Delores said. "I cook the rice in an old pot, not an electric cooker. I blend the pork mixture by hand, I stuff casings by hand—real casings, no plastic."

The results are so delectable that many customers start unwrapping their boudin, which is sold warm, before they leave the shop. They squeeze the stuffing from the casing directly into their mouths right there, or on the sidewalk outside, or in their cars or pickups. You never know when you'll be hit by lightning, and who would want to go without a bite of boudin?

As we drove west on Highway 14, from New Iberia to Abbeville to Kaplan, graceful white egrets sat in the sugarcane fields, watching the lumbering harvesting machines at work. Tractors towing green hoppers filled with cane inched toward mills emitting plumes of smoke like steel plants and dumped their loads into 100-foot piles to await processing.

But those industrious scenes were not matched everywhere. Along other roads, the landscape was littered with the detritus of the oil industry's booms and busts—deserted tanks, underpopulated trailer parks, rusting pickups—and in towns we saw signs flattened by hurricanes.

Between the boudin and the turtle, we tucked into some Atchafalaya oysters in Abbeville, the region's bivalve capital. There are three first-class oyster emporia in Abbeville (population 11,700): Black's, Dupuy's and Shucks, which is run by the people who used to cook at Dupuy's before it had a change in management. Urged on by Mr. Martin, ever the champion of the underdog, we chose Shucks, and we didn't regret it. The linoleum floors were a bit too brightly polished for my taste, but the neon beer signs were reassuring.

A dozen oysters on the half shell cost $4.50, a pittance by big-city standards. Perfectly shucked by a team of Vietnamese speed demons, they came on round plastic bar trays piled with ice chips. They passed all my tests. None of the precious oyster liquor had been spilled, and no shell fragments had been overlooked. The taste was clear, mildly saline, not obtrusively iodinic, with a slight hint of cucumber at the end.

Among us, we also sampled a big bowl of oyster stew topped with sliced scallion tops, creamy and buttery but perfectly balanced with plenty of briny juice; an oyster po'boy, ruined for me by a soggy roll; and a memorable dish of pan-broiled oysters, as nut-brown as chicken livers and loaded with big chunks of garlic. A tad too emphatic, perhaps, but great eating still.

There's plenty of routine eating in Acadiana, and not only beneath the Golden Arches, but we didn't encounter much. One night, driven off the road by a blinding storm, we took refuge at Café Vermilionville in Lafayette, a white-tablecloth place whose food was more complex and Frenchified than need be. But the gumbo was comme il faut, and the crayfish spring rolls had a nice spicy snap. Come breakfast time in Lafayette, there are bracing coffee and airy biscuits at Dwyer's Cafe and a superb shrimp and *tasso* omelette (it tastes best with a light dusting of Tony Cachere's Cajun seasoning) at the Hub City Diner.

To my great regret we could not eat at Café des Amis in Breaux Bridge, considered by many to be one of the region's premier restaurants. "I've gone there and gotten drunk just on the excellence of the food," Mr. Edmunds told me, and he's a discerning judge. After a devastating fire, it was closed for weeks but reopened late last month.

The cafe serves three meals a day five days a week, Wednesday through Sunday. It is one of the few places that still makes breakfast *couche couche*, a kind of cornmeal mush whose name obviously derives from the French *couscous*. Steen's cane syrup, made in Abbeville, is a perfect partner. And if you pass that way of a Saturday morning, you'll get zydeco with your meal.

Crayfish played only a minimal role in Cajun cooking until the 1950s. Before that, the little critters were often used as bait, but in the last half-century, they have become the focus of an annual mania. Which is probably appropriate, since they are the subject of an appealing local legend, telling how lobsters followed the Acadians south from Nova Scotia, growing smaller as the temperatures rose until they were tiny mud bugs.

Mud bugs, crawfish, crayfish, crawdads—call them what you like. Even Cajuns often seem unsure; a sign outside the Palace Café in Opelousas advertises crayfish bisque and crawfish étouffée (both terrific, by the way, as is the crayfish salad).

At the peak of the season, which runs roughly from mid-December to mid-June, devotees flock to joints that serve three-pound piles of crayfish boiled with cayenne and attack them with the same gusto Marylanders reserve for boiled crabs. Hawk's, lost in the midst of the crayfish ponds near Rayne, and Richard's Seafood Patio in Abbeville are prominent specialists.

Crayfish freeze well, certainly far better than shrimp. Several experts I consulted argued that if properly handled, frozen crayfish are only marginally inferior in cooked dishes to fresh ones. That was certainly my impression at a place with a peculiar but appropriate name: Joe's Dreyfus Store Restaurant, which is housed in an old general store in Livonia.

Joe Major, the chef, used to cook at the Petroleum Club in New Orleans, but now he produces more countrified fare of real quality. His crayfish bisque, silky smooth yet hearty, was enlivened by whole crayfish heads stuffed with piquant rice dressing.

I wasn't crazy about his underseasoned boudin smeared with pepper jelly. But that was his only flop. He topped a portobello mushroom with seafood and a roux-based gravy—an innovative dish full of Cajun style. And his crunchy, spicy soft-shell crabs topped with lump crabmeat were the stuff of a crustacean addict's reverie.

The Yellow Bowl, a cement-block restaurant on Highway 182 near Jeanerette, which began life as a bus stop cafe back in 1927, served us a quite spectacular crayfish étouffée, thickened with flour, rich with fat from the crayfish heads, bright with Tabasco and layered with flavors of celery, green peppers, parsley and scallions. We also had sweet, delicate, grease-free fried shrimp, just as scrumptious by themselves as on toasted rolls in a po'boy.

And then came what Kathleen Newland judged to be "a perfect, authentically thin Cajun gumbo," in sharp contrast to the thicker versions encountered in New Orleans. It was packed with seafood and based on a very dark roux, made from flour browned in oil. Ms. Newland, who brews a mean gumbo herself, said that it "tasted almost as if it had coffee in it."

More than any other dish, gumbo shows how the original Acadian settlers assimilated the traditions of other peoples. It is thickened with okra, an African (eventually African-American) vegetable, or file (ground sassafras leaves), first used by the regional Choctaw Indians, but never both. In addition, it often contains andouille, which owes a great deal to German sausage technique despite its French name.

Our mates having left the day before, Betsey and I finished our visit as the overnight guests of Mr. McIlhenny at Avery Island, which isn't really an island but a salt dome rising above the wetlands. The family cook, Eula Mae Doré, a true Acadian treasure, made us an andouille and goose gumbo, a deluxe version of the traditional chicken and sausage combination.

It was satisfyingly spicy, but not so spicy that the gamy taste of the goose, which Mr. McIlhenny had shot, was obscured. It was rich, not flour-rich but flavor-rich, thickened by Ms. Doré's own file, made from leaves plucked from her own sassafras tree, as she told us, "during the last full moon in August." The file was added not in the kitchen, but by each diner, at the table and at the last moment, lest the soup turn gummy.

The wine, as good as the gumbo, was a lush, round and fully mature 1991 Nuits-St.-Georges Les Pruliers from Daniel Rion.

"After God invented gumbo," said Mr. McIlhenny, a large man who epitomizes the Cajun love of exuberant living, "he invented red wine."

—Kaplan, Louisiana, December 4, 2002

A Lunchtime Institution Set
to Overstuff Its Last Po'boy

S am Uglesich grew up among mariners and fishermen off the coast of Croatia on rocky Dugi Otok, whose name means "long island," surrounded by the azure waters of the Adriatic. Twice he set out for the United States. The first time, he jumped ship in New York, but was caught and sent home. The second time, he made his break in New Orleans, then as now a more permissive city, and got away with it.

Naturally enough, he opened a seafood restaurant in his adopted city, specializing in the local shrimp, soft-shell crabs, lake trout and oysters. The year was 1924, the place South Rampart Street; Louis Armstrong had played gigs a few doors away.

Three years later, he moved to a modest frame cottage on Baronne Street. There, as the neighborhood around them crumbled, he and his son, Anthony, along with Anthony's wife, Gail, gradually built a reputation of legendary proportions. Grander establishments like Galatoire's, Commander's Palace and Antoine's loomed larger in the guidebooks, but the exacting standards of little Uglesich's (pronounced YOU-gull-sitch's)—everything bracingly fresh from lake and gulf and bayou, nothing frozen or imported, and absolutely no shortcuts—generated greater buzz.

Without benefit of advertising, word of Uglesich's big, tan, glistening oysters, its sweet, plump crawfish balls, its searing shrimp Uggie and its overstuffed yet feather-light po'boys spread across the city and then across the country. It mattered not to most people that it took no credit cards and served neither dessert nor coffee.

Five days a week, 11 months a year, lines have formed outside the ramshackle building, which displays a sign from the long-defunct Jax Brewery in one window. On Good Friday this year, customers began arriving at 9 in the morning, even though the restaurant does not open for lunch, the only meal it serves, until 10:30. Soon there were more than 200 people in line, and the sun was setting as the last of the day's 400-odd clients were being served.

All this with just 10 tables inside and 6 on the sidewalk outside.

Soon Uglesich's will close forever, at least in its present form. Anthony and Gail Uglesich are exhausted, worn-out by years of rising at 4:30 and working flat-out all day. Balding, bearlike, Mr. Uglesich, 66, told me he would shut the doors in mid-May, but he has renewed his liquor license, just in case he finds retirement miserable.

"I may go nuts," he said at the end of a particularly brutal day. "I doubt it, but I won't know until I try it. If I do climb the walls, I might try packaging our sauces for retail sale, or maybe do some catering— people are always offering me thousands of dollars to cook for their dinner parties—or reopen here for four days a week, with limited hours and a very limited menu, just appetizers. No more of this, though."

Mrs. Uglesich, 64, a petite woman whose regular customers call her Miss Gail, put the situation bluntly. "Our bodies are telling us we can't take it anymore," she said in the soft, liquid accent that marks her as a New Orleans native. "Anthony has missed only two days' work since we were married, and that was 41 years ago."

Neither of the Uglesichs' two children—Donna, 40, a business-woman, and John, 35, author of *Uglesich's Restaurant Cookbook* (Pelican Publishing, 2004)—has shown any desire to take over the business. "It's too hard," Mrs. Uglesich said.

With many New Orleans restaurants, including some of the most famous ones, relying these days on frozen crawfish tails and frozen soft-shell crabs and on shrimp and crabmeat imported from Thailand or China, Uglesich's stands out more than ever.

"Look," Mr. Uglesich said, peering through wire-rimmed glasses, "90 percent of the shrimp eaten in this country is imported. Local crawfish costs me $7 a pound, compared with $2.50 imported. People in restaurants here know they can get away with things. But I'd pay $10 for Louisiana crawfish, if that's what it takes. Otherwise, what's going to happen to our local fishermen? When we're gone, I don't know."

Two houses across the street from Uglesich's have been spruced up recently, but otherwise the neighborhood remains pretty insalubrious. A big parking lot for the trucks of Brown's Dairy occupies one corner, weed-filled vacant lots several others; the neighborhood seems miles, not just a few blocks, from both the imposing, pillared mansions of the Garden District and the busy shops and restaurants of the Central Business District.

A few weeks ago Mr. Uglesich was mugged late at night, but he still showed up for work the next day, battered and bruised, to stand in his usual position behind the counter, ready to take orders and to dispense seafood wisdom along with the wines that sat on a shelf behind him. He usually stocks 15 or 20 labels from France (Trimbach, for example), Australia (Penfolds) and California (Ravenswood). None sell as well as beer or Mrs. Uglesich's horseradish-, lime- and chili-spiked Bloody Marys.

The setup is utilitarian, to put it kindly: concrete floor, sturdy Thonet-style chairs, Formica-topped tables. Mrs. Uglesich makes the sauces and soups at home. Mr. Uglesich brings them to the restaurant in his car. The kitchen gear consists of a single eight-burner range, a fryer, two refrigerators and several sinks. There are only seven employees in the whole place.

"I was never tempted to get big," Mr. Uglesich said. "I can't find enough good produce as things stand now."

He is a notoriously picky buyer. Many days, he rejects what his suppliers offer him, like soft-shells he considers too small. He claims to be able to tell as soon as a sack hits the ground whether the oysters inside are good enough. He checks every delivery of fish and shellfish with a practiced eye.

Mr. Uglesich buys catfish only from Joey and Jeannie Fonseca in Des Allemands, a tiny place in the swamps southwest of the city; bread only from the 109-year-old Leidenheimer Baking Company;

and oysters only from the P Oyster Company, which was founded by two fellow Croats, John Popich and Joseph Jurisich.

Uglesich's focuses on relatively few main ingredients. It serves no meat at all, except for the roast beef po'boy, and only two kinds of fish: lake trout and catfish. K-Paul's made redfish famous, Lilette serves delicious drum, and the local pompano has been famous for a century, but Mr. Uglesich sticks to his longtime favorites.

Shrimp rules on Uglesich's tables. In addition to shrimp Uggie, you can order a shrimp po'boy (crisp fried shrimp in a long, toasted bread roll), shrimp and grits (shrimp in a delectably creamy sauce ladled over fried triangles of grits), grilled shrimp and onions, shrimp and country sausage with a Creole mustard sauce, shrimp in bacon with a sweet potato soufflé, firecracker shrimp with barbecue and horseradish sauce, shrimp rémoulade, shrimp Creole, shrimp stuffed with crabmeat, voodoo shrimp and volcano shrimp, among a long list of other dishes.

Voodoo shrimp, which contains black bean paste and is described on the menu as Asian Creole, and volcano shrimp, which includes ginger, soy sauce, black bean paste and Chinese red pepper, reflect the influence of recent migrants to south Louisiana, as does the Vietnamese dipping sauce that is now served with the crawfish balls.

Still, it is hard to top the raw oysters on the half shell served up on a side counter, cold and crisp and bereft of plate in the New Orleans manner, by the estimable Michael Rogers, once voted the fastest oyster opener in town. He makes his own ketchup-based cocktail sauce, but the oysters are so fresh that they almost beg to be eaten plain, with only a squirt or two of lemon juice.

"We heard from the president of the United States, a letter about our plans to close," Mr. Uglesich said, tearing up a bit. "That was very nice. We're nothing special here, just a couple of self-taught cooks. It's only a little hole in the wall."

Paul Varisco thinks otherwise. The owner of a restaurant-supply business, he has eaten lunch at Uglesich's three times a week for years. So often, he said when I caught up with him on Good Friday, "that I must be at least partly Croatian now, instead of Italian, French and German." One of the restaurant's best-selling specialties, Paul's Fantasy—pan-fried trout with grilled shrimp and cubed, sautéed new potatoes, all fearlessly seasoned—is named for him.

So, I asked, what will he do when Uglesich's closes? "I'll take Anthony out to lunch a lot," he replied, "almost anywhere to keep him out of Gail's hair."

Julia Reed, a writer who lives in New Orleans, is another regular. For her, Mr. Uglesich agreed to open on a Saturday night so she could give a birthday party in honor of her husband, John Pearce. It was a rare event; Mr. Uglesich has played host to private parties only a few times since he first did so in the 1980s, for a bash given by the record executive Ahmet Ertegun for the Fort Worth billionaire Sid Bass and his wife, Mercedes. Oscar de la Renta and Albert Finney were among the guests that time.

Ms. Reed dolled up the place with a giant silver punch bowl to cool the Pol Roger, masses of white lilies, linen tablecloths and monogrammed napkins. Bottle after bottle of Burgundy (Meursault les Chevalières 2000 from Joseph Matrot) and Alsatian riesling (Grand Cru Saering 2001 from Schlumberger) kept thirsts at bay.

The food was vintage Uglesich. One of the restaurant's idiosyncrasies is the liberal use of cheese with shellfish—liked by some and detested by others. Fried oysters with blue cheese opened the Pearce soiree, and I found myself in the first camp while my wife, Betsey, found herself in the second. But there was no dispute about what followed, including shrimp and grits, fried mirliton (a squash) with shrimp rémoulade and luscious crabmeat au gratin.

Chunky and intensely creamy, the crab dish is "made of all the things you're not supposed to eat," Ms. Reed informed us, including butter, evaporated milk, egg yolks, whipping cream, Swiss cheese and Cheddar cheese. It was divine. I must get the recipe, I thought; it would make a great advertisement for the dairy industry, not to mention a fine starter for my last earthly meal.

Mr. Uglesich saved the best for last. The afternoon before, he had bemoaned the tardiness of soft-shell crabs this year, which he attributed to cold weather. But at 7 o'clock that evening, a supplier showed up with the first of the season, still wiggling in a cardboard box lined with wet newspaper. They were mighty beasts, the size of salad plates, and magnificent when dipped in an egg wash, dredged in plain bread crumbs and fried until the tops and the legs were crisp and the undersides rich and creamy.

The tartar sauce that came with them was house-made, of course.

—*New Orleans, April 27, 2005*

MIDWEST

In the Midwest, a Sweet Tooth Is Nonpartisan

I t must be inborn. Show me a Midwesterner, and I'll show you someone with an incurable sweet tooth. A son of Ohio, I'm as bad as the next guy—worse, if you believe my dessert-averse wife, Betsey, who is made of sterner Southern stuff.

In most of the rest of the country, the third Saturday in October is just another day to admire the leaves or to watch football. But it is Sweetest Day in Michigan, Illinois, Wisconsin and Ohio, where the holiday was invented, a day when one bestows candy, posies and other gifts on husbands, wives and, yes, sweethearts.

I have been bouncing around the Midwest on campaign duty for the last couple of months, indulging in favorite sweets and discovering new ones: humble confections like the remarkable Bismarck doughnuts of Oak House Bakery in Madison, Wis., made with unbleached white flour, filled with real whipped cream and iced with chocolate, and fancier ones like the delectable lemon tarts with candied kumquat, each topped with exactly nine perfect swirls of meringue, at 40 Sardines, a wonderful restaurant in Overland Park, Kan., in the suburbs of Kansas City.

Pie has always been a Midwestern passion, and the cherry pie served at the Cherry Hut in Beulah, Mich., leads my list of all-time regional classics. Right there next to it is Ted Drewes frozen custard, dispensed from a tiny stand on old Route 66 in St. Louis, and the kringle made in Racine, Wis., by bakeries like O&H, which is the only Danish pastry in America that any self-respecting Dane would eat, and the loaf-size cinnamon roll adored by the customers of the Machine Shed in Urbandale, Iowa, near Des Moines, me included.

Comparable delights, almost all of them homemade, graced our family table in Akron in my boyhood decades.

Even today, almost half a century after I left the land of the Buckeyes to explore the wider world, I find myself daydreaming about my mother's party pieces, a velvety custard pie with a graham cracker crust and a raisin-studded spice cake whose not-so-secret ingredient was tomato soup. I discovered years later that one recipe came from the cracker box, the other from Irma S. Rombauer's *Joy of Cooking*. A Midwesterner herself, Aunt Irma (as my mother jocularly referred to her) was born in St. Louis in 1877 and died in 1962.

Daydreaming doesn't put on the pounds, but I do more than daydream. Plop me down in or near Cincinnati, and I can't resist stopping at one of Graeter's three dozen ice cream parlors, which have been in business for 133 years, using something called "the French pot process" to make dense, devilishly rich ice cream. With little air whipped into it, Graeter's frozen manna weighs nearly a pound a pint. In season, I always take the fresh peach, full of the flavor of ripe fruit. Try it; you'll understand how "peachy" came to be a synonym for "splendid."

Unfortunately I can't stay away from Marshall Field's in Chicago, either. It sells a product known as Frango mints, compact little cubes of dark chocolate infused with peppermint. Chicago purists complain that they're no longer produced in the region. (A nonunion plant in Pennsylvania has made them since Field's closed its 13th-floor candy kitchen in 1999.) But hey, they still taste the same to me, and for me taste trumps pride and provenance any old day.

Pie is to the Midwest as rice is to China. When Norman Rockwell wanted to conjure up an image of wholesome American life, he painted what I always took to be a Midwestern farmwife, apron on, carrying a pie to the dinner table. Not by happenstance do we say that something typical of our way of life is "as American as apple pie."

The Norske Nook in Osseo, Wis., up near the Twin Cities, is pie paradise. The cheerful, red-pinafored waitresses there will serve you apple pie if you like: standard-issue apple, Dutch apple or harvest apple. You won't be sorry if you order it. But there are far more exceptional items in the Norske Nook's repertory of more than two dozen pies, all made from scratch every morning according to the recipes of Helen Myhre, who founded the place. This, until recently, was the nation's premier dairy state, remember. So go ahead, take the plunge, and order the Farm Belt favorite, sour cream raisin, made from rich, tangy, extrathick Wisconsin sour cream, with a short, flaky crust and a fine pompadour of meringue, or maybe the lush banana cream, which won the National Pie Championship in 2003.

Seek, as you cruise the highways in the nation's midsection, and ye shall be rewarded (particularly if you have one of Jane and Michael Stern's helpful guidebooks in hand). In Huntington, Ind., Dan Quayle's hometown, Nick's Kitchen offers a beautifully burnished butterscotch pie. In Marshalltown, Iowa, Stone's serves a tottering wedge of lemon chiffon pie that is taller than it is wide. In Two Harbors, Minn., on the remote north shore of Lake Superior, Betty's Pies pairs blackberries and peaches in a North Woods version of a pie that wins plaudits from Georgia to Oregon.

Why pie? Pie has always been a small-town specialty. For the rural housewife, the ingredients were close at hand, easily produced on the farm or readily and cheaply bought, and all she needed to add was time, care and a few little tricks probably passed down from mother to daughter.

Beulah, Mich., where the Cherry Hut has been doing business since 1922, could hardly have shorter supply lines; not far from Traverse City, it stands in the midst of the country's most productive sour cherry orchards. Like many of these places, it started as a simple roadside stand and just grew and grew and g-r-e-w. Still family run, it now has three big dining rooms, plus a patio, and during its season— Memorial Day to Oct. 24 this year—there is often a line of hungry eaters waiting for a table. On the Fourth of July this year, the Cherry Hut sold 595 pies.

True to form, I ordered mine à la mode, and Betsey asked for a small piece, hold the ice cream, please. That was her last moment of restraint. She took one warm bite and closed her eyes in bliss. "I have shivers down to my toes," she said. "The crust is just perfect, and so is the tart-sweet balance. It doesn't hurt your teeth."

Brenda Case, who runs the place with her husband, Leonard, told us the recipe has never changed. Lard, always lard, in the crust. Fresh local cherries in season, frozen local cherries at other times. No cornstarch. The result is light and juicy, as if you had just plucked the cherries from a tree, and a million miles from the gooey consistency produced by canned pie filling.

There are cherries everywhere at the Hut to remind you why you're there. The menu is shaped like a cherry, the curtains are a cherry print and the waitresses wear candy-striped outfits in white and cherry red. Ours, Mrs. Case's astonishingly energetic 74-year-old sister-in-law, Lorayne, suggested a hot turkey sandwich as a modest hors d'oeuvre before the pie. It came garnished with a maraschino cherry.

Frozen custard was all over the Midwest when I was growing up, but it has lost its grip in most places. Not, happily, in Milwaukee and environs, where neon-clad Leon's (the inspiration for Arnold's joint in *Happy Days*) still serves terrific stuff, with a not-really-optional crown of hot fudge. Kopp's, whose Layton Avenue shop provides a fetchingly landscaped garden, complete with a waterfall, for your eating pleasure, has developed the flavor of the day into an art form. If vanilla or Dutch chocolate, always on offer, don't do it for you, you might just luck into caramel cashew or German apple streusel. On Sweetest Day this year, chocolate cherry kiss showed up for duty, and on Sunday, for Halloween, they promise pecan praline pumpkin pie.

The crew at Ted Drewes, in St. Louis, indulges in no such antics. There you can take your choice of vanilla or vanilla or vanilla. You can have it in a cone, in a dish, in a soda, in a sundae, in a "crater" (hot fudge, custard and devil's food cake), in a milkshake or in a "concrete"—the house special since the 1950's—a gravity-defying, extrathick shake, so thick you can turn it upside down without losing a spoonful.

"Keeping it simple makes service faster and quality control easier," said Travis Dillon, who runs the company along with his father-in-law, Ted Drewes Jr., son of the founder. "Too many variables gives too many chances for mistakes."

It's a philosophy reminiscent of Henry Ford, who made Model T's only in black, for nearly identical reasons.

The 30 add-ins and add-ons cover a delicious range, from crumbled Heath bars and Oreos to blueberries and bananas to pistachios and coconut. And the frozen custard itself is a paragon among iced desserts: at least 10 percent butterfat and at least 1.4 percent eggs by weight, which makes it smooth as a newborn's cheek. Honey has been the chosen sweetener since sugar rationing began during World War II.

Drewes retails more than 150,000 gallons of custard every year. It is made on the spot daily in small batches, because it tastes better when freezer fresh.

My favorite concoction, the butterscotch sundae, has the color of a lion's mane and the texture of satin, with the real roasted-sugar flavor usually found only in Scotland. Mr. Dillon told me he liked fudge and raspberries or peaches and macadamia nuts on his sundaes. His wife, Christy, he said, often orders chocolate sauce and almonds, or pecans and pineapple. That made me, as a single-topping man, feel like a piker.

• • •

One year Betsey showered 15 kringles upon our astonished daughter, Catherine, and her four roommates at Harvard. Betsey claims to have confused Racine's kringle, which serves six to eight, with the single-serving Danish familiar to New Yorkers. I don't believe a word of that; I put it down to excessive maternal anxiety.

Our good friend from Vietnam Les Aspin, who represented the Racine area in Congress before serving as defense secretary, turned us on to kringles. They were his unvarying Christmas present: horse-collar-shape rings of puff pastry, filled with almond paste and sparingly topped with white icing, so addictively scrumptious that I could easily plow through one in two days, instead of a week, if Betsey's back were turned, which it very seldom is.

Les having gone prematurely to his reward, we order frozen kringles for ourselves and our friends each year direct from O&H, the largest of the handful of bakeries still operating in Racine, which once had the largest Danish community in the nation. They come with fruit fillings—apricot, blueberry and cherry, among others—in addition to pecan and the original almond. I have to admit that I'm not crazy about a relatively recent addition, turtle, which incorporates caramel, chocolate and pecans. The puff pastry's fragility gives way under that onslaught of flavors and textures.

The delicacy of kringle, achieved by folding and refolding the pastry, partly by machine and partly by hand, and passing it again and again through steel rollers like those on a pasta machine, is what sets it apart. When the three days of folding, rolling and resting have been completed, the finished product has 32 distinct layers of dough and butter, each a mere two millimeters, or eight-hundredths of an inch, thick.

Well, not pure butter, for all of Wisconsin's pride in its dairy herds. A quantity of margarine is incorporated as well, to achieve the desired melting point.

Until three years ago, all the work was done by hand in a small bakery. But now O&H makes its kringles in an immaculate, hangarlike former machine-tool shop filled with machinery, much of which the company designed or adapted from other uses. It produces half a million a year, in more than 100 varieties. Of those, 40 percent are sold at two Racine retail outlets, the rest through mail orders or the Internet.

Eric Olesen, one of three brothers, grandsons of a co-founder of O&H, showed me around. The O in the company's name stands for Olesen, obviously; the H stands for Harvey Holtz, a bookkeeper who was his grandfather's early partner.

Why, I asked Mr. Olesen, does Racine Danish differ so radically from the rest of what Americans eat? "Here," he said, "we focus on the pastry, as they do in Denmark. Elsewhere in our country, people put the emphasis on the fillings, and because of that it isn't worth all the time and expense that goes into making puff pastry."

Finesse isn't as much of an issue with Iowa's favorite goody at breakfast (and lunch and dinner), the cinnamon roll. To satisfy the big eaters of the Corn Belt, sugar and spice are laid on with a trowel.

Cinnamon rolls have become a fad nationwide. Any self-respecting airport sells them. So does Stroud's, the down-home fried-chicken house in Kansas City. A calorie-laden variant, the Michigan maple roll (grilled, yet!) stars on the breakfast menu at Juilleret's cafe in Charlevoix.

But Iowans have a unique mania for cinnamon rolls. They take candidates in the presidential caucuses to places like the McNally Bake Shop in Emmetsburg, whose rolls one politician pronounced heavenly. They serve rolls to tourists in Amana. And the best home bakers, as many as 200 most years, enter their prize specimens in the contest at the Iowa State Fair, judged by a panel of home economists and experts from Tone's, the spice company, headquartered at Ankeny, Iowa. This year's winner, Marianne Carlson of Jefferson, earned $3,000, the fair's biggest food prize, donated by Tone's.

"When they bring 'em in, still warm, the whole building smells wonderful, and your sweet tooth drips," said Arlette Hollister, who has been the superintendent of food at the fair for the past 18 years.

I was a little embarrassed to tell Ms. Hollister that the best cinnamon roll I could remember eating—it's more like a half-dozen rolls masquerading as one—was served at the Machine Shed, a kitschy suburban establishment full of hay bales and impossibly corny signs, down-on-the-farm gifts and waitresses in bib overalls. Part of a regional chain, it serves herculean breakfasts, specializing, as my colleague, David Yepsen of the *Des Moines Register*, told Betsey and me, in the three basic Iowa food groups: salt, fat and sugar.

But maybe I'm not hopeless after all. Ms. Hollister, who had spoken glowingly of the fluffiness of Ms. Carlson's rolls, described the ones at the Machine Shed, which are approximately as fluffy as a bagel, as "very, very, very good." I also learned, just as I left Des Moines, that Chuck Offenburger, a former newspaper columnist who used to run an annual contest to pick the coffee shop or restaurant that served the best roll, had once rated the Machine Shed number one. Who am I to dissent?

—Chicago, October 27, 2004

The Meat That Made
Sheboygan Famous

Summer is nigh. The season of backyard barbecues and lakeside cookouts is at hand, which in most parts of the country means an orgy of grilled steaks, hamburgers and hot dogs lasting until Labor Day and beyond.

But not in Wisconsin, and certainly not in Sheboygan, a well-kept little city of 51,000 on Lake Michigan, about an hour's drive north of Milwaukee. This is the capital of the kingdom of bratwurst. A brat— the name rhymes with "pot," not with "pat"—is a pork or pork-and-beef sausage, spicier and stubbier than a hot dog. In Sheboygan, at least, it is also an object of veneration, taken as seriously as a lock of some medieval saint's hair.

"When it comes to the manufacture, preparation, serving and in-gestion of brats, we are right," says Sheboygan Brats, or *Come Fry with Me*, a leaflet published by the local convention and visitors bureau. "We are in first place. There is no second."

No self-respecting restaurant here, whether humble hole in the wall or soigné supper club, can make do without a proper charcoal grill, because the bratwurst catechism specifies that the stout little sausage must be grilled over charcoal, not boiled or fried or sizzled on a stove-top griddle.

No civic, charitable, religious, educational or sporting fund-raiser, not even in midwinter, is complete without a brat fry, which has nothing to do with frying and everything to do with grilling. They know their sausages here, but they sometimes have a little trouble with culinary terminology.

A few old-fashioned butchers and markets in and near Sheboygan make their own brats. Most add salt, pepper and nutmeg to the ground meat that is stuffed into natural casings to form sausages; some use mace, garlic, sage or ginger. But the little guys have been eclipsed in volume, if not quality, by Johnsonville Foods, now partly owned by Sara Lee. The enormous Johnsonville factory, rising from the farmland west of here like an auto assembly plant, cranks out millions of brats a year and sells them nationwide.

Once cooked, a Sheboygan brat must be served on a split hard roll called a *semmel*, which is rugged enough to hang together under attack from the torrents of savory juice released when you bite into it. The classic accompaniments are brown mustard, preferably coarsely ground; dill pickle slices, ketchup and raw onions, though some nonconformists opt for relish or sauerkraut.

"A few people do that, I suppose," said Charles K. Miesfeld III, a fourth-generation bratwurst manufacturer, with the air of a priest discussing a wayward parishioner. "But it's not traditional, not the Sheboygan way." Even worse: At Milwaukee Brewers baseball home games at Miller Field, and at tailgate brat fries before Green Bay Packers football games at Lambeau Field, brats are often served, not on semmel rolls but on brat buns, which are downsized versions of squishy hot dog rolls.

"What can you expect?" Mr. Miesfeld asked me when I brought this schism to his attention. "You're in Milwaukee and Green Bay, not Sheboygan."

Since this is Wisconsin, the dairy state par excellence, the cut sides of the rolls are slathered with plenty of butter before the sausage is inserted. And since the German-Americans who dominate the local population are big eaters, two bratwursts are usually squeezed into one roll, side by side.

"A double with the works, that's what I always have," said Mr. Miesfeld, 44. "A double, then you pop a cholesterol pill. It's a mortal sin here if you order a single."

Personally, I'd hold the ketchup, if I weren't afraid the Wisconsin condiment cops would nab me for heresy.

Bratwurst—generally a fresh sausage, neither smoked nor cured—originated in southern Germany, in what are now the *Länder*, or states, of Bavaria and Thuringia. Each region or city had its own specialty, and many still do. Coburg bratwurst, traditionally grilled over a fire fueled by pinecones, were known as early as 1530. Thuringer bratwurst are usually made of veal but sometimes contain pork. Regensburg bratwurst, roughly the size of your ring finger, are still served at the Historical Sausage Kitchen, a smoky little joint, founded in 1309, which stands along the Danube near an ancient stone bridge.

My wife, Betsey, ate a dozen or so *Regensburgers*, cooked over an open beechwood charcoal fire and lined up with Teutonic precision on a paper plate, when we visited the historical kitchen some years ago. She begged for more. "I was cold," she later explained, piteously.

The most famous German brats are probably those of Nuremberg. A little smaller than *Regensburgers*—the size of your little finger, maybe—these are made from neck or shoulder of pork, seasoned with marjoram, cooked over a wood fire and traditionally served on a pewter plate with sauerkraut, asparagus or potato salad. Six make a snack, they say, 14 a dandy lunch.

According to local legend, *Nürnbergers* are as slim as they are because they were illicitly passed through the keyholes of taverns after closing time.

My guess is that Sheboygan bratwurst are descendants of Nuremberg bratwurst, although they are much bigger—about six inches long and more than an inch in diameter. (Everything seems to grow when it crosses the Atlantic from east to west.) But this is no more than a hunch, I admit.

The local convention and visitors bureau, so good on most wurst questions, speaks less authoritatively on the matter of antecedents. The Germans who settled this region in the early to middle 19th century, the bureau says, substituted pork for veal in their brat recipes because they had more pigs than cattle. But why was that? Cattle were already plentiful in the United States, and as the passage of time has shown, Wisconsin is fine cow country.

Mr. Miesfeld has another explanation. His father and grandfather used a mixture of pork and veal, he said, but veal became too expensive in the 20th century and they went over to pork or pork mixed with beef.

Willy Ruef, 64, a master butcher from the Swiss capital city, Bern, who operates a meat market in New Glarus in the southern part of the state, still makes his bratwurst with veal. True, they cost more than pork brats, but New Glarus continues to attract immigrants from Switzerland, and they and his other customers are apparently glad to pay more for authenticity.

Usinger's, the famous Milwaukee sausage house, founded in 1880, makes fresh, mottled-red bratwurst with coarse-ground pork, corn syrup, lemon juice, salt and spices. It also makes a precooked version of that sausage, as well as precooked brats stuffed with pork and veal. Both are popular with people like tailgaters, who can't take the time, or don't have the facilities, to parboil their brats before slapping them on the grill. Parboiling in water or beer, or even beer and onions, which is de rigueur in Milwaukee, reduces the risk of sausage casings bursting over the coals.

"If that happens, you lose the juices and most of the flavor," said Jill Shibilski, a 15-year veteran behind the handsome old marble counters in Usinger's downtown Milwaukee shop. "And remember, never poke them with a fork, for the same reason. Turn them with tongs, or your fingers."

(Usinger's made the hot dogs, or frankfurters, as the firm prefers to call them, for the 2002 Winter Olympics in Salt Lake City. Sausage-starved souls stranded far from Wisconsin can order their brats, dogs and scores of other delicious sausages on the Internet, at www.usinger .com.)

True sons of Sheboygan view parboiling as foolishness. They acknowledge the danger of exploding brats, certainly, but they insist that the way to guard against it is to cook the sausages slowly, for 20 minutes or more, a respectful distance from coals that have subsided from red to gray-white.

Traditionalist that he is, Mr. Miesfeld vigorously espouses that view. But he is a canny businessman, as well, and his Triangle Market caters to every taste, no matter how perverse. In addition to his classic Grand Champion bratwurst, customers can choose 19 other kinds of brats, including all-beef, no-salt, chicken, turkey, garlic, garlic and onion, cheese, jalapeño, Cajun, chili and Italian. What? Italian brats? Can bratwurst pizza be far behind?

Betsey and I got some inkling of Mr. Miesfeld's virtuosity as a sausage maker at the Horse and Plow pub of the American Club, a handsome inn in the nearby village of Kohler. The grilled-sausage sampler there included a garlic brat, an apricot and Dijon brat, which tasted a lot better than it sounds, and a spicy, Slovenian-style sausage called a *kranski*, all from the House of Miesfeld, plus a mound of warm, vinegar-laced, bacon-dotted potato salad.

A towering glass of malty, amber-hued Maibock beer, a seasonal specialty from the Capital Brewery in Madison, did for the sausages what a bottle of good, flinty Chablis does for a plate of oysters. Only Miller remains of the many megabreweries that once graced Milwaukee, but dozens of small outfits have sprung up all over the state, producing beers of many varieties.

Everyone we talked to said the best semmel rolls come from City Bakery, and when we popped in for a visit, the young woman working behind the display cases, Kim Bannier, told us why: it has the only hearth oven in town. The rolls, about the size of a hamburger bun, are formed by hand, placed on a board dusted with cornmeal to rise, tapped with a stick to make the traditional crease in the top, then eased onto the oven's brick floor. The method, which produces a thin, notably crispy crust, has changed not an iota since 1937.

By now we had a passable working knowledge of brat and bun.

But we longed to set aside our table manners, to say nothing of our limited dignity, and sample the primal brat experience: smoky sausage and crusty semmel crumbling together in the mouth, condiments merging into a single slithery sharpness and buttery juices dribbling down the shirt.

We got our wish at Terry's Diner, a no-frills establishment housed in a battered, concrete-block building in a working-class neighborhood on Sheboygan's south side. Settling ourselves on a couple of stools and sipping Diet Cokes—an exercise in futility if I ever saw one—we watched the laconic grill man move the brats around an ancient charcoal grill that must have been there since the place opened in 1939.

Why, I inquired, didn't he use tongs, to protect his fingers?

"I was born and raised in Sheboygan," he answered, "and the only way I ever learned to cook brats is using my hands. You have to squeeze them. When they're soft they're not done. When they firm up, they are."

He knows his business. With our appetites stimulated by the sweet, fatty smoke coming from the grill, we tore into the sandwiches as soon as they appeared on the counter before us, wrapped in parchment paper, bereft of plate. Bingo. Best in show.

At Terry's the brats come side by side on the roll, but at our next stop, the Charcoal Inn North, an immaculate little cube of a restaurant with lace curtains, they are split and flattened before grilling, then served one atop the other. That method yielded slightly less juicy sausages, but it produced crunchy bits at the edges of the brats. A fair exchange, we thought, though we preferred the spicier flavor of the sausages at Terry's.

Bob Lauer, owner of the Hoffbrau, a wood-paneled supper club decorated with lots of sporting memorabilia, had a trick that lent his brats (and New York strip steaks) the flavor of wood smoke. Disdaining charcoal briquettes because he thought they sometimes gave food an oily taste, he used only natural hickory lump charcoal from Cedar Grove, Wis., containing no chemicals. Though the Hoffbrau is no more, the knockout flavor of its brats is remembered by many (including the two of us).

But no matter where we went, no matter whether the bratwurst was slightly or intensely smoky, filled with finely or chunkily ground meat, mild or spicy, one ratio remained constant: each sandwich required a minimum of six large paper napkins for the postprandial cleanup.

—*Sheboygan, Wisconsin, June 5, 2002*

Don't Look for Walleye in a Place Called Wobegon

When I was growing up in the Midwest more than half a century ago, mahimahi had not yet made it from the tropics to the flatlands, except occasionally in frozen form. To taste the real thing, you had to travel to Hawaii. To taste fresh red snapper, you had to go to Florida or New Orleans. To taste swordfish at its best, you had to visit Boston or New York.

In Ohio, cod and salmon and tuna came only in tin cans.

So we ate freshwater fish—trout and Lake Superior whitefish, yellow perch and walleye—and loved them. At the old London Chop House in Detroit, which was for many decades one of the best restaurants between the coasts, Lester Gruber served the pampered magnates of the Motor City a minor regional masterpiece that the menu described as "a mess of perch." In Chicago, top hotels regularly offered rainbow trout at breakfast.

To me, though, nothing beat fillets of flaky, fine-textured walleye, coated with cornmeal, sautéed until golden—always sweet-tasting and not at all fishy-smelling, in the pejorative sense, though my mother made my father cook them outdoors lest her dream kitchen be sullied.

Modern air shipment of fish from all points of the globe made monkfish and diver scallops, as well as Dover sole and ahi tuna, available almost everywhere. For many, the appeal of freshwater species quickly ebbed, and pollution in some lakes compounded the problem. When I ordered walleye a few years ago at a lakeside restaurant near Milwaukee, the waiter eyed me dubiously and asked,

"Why would you want walleye when you could have a nice orange roughy?"

But now my old favorite seems to be staging a comeback.

Taverns and roadhouses in Ohio still serve walleye, and you see it again on the menus of big-city restaurants in the Midwest. Happily, walleye never lost its hold on Minnesota, a state bloody-minded enough to elect Jesse Ventura, a wrestler, as governor and to turn its back on tasteless fad fish like orange roughy. Here, walleye is a cult.

Where else would they put up gargantuan statues of fish, like the 26-foot fiberglass walleye that graces a lakeside park in Garrison, Minn., north of the Twin Cities?

"Fishing for walleye, eating walleye—it's a secular communion," said Karal Ann Marling, a professor at the University of Minnesota who studies popular culture. "It affirms your identity as a Minnesotan."

You betcha. Almost every one of the state's 12,000 lakes contains a walleye or two; I take that to include Lake Wobegon, where all the fish are presumably above average, although I was unable to reach Garrison Keillor to confirm it. On the first day of the fishing season every spring, known locally as "the opener," the male half of the state's population heads for the north woods to stalk the elusive walleye, while the female half stays home.

Since the opener usually coincides with Mother's Day, you might think the women would take offense.

"Not at all," Professor Marling said. "They're happy to get those smelly men and their fishing tackle out of the house."

Judging from a fish story I heard from Kevin Cullen, executive chef at Goodfellow's, a well-liked Minneapolis restaurant, the men can be tolerant, too.

"I usually get four-pounders," he said, "but this one day I thought I'd hooked a rock. *Zzzzz!* goes the reel. It was a big walleye, went maybe eight or nine pounds. My wife, Patti, grabs the dip net and smacks him right in the mouth. The fish spits the hook. She says, 'Do you want a divorce?' and I say, 'Nah, just get me a beer.'"

•   •   •

In fact, the walleye performs better in the frying pan than on the hook. It's not much of a game fish, despite the annual angling frenzy in Minnesota. Battlers like smallmouth bass and salmon twist and leap in an effort to escape, but walleyes head for the bottom, tugging unhappily.

Catching one, said my friend Charles Eisendrath, a keen fisherman who teaches at the University of Michigan, "is just like catching an old sock."

Long and slim, with dark green backs and yellow sides, walleyes are so called because of their wide-set eyes, sensitive to light, which have an opaque, milky look.

They are often casually referred to as "walleyed pike" or "pickerel," but those are misnomers. Their scientific name is a jawbreaker—Stizostedion vitreum—but it identifies them as members of the Percidae or perch family, close cousins of the slightly larger Stizostedion lucioperca, a prized European food fish that is known as *fogas* in Hungary, *sandre* in France, *Zander* in Germany and pike-perch in Britain.

(Pike, on the other hand, belong to the Esox genus. Esox lucius is the French *brochet*, the basis of one of the glories of Lyonnais cooking, quenelles, or fish dumplings, traditionally served with rosy crayfish sauce. On this side of the Atlantic, Esox lucius is the carnivorous northern pike, valued in Canada as a fearsome game fish but reviled in California as a menace to the trout in Lake Davis. Officials there have recently mounted a campaign of electrocution, poisoning and precision bombing in a bid to eliminate it.)

On recent visits to the Twin Cities I have come across walleye beignets, walleye pot stickers, walleye spring rolls and walleye tacos. I have eaten stir-fried walleye with ginger and scallions, steamed walleye with Cambodian-style noodles and walleye cheeks with morel cream sauce. I have heard about walleye-on-a-stick, a favorite at the Minnesota State Fair.

But the dirty little secret hereabouts is that not a single piece of walleye served in a hotel, restaurant or club, or even at the state fair, comes from Minnesota waters. Commercial fishing for walleye is banned in this as well as most other states, principally to safeguard sport angling.

For a time, one Minnesota Indian tribe ran a commercial walleye fishery, but that was suspended when overfishing badly depleted the stock in Red Lake. Now most chefs buy Canadian fish, either from the Lake of the Woods, north of here, or from Lake Winnipeg.

In Michigan and Ohio, the walleye comes from Lake Erie by way of Canadian boats based in Ontario towns like Leamington and Kingsville, about 40 miles southeast of Detroit. One Cleveland dealer, State Fish Inc., sells 300,000 pounds of walleye a year, or about 130,000 pounds of fillets.

"Everyone in this state knows walleye, and most people like it," said Gary Rowan, a State Fish vice president. "You know why? We get four deliveries a week—caught one day, here the next, in the restaurant the day after that. Fresh. Very fresh. A lot fresher than any ocean fish available here. That's why it tastes so good."

But Midwesterners are not the only Americans who appreciate the walleye's mild, firm, snow-white flesh. New York chefs like Laurent Tourondel of Cello on the Upper East Side and Kurt Gutenbrunner of Wallsé in the West Village, attracted by its resemblance to European species, have put walleye on their menus, and New York retailers like Citarella and Jake's Fish Market often stock it.

In Europe, the Finns call pike-perch *kuha*, "the secret night-dweller of deep waters," in the romantic words of a cookbook published by Havis Amanda, a seafood restaurant in Helsinki. One recipe calls for braising it and serving it with asparagus. The Russians sometimes use the same fish in the aromatic soup that they call *solyanka*.

Years ago, without the slightest notion that I was tasting a relative of the plebeian walleye, I ate a sumptuous pike-perch preparation, *sandre au beurre blanc*, at Barrier in the Loire Valley, then a Michelin three-star. Talk about turning calico into cashmere! But even that pales in memory compared with a dish eaten earlier in a tavern in rural Sweden, whose name I have forgotten, if I ever knew it. Typically Scandinavian in its daring melding of seemingly disparate elements, it brought together sautéed walleye, cubes of earthy roast beets, salty capers and nippy horseradish.

A recent swing through the Great Lakes states, indulging myself in walleye three or four times a week, convinced me that more and more good chefs in the region have set their minds to preserving traditional methods and developing innovative ways of cooking this delicate freshwater fish. I missed Jean Joho's sautéed walleye with mustard sauce at Everest in Chicago and Michael Symon's herb-crusted walleye at Lola in Cleveland, and no doubt lots of other deserving dishes. But with my wife, Betsey, I tasted a lot of winners.

I started at the Diamond Grille in Akron, my hometown, where I have been eating walleye since the Johnson administration, when I first noticed it lurking on a menu dominated by steaks. I went to grade school with Nick Thomas, the owner, a man of the old school who thinks nothing of taking orders and clearing tables on a busy night. "Grille" it may be, but not when it comes to walleye; the direct heat is too intense, Mr. Thomas told me. So his fish is quickly pan-fried, sauced with a bit of melted butter and served with lemon on the side. A perfect benchmark, I thought, for the fancier dishes to come: would they succeed as well in catching the subtle essence of the walleye?

Almost everyone I asked in the Twin Cities said the best walleye around was at the Tavern on Grand, an unassuming spot a few blocks from James J. Hill's old mansion in St. Paul. For once, the vox pop had it right. "Serving Walleye All Day Every Day" says the sign outside, and for those who don't read signs, there is an eight-foot-long neon walleye in the window.

The fish at the tavern, again pan-fried, was firm and tender, less buttery but quite peppery. Lemon and tartar sauce, which seemed superfluous, came with my pair of fillets, and lettuce, onion, mayonnaise and tomato came on my wife's sandwich. More a shad fancier than a walleye fanatic, having grown up in the wrong section of the country, Betsey was nonetheless impressed.

When I asked David Wildmo, one of the owners, where he bought his fish, he started to hem and haw. "I hate like hell to lie to you," he began, and after a little prodding he decided not to. The walleye comes from a big marketing cooperative in Manitoba, 2,000 pounds of it a week, filleted by machine and frozen with the skin on. Yes, frozen, and to my taste (and contrary to my prejudices) none the worse for it. It's as good as fresh, Mr. Wildmo said, if you peel off the skin when it arrives, keep it on ice and sell it fast.

A stop at the bar of the St. Paul Hotel reinforced the message that less is often more in dealing with walleye. A perfectly fine fish that was delicious on its own could not survive being dusted with almond flour and served with pecan frangipane butter sauce. Walleye for dessert, anyone?

At Goodfellow's, a gorgeous Art Deco dining room with onyx-faced columns and glittering chandeliers, Mr. Cullen started us off with what he called "an urban take on north woods houseboat walleye"—a fillet first sautéed, then roasted and topped with chive crème fraîche, a crispy shallot and roasted, chopped and pickled Vidalia onions. Clever—three textures and three flavors from the onion family—but basically not so different from Betsey's sandwich back at the Tavern on Grand.

Moving rapidly uptown, Mr. Cullen paired sweetbreads with a walleye fillet, painted with pesto. And he sent out a third, more complex dish that showed the fish's (and the chef's) versatility. For this, he crusted another walleye fillet, like the others fresh from Lake of the Woods, with a mixture of Parmesan and *panko* (Japanese-style seasoned bread crumbs) and pan-fried it. It came to the table with mustard aioli and a few drops of 10-year-old balsamic vinegar. To add crunch and flavor contrast, Mr. Cullen added deep-fried vermicellilike potato strands dusted with cayenne pepper.

Paul Kahan also pairs walleye with aioli at Blackbird, his stark, sleek restaurant on the newly gentrified West Randolph Street in

Chicago. His seared walleye sandwich, on toasted, rough-hewn sour-dough bread, is dressed with arugula, roasted tomato and a lemon-and-herb aioli. Juicy, blooming with tart, peppery flavors, it's an everyday hit with the ladies (and gents) who lunch there.

"McDonald's had better watch its step," said our luncheon companion, Bill Rice, food columnist of the *Chicago Tribune*. "This could put the Filet-O-Fish out of business."

Maybe fish tacos, too.

—Minneapolis, May 29, 2002

WEST COAST

Stalking the Wild Morel
in the Woods of Oregon

Jack Czarnecki can't remember when he didn't hunt morels, those elusive aristocrats among mushrooms, but this is his first Oregon spring. So he was as psyched as a sprinter in the starting blocks when I met him at 6:30 one dewy Tuesday morning in late April.

"Morels," he said breathlessly. "My blood is up."

The roadsides were swabbed with color—cherry and pear and lilac, azalea and japonica and poppy, all blooming at once—as we drove into Portland to meet Ken Beckett, who edits the newsletter of the Oregon Mycological Society. But Mr. Czarnecki wanted to talk about the "fabulous rains" of the preceding days; rain, he said, "is the mushroom's sunshine."

An hour and a half later, after tooling down the majestic Columbia River gorge and crossing a bridge, we found ourselves standing on a fir-covered plateau near the hamlet of Glenwood, Wash., on the edge of the Gifford Pinchot National Forest. To the north rose the snow-covered flanks of 12,307-foot Mount Adams, one of the tallest peaks in the Cascade Range.

"I found 43 under a willow tree near here a week ago," Mr. Beckett reported as we took knives and wicker baskets—optimistically large, I thought—from his van.

Northern Europeans like Mr. Czarnecki's Polish forebears, as well as American fans, rank morels with truffles and caviar among the supreme delicacies. Heralds of spring, found in woodlands from mid-April to mid-June, they are curious-looking things, two to five inches tall, with spongy, honeycombed, cone-shape caps. The taste is haunting—musky, loamy, faintly sweet, hinting of caraway and bell peppers.

For three generations, Mr. Czarnecki's family ran Joe's Restaurant in the old railroad town of Reading, Pa., where the menu was built around morels (pronounced moh-RELS), chanterelles and 200 other varieties of fungi. His books, such as *A Cook's Book of Mushrooms* (Artisan, 1995), made the place nationally known.

But Reading missed the boom of the 1990s, and the neighborhood around the restaurant faded. After Jack's father, Joseph, died late in 1995, he decided to close Joe's, which had been in business for 70 years, head for the Northwest and start over at age 48.

In this village 35 miles southwest of Portland, he and his wife, Heidi, found an old building with white columns in front called the Joel Palmer House. They bought it and set about turning it into a restaurant. After endless tribulations, after running out of money and nearly quitting, they were bailed out by a Small Business Administration loan, and they opened last November.

The place has been a big hit, though the Czarneckis have had to cut a few corners here and there. They are using old knives, forks and spoons marked "Joe's," for example, until they can afford new cutlery. If anyone asks about it, Mr. Czarnecki just says the L has rubbed off.

Mr. Czarnecki began hunting mushrooms the minute he arrived, of course. Oregon's prolific mushroom supply was one of two reasons the Czarneckis chose to come here; the other was the region's flourishing vineyards. Having studied oenology at the University of California, Davis, he is a wine nut as well as a mushroom maven.

What with the mushrooms, with a forager who delivers things like seaweed and fiddlehead ferns to his door, with some of the best pinot noir vineyards in the New World a dozen miles down the road, with oysters and salmon and diver-harvested sea urchins close at hand, Mr. Czarnecki is only half kidding when he describes Dayton as "the culinary epicenter of the universe."

In 1997, he harvested 300 pounds of chanterelles himself, plus 100 pounds of *matsutakes*, the delicately scented mushrooms so beloved of the Japanese that they sometimes command prices as high as those of white truffles—as much as $700 a pound. "That's big game hunting," Mr. Czarnecki said.

It was my first mycological mission, but I have suffered from the dread morel mania for decades.

I first tasted the little devils by accident, 35 years ago. It was in France, south of Paris, I think, maybe in the Barbizon forest; the names of the town and the restaurant are lost to memory. I remember that I ordered a veal chop, something I had never encountered before—in Ohio, where I grew up, chops came in two flavors, pork and lamb—and when it arrived, it was swathed in a gray sauce studded with the most astounding mushrooms. I was hooked at once. Ever since, morels have carried me back to my youthful voyages of gastronomic discovery.

Gertrude Stein liked them, too. In *The Autobiography of Alice B. Toklas*, she told of searching for morels in the woods near the little town of Senonches, just northwest of Chartres, when "the fields were colored with the first poppies and cornflowers and hedges of blossoming hawthorn."

Curnonsky, the self-styled Prince of Gastronomes, advocated stewing a pound of well-washed morels, preferably plucked from the pine forests on the slopes of the Jura, near France's border with Switzerland, in three ounces of butter, four ounces of yellow vin d'Arbois and a quarter pint of thick cream, then turning the result, seasoned with salt, pepper and lemon juice, into puff pastry shells. But, of course, he never met Jenny Craig.

North of Lyon, they make a morel sauce for the famous chickens of the region, the patriotic *poulets de Bresse*, with their blue feet, red combs and white plumage. At Cartet, a lunch-only bistro near the Place de la Republique in Paris, the boss, a semiretired actress, used to make what remains for me the definitive morel dish: an exquisitely unctuous morel omelette.

In the United States, morels have been slow to build a following. They are not mentioned in *The Joy of Cooking* or Fannie Farmer or even James Beard's *American Cookery*, though Beard knew them as a boy in Portland. He recalled years later how repulsive he thought they looked when he first spied them in a market—"they resembled dried-up brains"—and how good they tasted.

Wild mushrooms started to seep into the American public's consciousness in 1985, when Phillips Mushroom Farms, a big producer in Kennett Square, Pa., began offering beefy portobello caps to commercial clients. Now, more than 10 million pounds of "specialty mushrooms," meaning all types other than the ubiquitous white buttons, are sold in this country every year.

In 1996, two of the country's most prominent chefs, Alice Waters of Chez Panisse in Berkeley, Calif., and Charlie Trotter, from Chicago, published vegetable cookbooks. Both included morel recipes, Mr. Trotter suggesting a preparation of morels stuffed with grits and served in their own juices with okra, and Ms. Waters recommending a fricassee of morels, onions and potatoes.

But there have always been many enthusiastic and successful morel amateurs, secretive souls who guard their happy hunting grounds as carefully as their PIN codes. One of the best regions is northern Michigan, and every year hordes of hunters head to Boyne City for the National Mushroom Festival there. Each contestant gets 90 minutes of search time.

The record was set in the mid-70s by a local enthusiast named Stan Boris. Sprinting all the way, he emerged from the woods with more than 900 morels.

Depending on supply and season, fresh morels cost $15 to $50 a pound retail in New York. Dried morels, which reconstitute very well, are available all year.

And now there are cultivated morels, too. These are grown in Auburn, Ala., by a Minnesota-based company called Terry Farms, using a patented process developed in recent years by university researchers. The flavor is less pronounced, but they are available year-round, about 1,000 pounds a week at the moment, and celebrity chefs like Charlie Trotter snap them up.

Still, Oregon morels dominate the market; New York's Daniel Boulud, a Frenchman, uses them instead of imported morels, as he wrote [in the "Food Section"] recently. Vitaly Paley, owner of Portland's bistro of the moment, Paley's Place, said he used Oregon morels when he cooked in a Michelin two-star restaurant in France, the Moulin de la Gorce, near Limoges, before coming to the United States.

Since it was the start of the season, we were looking for black or gray morels (Morchella angusticeps), which are actually tan when young, turning gray later. The best variety, the cream-colored Morchella esculenta, or yellow morel, had not yet appeared. (Morel taxonomy is tangled and disputed, but there is a variety that resembles M. esculenta, called M. crassipes, or "clubfoot morel," which is larger, as well as a variety that most authorities consider a close relative of M. angusticeps, called M. conica, which is smaller. M. deliciosa, the white morel, also called "dead elm morel" because of its breeding ground, is smaller still, but no less delicious.)

Unfortunately, black morels are the hardest to see, blending most completely with their surroundings. Just how hard, I soon learned.

Ken Beckett went in one direction with a chum of his, Jack Czarnecki and I in another. I had been briefed: look in disturbed areas, where there had been fires or a vehicle had left deep tread marks, or brush had been cut back. Morels seem to like that. No one knows for sure why.

"You can lower the odds by knowing the environment," Mr. Czarnecki said. "But they're infuriatingly elusive. You can be in the middle of a whole bunch, and still you don't see them. You get better at it after a little while, but this is completely new territory for me. In the East, we search under elms, but here you're looking in an evergreen forest."

I discounted that as modesty or poor-mouthing or both. But after wandering around for nearly an hour, poking with walking sticks in places where our quarry might lurk, cracking twigs underfoot as we went, our ingestible take was exactly zero—only a few gyromitras, or false morels, which are just marginally edible, and a few verpas. Those can be eaten, my companion said dejectedly, "if you cook them in three changes of water."

Like golf and fly-fishing, morel hunting teaches patience and humility, especially humility. As we came into a clearing, Mr. Czarnecki said, "We should find some here—unless, of course, we don't." We didn't.

Finally, Mr. Beckett rejoined us, and he spotted morels at once, near where we stood. "There," he cried, pointing with his walking stick to what looked to me like a pinecone. "And there, and over there, too." In five minutes, he had a dozen beauties, some of them two inches tall. Some were hidden by shadow, some by fir needles, some by a fallen tree limb.

"I just went through there," Mr. Czarnecki muttered, wounded.

Mr. Beckett, 56, arranges financing for equipment rentals when not busy in the forest. He decided that radical measures were now required. We would visit his secret willow tree. Back into the van, down the highway, and there it was. But so was a man in a pickup, just pulling away—a "commercial," as amateurs call them, a professional collector and seller of mushrooms in a trade that has become so profitable that some carry guns to ward off thieves. This one was a long-haired logger; others are Cambodians and Mexicans.

"That's an absolute low in my mycological career," Mr. Czarnecki said, dripping contempt. "One of them, in one of Ken's best spots."

Undaunted, Mr. Beckett headed for his tree anyway and proved that amateurs sometimes outshine pros. He was soon spotting big morels in hidden crannies. "Watch out," he yelled at me at one point. "You're standing on two or three." I had no trouble spotting them once I knew where they were.

Finally, we had to head for home. Mr. Czarnecki fretted all the way about dinner, which he was cooking for my wife, Betsey, and me, and some winemaking friends. Mr. Beckett came to the rescue, donating not only his entire day's take but also some of the morels he had found earlier in the week.

That night we had a feast: not only wines from Archery Summit and Eyrie and WillaKenzie, three of the Willamette Valley's best vineyards, not only *matsutakes* in wontons, the first time I had sampled that elusive flavor, but also Mrs. Czarnecki's smashing three-mushroom tart (made "with cipes and other things," she said with studied vagueness) and lamb with shiitakes and morels Rosenthal—gently braised morels in a nest of crisp phyllo strands called *kataifi*.

It made us forget all about our failures in the forest.

—*Oregon, May 20, 1998*

● ●

MORELS WITH RUFFLED PASTA

(Adapted from Jack Czarnecki)
Time: 30 minutes

    6 ounces ruffled pasta (radiatore), tricolor or plain
    6 ounces fresh morels, cut into approximately the size of the
       cooked pasta
    2 tablespoons vegetable oil
    1 small onion, thinly sliced
    1 small red or green bell pepper, thinly sliced
    ¼ teaspoon salt
    1 teaspoon sugar
    1 tablespoon soy sauce
    1 tablespoon arrowroot mixed with 1 tablespoon cold water

1. Bring about 6 quarts of lightly salted water to a boil, and add the ruffled pasta. Cook until it is al dente, about 8 minutes.

2. While the water is coming to a boil, prepare the mushrooms: in a large skillet over a medium-high flame, heat the oil and add the onions and bell peppers. Sauté until they are slightly softened, about 2 minutes. Add the morels, salt, sugar and soy sauce. Stir well, and simmer for 1 minute. Add the arrowroot mixture, and simmer until the sauce thickens, about 1 minute more. Adjust the salt to taste.

3. Drain the pasta, and transfer it to a serving bowl. Add morels and sauce, and mix gently. Serve immediately.

Yield: 2 servings

MORELS ROSENTHAL IN KATAIFI NESTS
(Adapted from Jack Czarnecki)
Time: 1 hour

12 ounces *kataifi* pastry (available at Greek and specialty markets), divided into four long bunches
7 tablespoons butter
½ cup chopped fresh herbs, like savory, thyme, oregano or basil
⅓ cup thinly sliced onion
⅓ cup thinly sliced red bell pepper
1 pound whole fresh morels
2 tablespoons flour
½ teaspoon salt
1 teaspoon sugar
1 tablespoon soy sauce

1. Heat oven to 300 degrees. On a nonstick baking sheet or a baking sheet lined with parchment paper, form each bunch of *kataifi* strands into a circle about 4½ to 5 inches in diameter, allowing

some strands to form the bottom of the nest. Melt 3 tablespoons butter, and drizzle over the *kataifi*. Sprinkle the fresh herbs on top. Bake until lightly golden and crisp, about 15 minutes. Set aside at room temperature. (Nests may be made up days in advance if stored in an air-tight container and kept cool.)

2. In a large sauté pan over a medium flame, heat 2 tablespoons butter and add onion and bell pepper. Saute until slightly softened, about 1 minute. Add morels, and stir. Reduce heat to low, cover pan and allow morels to braise for about 15 minutes.

3. While morels are braising, prepare a roux: in a small sauté pan over medium-low heat, melt the remaining 2 tablespoons butter. Add flour, and stir with a wooden spoon until smooth. Continue stirring until roux is golden brown, 5 to 7 minutes. Remove from heat and set aside.

4. Add salt, sugar and soy sauce to the morels, and stir well. Bring liquid to a simmer, and stir in just enough roux to thicken the sauce. All of the roux may not be needed; the mixture will continue to thicken as it stands.

5. To serve, place the *kataifi* nests on four serving plates, and fill each with morels. Serve immediately.

Yield: 4 servings

A New Normandy, North of the Golden Gate

C
an this be the place? Dubiously, you drive up a muddy, un-marked road potted with water-filled holes, park next to a worn army-surplus generator, poke your head into a metal farm building and peer down a corridor.

At the far end stands a pink-cheeked woman with short-cropped gray hair topped by a fluorescent lime-green baseball cap, energetically stirring the contents of a stainless-steel tank with a wooden paddle. This, it turns out, is Cindy Callahan, Sarah Lawrence alumna, nurse, graduate of the University of California's exacting Hastings Law School, mother, cheese maker.

With her husband, Ed, a doctor who died several years ago, Mrs. Callahan forsook the pleasures of cosmopolitan San Francisco in 1986 to begin raising sheep in southwestern Sonoma County. This is not the Sonoma of obsessively tended vines and chic shops. Here vast pastures roll rhythmically into the distance, punctuated by rough granite outcrops and enormous eucalyptus trees. In the mist of a late-November morning, the dark bulks of Angus cattle loom large on the hillsides; small, vulnerable-looking sheep huddle in the foreground.

Now 66, Mrs. Callahan runs Bellwether Farms with her two sons, Liam, 35, and Brett, 32. They produce handmade goat's- and cow's-milk cheeses of rare excellence, including a firm, sweet, slightly caramel-flavored ricotta. It bears no resemblance to the wan, wimpy stuff that Americans are accustomed to. Thomas Keller of the French Laundry in the Napa Valley, who uses it in ravioli, describes it as the best he has ever tasted in the United States.

Amazingly, this profoundly rural area, much of it beyond the reach of cell phones, lies only 50 miles or so north of the Golden Gate. More amazingly, it has evolved in recent years into one of the nation's prime centers of artisanal cheese making, a New World counterpart to Lombardy and Normandy. At many of the best dairies, as at Bellwether Farms, women play leading roles, like their Old World sisters.

Up the road, near Sebastopol, Jennifer Bice (rhymes with "dice") owns Redwood Hill Farm, a producer of goat's milk yogurt and cheeses sold nationally in Whole Foods markets, among others. Down south, near Point Reyes in Marin County, where the landscape looks less like Wales and more like Scotland, three Giacomini sisters oversee the making of California's first blue cheese, and Sue Conley and Peggy Smith, the head cowgirls at Cowgirl Creamery, turn Ellen Straus's gorgeous organic cow's milk into all manner of delights.

My wife, Betsey, and I had tasted one or two of these cheeses in the East, but it was only last summer that we learned just how much we had been missing. Toward the end of an excellent dinner at Gary Danko, one of the premier restaurants in San Francisco, I did what I have done hundreds of times in England and France and Italy: I asked to taste some local cheeses.

Lynn Andrews, the resident cheese expert, who matures some of the cheeses she sells in an in-house cooler, did not let us down. She brought out eight of them and, Scheherazade-like, spun an intriguing tale about each of them in her soft voice.

We tasted. We talked. We surrendered. No inner voice whispered, "Yes, but." We felt no longing whatsoever for the great cheeses of far-off Europe.

California is the nation's largest dairy state and its second-largest cheese producer; some expect it to take the lead from Wisconsin by 2005. Cheese is made all over the state, even near Los Angeles, in Winchester, where the Netherlands-born Jules Wesselink and his daughter, Valerie Thomas, produce a granular, aged Gouda whose hauntingly nutty, salty flavor dazzled Mr. Keller and his cheese manager, Lachlan Patterson, when I took a big chunk by for them to taste.

We were much intrigued, after our tasting session at Danko, by the involvement of so many women in Marin and Sonoma cheese making. Traditionally, men herd the sheep, goats and cows on the European continent, while their wives make cheese. In England, Mrs. Kirkham, Mrs. Montgomery and Mrs. Appleby—they are known by their family names alone—have helped to keep the tradition of farmhouse cheese alive.

The same pattern seems slowly to be developing in the United States, through the efforts of women like Sally Jackson, who makes cheeses of unusual complexity in Washington State, near the Canadian border; Paula Lambert, who makes a broad range of Italianate cheeses in Dallas; Dr. Patricia Elliott, a physician in Rapidan, Va., near Charlottesville, who specializes in hard sheep's milk cheese; Mary Keehn, who makes the unparalleled Humboldt Fog in far northern California; and, of course, Laura Chenel, whose Sonoma County goat cheese began the California boom in the 1970s. She has been so successful that her cheese is now made by machine, not by hand.

Bellwether Farms deals in meat as well as cheese, selling spring lambs, less than six weeks old, to San Francisco restaurants like Masa's and Rubicon. The dressed carcasses weigh only 20 pounds, a bit more than the baby lamb, or *abbacchio*, that forms the centerpiece of Easter feasts in Rome.

Lambs are born here in late winter or very early spring and weaned 35 to 40 days after birth. Only after they go to market do the Callahans begin to milk the ewes in their flock of East Friesian sheep, continuing until October. When no sheep's milk is available, they buy cow's milk from a neighboring farmer, but the sheep cheeses have made Bellwether's reputation.

All are grounded in the lessons Ed and Cindy Callahan learned at farms in Tuscany and Umbria when they visited Italy early in their cheese-making careers. Liam Callahan's favorite among them, and mine, is San Andreas, which is named after the earthquake fault line that passes near the farm. It is made from unheated milk and shaped into fat wheels that weigh about four and a half pounds when they are fresh.

After two to four months on pine slats in an aging room, where the temperature is held at a constant 50 degrees, they are down to three pounds. In the process, the cheeses lose moisture and develop surface mold. When mature, they are firm in texture, with a clean, mild flavor and a tangy finish; you can taste the full flavor of the Friesian milk in the finished product. Though softer than pecorino, they have a similar bite.

Bellwether makes a Tuscan-style cheese studded with peppercorns, called Pepato, and a cow's-milk version of San Andreas called Carmody, after a nearby road, as well as impossibly unctuous crème fraîche.

The prize-winning ricotta is a byproduct of San Andreas and Carmody. Once the curds have been separated from the whey and poured into molds, the whey is pumped into another vat, topped up with whole milk and heated rapidly, to 180 degrees for sheep's milk, 192 for cow's milk. When vinegar is poured into the tank, soft curds form in less than two minutes.

This is tough, repetitive physical labor, from which there is no shirking. Liam Callahan said with a sigh of resignation, "It sure gets you into a rhythm."

But the rural life has never lost its allure for his mother.

"We had a professor at Sarah Lawrence named Joseph Campbell," she said. "He was a famous guy, a philosopher. He used to tell us, 'Follow your bliss.' Well, I'd say it's pretty blissful out here."

Jennifer Bice, a gentle but determined woman, sometimes wears a silver goat pin on the lapel of her sweater. She dotes on the 400 goats she keeps at Redwood Hill, giving each a name. She breeds Alpines and Nubians, LaManchas, Saanens and Toggenburgs—the five major types of dairy goats in the United States. And she serves regularly as a judge at major goat shows.

Her parents started the dairy, located among towering trees just south of the Russian River, in 1968, and young Ms. Bice worked with the goats as 4-H projects. She and her husband, Steven Shack, took it over in 1978 and built it into one of the best of its kind in the country, producing cheeses of remarkable delicacy with traditional methods. Mr. Shack died of cancer in 1999.

Ms. Bice said that she found it difficult to attract American workers to the area because of the high cost of living. So much of the work at Redwood Hill is carried out by foreigners, recruited at agricultural colleges abroad and brought here on special 18-month work visas. At the moment, she has several Bulgarians, a Danish woman and a young Tanzanian on the payroll.

The goats, fed on hay and grains, are milked twice every day, at 6 a.m. and 5:30 p.m. Their milk is cooled from 103 degrees to 38 degrees in five to seven minutes to retard the development of bacteria, then pasteurized. A starter culture is added to form a soft curd, a process that takes much longer than using rennet, a substance taken from animals' stomachs. The cheese takes 16 to 18 hours to coagulate and two days to drain; with rennet it takes no more than 24 hours. The advantage is a smoother and more delicate texture.

"Can't make good cheese from bad ingredients," Ms. Bice admonished me as she showed me around her tiny "factory"—actually, one big room where the cheese is made and packaged, with a mini-laboratory tucked into a corner. The cheeses are matured in a pair of adjacent rooms where they are first dried and then aged, the delectably edgy Camembert-style Camellia for as much as four weeks.

Of the 30,000 pounds of cheese Redwood Hill makes every year, one of the most successful styles is called California Crottin, in homage to the white disks so popular in France. With a pale yellow rind and a robust, earthy taste, it is an ounce and a half of pure joy. But unlike the French, who offer *crottin* in fresh, medium and mature versions, Ms. Bice sells it only fresh.

A lover of goat cheese when it is old and chalky, I asked why.

"When we started, we sold a well-aged *crottin*," Ms. Bice said, "but people complained. Americans want it fresh, so that's what we give them."

Redwood Hill stands on a hilltop just above Iron Horse Vineyards, and my friend Joy Sterling, a member of the family that owns the winery, jokes that Ms. Bice's cheeses taste so good "because her goats spend their whole lives looking at my vines." Maybe she's on to something there. Maybe visually soothed animals give sweeter-tasting milk. Certainly Bob Giacomini's herd of Holstein cows, from whose milk his family produces Point Reyes Original Blue, the hottest new handmade California cheese in many years, have a view to die for.

"Brigadoon," Betsey said when she saw the landscape. Its verdant moors, punctuated here and there with yellow gorse, slope down to firthlike Tomales Bay, and on most mornings horizontal stripes of low-lying fog cling to the hillsides beyond. No wonder there are villages and roads with names like Argyll and Aberdeen and Inverness.

Mr. Giacomini has run a dairy in the area since 1959, but the cheese has been on the market only since January. It came into being because he wanted to reduce the size of his 500-head herd, whose manure was threatening to pollute the oyster beds in the bay, without reducing his income. And because he wanted to lure at least some of his four accomplished daughters back home.

Three of them, all with business degrees, are here now: Karen Giacomini Howard, 41; Lynn Giacomini Stray, 35; and Jill Giacomini Basch, 31. They work with Monte McIntyre, the cheese maker, who was born on a dairy farm in South Dakota and perfected his craft making Maytag, which many experts consider the nation's finest blue cheese, in Newton, Iowa.

"We've always been a family of foodies anyway," Ms. Basch said.

The succulent new cheese has caught on quickly, gaining a place in stores across the country (including Murray's Cheese Shop in New York) and restaurants all over California (at Miramonte, the comfort-food genius Cindy Pawlcyn's sparkling new place in St. Helena, it appears on the Super Supper Burger). The only question is whether it can build a sufficiently large following to justify the Giacominis' investment.

Two 1,500-gallon vats give their shiny new plant a capacity of 250,000 pounds a year; they are producing 15 percent of that, making cheese only a day or two a week.

The milk is not pasteurized, but it is homogenized, which breaks up fat globules and encourages the formation of holes in the curd, so air can penetrate to the interior and help mold to grow. (Later, more are mechanically punched into the cheese.) A liquid mold, penicillium roquefortii, is added to the milk, along with rennet, and the resulting curd goes into round forms. After draining overnight, the nascent cheeses are taken into a cold, humid room—"a kind of artificial cave, since we don't have real ones here," Mr. McIntyre explained—where they are sprinkled once a day for three days with kosher salt.

Encased in Cryovac bags, the cheeses age for six to eight months. It is this technique, I suspect, that makes them so much moister than Stilton. They are less pungent than Roquefort because they are made with cow's milk, not sheep's milk. Their remarkable richness, reminiscent of Gorgonzola, is a family secret, at least for now.

Cowgirl Creamery is something different, a glass-enclosed room inside Tomales Bay Foods, a hangarlike store in the hamlet of Point Reyes Station (population 350). It was started five years ago by Ms. Smith, 48, a former co-chef at Chez Panisse cafe in Berkeley, and Ms. Conley, 49, who developed what must be the creamery's greatest treasure—a rich, creamy, subtly tart, triumphantly cheesy cottage cheese that puts soupy commercial rivals to shame.

The store sells oils, wines, prepared food to go and cheeses made by others, in the United States and abroad, whom the cowgirls admire (www.cowgirl creamery.com) It is where I first tasted Mr. Wesselink's and Dr. Elliott's cheeses, and it stocks the wonderful English cheeses from Neal's Yard in London. (One of the cowgirls, Kate Arding, who manages the cheese counter, used to work there.)

But the main feature is the Cowgirl cheeses, made from the phenomenally rich, thick Straus milk, which comes from a single herd of Holsteins, the first herd of any breed west of the Mississippi to be certified organic. They graze along Tomales Bay near Marshall, about 10 miles north of Point Reyes Station.

"It's the milk that makes the difference," said Ms. Smith, an earnest, engaging woman with steel-gray streaks in her dark hair. "The herd has an individual character. You can taste the changes of the grasses and the seasons in the milk."

Straus milk is an unlikely byproduct of Nazi persecution of the Jews in Europe. Ellen Straus, born in the Netherlands, and her husband, Bill, born in Germany, are both refugees, who met in the United States. Their son, Albert, helps run the family farm.

In addition to cottage cheese, Cowgirl makes *fromage blanc,* crème fraîche and *mascarpone*—all velvety, all delicious, all tantalizingly unavailable outside the Bay Area. They need to be eaten quickly, Ms. Conley said, preferably within three days, so they are not well adapted to shipping.

But the creamery's soft-ripened cheeses can be ordered by mail, and they are every bit as beguiling. The triple-cream Mt. Tam (after Mount Tamalpais, just down the coast) is available all year long; buttery yet not cloying, it has an earthy flavor reminiscent of mushrooms. Three others are available seasonally—St. Pat, wrapped in nettle leaves, in the spring; Pierce Point, washed in Quady Essencia, a Muscat-based sweet wine, and rolled in dried herbs, in the fall; and my pick of the litter, Red Hawk, a more pungent, washed-rind triple-cream, ideal for winter, best when aged for six weeks.

Oh yes, the name. When Ms. Smith and Ms. Conley were setting up shop, Mrs. Straus said to them, "Remember, girls, this is the Wild West."

—*Valley Ford, California, November 28, 2001*

An Asian Odyssey, Seconds from the Freeway

Here in the San Gabriel Valley, northeast of downtown Los Angeles, more than 500 Chinese restaurants vie for your business. This is no worn, close-packed, inner-city Asian neighborhood like those in New York and San Francisco, but a spacious, suburban, shopping-center Chinatown, crossed by freeways and punctuated by signs covered with the bold strokes of ideographs.

More Asian-Americans live in metropolitan Los Angeles than anywhere else in the country. According to the 2000 census, 10.4 percent of the area's 16.4 million people, a total of 1.7 million, are Asian-American, including 415,000 Chinese. Many live in Monterey Park, the first Asian-majority city in the mainland United States, where it is easier to buy bok choy than iceberg.

For Asians, as the food historian E. N. Anderson commented several years ago, especially well-heeled Asians like those in Monterey Park, "even the most trivial matters are occasions for a feast."

Hereabouts, it is a feast for all the senses: dumplings so delicate they shimmy like your sister Kate when the waitress sets the steamer on the table. The fattest, crunchiest *cha gio* (Vietnamese spring rolls) you ever hope to put in your mouth. Ethereal, exquisitely flavored rice cooked in the style of Hainan Island. Complicated and indefinably delicious Thai aromas and flavors, a rebuke to every mail-it-in, one-spice-fits-all clip joint in the land.

The foods of Korea, Thailand and Vietnam, Shanghai, Taipei and Tokyo, pour from a thousand kitchens in astonishing abundance, from holes in the wall and coffee shops and strip-mall dining rooms

126

in burgs with names like Gardena and Arcadia and Alhambra. Because most of the chefs, like most of the customers, are relatively recent arrivals from Asia, the dishes they serve retain the true tastes and the modest prices of their homelands.

Like so much else in Los Angeles, the Asian food scene, by all accounts the country's richest, always seemed chaotic and unfathomable to me, though I lived for three years in Asia. Frustrated, I had to content myself with nibbling at the edges. But last winter, I ran into the Hollywood producer Sean Daniel, a much more diligent eater than his lean and hungry look would suggest, and he offered to act as a guide. That sounded just fine to me.

So with my wife, Betsey, I took the plunge. We ate alone or with a shifting cast of supporting eaters including Mr. Daniel; the writer-director Gary Ross (*Big, Dave*) and his wife, Allison Thomas; another writer-director, Phil Robinson (*Field of Dreams*), and his friend, the singer Carole King; and Bill Carrick, a Los Angeles-based Democratic campaign consultant, and his wife, Beegie Truesdale.

To Mr. Daniel's ideas, I added others from S. Irene Virbila, the restaurant critic of the *Los Angeles Times*, and I pored over *Counter Intelligence* (St. Martin's Press, 2000), the indispensable survey of L.A.'s ethnic eateries by Jonathan Gold, now the New York restaurant critic of *Gourmet.*

Almost without exception, we were bowled over by the food and pleased by the warmth and helpfulness of the service, even when we were on our most thickheadedly Occidental behavior. If one or two places were rated B rather than A by the health department, none was downright grubby, and hey, at these prices, what kind of nut expects décor by Adam Tihany?

The climax to a memorable week in the gastronomic trenches came on a rollicking Saturday evening, when a bunch of us, fatter and happier with each passing hour, tried three restaurants, ferried by van from one to another by an abstemious driver. The generous Mr. Carrick, sommelier for the nonce, produced several fine bottles from his cellar, including a mature, spectacularly rich 1997 Williams Selyem Russian River pinot noir. We drank some in the one restaurant with a BYOB policy; the rest we finished off in the van.

In three years as a correspondent in Saigon, I must have eaten spring rolls at least twice a week. I got pretty sick of them. But I doubt I would ever have tired of the *cha gio* they serve at the Golden Deli, a lively, ever-crowded cubbyhole in San Gabriel.

Knobby, crusty, golden, these are Paul Bunyanesque spring rolls, longer and fatter than any I have seen, good for four ample bites each. Layers of rice paper, fried to a magnificent crispness, enclose a mixture of ground pork, crab meat, cellophane noodles (but not too many), minced onions, grated carrots and wood-ear mushrooms, seasoned with black pepper and fish sauce.

Eating *cha gio* entails ritual. You wrap the roll in a romaine leaf, tucking in one or more herbs from a spectacular assortment on the table—spearmint, licorice-scented purple basil and sharp, spicy *rau ram*, also called Vietnamese coriander. Then you dunk the end of the package in a little saucer of *nuoc cham*, a potent dip made from fish sauce, diluted with water, plus lime juice, chilies, sugar, garlic and scallions. It is to Vietnamese cooking as soy sauce is to many other Asian cuisines, but much subtler.

The Golden Deli has other joys, including several varieties of *pho*, the aromatic noodle soup, garnished with *ngo gai*, or saw-leaf herb, a member of the coriander family. *Goi cuon*, or summer rolls, are over-stuffed with fat pink shrimp, which show through the translucent rice paper enclosing them. But the spring rolls are worth a journey from Beverly Hills or Brooklyn.

So are the dumplings—gorgeous pleated things, fashioned from pastry of exquisite fragility—at Din Tai Fung in Arcadia, right in the shadow of the Santa Anita racetrack. A branch of a storied establishment in Taipei, this, too, is chronically SRO. But here it's fun to wait, because you can watch the young men in their glass-walled room, dressed in white from shoes to baseball caps, as they make the dumplings by hand with the aid of tiny rolling pins.

If you go on Saturday or Sunday morning, you can sample *xiao long bao*, small dumplings filled with broth, often called Shanghai soup dumplings. You will find no better example of this delicacy anywhere. But pork dumplings and a pork and crab combination are no less juicy, nor are the open-topped *shao mai*, redolent of five-spice, which resemble tiny pomegranates.

Change of pace? Have a tossed salad in a sack, in the form of vegetable dumplings, densely packed with chives and greens.

Los Angeles has a wealth of Japanese restaurants. Sushi Sasabune has the bossiest chef and famously warm rice, Matsuhisa begat Nobus with similar fare in a half-dozen capitals and Ginza Sushiko may well be the best Asian restaurant of any kind in the United States. But all are expensive (Ginza Sushiko hideously so, often more than $1,000 a couple), all are in the West End and very few have predominantly Japanese clienteles. We wanted something else. We found it at Tsukiji. Named for the fish market in central Tokyo, tucked into a Gardena minimall full of Japanese businesses, with big Japanese companies based nearby, it attracts workers at lunch and families at night. You notice at once how immaculate the cramped space is and how softly people speak.

You notice the food, too. Tsukiji specializes in *tataki*, an uncommon style of sashimi—notably finely chopped Spanish mackerel, seasoned with velvety, heavily serrated *shiso* leaves, and *negi*, a kind of leek. Tsukiji's sushi is exceptional. The fish is less cold than usual, which enhances its flavor. The ginger served with it is white, not purple-pink, and milder than usual. Octopus is miraculously tender. Creamy *uni* (the ovaries of sea urchin), for me the greatest of marine delicacies, towers pale orange above its collar of nori. I find two short words in my notes: "Oh, my!"

Here is the proof of the pudding: We found ourselves using less soy, with less wasabi in it, and eating less pickled ginger, because the sushi itself was so completely satisfying.

The intersection of Del Mar Avenue and Valley Boulevard in San Gabriel forms the commercial nexus of the San Gabriel Valley, with the sprawling Ranch 99 shopping center on one corner, anchored by a big Asian supermarket. Among the mall's many restaurants, one stands out, called Tung Lai Shun.

Transplanted from Beijing, Tung Lai Shun features awful doo-wop music; moist, multilayer sesame bread, shaped like a plump discus, with herbs and scallions inside; and lamb in every guise imaginable.

This is not lamb for the timid of taste. This is lamb that aspires to muttonhood, as robustly flavored as game, a reminder of the semi-wild sheep that graze on the grasslands of Mongolia, where this style of cooking originated. It is served cold in a garlic-flavored jelly as an appetizer, and as a main course with pancakes, in dumplings bursting with juice, in a hot pot with cabbage and in a stir-fry with scallions.

Not all the food thrilled us. Tea duck was dry and stringy, for example. But what was good was very good indeed, including all of the lamb dishes, and much is extremely difficult to taste anywhere else.

Shiang Garden offers something altogether different—the spicy food of Hunan Province, prepared with remarkable sophistication. You sense that when the waiter shows you a tray of cold appetizers, including minuscule anchovies, dry-fried with chilies and glossy, succulent black mushroom caps. Slices of Hunan ham, glazed with honey and firm to the tooth, are meant to go into hinged pieces of steamed (Wonder?) bread.

Three decades ago, at Cecilia Chiang's wonderful Mandarin restaurant in San Francisco's Ghirardelli Square, I first tasted a dish of minced squab in a cup of iceberg lettuce. Shiang Garden plays the same game with shrimp, chopping them fine, adding garlic, tossing them with bits of sautéed bread and spooning the mixture, still warm, into cool, crisp lettuce wrappers. But even that didn't delight us as much as the house bean curd, which arrived in a ceramic pot shimmering with heat. Inside were cubes of creamy tofu, meltingly soft at the center, with a taste as fresh as spring water, and flavored with black beans, scallion tops, chilies and garlic. Real alchemy, this dish; it made a believer out of me, a tofu skeptic.

Lake Spring Cuisine plays in the white-tablecloth league, with décor marginally less jarring and lighting marginally less glaring than the norm in Chinese restaurants. But it's not the look of the place that has made it legendary among local devotees of Chinese cooking. Lake Spring Cuisine is famous for the dish listed on the menu as "pork pump," a glistening, deep-brown, not-very-appetizing-looking lump that you see on almost every table. Order it. But first you should order another dish, jade shrimp, which is as subtle as pork pump is overwhelming—a platter of small pink shrimp in a pale, translucent green glaze of puréed spinach and garlic.

The pork is, in fact, red-cooked pork shoulder, a Shanghainese classic; Bruce Cost gives a comprehensive recipe in *Asian Ingredients* (William Morrow, 1988). "Pork pump," as Mr. Gold explains, is a typo (for pork rump) that has persisted on local Chinese menus since the 1970s. At Joe's Shanghai in Flushing, the dish is correctly named but not nearly as memorable as at Lake Spring Cuisine. So perhaps nomenclature counts for something, after all.

Superslow cooking is the secret. The meat, encased in a thick layer of fat, simmers for hours in soy sauce, star anise, ginger, orange peel and rock sugar, causing some fat to melt into the meat, giving it a miraculously unctuous texture. A quick probe with chopsticks is rewarded with strands of sweet, lush pork, as perfectly piggy as prime Carolina barbecue.

China tea cuts the richness of the meat and its syrupy sauce. Plain steamed rice provides ballast, and you need nothing more.

Boisterous Soot Bull Jeep is in Koreatown, near downtown; its neighbors include Korean dry cleaners, accountants and photo finishers. But next door is Pico-Union, the most densely packed neighborhood of Central American immigrants in the country, and this is the heart of the notorious Rampart Division, where rogue cops started their own gang. Not quite Rodeo Drive.

Inside, a glass case holds the Chivas stocks of Korean habitués, and hardwood charcoal burners are built into the Formica-top tables. Ventilating fans can't keep up with the smoke, so some hangs in the room, a pall of smog, staining the walls the color of butterscotch pudding.

You order whatever you like to grill on the screen atop the brazier, whose charcoal gives food a pungency that more common gas flames cannot match. We liked the thin strips of Spencer (aka Delmonico) steak best, with crisp ends and pearls of juice drawn out by the heat.

Short ribs, shrimp, squid, chicken and sweet, oily eel went down the hatch in a hurry, but I found the tripe and octopus tough. Maybe we cooked them too long or not long enough.

Tips: Pay attention, and pull the cooked bits off to the side before they turn into cinders. Don't neglect the unashamedly garlicky, chili-laced kimchi or the steamed spinach that come with the meat. And wear old clothes. This Seoul food is messy eating (even our deft waitress had a mishap, staining her white turtleneck with squid ink). Klutz that I am, I singed my fingers as I maneuvered things over the flames. Oven mitts for me next time.

At Yazmin, a gaudy storefront in Alhambra, south of Pasadena, you'll eat off melamine plates, but never mind. They'll serve you faithful renditions of dishes from Penang, Singapore and Jakarta, plus exotic Nonya specialties created long ago by immigrant Chinese women for Malay husbands.

Yazmin offers most of the repertory of the famous Singapore street vendors, including *rendang*, a grainy, slow-simmered, comfortingly hearty beef stew made with coconut milk. It's fabulous, especially if you ask for chili-based *sambal olek*, a condiment, and add it in judicious proportions. Hainan rice, steamed in the style of an island in the South China Sea, with ginger and garlic in a mild chicken broth, makes an admirable accompaniment.

And then there is *rojak*, a midsummer California night's dream, cooling and palate-stirring: pineapple, cucumber, mango, jicama, crispy tofu, peanuts and hot pepper. It makes a world-class salad, colorful, enlivened by vivid contrasts in texture, sweet and salty, mild and peppery.

Sanamluang Cafe is a tiny L-shape place on Hollywood Boulevard, a couple of miles (and a couple of civilizations) from Grauman's Chinese Theater. It's the kind of spot where babies are propped on some tables while Gwyneth wannabes eat at others. The Sunday we were there, three cops—one black, one white, one Thai—were devouring carry-out lunches in the parking lot.

Try the General's Noodle Soup—a stirring, garlic-laced broth with egg noodles, duck, bits of ground pork and shrimp, to which you add as many *nam prik* (green chilies) as you can take. If you don't overdo it, you can taste each ingredient. Several dishes are made with scrumptious, deep-fried belly pork; fish sauce or kaffir lime leaves spike others. But unlike many Thai chefs, this one doesn't dump lemongrass and coriander milk into everything.

Don't order too much. You must, on pain of excommunication, save room for irresistible coconut-flavored griddle cakes, the size of a silver dollar, crisp on the outside, molten on the inside, which a guy cooks on a grill outside the restaurant. Buy a dozen, and devour them on the freeway.

For as much as we could eat: $18.56 plus tip. Astounding.

—*Monterey Park, California, April 17, 2002*

Behind the Redwoods,
a California Dream

When you turn off busy Route 101 at Cloverdale and head up into the hills, you leave one world behind and enter another. The lumberyard, gas stations and fast-food joints quickly disappear as Route 128 twists its way northwest through scrawny, moss-covered trees. Only a scattering of houses can be seen.

Forests of evergreens begin to appear as you drop down the western slope of the coastal ridge into the Anderson Valley, California's own Shangri-la. After passing through downtown Boonville, all seven blocks and 974 souls of it, you start to see grapevines growing in orderly ranks. But this is a vineyard region with a difference, still largely untouched by developers and weekenders. In Napa and Sonoma, the landed gentry drive Range Rovers and wear loafers; here, they drive pickups and wear muddy boots. It is, as Bruce C. Cass observes mildly in *The Oxford Companion to the Wines of North America*, "an isolated and somewhat eccentric district."

Early in the last century, the locals developed a lingo that they call "boontling," in which Boonville is called "Boont" and Philo, the only other town of significance, is called "Poleeko." A few people still speak it.

The main purpose appears to have been to confuse outsiders, including the police. The valley and the slopes above it have long sheltered a motley crew of tax evaders, back-to-the-earthers and other unconventional citizens, including, at various times, Charles Manson and Jim Jones. Marijuana is a major cash crop; last summer the police uprooted 24,500 plants in two days, but the district attorney, a man of sturdy libertarian principles, refused to prosecute.

No one asks at local dinner parties whether it's O.K. to light up a joint. It's standard practice.

"A lot of people still come here to get lost," said Don Schmitt, himself a refugee from the Napa Valley, where he and his wife, Sally, operated the French Laundry before selling it to the superchef Thomas Keller. They now run a 32-acre organic spread called the Apple Farm with their daughter, Karen, and her husband, Tim Bates, where they grow 85 varieties of apples, including heirloom beauties like Gravensteins, Spitzenbergs and Arkansas blacks.

But the wines are the big noise in the valley, and the big money spinner. Roederer Estate, owned by the French Champagne house of the same name, produces what many experts (and many enthusiasts, like me) consider the best American sparkling wine, and Navarro bottles a range of outstanding still wines, including a luscious late-harvest gewürztraminer with hints of lychee.

It is geography that makes the vineyards here special. Unlike the Napa and Sonoma Valleys, the Anderson Valley opens onto the Pacific Ocean at its far end, and its floor slopes from 1,300 feet above sea level in the southeast to 800 feet in the northwest. Fog slides up the valley in the mornings, slowing the ripening process, to the benefit of cool-weather northern European grape varieties like riesling, pinot noir and chardonnay.

Driving along the ridge above the valley one day early last November, my wife, Betsey, and I felt as if we were on an island surrounded by vast, fleecy seas of cloud. But that same afternoon, as we tasted wine at a vineyard below, we luxuriated in bright sunshine that had burned through the fog.

Inevitably, the valley is attracting more and larger growers, such as Kendall-Jackson and Duckhorn Vineyards, which now produces an intense, weighty pinot noir on its Goldeneye property here. Mr. Schmitt told me he frets about absentee ownership, about limited water resources and especially about the possibility that the valley will become monocultural, with orchards and sheep pastures being converted to vastly more profitable use as vine-yards.

The cultural impact has been substantial. In 1971, there were virtually no Spanish speakers in the region. Now, following the im-portation of skilled Hispanic vineyard workers, more than half of the elementary and high school students speak Spanish. The valley is becoming a bit less insular.

"We feel a little like Oregonians," said Milla Handley of Handley Cellars, one of the pioneering Anderson Valley operations, which she and her husband, Rex McClellan, started 21 years ago in their base-ment. "We love where we live. There is something comforting about the isolation of the Anderson Valley. It's small and finite, defined by the mountains. We can live by ourselves.

"There's a strong community spirit—the true hippies, the old log-gers, the winos like us, the commune people, we all play softball to-gether, we all take part in the variety show every year. We don't hate visitors, not at all, but we don't want to see the valley overrun by tour-ists or grapes.

"I don't want to wait to make a left turn. That worries me."

But it seems unlikely that the valley will be Napa-ized anytime soon, for all its attractions and all the Silicon Valley millions waiting to be invested. "We're too far from the Bay Area," said a young woman pouring zinfandel at the octagonal Greenwood Ridge tasting room. "There's nothing to get people here—no freeways—and noth-ing to anchor them here—no shopping, and not very many hotels or restaurants."

Thirty years ago, Louis Roederer of Reims, which produces the luxu-rious Cristal Champagne, went looking for a place to make sparkling wine in the New World. Its chairman, Jean-Claude Rouzaud, sought growing conditions as close as possible to those in France. After scouring New Zealand and Tasmania, he chose California, but not the Napa Valley, as most of his competitors did.

"Here in the backwoods he found a good balance between heat in the daytime and cool temperatures at night and in the early morning," said Arnaud Weyrich, the 33-year-old Alsatian who is scheduled later this year to take over as winemaker from Michel Salgues, who is retiring.

Another advantage was the temperature gradient in the valley, which is cooler at the ocean end, hotter at the inland end. Planting began in 1982, and the first wine was released in 1988. Roederer now has 125 acres of pinot noir and chardonnay vines near the ocean, 160 in the center, around Philo, and 117 at the warmer end, which gives it a variety of lots from which to blend.

The whole Roederer operation was conceived in lavish but understated terms, with handsome stone walls and iron gates surrounding the main property, and the winery tucked carefully behind the brow of a hill to avoid overwhelming the landscape. The public tasting room is furnished with tapestries, antiques and Oriental rugs.

Although the soil here differs from that in Champagne, and lime must be added to lower its acidity every two or three years, Roederer's basic California fizz, known as Roederer Estate brut, can be hard to distinguish from the old-country product. Pale, complex and truly dry, it contains a generous proportion of reserve wines, aged up to five years, as well as wines of the current harvest. The brut bottled in magnum is markedly richer and creamier.

Roederer also makes a rosé here, which has more body than most, and a magnificent vintage brut called L'Ermitage, which is comparable to Cristal in its finesse. Made only in the best years, it has tiny bubbles and deliciously yeasty and nutlike flavors.

Navarro is an entirely different bunch of grapes, planted in 1975 by Ted Bennett, who had made a fortune in the retail stereo business. Experts like Darryl Corti, the Sacramento wine and food maven, told him he'd never sell his gewürztraminer (and other aromatic varieties in which he wanted to specialize) through conventional channels. So he developed innovative techniques.

The Mendocino coast, north of here, was just becoming a destination resort at the time, and Mr. Bennett persuaded people headed there from San Francisco to stop and buy at his tasting room. His wife, Deborah Cahn, an advertising copywriter, began turning out a stylish, witty quarterly newsletter. The Internet beckoned. And restaurants like Ducasse in New York and Peristyle in New Orleans came shopping.

Jim Klein, the winemaker, who was wearing blue wraparound sunglasses when we spoke at an outdoor table next to the Navarro tasting room, told me that Mr. Bennett had bought land cheap and had therefore been able to keep prices low. He sold his 2001 chardonnay for $9.75.

"He's very cost-oriented," said Mr. Klein, who was named winemaker of the year in 2002 by the *San Francisco Chronicle*. "That obviously helps. When most people were hit by the post-Sept. 11 slump, we didn't see a beep, and 95 percent of our sales are direct. Only 5 percent goes to distributors."

In addition to bargain-basement chardonnays, crisp pinot gris, ethereal gewürztraminers and zingy rieslings, Navarro makes excellent pinot noirs, light-bodied but subtle and age worthy, from grapes grown high on the slopes above the winery, where they are exposed to the cool, maritime breezes.

Milla Handley, a great-granddaughter of the founder of Blitz-Weinhard, a regionally renowned brewery in Portland, Ore., graduated from the nation's premier oenological school, at the University of California at Davis. Politically aware and socially active, she operates according to firm principles. She said she is absolutely determined, for example, "never to buy grapes for $3,500 a ton from some yuppie grower, which would put my wines beyond reach of the average consumer."

The Handley Cellars press kit says: "Milla encourages balance between work and family by promoting a family-friendly atmosphere that leads to the gathering of employees' children after school, and flexible scheduling to accommodate family priorities." Now there's the authentic Anderson Valley ethos speaking.

My own favorites among Ms. Handley's wines are the lean, slightly mineral Anderson Valley chardonnay, which tastes more European than Californian, with none of the overripe butterscotch flavor produced in hot climates, and a pinot noir with overtones of ripe cherries, which she terms "the challenging child."

Others have other specialties. Husch, whose gewürz was the first Anderson Valley wine I ever tasted, 25 years ago, still does a fine job with that grape. Greenwood Ridge excels at merlot and zinfandel. Lazy Creek's young owners make highly concentrated pinot noir from the fruit of old vines. The local weekly, the *Anderson Valley Advertiser*, is as unconventional as the valley itself. Its editorial philosophy may be deduced from its front-page mottos, "Peace to the cottages! War on the palaces!" and "All happy, none rich, none poor." Not surprisingly, the local establishment, such as it is, doesn't agree very often with the paper's feisty self-description: "The country weekly that tells it like it is!"

Its editor is Bruce Anderson, 63, a tall, bearded, surprisingly courtly man who sports a beat-up fedora much like the one Averell Harriman used to wear. He prints 4,000 copies of each issue, some of which go to subscribers who live as far away as New England. In addition to printing the kinds of local tidbits that once filled many American newspapers, plus two or three pages full of readers' letters, he runs a column for the marijuana crowd called "CannabiNotes" and a weekly essay by Alexander Cockburn, the left-wing British journalist, who lives up the coast in Humboldt County.

But the paper's staple is long articles excoriating officialdom, local, national and international, contributed by freelancers who relish seeing their stuff run uncut. (Mr. Anderson pays $25 a piece). One week in early November, targets included American imperialism, the California Fish and Game Commission and President Bush's decision to withhold all federal funds from the United Nations Agency charged with population control and maternal care.

Mr. Anderson is a relentless campaigner. He has hammered away on the case of a friend named Judi Bari, an environmental activist who was permanently disabled by a bomb (and seven years later died of cancer). The bomber, he told me, "is still unpunished, and no serious effort has ever been made to find the truth, 12 years down the road." He suspects her former husband.

Sometimes the *Advertiser* goes off the deep end, but always entertainingly. For months, Mr. Anderson promoted the idea that a certain Wanda Tinasky, who wrote regular letters to the paper, was in reality the reclusive novelist Thomas Pynchon, and that Mr. Pynchon was living in hiding somewhere in the region.

"In fact," the editor said, "Tinasky was nothing but an erudite old hippie who later murdered his wife and killed himself. I was wrong—at book length."

The general air of zaniness in the valley is enhanced by boontling. Despite the efforts of Heidi Haughy Cusick of the Mendocino County Alliance, we never managed to find a boontling speaker. But the lingo is all around you. A cafe in Boonville is called "Horn of Zeese" (cup of coffee), a booth on the main drag is labeled "Buckey Walter" (pay phone) and fanciers of the grape refer to good wine as "bahl seep." Handley makes a gewürz-riesling blend called Brightlighter, which means "city folk" in boontling.

There is plenty of "bahl gorms" (good food) in the valley. On the more casual side, Boonville's Redwood Drive-In produces a knockout Ortega burger, made with an Ortega chili and pepper Jack cheese, and Libby's Restaurant in Philo, a funky Tex-Mex place with a hand-lettered "Mendocino County Mobilization for Peace" sign in the window, makes everything from scratch—mole sauce, guacamole and vibrant *salsa fresca*. It also stocks 25 local wines.

Johnny Schmitt, son of the French Laundry's old proprietors, runs the 10-bedroom Boonville Hotel, which from the outside looks like something on the Paramount back lot, with a broad, two-tiered cow-town veranda. Inside, it's Sante Fe—all autumnal colors, sisal rugs and updated Shaker-style furniture—plus a good dining room.

Mr. Schmitt doesn't mess around at the range. He coaxes real flavors from real ingredients: a rich tomato and white bean soup with spicy sausage, a Caesar salad with superlative romaine (after all, this is California, folks), a thin-crust pizza with cherry tomatoes and killer applewood-smoked bacon, and a rare rib-eye steak and mushrooms on a bed of spinach with proper horseradish cream.

After that feed, there was nothing to do but drive back to the coast, where we were staying, along the glassy Navarro River and through a canyon of second-growth redwoods. Stumps the size of Volkswagens stood among the trees that towered above our heads. The ground was carpeted in fallen red needles, and the air smelled spicy.

The Pacific was foaming and churning when we approached the Elk Cove Inn, our local headquarters, in the waterside hamlet of Elk. As the sky spun through its kaleidoscopic changes, from gold to pink to lavender, fearsome waves crashed into offshore rocks that looked to us like Monet haystacks that had drifted out to sea.

"Perfection," said Mrs. A, who can never resist a good sunset.

—Boonville, California, January 8, 2003

How to Grow a Giant Tuna

Tooling his black BMW south along Interstate 5, Philippe Charat banters with his passengers and chats on his cell phone in English, Spanish and French. No matter what the language, the subject remains the same: fish.

We're headed from San Diego to this booming city of 400,000 in Baja California, 75 miles from the international border, and from there by launch out into the ocean, around a headland called Punta Banda and into Puerto Escondido Bay. There, Mr. Charat runs an unusual aquaculture business—an underwater feedlot for the creatures that he calls "the kings of the sea": Thunnus thynnus orientalis, or Pacific bluefin tuna.

This is the fish prized above all others by connoisseurs of sushi and sashimi, the one whose belly meat, called *toro*, commands the highest prices on Japanese restaurant menus (with the exception of the potentially poisonous *fugu*, or blowfish, which is not nearly as widely sold). At its best, when the fat content is high, when the fish has been meticulously handled, the flesh is fabulously tender and buttery, ranging in color from a soft pink to a deep, winy red. Obviously too luscious to cook. Begging to be eaten raw.

Unlike salmon, tuna has not yet been successfully farmed—that is, raised in captivity from egg to maturity—though Mr. Charat predicts it will happen one day. For now, all bluefin must be caught in the wild, not only the Pacific species but also its giant, biologically similar Atlantic cousin, which is perhaps slightly less desirable from a gastronomic viewpoint.

What Mr. Charat has done here, building on the experience of an operation that he studied in Australia, is to ensure that all the bluefin he catches, not just a few, become prime specimens. His boats net the fish, tons at a time, as they cruise along the coast, 20 to 30 miles offshore.

Then, the tuna are towed at less than two miles an hour, still in the water in specially designed enclosures, to Puerto Escondido Bay. There they live the life of Riley, splashing happily about in 16 huge circular pens, gaining weight and building their fat content on a sardine diet—all the fish they can eat, three times every day, six days a week, for four to eight months.

"You take a run-of-the-mill fish, a so-so fish, and turn it into a superstar," Mr. Charat said.

The tuna are caught between June and August, as they swim between Magdalena Bay, near the southern tip of Baja California, and Monterey Bay, south of San Francisco. They are sold between October and March, by which time they weigh up to 190 pounds.

When Mr. Charat's company, Maricultura del Norte, gets an order, an appropriate number of fattened tuna are harvested. That gives him an edge over conventional suppliers: they have to sell as soon as their boats dock, whether the demand is high or not. He sells, as he said, "when I want to."

One day in January, my wife, Betsey, and I visited the feedlot with Mr. Charat and our mutual friend, Sam Popkin, a tuna-crazed professor of political science at the University of California at San Diego. It was harvest day, with the sky blue and the sun hot at midmorning. Maricultura's agent at Tokyo's fish market, Tsukiji, had ordered 100 large and 300 small bluefin.

At Christmastime, when the demand peaks, Maricultura sometimes harvests as many as 900 tuna in a single day, working from sunrise to sunset.

Tsukiji pays the highest prices in the world, but its buyers insist on quality—tuna without bruises or blemishes, with vividly colored flesh, with maximum oil and fat content. The current price for a gutted bluefin, with head and tail on, runs about $9.50 a pound for small fish, $12.75 a pound for medium fish and even more for larger fish. A 410-pound tuna was sold at Tsukiji for a record $160,000 last year.

The meat sells at retail for as much as $45 a pound, despite the lasting slump in the Japanese economy.

Mr. Charat takes extraordinary steps to meet Tsukiji standards— some during the harvest, others before it starts. The fish are towed here very slowly to minimize enzyme stress, which can adversely affect flavor. Those to be harvested at a particular time are isolated from those which are not, lest they thrash about and damage one another. The sardines they are fed, caught locally by Maricultura's own trawler, the *Noble Provider*, are so good that Mr. Charat distributes a few from time to time to friends in the food business, who consider them vastly superior to those on sale in fish markets.

To avoid damage to their livers from overeating, the tuna are fed only six days a week; it would never do to have a bay full of fish with *crises de foie*. And on those six days, the sardines are broadcast across the surface of the water to force the big fish to compete aggressively for food. Some farmed salmon are criticized because, having no need to work for nourishment, they develop a flabby texture.

"It takes a tough man to make a tender tuna," Professor Popkin observed as each of the various procedures and safeguards was explained to us.

The harvest was a gaudy, melodramatic spectacle in primary colors, like a picture fashioned with a child's poster paints. The workmen wore green or yellow rubberized trousers with orange bibs; a blue tarpaulin on the work barge was stained a vivid red by streams of fish blood as the day wore on. Yet everything was done so efficiently and so quickly, with so little apparent suffering by the fish, that it scarcely seemed as primal as it clearly was.

Divers in black wet suits and yellow flippers started by raising a barrier inside one of the pens, separating a dozen or so tuna from the rest. Next they grabbed the fish, one by one, one hand on the tail and the other in the gills, and hoisted them onto the barge, where another crew of workers held them in place. Instantly that team spiked each tuna in the head, killing it, cut a main artery behind the gills to bleed it, and ran a fine steel wire down the fish's spinal column, paralyzing it immediately.

Another team, astonishingly deft like the first, then took over, cutting out the gills and guts in one swift motion and tossing the bluefin into a 32-degree saline water solution.

The whole process took only about 50 seconds—a short enough period, Mr. Charat told us, to preserve the tuna's quality in two ways: by avoiding the formation of excessive lactic acid and by preventing the fish's blood temperature from rising after it has left the sea.

When the workers took a break, they presented their visitors with a late breakfast, a pailful of sea urchins fresh out of the ocean. A whack with the back of a knife and the rich, creamy roes were laid bare. The taste of the first startled us. It was overwhelmingly salty, but the rest, rinsed in fresh water, were blissfully sweet and custardlike, with no hint of the metallic flavor that mars the elderly *uni* served at second-rate sushi bars.

They sure beat doughnuts.

A twisting trail brought Mr. Charat, who is 62, to Ensenada. The son of a French mother and a Russian father, he left Paris with his family as an infant. They lived in Cuba and in Texas, but by 1957 the elder Charat was in the fishing business in Mexico. The son showed an entrepreneurial flair at Harvard, helping two friends start the Harvard Student Agencies, which have gone from strength to strength, publishing, for example, the widely read *Let's Go* guides. He went on to the Harvard Business School.

In 1973, Mr. Charat entered the shrimp fishing business in the Gulf of Mexico. But in 1981 his company was nationalized. In 1983, he bought three tuna purse seiners, selling his catch in Mexico and in Samoa.

Thirteen years later, he started his present business, following a visit, as part of a Mexican delegation, to a tuna-fattening operation at Port Lincoln in South Australia, west of Adelaide. The Australians utilized frozen sardines; he could do a lot better, Mr. Charat reasoned, with the fresh sardines in ample supply in this corner of the world.

And so he has. A Mexican citizen, he holds a 50-year concession from the Mexican government. Maricultura fattened 30 tons of tuna the first year, 60 the second, 100 the third, 300 the fourth. Another big increase is expected this year. Before too long Mr. Charat hopes to begin fattening yellowfin tuna and yellowtail, a kind of amberjack that the Japanese call *hamachi*, at a new installation in Magdalena Bay, which is 600 miles south of here.

He already has one competitor in this region, and five more have been authorized by the government. The business is well established in Australia. And according to Chris Purcell of Ocean View Fisheries, a fish wholesaler in Halifax, Nova Scotia, about a dozen fishermen in nearby St. Margaret's Bay fatten Atlantic bluefin on a small scale, maybe 40 to 50 fish each.

The world's, and especially Japan's, appetite for tuna seems insatiable. The question is whether stocks of bluefin can withstand the pressure. Already, the giant Atlantic bluefin, which can reach up to 1,500 pounds, is listed as endangered by the Monterey Aquarium, which monitors such matters. The southern Pacific bluefin, which is caught off Australia, has also been overfished, but so far the northern Pacific bluefin, caught here, appears to be in better shape.

About 95 percent of Maricultura's output goes to Japan, with about half of that ending up at Tsukiji, where it is labeled "LAX" after the airport from which it is shipped—a mark that guarantees it a premium price. The other 5 percent is sold in San Diego and Los Angeles, mostly to top restaurants.

Chilly from their cold-water bath, the fish are cleaned, weighed, tagged and measured before being placed with cold gel packs in plastic-lined boxes to keep them fresh. If they are harvested on Thursday, for example, they are packed on Friday morning and trucked to Los Angeles International Airport on Friday afternoon. They arrive in Tokyo on Sunday, local time, and go on sale at 5 a.m. Monday. Most of them will be consumed by Wednesday at the latest.

That may sound like a very long time. But in fact it is almost ideal;

like a number of other fish, such as Dover sole, bluefin only reaches peak flavor and texture four to six days after it has emerged from the water.

Mr. Charat demonstrated that the night before we visited Ensenada. At George's at the Cove, one of San Diego's leading restaurants, the chef, Trey Foshee, prepared a loin of two-day-old Maricultura tuna in several ways. A grilled rib steak was superb, but a slice of the same fish, served raw, was not quite as rich-tasting, and not at all as tender, as we had expected.

"Wait two or three days," Mr. Charat said. "It's not ready."

Professor Popkin took a piece of the bluefin loin home, kept it in his refrigerator for 48 hours and then served it as sashimi to his family. It was perfect, he reported, the melt-in-the-mouth stuff you dream about.

—Ensenada, Mexico, April 3, 2002

SOUTH AMERICA

New Heights for Andean Wine

The awesome crags of the Andes glitter like icebergs in the early morning sunlight as the plane lets down here in western Argentina, across the grassy Pampas from Buenos Aires.

Runoff from the melting Andes snows, diverted into canals built by the Tehuelche Indians as early as the 16th century and improved by the Incas and the Spanish, makes Mendoza bloom. Although located at the edge of the Cuyo desert, this is a city of plane trees and sycamores, shady parks and broad plazas, fountains and rose gardens.

That same water nourishes the vineyards surrounding the city. Mendoza wines have helped to make Argentina the world's fifth-largest producer, a reliable source of inexpensive red for the country's thirsty population, much of which traces its origins to Italy. But until recently they have never counted for much in world markets.

Dr. Nicolás Catena is changing things; not single-handedly, exactly, any more than Michael Jordan single-handedly won pro basketball

148

championships for the Chicago Bulls. But he has shown customers in North America, as well as friendly rivals here, what Mendoza can do at every price level. At 61, slight, soft-spoken and studious-looking in rimless glasses, he is the acknowledged star, the pacemaker, the public face of the Argentine wine industry.

It is an industry in rapid ascendancy. More first-class wines appear with each vintage, and critics and consumers around the world have taken notice. On the shelves of shops in the United States, labels like Balbi, Flichman, Norton, Santa Ana and Terrazas have won space, along with Catena, of course.

Despite the country's debilitating economic troubles recently, foreign millions continue to pour in to finance new vineyards and wineries.

Beginning with Dr. Catena's grandfather in 1902, the Catena family established a local reputation for red wines. These wines, made largely from the *criolla* grape, were too sweet and too often oxidized.

"We never imagined," Dr. Catena said, that "anyone here could compete with the Europeans—perhaps 10 percent as good, no more."

Dr. Catena's great awakening came when he went to the United States. Already armed with a Ph.D., he studied economics and mathematics at Columbia University during the turbulent late 1960s and then, in 1982, found himself at Berkeley as a visiting professor. Inevitably, he visited the Napa Valley. Almost as inevitably, he fell under the spell of Robert Mondavi, whose winery was at that time helping to establish lofty new standards for American wines.

"I discovered what investment, research and enthusiasm could achieve," Dr. Catena told me and my wife, Betsey, over a candlelit dinner under the maple trees at 1884, the restaurant that he has set up in his century-old Bodega Escorihuela. "I saw that the Americans had done in 10 years what the Europeans took over 300 years to do.

"I decided that I had to do something similar. I thought we needed to make cabernet and chardonnay, even though we didn't use those grapes much in Argentina at the time. They were the best, obviously, and I wanted them."

After a time, Dr. Catena got to know the peripatetic Mr. Mondavi, and they discovered that their families had come from the same part of Italy—the Marche, on the Adriatic coast.

Top Catena cabernets and chardonnays have been exported to the United States for a decade now, and they have received enthusiastic notices from the world's wine critics—easily the equal of the reviews accorded to the much better-known vintages of Argentina's neighbor to the west, Chile.

Unlike some Chilean producers, Dr. Catena has been careful not to price himself out of the North American market. The number of wine drinkers in New York or Los Angeles willing to pay $50 a bottle and more for his top-of-the-line Zapata reds may be limited, but for those who are not, there are Catena wines at more modest prices, sold under Catena Alta, Catena and Alamos Ridge labels.

"In the end," said my English friend Bill Baker, one of his country's most respected wine merchants, "Argentine wines will be better and better priced than their Chilean competitors."

I tasted Catena Alta cabernets, merlots and malbecs from 1997 and 1999 with Dr. Catena, and they were only slightly less aristocratic than their Zapata counterparts, which had not yet been released. They had just as much fruit, just as much robustness of flavor, perhaps a little less opulence and complexity. The Alamos Ridge wines, tasted in the United States, made a less vivid impression, of course, but they struck me as good values at around $10 a bottle.

The Argentine wines that interest me most are the ones made almost nowhere else, including the chunky, chewy, spicy malbec among the reds and the tangy torrontés among the whites.

Malbec, which is also called Auxerrois by the French, was once an important grape in Bordeaux, used extensively in the days before the great phylloxera epidemic of the 19th century in wines like Château Latour. Now it is used only in Cahors in southwestern France, where it traditionally produced heavy, intensely tannic wines, almost black in color, which were often not ready to drink until they had spent two decades in the bottle. Modern Cahors is a bit gentler.

Argentine malbec is different. The deep violet glints in the glass are similar, as are the jammy flavors of ripe berries. But where the tannins in Cahors can be quite harsh, those in the best Argentine malbecs are sweet and silky, and the wines give no impression of heaviness at all despite their power. They make perfect companions to Argentina's great beef or to our own.

In 1960, Argentina had 120,000 acres of malbec, but then came the stampede to "international" grape varieties like cabernet. Now there are only 25,000 acres left, but the best of those vines, including several owned by Catena and by the Austrian-controlled Bodegas Norton, are 70 to 100 years old. At the moment, Pedro Marchevsky, the Catena vineyard manager, is conducting experiments with 135 malbec clones in the company's Tikal vineyard.

The torrontés vineyards are some of the world's highest, many more than a mile up, near the village of Cafayate in the northwestern corner of the country, not far from the Bolivian border. No movie theater or bright lights there, "just work," laughed Susana Balbo, a highly regarded Argentine winemaker who toiled for a time in Cafayate. Two of the best examples are made by Etchart and Michel Torino, both reminiscent of albariño and viognier in their jasmine-scented bouquets and fresh tropical-fruit flavors (mango? pineapple?).

Another, only slightly less appealing torrontés, easier to find in the United States and irresistibly priced at about $7, is made by Santa Julia.

At the moment, the light of Dr. Catena's life is a striking new winery near here, built of cream-colored local stone and pale, indigenous hardwoods in the shape of a Mayan pyramid. It opened earlier this year. His daughter Laura Catena, the company's export director, a Harvard- and Stanford-educated physician who somehow combines the practice of medicine in San Francisco with her work in the wine trade in Argentina, commented recently that the $12 million building "shows our pride in our own culture."

So does 1884, the Catena restaurant. The family recruited Argentina's premier chef, Francis Mallmann, to create a menu that celebrates the Incan influence in the region, with dishes incorporating corn and pumpkin, as well as the beef of the Pampas—not to mention, of course, the wines of Mendoza.

Much of the cooking is done in the courtyard in traditional igloo-shaped mud ovens, or *hornos*. We sampled bitter, palate-cleansing chicory, seared at 600 degrees, with almonds and sun-dried tomatoes; empanadas made the old-fashioned way with hand-chopped instead of ground beef; a tart of onions and leeks and magnificently juicy goat, scented with lemon and oregano, roasted in an iron box—all the while talking politics, monetary policy, Machiavelli and wine prices with Nicolás Catena.

On the latter subject, he said, "I have known from the start that if I charged $40 a bottle, the wine had to be comparable with a French wine selling for $60 or $80, because people are not used to costly wines from here." And he acknowledged that like Mr. Mondavi and his Italian friend Piero Antinori, he makes far more money on his cheaper wines than on his prestige products.

But he pours his passion into the top of the line. He has raised the quality bar in Argentina by limiting production through the pioneering use of controlled irrigation and by rigorous thinning of his grapes. He has planted vineyards at altitudes as high as 4,900 feet, which provide the cooler temperatures and lower humidity that help to produce premium grapes. He has imported French barrels and computerized European winemaking gear, installing them in immaculate wineries that contrast starkly with the unhygienic facilities and poor barrels that plagued wine production in Argentina for decades.

Others have joined him here in the pursuit of modern excellence. Hiram Walker, Moët & Chandon, Pernod Ricard, Kendall-Jackson, Allied Domecq, Sogrape of Portugal and several Chilean companies have made huge investments. Exports have grown to about $140 million from $40 million in the last five years.

Norton, which was founded in 1895 by a British engineer who had worked on the railway across the Andes, now belongs to the family that controls Swarovski crystal. Carlos Tizio Mayer, the technical manager, described its strategy: to keep prices down—no more than

$15 for the top blend, marketed as Norton Privada—"so we can earn a little money and a lot of customer loyalty."

"It's easy to produce very expensive wine here, but it's not so easy to produce good value," he told us as we toured the winery, which is surrounded by spectacular rose gardens. "We want to make our name and attract our customers now, because in the next few years only three or four Argentine names will loom large in the international market, and we intend to be one of them."

I was taken with Norton's 2000 sauvignon blanc, a crisp yet fruity wine with just the right sharpness, but there, too, it was the malbec that turned my head. The 1999 exhibited had a nose like a magnet that drew you right into the glass, and a typical big-shouldered, almost rowdy style on the palate.

Never contaminated by phylloxera, the Argentine malbec, as Mr. Tizio said, "is a natural treasure in its genetic purity." It can make great wine.

—Mendoza, Argentina, August 22, 2001

A New World Banquet,
Flavored by Africa

This is where the strands came together, where the native Brazilians and the Portuguese settlers and the African slaves whom they shipped across the South Atlantic to harvest sugar began fashioning a vivid new culture.

Today things that began in this beach-fringed coastal region, a two-hour flight northeast of Rio de Janeiro, have spread across Brazil and far beyond—the candomblé religion, a mélange of Roman Catholicism and animist tradition; popular music, heavily influenced by African drum rhythms and by Bahian innovators like Gilberto Gil; and the distinctive, delicious local way with seafood and spices.

"Everything that happens here is of universal interest," wrote the novelist Jorge Amado, overstating the case the way hometown boys often do, but not by much. A growing tide of visitors from abroad is discovering what he meant.

Although Salvador is now a spirited city of two million, where dazzlingly white office blocks jostle with gilded Baroque churches, it has the smell of an African village, with the scents of palm oil and coconut milk, chilies and cilantro borne on every breeze. I ate dishes in Salvador I had not tasted since I tasted them (or their cousins) when I lived in West Africa more than three decades ago.

None of which should be surprising; nine of ten Salvadorans are wholly or partly of African ancestry. It was African women, first as slave cooks and then as servants, who kept African culinary traditions alive here and adapted them to the New World, incorporating European ingredients like salt cod. Now you see their descendants, wearing long, lacy white dresses and turbans, cooking on street corners in the colonial district known as the Pelourinho, whose very name is a reminder of harsher days; *pelourinho* means flogging post in Portuguese.

McDonald's has come to Bahia, but the Baianas, as the street cooks are known, have easily held their own.

From their sputtering pots of dendê oil (a yellow palm oil usually colored with a healthy dose of red pepper), they serve fritters called *acarajés,* which are made from a bean purée, ginger, onion and ground dried shrimp. Often the fritters are stuffed with a yellow paste called *vatapá* or served with a sauce incorporating cilantro and (lest your taste buds tire) scorchingly hot malagueta chiles.

I wouldn't swear to it, because nobody's taste memory is that good, but I think I once ate something very similar in Benin, the long, narrow country just west of Nigeria, which gave birth to voodoo.

Acarajés are as popular here as hot dogs in the United States. A character in one of Amado's novels writes an ode to them in which he rhymes kitchen with bewitchin'.

Sweet tidbits are available, too, laid out on trays. Bolinhos estudantes turned out to be delicious sweet buns of cassava and coconut. My wife, Betsey, and I especially liked the quindims, custardy confections of eggs and coconut—perhaps because they seemed so reassuringly nurserylike in the midst of so many exotic flavors.

Bahian street food is only the overture. We got a taste of more sophisticated stuff at Senac (Serviço de Educação Nacional de Artes Culinarias), a government-run restaurant where chefs and waiters are trained. In a second-floor dining room with tall windows and wide-plank floors, an array of dishes, almost 40 of them, were laid out on a lunchtime buffet, each carefully labeled with names that were sometimes comprehensible, sometimes not. Like almost everyone we encountered in Bahian restaurants, the trainee waiters were all smiles, all the time.

Amid the moquecas, which are stews of shrimp, skate, crab, tripe, mussels or whatever else comes to hand, Betsey noticed things that reminded her of Charleston, S.C., where her family settled in 1680.

Yes, a bite or two confirmed, that was a Bahian version of low-country Hoppin' John, made from rice and black-eyed peas. And, yes, that delectable dish labeled caruru was a kind of shrimp-and-okra gumbo. But of course. Many Africans shipped to South Carolina to work in the rice and indigo fields, folk whose descendants live on the barrier islands to this day, came from the same places as those brought to Salvador.

Then we noticed that at Senac quindims were labeled quindims de yaya—literally young girls' quindims. We had seen that word "yaya," a survival from the days of slavery, much closer to home. Betsey had read Rebecca Wells's book *The Divine Secrets of the Ya-Ya Sisterhood,* which tells of women's interwoven lives in a Louisiana town. We had both eaten gumbo yaya in New Orleans.

"This is like an echo chamber," Betsey said.

The moquecas? This is as good a time as any to say that the best of them, to my taste, are made by the chefs with the lightest touch on the dendê oil. A little of it adds an inimitable musky accent to Bahian cooking; a lot of it overwhelms the more delicate flavors in a dish. It can also play havoc with your cholesterol count. Senac's scrumptious crab moqueca avoided these hazards. Not all the others did, and there was a second problem. My guess is that since the restaurant is patronized almost entirely by visitors, the heat in most dishes had been toned down, but that was easily fixed. A shot of one of two malagueta sauces on the table brought the flavors to life.

At the Casa da Gamboa, we ate an inventive dish called casquinha di siri (crab taken from the shell, mixed with bread crumbs and seasonings, and put back in).

We ate superb grilled vermelho (red snapper) and robalo (a kind of saltwater bass). And of course we paid the obligatory visit to one of the two restaurants run by Salvador's most famous cook, Dadá. The one we chose, Sorriso da Dadá, is down the cobblestone street from the theater where the Balé Folklorico da Bahia performs its thunderous routines; the other, smaller one, the original, is called Tempero da Dadá. Dadá who? I asked Silvia Vanucci, a font of information on things Bahian who showed us around town.

"Last name?" she replied. "Ah, Dadá. I have no idea."

Never mind. The food was stunning, perhaps the best we ate in Bahia, particularly the house specialty, bobó de camarão, a mixture of jumbo shrimp, dried and grated sweet cassava, onions, green peppers, onions, tomatoes and coconut milk, among other things. It came to the table bubbling hot in an earthenware dish, the bright pink shrimp bathed in a golden sauce as beautiful as it was luscious. Drummers in the street outside were pounding out a vigorous tattoo—in its honor, maybe?—as it arrived.

Dadá's only real competition, we thought, came from a harborside restaurant called Trapiche Adelaide. Fitted into an old warehouse, as modern as the day after tomorrow, it pays fond, subtle homage to regional culinary traditions.

Ingredients like taro root, coconut, mangoes, banana leaves and mandioquinhas, potatolike tubers with bright yellow pulp, dot the menu, but it is the utter freshness of the fish and the precision with which they are grilled or fried that sets Trapiche Adelaide apart. The sophistication of Claude Troisgros, Rio's top restaurateur, who serves as a consultant here, is evident.

A visit to the public market on the waterfront gave some measure of the vast range of raw materials available to the Bahian cook. The whole place smelled of cilantro. The aisles were lined with great stacks of sugar cane, piles of jackfruit the size of basketballs, mint leaves six inches across, bales of gray-green kale and baskets of plump, tiny, silver-red sardines.

Most striking of all were the dozens of fruits whose names I had never heard and whose flesh I had never tasted: the lumpy ata, or sugar apple; the umbu, which looks like a greengage plum and tastes like an orange; the acerola, or Barbados cherry, sour but very rich in vitamin C; the caju, or cashew apple, shaped like a bell pepper, which grows beneath the cashew nut, and the caffeine-rich guaraná from the Amazon.

Brazilians are nuts about the juices of these strange fruits, and you see signs offering sucos everywhere. At a tiny lancheria, a roadside lunch counter, in a seedy section of Salvador, we sampled several, all freshly squeezed, some plain, the tarter ones sweetened a bit. With them came little sandwiches on soft, flattened buns—thin sizzled beef, or chicken, or cheese. Eden for a couple of bucks.

—Rio de Janeiro, July, 25, 2001

• •

BOBÓ DE CAMARÃO
(Adapted from Sorriso da Dadá, Salvador da Bahia, Brazil)
Time: 35 minutes

For the cassava cream:
½ cup extra virgin olive oil
1 pound cassava (yuca) root, peeled and finely grated
1 large onion, peeled and finely chopped
1 green bell pepper, cored and finely diced
1 large ripe tomato, cored and finely diced
½ cup packed cilantro leaves
1 cup coconut milk

For the shrimp:
½ cup extra virgin olive oil
1 large clove garlic, peeled and minced
1 large onion, peeled and cut into 1½-inch chunks
1 small green bell pepper, cut into 1½-inch chunks
2 large firm tomatoes, cored and cut into 1½-inch chunks
12 to 16 jumbo shrimp, shelled
2 cups coconut milk
½ cup packed cilantro leaves
Salt
2 tablespoons palm oil (optional)

1. Prepare cassava cream: In a large saucepan, heat olive oil over medium-high heat. Add cassava, onion and bell pepper and stir until mixture starts to soften, about 3 minutes. Stir in tomato

and cilantro, and gradually add coconut milk. Continue to stir until mixture is soft and thick and begins to pull away from sides of pan, about 10 minutes. Remove from heat and reserve.

2. For shrimp mixture: In a large sauté pan, heat olive oil over medium-high heat. Add garlic, onion and bell pepper. Sauté until onion is translucent and pepper is tender, about 3 minutes.

3. Add tomatoes and shrimp, and stir until shrimp just begin to turn pink. Add coconut milk and cilantro, and stir for 1 minute. Slowly add reserved cassava cream, stirring until mixture is heated and shrimp are pink, about 5 more minutes. Season to taste with salt, and drizzle with palm oil just before serving. Serve hot, accompanied by white rice.

Yield: 4 servings.

UNITED KINGDOM AND IRELAND

UNITED KINGDOM

Best Fishing Hole in St. James's

For those who can afford it, the Englishman's fish of choice has always been Dover sole. And the lucky ones who can afford it have always repaired to Wiltons to enjoy it.

Well, not quite always. George Wilton didn't open for business until 1742, and for the first few decades the family establishment dealt mainly in oysters and shellfish. But for 150 years it has been famous for its superlative and now mortifyingly expensive sole ($38 grilled, fried or à la meunière, with first course, vegetables and dessert extra).

Situated in the heart of St. James's, London's clubland, Wiltons is rather clubby itself: discreet, masculine, unchanging, understated. But of course the food is vastly better, women are just as welcome as men and business or political documents may be placed on the table or passed from hand to hand—heinous activities that are forbidden at White's and the other tony clubs that thrive on the fiction that they exist only for social purposes.

"It's a kind of business annex to White's," said Andrew Phillips, the general manager of Dukes, a small, quietly elegant hotel tucked into a tiny St. James's courtyard.

Aristocrats, art dealers, city gents and political grandees constitute the clientele, along with "businessmen, bankers and bounders," as a house history puts it. Many of the patrons have luxuriant hair, as if they had just left Trumper's, the top people's stylist just down the street.

Sit on the little bench inside Wiltons's door at 55 Jermyn Street and listen to Robin Gundry, the pinstriped general manager, greet his customers at lunchtime: "Good morning, my lord . . . Can I help, sir? . . . Do come this way . . . Won't keep you a minute . . . Oh, you are a star, sir. . . ."

Rex Harrison liked to stay at the Ritz, right around the corner. In this part of town, he once said, every last want of a gentleman (or an actor impersonating a gentleman) could be attended to: "I can walk to my tailor's in Jermyn Street, get my shirts from Turnbull & Asser, Lobbs for my boots, Locks for my hats, Wiltons for a little fish, Berry Brothers for the booze, Hatchards for books, and George Trumper for my hair."

You might start with a half-dozen oysters. They will set you back $25, but then they are elegant creatures, five inches across, pale beige rather than silver-gray, in shells as flat as saucers. They come from West Mersea, on an island off the Essex coast, from beds that are harvested exclusively from rowboats, lest oil or gasoline pollute the waters. They are opened by London's best oysterman, Patrick Flaherty, a 37-year veteran. None of the briny juices escape. No nasty bits of shell creep in.

That's the way it is at Wiltons. The point is the raw materials, not a saucier's legerdemain. The restaurant has bought its smoked salmon from the same East End supplier for 50 years, and the wet-fish merchants it deals with "know exactly what we require," Mr. Gundry said, "and know that we'll pay top price for it."

If you demand wild salmon from the River Spey in Scotland, rather than a flabby specimen from some fish farm in lord-knows-where, and grill it for exactly the requisite time, you need not be a culinary wizard.

The same thing is true of Dover sole. That would be Solea solea, a thick, white, meaty flatfish, not to be confused with the European lemon sole or the host of North American pretenders like flounder on the East Coast and petrale on the West. It is much firmer and sweeter than most of its cousins; its only real European rival is the lordly turbot.

According to the 19th-century expert Francis Day, quoted by Alan Davidson in his new *Oxford Companion to Food*, the sole's name comes from the Greeks, who thought a fine one "would form a fit sandal for an ocean nymph."

Dover sole runs as large as three or four pounds or more (the fishermen call those tombstones) and as small as six inches long (their nickname is "tongues"). The ideal eating size is about a pound, just big enough to feed one person amply. No matter what the size, they are white on the bottom, brown on the top, an elongated oval in shape with two eyes placed extremely close together on the darker side.

In Escoffier's time, sole was subject to all manner of indignity. Fillets were the order of the day, their taste masked by preparations involving cheese (Mornay), crayfish (Nantua), mushrooms (*bonne femme*) and grapes and cream (Véronique, probably the best of the lot). Dozens upon dozens of recipes are paraded through the columns of the *Larousse Gastronomique*, but the Wiltons menu mentions only two of the fancier preparations—sole Colbert, in which the fish is split open before deep-frying and the cavity then filled with herb butter, and sole Walewska, which involves cheese, mushrooms and lobster.

That venerable standby sole *meunière* (named in tribute to the floury hands of a miller's wife who, one day in the dim, distant past, prepared a fish to be sautéed in butter) is one of the favorites at Wiltons. But whole, grilled sole is the overwhelming choice of English connoisseurs: brushed with melted butter, sprinkled with salt and pepper, turned quickly on the grill in such a way that the grill bars burn a dark lattice pattern into the fish, then cooked under the intense heat of the broiler for roughly 12 to 15 minutes.

Perfectly simple, simply perfect and entirely sufficient. This is the porterhouse steak of fish. No sauce is needed, partly because cooking the fish whole ("on the bone") helps to keep it moist. You may well come across an occasional apostate who insists upon tartar sauce (too robust, in my view) or hollandaise (too rich). A squirt of lemon is enough.

"Nothing on this planet could possibly taste better," said Rick Stein, the British cookbook author and television chef, whose restaurant at Padstow in Cornwall faces out toward the Trevose Bank, a small corner of the North Atlantic that yields some of the very finest of Dover sole.

"The grill and the sole are a match made in heaven," said William Black, another of the country's leading authorities on fish.

Relatively few Dover sole are actually landed at Dover, the Channel port southeast of London. They come from ports in the West Country like Brixham and Padstow and Looe, from the North Sea or from Ireland. Mr. Stein says that good ones come from the Bay of Biscay, which lies between Brittany and Spain. But Dover was the main source in the 19th century, when sole came into fashion, and the name has stuck.

Unlike most fish, which deteriorate rapidly once caught, sole tastes best when about three or four days old. Flippingly fresh, just out of the water, they are tough; like game, they improve with a bit of age. Therefore they can be successfully air-freighted across great distances. If they are shipped soon after they are caught, they land in New York or Tokyo fish markets in prime condition, unlike more fragile species like *daurade* and *rouget*. Which, of course, exponentially increases the demand for Dover sole and drives up the price; large quantities of sole are air-freighted every day from Amsterdam as well as London. At the Four Seasons in Manhattan, a plainly cooked Dover sole will set you back an elaborately garnished $46. Before too long, many British fishmongers predict, Dover sole will be as expensive as caviar.

A certain amount of ceremony and tradition surround the eating of Dover sole in England—and for that matter other kinds of seafood. Smoked salmon and oysters, for instance, are always served with thinly sliced, buttered brown bread. A grilled sole must be boned without turning the fish over, which is easier than it sounds; a nautical legend says that flipping the sole onto its back would cause the ship that caught it to capsize.

But nothing quite matches the traditions of Wiltons itself—dishes like mushy peas and bread and butter pudding and Arnold Bennett omelette, an unlikely concoction of smoked haddock, cream and Parmesan cheese.

Service is provided by waiters in dark suits and waitresses in white nurses' uniforms (which, I have always supposed, is meant as a subliminal reminder to the customers that they are eating real nursery food). Nicholas Lander, the restaurant critic of the *Financial Times*, says Wiltons has much faster service than most other London restaurants, because "board chairmen will bang the table if they're kept waiting."

The place belongs to the Hambros, a banking family, originally from Denmark. One evening in 1942, Olaf Hambro was eating oysters alone at the bar when a bomb landed in Piccadilly, only a block or two away, shaking the restaurant and its proprietress, Bessie Leal. She folded her tea towel, unpinned her apron and announced, again according to the official Wiltons history, that she was going to close the place and head back to her native Cornwall.

Mr. Hambro made her an offer, which she accepted forthwith.

"Put it on the bill," he said, and Mrs. Leal did just that.

The next day, Mr. Hambro hired Jimmy Marks, the oysterman at Bucks Club, to run the place. He did so until his death in 1976, four days short of his 90th birthday; his widow, Lucille, took over for the next eight years.

In those days, the restaurant had curtained booths for those who sought privacy, whether for needs of security or reasons of the heart. There are still curtains between some tables, but only a fool would expect to hide anything behind them.

Mr. Marks once told me toward the end of his life about packing hampers of food and carrying them himself to nearby St. James's

Palace—clandestine picnic suppers for the Prince of Wales and his mistress, Wallis Simpson. As an admirer observed, Mr. Marks was a bit like an oyster himself: "hard shell, compact build, self-sufficient, a certain cool acidity." He feared no one.

During the war, it is said by old-timers on the restaurant staff, Winston Churchill, a great devotee of oysters and caviar, visited Wiltons often. At one point, he let his bill run on for 18 months, until Mr. Marks approached the great man for payment.

"Mr. Churchill, sir, I think your secretary must have overlooked your account," the redoubtable Mr. Marks said. Having held off the Nazis, Churchill was not about to be quickly bested by a maître d'hôtel.

"Good heavens, Marks," he said. "Didn't know you were hard up."

Another time, at the height of the IRA bombings in London in the 1970s, a police inspector urged that the bar and front tables be cleared.

"Nah," Mr. Marks replied, according to the house history. "That there table is Lord Ashcombe's. If Lord Ashcombe wants his lunch there, Lord Ashcombe will have it there."

—*London, June 14, 2000*

This Blessed Plot, This Realm of Tea, This Marmalade

It is made from exotic fruits that grow far away, bitter oranges that hang like golden baubles amid the shiny leaves of trees near Seville in southern Spain. Its name comes from *marmelo*, the Portuguese word for "quince." It has been eaten in one form or another since the days of the ancient Greeks and Romans.

Yet for more than 250 years, marmalade has been a quintessentially, unmistakably British product, as much a part of a proper Scottish breakfast as oatmeal, and as much a part of a proper English tea as Cornish cream. A supply of marmalade went to Antarctica with the ill-fated Robert Falcon Scott in 1911, and cans of this mellow citrus preserve followed the Union Jack to the most distant imperial outposts.

For a time, late in the last century, marmalade seemed to be losing favor with the British consumer. But recently it has made a comeback.

"I don't quite understand it," said Peter J. Wilkin, chairman of Wilkin & Sons Ltd., the highly reputed marmalade and jam manufacturer, founded by his great-grandfather in 1885. "People don't really have tea now. They don't have breakfast, either, except on the weekends.

"But our marmalades are our biggest sellers, and they're much more popular than they were 15 years ago—here in Britain and abroad, too."

Rightly so, in my view. Properly made marmalade (which to my taste means dark and treacly stuff, generously endowed with rough-cut strips of peel) has no peer as the crowning glory on a piece of hot, buttered toast. On a morning dark and drear, it is superbly restorative, a welcome lift as the new day begins, sweet but not cloying, a ray of sunshine spooned from a jar.

Observations on marmalade's place in British life dance through the pages of literature. James Boswell, for example, remarks that he and Samuel Johnson were offered it at breakfast in Scotland in 1773, along with a semiobligatory dram of good Scotch whiskey.

When Louisa May Alcott visited Britain in the 1800s, she described "a choice pot of marmalade and a slice of cold ham" as "essentials of English table comfort."

At Oxford in the upbeat 1920s, Charles Ryder, the protagonist of Evelyn Waugh's novel *Brideshead Revisited*, ate his "scrambled eggs and bitter marmalade with the zest which in youth follows a restless night." And in the more downbeat 30s, in *The Road to Wigan Pier*, a jar of marmalade on a sideboard, "an unspeakable mess of stickiness and dust," epitomized for George Orwell the complete squalor of a working-class household.

Americans have been fans of marmalade since Colonial days, and still are. My wife, Betsey, recently showed me a marmalade entry in the "receipt book" compiled in 1770 in South Carolina by her ancestor Harriott Pinckney Horry. It resembles the recipe given by Hannah Glasse, the pioneering English food writer, in her collection, first published in 1747, and the one used by Wilkin in some of its marmalades, whose top export market is the United States.

I would have known I was in the right place if I had been wearing a blindfold. In the wintertime, a captivating bittersweet aroma—a marmalade-scented canopy—hangs over Wilkin's plant here at Tiptree in Essex, a 50-minute train ride northeast of London. Marmalade is manufactured three months each year, from January through March, when the Seville oranges (Citrus aurantium) are at their ripe, sharp-tasting, thin-skinned best.

Marmalade making consists of disassembling oranges and putting the parts back together. Most of Wilkin's competitors save money by beginning that operation in Spain, but Wilkin brings in whole fruit, which it processes in small batches, partly by hand, partly by machine.

In the small, modern, surgically clean factory here in Tiptree, oranges are first scrubbed, then frozen to soften their skins, then boiled in stainless-steel tanks that hold 1,750 pounds of fruit each. This not only completes the softening process but also releases the pectins, natural jelling agents that are present in the skins and the seeds. After four hours, the heat is turned off and the oranges cool overnight, steeping in their own juices to intensify their flavor and lend them a slight taste of caramel.

The operation varies, depending on which type of marmalade is being produced. Wilkin makes 14, some clear and jellylike, some opaque; some with mere threads of peel, some with thick strips of peel, some with no peel at all. Most are made with oranges, but other citrus fruits, including grapefruit, tangerines, lemons and limes, are also used, either alone or together.

For Tawny, the company's classically dark, thick-cut marmalade, the softened oranges go to a room where pairs of women, using only their hands, split the fruit into two pieces and scoop out the flesh. The flesh moves on to a separator, which divides the fruit mash from the seeds, which are discarded. The peels are thrown onto a conveyer belt that runs between the women's workstations, to be inspected for quality and sliced by whirling knives into strips about a quarter-inch wide.

Finally, for a second boiling, the peels are combined with the mash, orange-infused water from the first boiling and sugar. In 150-pound batches, the mixture is cooked twice at 220 degrees for 10 minutes or so, before being poured into 56-pound containers, where it rests for 24 hours to darken and caramelize further. These second boilings are done in traditional copper-lined, stainless-steel pans, 14 of them, at normal atmospheric pressure.

"The equipment is all new, installed last year," Mr. Wilkin told me. "It cost thousands and thousands of pounds, obviously. It is electronically controlled and more modern in other ways. But the pans and process are the same. We tried pans without copper linings, we tried pressure cookers, we tried vacuum cookers. But we couldn't get the taste we were used to."

The label is terse: "Ingredients: sugar, oranges. Prepared with 47 grams of fruit per 100 grams. Sugar content 67 grams per 100 grams."

Walter Scott, the company's production manager, was rather more lyrical. "The elixir of life," he said as he watched marmalade flowing into hot jars on the speeding bottling line.

Wilkin's attention to detail and refusal to cut corners costs money; it adds neither caramel nor preservatives, as many manufacturers do. But this also enables it to command premium prices, not only for its marmalades but also for its 45 jams, including Little Scarlet strawberry, made from premium fruit grown near Tiptree; loganberry, whose production dates back to plants brought from California by Peter Wilkin's great-uncle; and rarities like medlar, guava and ginger-rhubarb.

Compared with many of its competitors, Wilkin is a tiny company, with 170 employees and sales of about $15 million a year. It is one of only three family-owned companies left in the industry, along with Baxter's of Fochabers, in the Scottish Highlands, and Manchester-based Duerr & Son.

Yet Wilkin wins shelf space in elite shops like Fortnum & Mason in London and Legrand in Paris as well as in supermarkets.

Many mass-produced marmalades are no longer quite what they appear to be. Frank Cooper's Oxford marmalade, which introduced the coarse-cut, aromatic style in 1874, is no longer made in Oxford, nor do his descendants play any role in making it. The trademark belongs to a conglomerate. Though it is still labeled "Seville Orange Dundee," Keiller's is made by Robertson's, the biggest British producer, in its plant across Manchester from Duerr's.

There's more. Not only has Keiller been absent from Dundee for decades; the romantic, oft-told story of how a grocer's wife named Janet Keiller "invented" marmalade in 1797, using Seville oranges bought from a storm-tossed ship in Dundee harbor, has been decisively disproved by food historians, including C. Anne Wilson in *The Book of Marmalade* (University of Pennsylvania Press, Rev. Ed., 1999).

Wilkin marmalades do battle in the supermarkets with the less expensive market leaders like Chivers and Robertson's, and at Fortnum & Mason and similar stores with more expensive house brands. Fortnum's has 18 of its own-label varieties, including lemon with Earl Grey tea; orange with Champagne; orange with whiskey; lime, kumquat and blood orange—this last a favorite of Christopher Watson, the salesman who showed the line to Betsey.

The choice, in other words, is more or less infinite (I counted no fewer than 39 different varieties at a supermarket near our cottage in the Cotswolds). Nonetheless, an astonishing number of people in Britain, by no means all of them demented foodies, insist on preparing their own marmalades. Elegant hotels pride themselves on serving marmalade made in their own kitchens. Recipes are handed down from one generation to the next like heirlooms.

My friend Bill Baker, a prominent English wine merchant, detects "a bitter, burned taste" in a lot of commercial marmalade. The marmalade that his mother made every year until her recent death, he insists, was sweeter and more "orangey" in flavor, with more precisely cut strips of peel.

Come next year, he vows, "I'll make up a batch myself."

Lady Owen, an American from St. James, N.Y., on Long Island, spends three evenings late each January boiling oranges, sugar and a few lemons (for extra snap), rigorously following the recipe given to her by her mother-in-law. Lord Owen, the former foreign secretary, said homemade preserves were a tradition in his family—"My mother never bought anything she could make," he said—a tradition reinforced by shortages during World War II.

"I had never seen Seville oranges before I came here," Lady Owen said. "I was so thrilled that an American kid could turn them into this delicious thing, with such a special taste, that I kept at it."

The Greeks made a product called *melomeli*. For this, according to Ms. Wilson, they preserved quinces in honey, and ate them as an aid to digestion. Martial, the first-century Latin poet, mentions a similar

Roman preparation, and medieval manuscripts make it clear that the Portuguese learned the process, perhaps from the Arabs. They substituted sugar for honey, giving birth to what they named *marmelada*.

In the first half of the 15th century, the English made a spiced jelly called chardequynce from quinces (or quinces and pears) and honey (or sugar). Then in 1495, only three years after Columbus's first epic voyage to America, a Portuguese ship's captain named Farnando Yanes delivered to the port of London the first consignment of *marmelada* ever to arrive in Britain.

The English initially ate it as a sweetmeat or as an after-dinner digestive. It was solid, not liquid, and it came in a box, not a pot. But gradually cooks began to experiment with other fruits, using apples at first to aid the jelling process. The first printed recipe for "modern" orange marmalade was published in 1714 in Mary Kettilby's *Collection of Above Three Hundred Receipts in Cookery, Physic and Surgery.*

It was the Scots who moved marmalade to the breakfast table, complete with finely cut peels, or "chips," to use the Scottish term. There it joined scones, sausages, game pies, trout, roast beef and sometimes a haunch of venison on the sideboard. The traditional Scottish breakfast was certainly not for the meek.

Not until well into the 19th century did the English follow the Scottish example and abandon the eating of marmalade in the evening.

Mrs. Kettilby's formula called for whole oranges, lemon juice and sugar. A contemporary recipe for homemade marmalade, that of Shaun Hill, owner of the Michelin one-star Merchant House in Shropshire, differs only slightly, using whole lemons along with the oranges and sugar.

"Homemade marmalade," he says, "is superior to anything you can buy," and he made 20 cases of Seville oranges into marmalade each January when he cooked at Gidleigh Park in Chagford, Devon, a prominent country-house hotel.

A few days ago, Betsey came across a pot that he must have given us around 1990, hidden at the back of our larder. Mr. Wilkin and others had told me that marmalade improved with age, like wine, so we opened the elderly pot and spread a little of the glistening, mahogany-colored preserves on toast.

I won't swear it was the best marmalade I've ever eaten, but it was certainly up there. In a way that almost never happens with even the best marmalades, the bitterness of the oranges and the sweetness of the sugar had miraculously dissolved into a rich, syrupy harmony.

—*Tiptree, England, March 27, 2002*

The Sauce Secrets of Worcester

The sun has set on the British Empire, but not on a handful of products that followed the Union Jack overseas. Colman's mustard, Gilbey's gin and Lipton's tea remain familiar in English-speaking countries and many others, and Lea & Perrins Worcestershire sauce is as ubiquitous as taxes.

Lea & Perrins bottles, with their characteristic long necks, designed to make it easy to Shake Well Before Using, have turned up in shipwrecks, encrusted with barnacles; in the forbidden city of Lhasa, Tibet; and in the excavations at Te Wairo, New Zealand, which was buried by a volcanic eruption in 1886. I came across one during the Vietnam War in a semidefunct colonial hotel in Dalat and another in a bar in Samarkand in what was then Soviet Central Asia.

Very few food products have been made to the same formula for so long. Lea & Perrins Worcestershire was first formulated in 1835. Its name was registered as a trademark in 1892, and it has been manufactured since 1897 in a handsome redbrick Victorian factory on Midland Road in Worcester, a mile from the city's fine medieval cathedral and 125 miles northwest of London.

As early as 1848, a batch of old letters in the company archives show, crates of the sauce were dispatched to Gibraltar, Malta, Singapore, India, Australia and New Zealand, Mauritius, South Africa, Argentina, Chile, Peru, Canada and Jamaica, and in the United States, to New Orleans and Cincinnati.

Today, 25 million bottles a year are produced here and shipped around the world. Sauce concentrate is shipped to other countries, to be diluted and bottled there, and the stuff is made from scratch in

Fair Lawn, N.J., in a plant where 10 employees won brief fame in 1996 by hitting the lottery for $14.3 million. The formula is the same everywhere, unlike that for Coca-Cola, which adapts its recipe to suit local variations in taste.

In all, Lea & Perrins Worcestershire is sold in 140 countries. Not even the tribulations of wartime have interrupted the cascade of condiments. A bombing raid during World War II resulted in the temporary disappearance of the familiar orange-and-brown labels, but not of the bottles; they continued to roll off the line, in the standard 5- and 10-ounce sizes, bearing utilitarian, black-and-white labels that announced, "Messrs. Lea & Perrins are compelled to issue this label owing to the destruction of their printer's establishment by enemy action." What phlegm! What stiff upper lips!

There are other manufacturers of Worcestershire sauce, of course. It is one of Heinz's many varieties. But as Dave Clements, 35, the good-humored factory general manager for Lea & Perrins, asked me when I visited the plant, "If Heinz does it better than we do, why isn't it called 'Pennsylvania sauce'?" Besides, a British high court ruled in 1906 that while anyone could call a sauce Worcestershire, no matter where it was made, only Lea & Perrins could use the words "original and genuine" to describe its product.

It is hard to escape the conviction that early on, before the invention of refrigeration, Worcestershire sauce was used to compensate for culinary ineptitude and ingredients that had passed their prime. Raymond Postgate, the founder of the *Good Food Guide*, said of Worcestershire and its bottled brethren, "They were provided on the justified assumption that you would want to hide completely the taste of what you would be offered to eat."

The sauce is all but indestructible, whether by heat, cold or time, which made it a welcome companion on long sea voyages. But its flavor—it is piquant, salty, vinegary, slightly fishy and perhaps vaguely fruity—also had a broad appeal that has never waned.

●　●　●

For Americans, it is perhaps best known as an indispensable ingredient in the Bloody Mary, a cocktail perfected in the 1920s at Harry's New York Bar in Paris by Fernand Petiot, the head bartender. Worcestershire sauce is also a popular seasoning for steaks and a must in Welsh rarebit, the classic end-of-meal savory, out of style but never, at least in my house, out of mind.

The United States uses more Worcestershire sauce than any other country. Other strokes for other folks: In Japan, it is widely used as a soy substitute, with sushi and other dishes. In New Zealand, the largest consumer of Worcestershire sauce per capita, it for many years relieved the monotony of a diet overladen with lamb. El Salvador, for reasons that make officials here scratch their heads, consumes 450 tons of sauce every year—2.5 ounces for every man, woman and child in that little Central American nation—and has spawned counterfeit labels seeking to mimic Lea & Perrins.

A few epicures may turn up their noses, and Worcestershire sauce gets no entry in the *Larousse Gastronomique*. But it has plenty of defenders.

"It is a valuable flavoring when used with skill and moderation," writes Tom Stobart in *Herbs, Spices and Flavorings* (Overlook Press, 2000). "Cooks do better to steer clear of made-up flavorings, but an item which has been popular and unchanged for over a century, and is used by chefs in so many countries, must be an exception. Indeed, one could almost say that it has graduated as a basic natural ingredient."

The sap of the wonderful Worcestershire tree, you might suppose. No, not really. So what actually goes into the sauce? How is it made? In keeping with long-standing tradition, Mr. Clements was willing to explain just so much and no more. The ingredients are stated on the label: vinegar, molasses, sugar, salt, anchovies, tamarinds, onions, garlic, spices and "flavoring."

Those last three words hide more than they reveal; I was able to pry nothing more specific from Mr. Clements than the fact that there are chilies and cloves in the mix and one "secret ingredient," as well.

"If I told you what it was," he said, putting on his best mock-MI5 cloak, "I would have to shoot you."

Ginger, perhaps? Sassafras? Elixir of bus driver's glove? Something as mundane as soy? Another tropical fruit to complement the tamarind?

Worcestershire sauce is an advertisement for free trade, in its manufacture as well as its distribution. The anchovies come from Spain, Italy or sometimes Morocco. The cloves come from Southeast Asia or Zanzibar, the garlic and chilies from China and the tamarinds—dark brown pods containing a juice widely used as a souring agent—from northeastern India.

Each major ingredient is treated separately. The anchovies are preserved in salt, for example, and aged for three to five years, in a process similar to that which produces *nam pla* fish sauce in Thailand, while the vegetables are pickled in vinegar. All are stored in small blue barrels, which are labeled with the name of the ingredient and the date. One that I spotted said "Pickles, 1997 season, shallots, 100 kilograms, malt vinegar, 100 kilograms."

At the appropriate moment, the aged and unaged ingredients are combined in huge fiberglass maturing tanks, holding up to 30,000 liters each (more than 7,000 gallons). These have replaced more romantic but less manageable oak casks. The mixture is never cooked (though it is heated just before bottling to pasteurize it). It just sits there, perfuming the air with an acrid smell. A stroll through a cellar filled with wine vats evokes a smile; here in Worcester, a walk through the mixing room is more likely to produce a cough or sneeze.

After several months—Lea & Perrins has never divulged the exact length of time—the solids are filtered from the brew, and it is bottled.

Secrecy has always been big at Lea & Perrins. Once, when a foreign government demanded a list of ingredients for all imported food products, the firm laid plans to supply it with a fraudulent formula, which excluded the "secret ingredient" and included spurious ones. At one time, the ingredients had code names, known to a few, beginning with the letter B—bulimay, buggy, bugbear, bugler, building, bulldog, buglehorn, bullcalf, bullace and bulletin, but no birdseed.

* * *

The consequence of decades of caution—dare one say paranoia?—is that no one knows how the sauce originated. Legend, handed from generation to generation, has it that a Lord Sandys (presumably an ancestor of the Duncan Sandys who married one of Winston Churchill's daughters) came home from service as governor of Bengal, in India, with a recipe that he presented one spring day in 1835 to the proprietors of the Lea & Perrins shop in Broad Street, Worcester.

"Make it up," he said, and they did. But when they tasted it, it was revolting, so they consigned it, in a stone crock, to the basement. There it languished, only to be rediscovered and retasted many months later. This time it bowled the partners over, and for years they presented their sauce as the product of a "recipe of a nobleman in the county" (Worcestershire).

Unfortunately, from the perspective of the spinner of stories, a former Lea & Perrins employee, Brian Keogh, found otherwise in the course of his research for *The Secret Sauce*, a history of the firm that was published privately in 1997 to mark the 100th anniversary of the Midland Road plant. "No Lord Sandys," he wrote, "was ever a governor of Bengal or, as far as available records show, ever in India."

Mr. Clements winced when asked about the sauce's origins. Since Mr. Keogh's discoveries, he said, "We have had to say that the saga of Lord Sandys may not be God's own truth."

Only 40 people work at the factory here, and only four or five know the formula. Each batch of sauce is made by one of two "head makers"—either Malcolm Taylor or Joseph Neary, both longtime employees. Head maker, Mr. Clements said, is "a position of enormous trust," because an unscrupulous individual privy to the firm's secrets could sell them to a rival. Until the late 1960s, head makers automatically became head magistrates of Worcester.

John Wheeley Lea and William Henry Perrins, the firm's founders, and their descendants ranked among the city's leading figures, along with the composer Edward Elgar. Leas and Perrinses served as mayors of Worcester, and a Perrins rescued the Royal Worcester Porcelain Factory from ruin.

Like the man who formulated Coca-Cola, John Stith Pemberton of Atlanta, Messrs. Lea and Perrins were chemists, or pharmacists. Their shop offered all manner of things, from surgeons' tools and leeches to Locock's Lotion for the Hair. And like Pemberton, Lea & Perrins first touted the health-giving qualities of its tonic. Worcestershire sauce, an 1851 newspaper ad claimed, "enables the stomach to perfectly digest the food," and thus "the daily use of this aromatic and delicious sauce is the best safeguard to health."

Today's claims are more modest. "Adds instant richness," the label on the Lea & Perrins sauce asserts.

Leas and Perrinses no longer run things. Lea & Perrins was sold in 1930 to H.P. Foods Ltd., a company built around HP sauce, more famous in Britain than in the United States, which resembles A1 sauce. After reorganizations, H.P. Foods passed into the hands of the French Danone Group, which also makes Evian water, Dannon yogurt and Kronenbourg beer.

But no Frenchman, people here whisper, has learned The Formula.

—Worcester, England, June 21, 2000

● ●

BLOODY MARY
(Adapted from the King Cole Room)
Time: 5 minutes

> 1 dash fresh lemon juice
> 2 dashes salt
> 2 dashes black pepper
> 2 dashes cayenne pepper
> 3 dashes Worcestershire sauce
> 1½ ounces vodka

2 ounces tomato juice
1 lime wedge for garnish

Combine lemon juice, salt, pepper, cayenne and Worcestershire sauce in shaker glass. Add ice cubes, vodka and tomato juice. Shake and strain into highball glass with a few ice cubes. Garnish with lime, and serve.

Yield: 1 serving

The Rich Source of Indulgence

William Ewart Gladstone, the great Victorian prime minister, called clotted cream "the food of the gods." George Blake, a Briton who spied on his own country and now lives in exile in Moscow, said recently that the only thing he really misses from his homeland is clotted cream to crown the Christmas pudding that he makes for himself every year.

Magnificent stuff it is, too—rich, luxuriously thick and golden, the very essence of self-indulgence. It has been made here in the southwest corner of England, principally in the counties of Devon and Cornwall, which face each other across the River Tamar, for at least 600 years. The poet Edmund Spenser mentions "clouted cream" in "The Shepheard's Calendar" (1579).

Because a similar product is made in the East, notably in Lebanon and Afghanistan, the food historian Alan Davidson theorizes that the recipe may have been brought to Cornwall 2,000 years ago by Phoenicians who sailed here to trade in tin.

Clotted cream is made by scalding either whole milk or fresh cream. It is a tricky process. Get it too hot and the cream develops a gritty texture. If it is not hot enough, the result is bland.

The finished product can be spooned or spread but not poured; it has a consistency somewhere between that of butter and that of whipped cream. In winter, when the cows must eat fodder, the clotted cream is the color of hazelnuts, but when the grass in the pastures is green, the cream is yellow as a jonquil.

As a topping for desserts—apple pie, for instance, or the steamed ginger and rhubarb pudding at the delightful Arundell Arms Hotel in Lifton, Devon, or a simple bowl of fresh, downy berries—clotted cream is nonpareil. As an ingredient in cooked dishes, sweet or savory, it adds an unmistakable lushness. But it achieves its apotheosis when slathered shamelessly onto a warm scone, together with homemade preserves.

A. E. Rodda & Son, based at Scorrier in Cornwall, is the largest producer, using the milk of more than 7,000 cows during the peak season. Rodda cream was served at teatime by the late Queen Mother. It is served on British Airways planes, and it is also exported to the United States, Japan, Australia and many other countries.

In my view, though, the best, most sensually satisfying clotted cream comes from small producers using methods handed down through generations. Perhaps the most tradition-minded of all is Barbara Lake, 58, who lives near this hamlet in the 300-year-old house in which she was born.

The house is approached down a narrow lane lined with eight-foot hedgerows so extravagently studded with pink, yellow, blue and white wildflowers that my wife, Betsey, said she felt as if she were driving through a roll of wallpaper.

Ms. Lake, a stocky woman in trousers, flowered sweater and boots, keeps 11 cows, about half Jerseys and half Guernseys. These fawn-colored breeds, both of which originated in the Channel Islands, off the French coast, produce milk with an exceptionally high percentage of butterfat.

A one-woman show, Ms. Lake milks her herd morning and evening, separates the cream from the milk and puts the cream into a shallow enamel pan. (She feeds the skim milk to her pigs.)

She took me into a square, low-ceilinged room, about 12 feet by 12 feet, which contains a table piled high with newspapers and magazines, a few chairs, a television set, a small sideboard and an old oil-fired Rayburn stove. She cooks her meals on the stove, and she cooks her cream there, too.

The enamel pan floats in a larger aluminum pan filled with hot water, forming a primitive sort of bain-marie or double boiler. Ms. Lake heats the cream to no more than 85 degrees Celsius, which takes about an hour and 45 minutes. It must not boil. After a time, small bubbles rise to the surface, and then the cream darkens as a blister-marked crust forms on top.

Having cooled for two or three hours, the clotted cream goes into the refrigerator. When Ms. Lake gets an order, she ladles some into a quarter-pound container—"a little crust from the top, a little smooth from the bottom in each one, for the best texture," she told me. She charges 65 pence, $1.07, if the customer picks it up.

The week I visited her, Ms. Lake made 42 pounds of cream on her stove. Using specially designed high-speed ovens, Rodda's makes about 10 tons a day.

In spring and summer, you can't move a mile in the West Country without seeing signs offering cream teas, posted by hotels, restaurants, cafes, teahouses and working farms. No vacation in the region is considered complete without one. A cream tea is as essential a part of a visit here as a lobster dinner is to a trip to Maine or a bowl of clam chowder is to a weekend on Cape Cod.

English eyes sparkle when the talk turns to cream teas, and rigorous standards are enforced. The tea itself should be freshly made in a pot, of course, without resort to tea bags. The scones, which are large, firm biscuits, slightly sweetened and leavened with baking powder, should still be warm from the oven, but not hot. If they are hot, the cream will get runny; if they are cold, they will crumble in the hand.

Bonus points are given for a choice of teas—say, English breakfast and Darjeeling and Earl Grey—and an assortment of scones—say, plain, with raisins and with cherries. (The word "scone," incidentally, rhymes with "prawn," not with "bone.")

The customer splits the scone, loads up each half with clotted cream and adds jam, usually strawberry or black currant. Here arises a perfect expression of the rivalry between Devon and Cornwall, each of which considers its clotted cream utterly matchless. In Cornwall, the jam goes on first, with the cream on top; in Devon, the cream is first, like butter, and the jam second.

So which is best, Cornish cream or Devonshire cream? Isabella

Beeton, the Fannie Farmer of Britain, used the terms "clotted cream" and "Devonshire cream" interchangeably, which ought to settle the issue.

But I was constantly reminded in Cornwall that "Cornish clotted cream" is registered with the European Union as a Protected Designation of Origin, while "Devonshire clotted cream" is not.

Neither Betsey nor I is an habitual drinker of tea, at least at 4 o'clock in the afternoon, when cream teas are meant to be consumed. (This might be a good time to point out that contrary to widespread American belief, "afternoon tea," whether a West Country cream tea or the more formal ritual at the Ritz in London, is not "high tea." High tea is a heartier, working-class meal usually served at about 6 p.m.)

This time, we yielded to temptation and stopped at the Primrose Cottage, a thatched tearoom, painted buttercup yellow, in the dreamy Devon village of Lustleigh. It looked as if it must be inhabited by dainty mice wearing pinafores, but in fact it is the province of Caroline Baker, 35, a microbiologist, and her husband, Simon, 38, who moved there from Bristol in search of a new, more serene life.

"I was doing stem-cell work," she said. "I was completely stressed-out."

Always a keen home cook, she bakes scones every day, as well as enough cakes to fill a glass-fronted case. Her superb scones, light and easily split, never visit a microwave. Her jams and clotted cream are local. The sumptuous cream, a great mound of it from Higher Murchington Farm on Dartmoor, formed stiff peaks like a meringue when I dropped a dollop onto a scone.

Apart from its cooked, slightly nutty taste, what sets clotted cream apart from other creams is its high butterfat content, which often reaches 63 percent. British single cream is 20 percent butterfat, American table cream 25 percent, American whipping cream 35 percent and British double cream 48 percent. A bacterial culture ferments and thickens sour cream, which ends with 18 percent butterfat; French crème fraîche, similarly made, has 35 percent.

Everything depends on the cows, of course. Harold Dunn, who owns a dairy farm near Whiddon Down, in Devon, puts his 120

Holstein-Friesians, a breed that originated in northern Germany, into the barn only for the worst days of winter. Usually they come indoors on Boxing Day, Dec. 26, and go out again on Feb. 10.

"The cream tastes better when they are out in the fresh air, even when it's cold, and eating the grass, even when it's pretty puny," the pink-cheeked, dungaree-clad Mr. Dunn said. "They love it. If I don't let them out, they shout."

Friesians produce more milk than the Channel Island breeds, with a bit less butterfat, and Mr. Dunn swears by them. He calls each of his cows by name, and he scratched the back of Emily, a favorite, as he explained his methods to me.

Dunn Farms clotted cream is extremely smooth, because it goes into the cartons still hot from the cooker. After chilling for several hours, a crust forms on the top and stays there, which customers describe as "the cream of the cream."

George Trenouth, the owner of Trevose Farm in western Cornwall, a few hundred yards from the Atlantic surf, told me he used "exactly the same process as my gran." The farm has been in his family since 1890. His 32 cows, almost all Jerseys, graze on grass enriched by minerals deposited by sea mists, and the cream has a special, slightly salty tang.

"In theory, you ought to be able to make clotted cream anywhere," Mr. Trenouth said. "They've tried pilot schemes in several other parts of the country, but they didn't work. The cream didn't taste quite right. Don't know why; maybe the weather and soil have something to do with it."

At 75, Mr. Trenouth still works eight- and nine-hour days, wearing an old flat-topped checked cap as he lugs heavy stainless-steel milk pails, with his border collie, Jazz, at his heels. His son, Richard, tends to the farm's herb and vegetable crops, but he is not so interested in clotted cream.

"Once my days are finished," the farmer said, "my cream business will be finished, too," which is a shame, since I tasted no more unctuous, no more brightly flavored clotted cream anywhere in my wanderings.

—*Coad's Green, England, June 11, 2003*

In England, There
Will Always Be Whim Wham
and Apple Dappy

For American kids, pudding means the gloppy, yummy stuff, usually chocolate or butterscotch, that comes out of a cardboard box.

Unless the kids grow up around Boston, where they might encounter Indian pudding, a confection of cornmeal, milk and molasses that dates back to the Pilgrims. Or unless Mom and Dad are Anglophiles, given to serving a suet pudding at Christmas dinner—"like a speckled cannonball, so hard and firm," as Dickens described it, "blazing in half of half-a-quartern of ignited brandy, and bedight with Christmas holly stuck into the top."

In Britain, though, a fabulous array of soft, warm, sweet puddings—so many that a resourceful mum could easily turn out a different one every day of the month—light up childhood mealtimes and linger reassuringly decades later in the memories of 50-somethings and 60-somethings. They are the quintessential nursery food, comforting to both body and spirit, and you will find them on the menus of proletarian pubs and elitist clubs alike.

A few classics, like bread-and-butter pudding and rice pudding, have found their way into the American repertory of desserts for grown-ups. Though delicious when homemade and served on a chilly night—especially, for some reason, a Sunday night—they are tame and a little bit bland, and they do not hint at the splendor of some English favorites.

Some puddings, like whim wham and chocolate puddle and jam

roly-poly, apple dappy and rhubarb hat and spotted dick, have agree-ably eccentric names that only enhance their appeal. (If the last seems just too naughty for Americans, and "more decorum is required at the dinner table," a solicitous English cookbook advises, it "can also be called 'spotted dog.'")

The English have always been great fruit lovers, but the growing season here is short, and in the days before canning and freezing were developed, only dried fruit was available for more than half the year, along with jams and jellies. Many favorite puddings, accordingly, are based on dates, prunes, sultanas (golden raisins), figs and apricots. Steaming the pudding restores some of the fruit's fresh, peak-season flavor.

In the cold, damp climate that prevails here in fall, winter and early spring, human bodies crave heat. Until well after World War II, central heating was rare, so people took many of their calories inter-nally, often in the form of suet, or beef fat, used in making puddings. Puddings earned a place on the British menu, it might be said, for the same reason Shetland and cashmere sweaters found their way into the British wardrobe.

Today, most cooks no longer use suet, the best of which surrounds calves' kidneys, in its original form. Many substitute butter or vegeta-ble shortenings, but some use a product called Atora (unavailable, so far as I know, in the United States), which looks like half-inch bits of dried spaghetti. Made from suet mixed with a small quantity of flour, then extruded through nozzles, it is easier to handle.

Sinful, sugary, awash in calories, as gastronomically incorrect as peanut butter and jelly, puddings fell out of favor in the health-obsessed 1970s and 1980s. But like American steakhouses, English puddings have been undergoing a renaissance of late. "The rib-stickers especially," said Simon Hopkinson, a leading English chef and food writer, "are back in fashion in a big way."

Sweet puddings, that is. The British never stopped eating what they call savory puddings, including Yorkshire pudding, that indispensable companion of roast beef (memorably defined by Ogden Nash as "a sort of popover that's tripped and popped under"). Other unchanging standbys are steak and kidney pudding; pease pudding, a puree of split peas; and black pudding, *boudin noir* to the French, which is a rustic blood sausage.

So exactly what is a pudding? The word, a British gastronome wrote a hundred years ago, has been extended "so widely by the fancies and tastes of cooks that it is difficult to assign any limitation to its application." Suffice it to say that even if he cannot define a pudding, an Englishman knows when he is eating one.

The revival in traditional sweet puddings began in the Lake District. A young cook named Francis Coulson arrived there in 1949, with pots and pans clanging against the spokes of his bicycle, and set about creating what became one of the country's first and most popular rural retreats, Sharrow Bay Country House Hotel. With his partner, Brian Sack, he slowly built a national reputation for unpretentious hospitality and sound English food, not least an irresistible dish he called sticky toffee pudding.

Spongelike, with fragments of crust here and there, the pudding is bathed in a viscous butterscotch sauce, with ice-cold cream poured over the whole shooting match at the last minute.

The texture and the dishearteningly delicious taste owe a lot to the pitted dates in the batter. It is still on the menu at Sharrow Bay, though Mr. Coulson died last year, on the day the hotel opened for its 50th season. Other versions, good and less good, are featured on menus across the land.

Another boost came from the Pudding Club, started by a bunch of die-hard chauvinists determined to beat back the assault of frozen supermarket Black Forest gateaux. They got together in 1985 at Three Ways House in Mickleton, a crossroads hotel in the Cotswolds, near Stratford-on-Avon, and their successors still meet there, usually the first and third Friday of each month. At each gathering, seven puddings, cooked in basins shaped like mixing bowls, are paraded before the guests and carried to a buffet.

You can go back as often as you like and take as big a chunk out of the moist, dark hemispheres as you care to, but only after clearing your plate each time. Loose clothing recommended. And no mixing: only one pudding at a time. Cream and custard are always offered—not crème anglaise, which is scorned as much too foreign and too effete, but properly Edwardian, slightly lumpy stuff made from a pre-mix called Bird's custard powder. (Me, I always go for the effete stuff.)

Anyone, member or nonmember, can attend the meetings, although enthusiasts tend to join on the spot. There are now more than 500 members. Pudding Club cookbooks and neckties, British television shows and a site on the Internet (www.puddingclub.com) have helped them to spread the gospel.

The evening I stopped by with my wife, Betsey, and the kids, the hotel put out three hearty puddings for us to enjoy, including the commonplace syrup sponge, the more unusual chocolate-nut and the obscure Lord Randall's pudding. Milord's favorite, based on apricots and marmalade, is named "for a Victorian philanderer," I was told (not entirely seriously, I suspect).

Lacking proper training, lacking the requisite bloodlines, we failed to make much of a dent in the spread. But many pudding heads go wild. Peter Henderson, one of the hotel's owners, said that the record, 18 helpings, was dispatched one cool night in November 1997, by "a guy from near here, a guy we never saw again."

Nowadays you come across first-class puddings all over Britain. Not long ago, for example, I ate a delicious ginger pudding—made with ginger marmalade, ground ginger and candied ginger—at the Dartmoor Inn, a pub at Lydford in remote, windswept southwestern England. A lot of people must have thought it was as fabulous as I did; the young pastry chef, Nicola Butt, was ready with a detailed recipe when I asked how it had been made.

Soon afterward, I started noticing puddings on the tables of some of London's celebrated chefs, often with a fresh twist. Alastair Little, who spends a lot of time in Italy when not cooking at one of his London bistros, makes a bread-and-butter pudding with slices of panettone, the light, yeasty Italian Christmas cake, and with raisins well-soaked in grappa.

Gordon Ramsay, the talented, turbulent former soccer star whose eponymous restaurant earned two stars in the latest Michelin guide, ennobles the plebeian rice pudding by adding a touch of crème anglaise.

At an annual New Year's house party that we attend near Bath, Simon Hopkinson sometimes makes a pair of unusual but traditional puddings as notable for their appearance as for their heartwarming flavors.

In a recent book, *Gammon and Spinach* (Macmillan, London, 1998), he describes one of those, which is called apple hat, as a "steaming damp dome sitting in a moat of yellow custard." Boiled for two hours or more, it gets a final enrichment from a tablespoon of thick cream, poured into a hole cut in the top of the dome, which quickly melts down into the pudding.

The other, Sussex Pond pudding, was judged by Jane Grigson, the great advocate of English cooking, as the best of all the English puddings. It was invented in the county of Sussex, south of London, in the 17th century. Whole lemons are steamed inside, and the citrus tang of their juices mingles with sugar and butter to form a "pond" around the pudding that is rich but uncloying. The lemon itself emerges soft enough to cut with a fork.

Great stuff. But for me, there is no beating Francis Coulson's sticky toffee pudding—sometimes he got carried away and called it "icky sticky"—during the colder months. I cannot keep myself from ordering it when I see it on a menu, any more than an elephant can resist peanuts.

Come summer, when berries are at their peak, when raspberries and blackberries are abundant and currants are bursting with juice (if you are lucky enough to find them at a farmers' market or provident enough to keep a bush of your own), the king must yield to the queen: summer pudding. Until I came across it 25 years ago, I thought strawberry shortcake, the all-American midsummer treat, was the greatest of berry desserts, but no more.

Summer pudding is simplicity itself—berries and currants barely simmered with sugar to release their juices, then poured into a pudding basin lined with slices of slightly stale white bread. Weighted and chilled for 24 hours or more, the bread, juices and fruit merge, with the flavors of the berries balancing one another, sweet and acid in equilibrium.

If you are in England, you serve the lovely purple mound with a pitcher of thick Jersey cream. But I use crème fraîche when I make a summer pudding at our weekend place in Pennsylvania, I substitute blueberries for currants when I have to and once, unable to find blackberries, I sneaked in a few strawberries, even though no one in England ever does that.

But then, as Cervantes said (or was it Addison?), "the proof of the pudding is in the eating."

—Mickleton, England, March 22, 2000

• •

STICKY TOFFEE PUDDING
(Adapted from Francis Coulson)
Time: 1 hour

For the batter:
4 tablespoons butter, at room temperature
¾ cup sugar
1½ cups plus 2 teaspoons all-purpose flour
1 teaspoon baking powder
1 large egg, lightly beaten

Vegetable oil or nonstick cooking spray
1¼ cups pitted dates
1 teaspoon baking soda
1 teaspoon vanilla extract

For the toffee sauce:
3 tablespoons butter

⅓ cup brown sugar

2 tablespoons heavy cream

1. To prepare batter: Preheat oven to 350 degrees. Using an electric mixer, combine butter and sugar. Beat at medium speed until fluffy, about 2 minutes. Sift 1½ cups flour with baking powder. Add egg and about ½ cup of flour mixture to batter. Blend. Add remaining flour mixture and beat until blended; batter will be crumbly.

2. Oil a 9-by-9-inch cake pan. In a bowl, combine dates with remaining 2 teaspoons flour. Toss to coat. In a food processor, finely chop dates. Return dates to bowl, and cover with 1 cup boiling water. Add baking soda and vanilla and stir. Add date mixture to batter and blend. Transfer batter to cake pan. Bake until dry in center, about 35 minutes. Remove from oven; keep warm.

3. To prepare toffee sauce: In a small saucepan over low heat, melt butter and add brown sugar and heavy cream. Simmer until golden brown, about 3 minutes.

4. Preheat broiler. Cut warm pudding into squares. Cover with a spoonful of toffee sauce, and place under broiler just until it bubbles; do not allow to overcook. Remove from heat and serve immediately.

Yield: 6 to 9 servings

SUMMER PUDDING

(Adapted from Jane Grigson)

Time: 30 minutes, plus overnight marinating and 24 hours' refrigeration of pudding

2 pounds (about 7 cups) mixed raspberries, blackberries and currants (or blueberries)

⅔ cup superfine sugar
About 1½ pounds good-quality white bread, unsliced

1. In a bowl, combine berries and sugar. Cover and rest at room temperature overnight.
2. Transfer berry mixture to a large saucepan; place over medium heat and bring to a boil. Reduce heat to low. Simmer gently to allow fruit to release juices, about 2 minutes. Remove from heat and set aside.
3. Cut bread into slices ¼ inch thick; remove crusts. Cut a circle of bread to fit bottom of a round 5-cup bowl. Cut wedges of bread to fit around sides of bowl, leaving no gaps. Reserve ¼ cup of berries and juice for garnish; cover and refrigerate. Pour half the remaining berries and juice into bread-lined bowl. Place a slice of bread in center of bowl; top with remaining half of unreserved berries and juice.
4. Cut slices of bread to make a layer completely covering top of bowl. Top with a plate that will fit snugly in bowl. Weight with a heavy can and place in refrigerator for 24 to 72 hours. To serve, remove plate and run a thin knife around inside edge of bowl to loosen pudding. Place a large serving plate over top of bowl, then turn plate and bowl over. Remove bowl. Garnish pudding with reserved berries and juice.

Yield: 8 to 10 servings

GINGER PUDDING
(Adapted from Nicola Butt)
Time: 1 hour 10 minutes

For the pudding:
2 12-ounce jars ginger preserves or ginger marmalade
1 teaspoon baking soda

11 tablespoons butter, more for greasing ramekins, at room
    temperature

¾ cup brown sugar

2 teaspoons ground ginger

Pinch of salt

4 large eggs, lightly beaten

2 cups self-rising flour

4 to 6 pieces stem ginger in syrup, finely chopped

2 tablespoons syrup from stem ginger in syrup

For the ginger sauce:

¾ cup dry sherry

5 tablespoons syrup from stem ginger in syrup

4 tablespoons butter

2 tablespoons brown sugar

1 teaspoon ground ginger

¾ cup heavy cream

1 teaspoon freshly squeezed lemon juice

1. To prepare pudding: Preheat oven to 350 degrees. In a small
   saucepan, combine ginger preserves and baking soda. Place over
   low heat, and stir just until warmed and fluid; set aside. In a
   mixer, blend 11 tablespoons butter, brown sugar, ground ginger
   and salt. While beating at low speed, add eggs, then ginger preserves. Add flour and mix until well blended.

2. Bring a teakettle of water to a boil. Lightly butter 12 1-cup ramekins. Place equal amounts of chopped ginger and syrup in each
   ramekin. Divide pudding batter equally among ramekins. (There
   may not seem to be enough batter, but puddings will rise.) Cover
   each ramekin with foil, and put in a large baking dish. Add boiling water to about halfway up sides of ramekins. Bake until puddings have set, about 40 minutes.

3. To prepare ginger sauce: In a medium saucepan, bring sherry to
   a boil, then simmer until it is syrupy, about 15 minutes. Add ginger syrup, butter, brown sugar, ground ginger and heavy cream.

Bring to a boil, then reduce heat to low. Simmer, whisking until mixture is slightly thickened, smooth and ivory in color. Remove from heat, and whisk in lemon juice. Set aside. Keep warm.

4. Place each ramekin on a plate. Remove foil, and top each with about 1½ tablespoons of sauce. Serve warm.

Yield: 12 servings

A Rugged Drink for a Rugged Land

Ian Urquhart, a gently spoken, 55-year-old Scotch whiskey man who heads the firm of Gordon & MacPhail, led the way through his firm's 6,000-barrel warehouses here in northeastern Scotland, identifying some of the choicest lots for an overseas visitor.

"That's 60-year-old Mortlach," he said fondly. "We bottled some of it in 2000 and more in 2001. There's still a little left. That cask was filled for my grandfather. It slept right through my father's generation."

He walked past a cask of 1949 Benromach with the comment, "Haven't decided when to bottle that," past 10 casks of 1951 Glen Grant in an aisle with barrels piled eight or nine high, past 1957 Glenlivet and 1988 Highland Park—the best all-round malt, many say—and on to the "graveyard." Whiskeys from defunct distilleries rest there, quietly eking out a kind of afterlife.

"Hillside," Mr. Urquhart said, in the tone of a man mourning a lost friend. "Demolished for a housing scheme. Seventy-eight Millburn. Millburn's gone, too. It's a Beefeater Steak House these days, outside of Inverness." Scots take their whiskey seriously, and not just because they fancy a wee dram themselves. (Or not so wee a dram; Lord Dundee, who drank his whiskey by the tumblerful, once said, "A single Scotch is nothing more than a dirty glass.")

The word "whiskey," after all, evolved from the Gaelic word *usquebaugh*, which means "water of life," exactly like eau-de-vie in French and aquavit in Scandinavian languages.

Like tartans, tam-o'-shanters, bagpipes and kilts, whiskey has epitomized Scotland for centuries. Much of the best is distilled on remote, windswept islands like Orkney and Islay, often in view of seals and otters frolicking in the sea, or in the valley of the rushing, moor-girded little River Spey, which empties into the North Sea just east of Elgin. It is a rugged drink, always tasting of peat and often of heather or seaweed, made by rugged individualists amid rugged landscapes.

More than 11,000 people are employed, directly or indirectly, in the whiskey industry here. Scotch is Britain's fifth-largest export industry, with about 90 percent of production consumed abroad.

Recent years have been challenging ones for the whiskey industry. After a boom in the 1970s, a long period of stagnation set in, and more than a dozen distilleries were closed, mothballed or destroyed. According to a recent parliamentary document, British consumption has declined by 30 percent since 1985. Worldwide exports a decade ago totaled 917 million bottles; last year the figure was 943.4 million. Exports to the United States, where other spirits have cut into Scotch sales, declined during the same period to 108 million bottles from 144 million, the Scotch Whiskey Association reports, although the United States ranked as the number one consumer in terms of value.

But those statistics conceal a success story. While familiar, heavily advertised blends like J. Dewar's and Cutty Sark, which constitute the bulk of sales, have had their troubles, the sales of single malts have soared. Malt exports to the United States, for example, rose to 8.4 million bottles last year from 5.3 million in 1993.

Shuttered distilleries that escaped the bulldozers are being re-opened, primarily to produce whiskey to be bottled as single malts. (All distilleries sell some of their output to blenders.) Glenmorangie, whose own whiskey is the best-selling malt in Scotland, restarted Ardbeg in 1997; Gordon & MacPhail refired the stills at Benromach four years earlier. A new distillery, complete with traditional pagoda-roofed towers, was built on the island of Arran in 1995.

All of that puts history into reverse. Single malts—the products of single distilleries made in pot stills similar to those used in Cognac from malted barley dried over peat fires—were the original Scotch. Not until the invention of the cheaper, faster columnar or patent still by Aeneas Coffey in 1830 did the Scots begin making spirits from a mixture of malted and unmalted grains. Lighter and much less robust in taste, these grain whiskeys were and are used to soften the flavors of malts in proprietary blends.

"The best of the blends have great character and complexity," wrote Michael Jackson in his *Malt Whiskey Companion*, first published in 1989, "but it is a shame so many are so similar, and that for so many years orchestrations drowned out the soloists."

Blenders do not disclose the proportions they use, but people in the industry told me that most use 20 to 30 percent malt whiskey and 70 to 80 percent grain. Premium blends like Johnnie Walker Black Label, Chivas Regal and Famous Grouse contain more, and more mature, malt whiskey.

Most Scots and connoisseurs from other countries drink blends, which are generally less expensive, if they want to mix their whiskey with water or soda in a predinner drink, and take their single malts neat, either before, during or, most commonly, after dinner, like Cognac or Calvados. The addition of ice to a blend is tolerated as an American eccentricity; the addition of ice to single malt is treated as near-sacrilege.

Each malt whiskey has a unique flavor, just as every classed, chateau-bottled claret differs from every other one. But those distilled in any given region share certain characteristics. The smokiest, peatiest, most iodinic malts come from Campbeltown, on a West Coast peninsula known as the Mull of Kintyre, whose mists were celebrated by the band Wings, and from Islay (pronounced EYE-la), an island near it. Springbank is a notable Campbeltown; Laphroaig, Lagavulin and Ardbeg are classic Islays.

Other islands also produce distinctive flavors. Talisker, from Skye, delivers the sharp tang of seaweed but also an explosive blast of salt and pepper.

The mildest and most subtle of malts, like Auchentoshan, come from the lowland distilleries near Edinburgh and Glasgow.

But the heartland of malt whiskey, with more than half the distilleries, is Speyside, which stretches from Inverness almost to Aberdeen, encompassing not only the sparkling Spey but also smaller streams like the Findhorn, the Isla and the Livet. Moor and glen, fir and gorse, burn and brae combine there with the changing patterns of sun and cloud to conjure scenic magic.

One day during a visit in June, my wife, Betsey, and I saw five perfect rainbows in just half an hour. On another day we were invited along with Ishbel Grant of Glenfarclas into an Arcadian setting—a fishermen's barbecue along the banks of the Spey.

Glenlivet, the largest-selling malt in the United States, is made in Speyside. Granted a government license in 1824, the first distillery to receive one after generations of illicit whiskey making, Glenlivet became so widely known that other distilleries added the word "Glenlivet" to their names. Finally, in a famous legal case in 1880, it won the exclusive right to call itself "The Glenlivet."

Another of Speyside's stars is Glenfiddich, the largest-selling malt worldwide, which is owned by William Grant & Sons, an independent company. Faced with giant competitors, it decided in 1963 to bottle much of its output as a single malt at a time when few were on the market. Its success emboldened many others to follow suit.

Like most Speyside whiskeys, Glenlivet and Glenfiddich have a distinctively light, fruity and honeyed taste.

A number of Speyside inns stock 100 or more malt whiskeys in their bars, including Minmore House, just down the road from Glenlivet, whose dining room features the accomplished cooking of Victor Janssen, a South African who operates the place.

Once upon a time, whiskey was an artisanal product, produced by farmers in the wintertime when they could not work out of doors. The process is simple, if exacting, as Johnny Miller, the distillery manager at Glenfarclas, showed me. After threshing, barley is first of all allowed to germinate by soaking in water, then dried (usually over peat fires) to halt germination.

Ground and mixed with hot water in a huge vat called a malt tun, the malted barley becomes wort. Mixed in another vat, called a washback, with yeast—water, barley and yeast are the only ingredients permitted in making whiskey—the wort is transformed in about 48 hours into "a kind of sour beer," as Mr. Miller explained, in a seething, noisy and rather smelly process.

The "sour beer," known as "wash," is then run successively through a pair of heated stills, bulbous at the bottom, narrow at the top, with a swan's neck extending down to a coiled copper pipe in a tank of cold water that converts the resulting vapor back into liquid. The first part of the run (the foreshots) and the last (the feints), both full of impurities, are eliminated.

What results may not, by law, be called whiskey; it must be aged in wood for three years before it earns that name. Mr. Miller let me taste some, and I was astonished. Though fruit, of course, had played no role in distilling it, it tasted distinctly of pears and plums, like French eaux-de-vie.

The amount and type of peat burned helps to shape the taste of the whiskey. So does the character of the water; what is used at Glenfarclas flows down from a granite mountain called Ben Rinnes.

Glenfarclas is one of the last distilleries in private hands. Most of the others are owned by big international corporations with roots in France (Pernod Ricard), Japan (Suntory), Cuba (Bacardi) and Spain (Allied Domecq), as well as in England and Scotland. All operate in basically the same way, with subtle yet important differences.

Jim Cryle, the master distiller at Glenlivet, a muscular man with steel-gray hair, offered me insights into the process, along with sips of his 12-, 18- and 21-year-old Scotches, among others, of which the flowery, creamy 18 was my favorite. The following, he said, are among the most important determinants of flavor:

The size and shape of the still (tall ones, he thinks, are best) and how it is heated (by internal steam coils or fires); what kind of cask is used (old bourbon barrels, old sherry butts, new oak), how long the whiskey is kept in wood (once it is bottled, the maturing process stops), where (a damp cellar or a dry one) and by whom (the distiller or an independent merchant like Gordon & MacPhail or William Cadenhead).

Though not as much as with wines, the year of production has an impact, too. Macallan, a highly regarded distillery surrounded by fields of highly regarded Golden Promise barley, offers 26 vintages; an American recently paid $140,000 for a fifth of each. No wonder Macallan's stills are pictured on the reverse of the Bank of Scotland's £10 note.

—Elgin, Scotland, July 16, 2003

IRELAND

Much Too Good for a Bagel

It's a beautiful, beautiful animal," Frank Hederman said, holding up a silvery 12-pound salmon, bright of eye and red of gill, less than 10 hours out of the sea. "These guys swim 4,000 or 5,000 miles to get here. By comparison, the farmed salmon, the ones who live in those cages off the coast, are essentially goldfish."

Mr. Hederman smokes fish, which is a little like saying Steinway makes pianos. Savvy fish fanciers in England and Ireland—many of them, anyway—prize his smoked haddock, his smoked eel and especially his smoked wild salmon above all others. Which is what makes you shake your head a bit when you drive up to his place of work.

To get there you cross a small stone bridge onto Great Island, which sits like a cork in the bottle of Cork Harbor. Mr. Hederman, a fit, droll 40-year-old, has lived on the island all his life. You turn right at the evocative remnants of Belvelly Castle, built in the 13th century, towards Cobh (pronounced *cove*), once called Queenstown. Cobh is the port where hundreds of thousands of nearly penniless emigrants boarded ships in the late 19th and early 20th centuries for North America; it was also the *Titanic's* last port of call on her fateful final voyage in 1912.

You're not headed for Cobh itself, or at least my wife, Betsey, and I weren't. We turned off the road at a roofless house, with a bunch of ramshackle buildings behind it—just old limestone walls with corrugated metal roofs thrown over them. They had been the kennels for a previous owner's hunting dogs, Mr. Hederman told us.

But this is about flavor, not architecture, and Mr. Hederman's salmon has that in spades—a subtle, elegant, elusive flavor, with a slight tang of salt and an uncommon balance between the clean taste of the fish and that of the smoke, which sneaks up on you. The color, a pale, appetizing hue that reminded me of cantaloupe, and the texture, smooth without a hint of oiliness, are equally appealing. The three elements—color and taste and texture—are uniform right through the side.

It took time to get it right. Mr. Hederman rejected, right at the start, the chipboard sawdust many smokers use, because it contains glue particles as well as wood. He tried burning staves from old whiskey barrels, but that, he concluded, deposited too many tars and tannins on the finished product.

Some tarry substances are an integral part of smoking; deposited on the fish, they form a barrier against airborne bacteria, helping to retard spoilage. That has been the main goal of smoking food, as well as drying it, for thousands of years. Flavor is a fringe benefit.

But as he worked amid smoke from the oak, Mr. Hederman found dark stains on his forearms—"like a deep suntan," he said. Too much tar, he decided, and he switched to beechwood chips, which not only cut down the tars but gave the fish a milder flavor. Each smoker has favorite woods; Bill Casey of Ballycotton imports his from England.

Mr. Hederman also decided that laying fish in trays, to be smoked horizontally, tends to produce a hard crust on top, which results in turn in uneven penetration of the smoke. So he leaves the "collar"—a ring of cartilage at the "neck" of the salmon—on the fish when he guts them and beheads them. That way, he can anchor a hook firmly in the collar to suspend the fish for processing.

The hook, a fearsome-looking steel gadget, is called a tenterhook, by the way. It was adapted from the linen trade. So why do we say we're "on tenterhooks" when we're nervous? I asked the expert. Sometimes, he explained, things fall off, "but you never know when that's going to happen, so you're apprehensive."

You learn something new every day.

Like Norway, whose blandly flavored smoked salmon is favored by the French, and Scotland, where the smokiness is more pronounced, Ireland is famous for its smoked salmon, often eaten with buttered soda bread. We went to see Mr. Hederman partly because of the results of a comparative tasting arranged for us by Myrtle Allen, the owner of Ballymaloe House at Shanagarry.

All of the samples she provided came from County Cork, Ireland's gastronomic heartland. In addition to Mr. Hederman's wild salmon, which we liked best, we tasted (in order of preference) a wild salmon, almost mahogany in color, from Anthony Creswell in Timoleague, which had a punchy, oaky flavor and a texture we found just the slightest bit mealy; a farmed salmon from Mr. Casey of Ballycotton, coral in color, thrillingly silky in texture but, to us, one-dimensional in flavor; and a much less satisfying salmon from Sally Barnes in Castletownshend. It tasted slightly of petroleum; Mrs. Allen did not know if it was farm-raised or wild.

We're talking here, of course, about Atlantic salmon (Salmo salar), whose range runs from Portugal to Norway to Greenland and down the Atlantic Coast of North America, though the population has been reduced by pollution in the rivers where the fish spawn. Norwegian, Scottish and Irish smokers all use the same fish, as do those that produce the Nova so beloved of New Yorkers; smoked salmon from the Pacific Northwest is altogether different, made from fish—whether coho or chinook or sockeye—that are distant cousins of Mr. Salar.

Time was, the best Irish salmon, indeed most of the best Irish fish, was either exported or netted by Spaniards working here. Although surrounded by water, the Irish had no special affinity for fish and none of today's passion for freshness and quality.

"It was poor people's food, Friday food," said Maire Flynn, an owner of the Tannery, just up the coast from here, one of the best of Ireland's new restaurants.

Just so, Mr. Hederman said.

"When I was a kid," he said, "what was available was really appalling. The smoked salmon was low cost, high volume, so I decided when I was 22 to try for low volume, high value. I knew our main resources here, our coasts and our grasslands, were underused. But it took a certain amount of passion, a lot of years of being penniless and my wife leaving me not once but twice, to get this business built and running."

Now he smokes about 25 tons a year, an average of half a ton a week. Besides salmon, he does cheese, mussels, chicken, haddock, mackerel and eels. His eels, by far the best I have ever tasted, come from the local power company, which takes them from the warm water at the intakes of its generators.

Hederman products are available at the English Market in Cork, the Farmers Market in Midleton, near here, and the Temple Bar Market in Dublin, as well as Fortnum & Mason in London. They are not sold in the United States or on the Internet. But Mr. Hederman is happy to ship salmon by DHL Worldwide Express (about $30 a side, excluding freight; www.frankhederman.com). To limit the freight charges, it is best for several people to combine orders. Mr. Creswell's excellent smoked wild salmon from Timoleague can be ordered on the Internet at www.ummera.com; it is also air-freighted by DHL.

No one doubts that wild salmon tastes better, whether fresh or smoked. Because it gets so much exercise, it has none of the unpleasant fattiness that plagues some farmed salmon. But wild salmon may be legally caught and sold in Ireland for only 32 days a year—eight weeks of four 12-hour days each. During that period, which falls in June and July, Mr. Hederman smokes the shining fish as they are delivered by fishermen, who catch them on lines trailed from small punts when the fish gather offshore before heading upriver.

"They fish out of Ballycotton, Cobh and Cork," one of Mr. Hederman's workers said. "They all talk out of the side of their mouths in an impenetrable accent. I'm from Dublin, and I need subtitles to understand them."

The rest of the year, Mr. Hederman and his colleagues in the trade have to rely on farmed salmon or frozen wild salmon, which works fairly well, if it is frozen fast enough and soon enough after it is caught, though there is always some damage to the fish's cellular structure. Lately, improved salmon raised organically in deep-water cages in Bantry Bay, where it develops muscles struggling against the strong tides, has begun to come on the market.

Salting, an intermediate step, cures and preserves the fish, helping to kill bacteria and to draw moisture from the fish. At Mr. Hederman's Belvelly Smoke House, coarse-grain Spanish salt is poured sparingly onto the split salmon, left there for four to six hours, then washed off. Next the sides go into a drying room, where a fan pulls fresh air across them.

Inside the smokehouse, the beechwood chips smolder in a barrel, which contains the smoke. Mr. Hederman built the smoker to a design he picked up in Scheveningen, a Dutch port and resort town near The Hague, from a man who had brought it from Germany.

How long the fish stay inside depends on the temperature outside. At Christmas, which is not only the coldest time of the year but also the busiest at Belvelly, the salmon can take up to 35 hours to finish smoking.

"You start with the best raw material you can get," Mr. Hederman said, as if the whole process were easy as pie, which it obviously is not. "The rest is just salt, smoke and time."

—Cobh, Ireland, October 25, 2000

EUROPE

FRANCE

Taillevent

The Paris restaurant Taillevent (named in honor of the author of the first cookbook ever published in France, in 1365) has stood near the top of the world's gastronomic pecking order for a very long time. André Vrinat opened it at 30, rue St.-Georges in Paris in 1946, having served in the Resistance in the Loire Valley during World World War II. It won its first Michelin star in 1948, moved in 1950 to the magnificent 19th-century town house of the Duc de Morny at 15, rue Lamennais, not far from the Arc de Triomphe, won a second star in 1954 and reached the apex, with three stars, in 1973. It has stayed there ever since, during "32 years of anxiety," as Jean-Claude Vrinat, who joined his father in 1962, remarked recently over lunch in one of his luxurious private dining rooms.

Maybe he should stop worrying. No other current three-star Paris restaurant has held on to that distinction as long, and only three places in the provinces have done so—Paul Bocuse and Troisgros in the Lyon region and the Auberge de l'Ill in Alsace. In my judgment,

Taillevent is the best all-around restaurant anywhere, taking into consideration not only the food but also the décor, ambiance, service, value for money and wine list.

When I told Vrinat as much, he answered with typical drollery, "Some people think so, but in my opinion, Taillevent is the greatest restaurant in the rue Lamennais." The rue Lamennais, exactly one block long, boasts exactly one restaurant: Taillevent.

The food produced by Alain Solivérès, the latest in a succession of chefs who have manned Taillevent's kitchen, bears a strong resemblance to that turned out by Claude Deligne, his most illustrious predecessor. Little affected by the latest food fads, simple and thoroughly grounded in tradition, it stands well back from the cutting edge, but it does not shrink from the modern and the inventive. My main course at lunch, the tiny loin and tinier rack of succulent rabbit, served on puff pastry in the style of Moroccan *pastilla*, with shallots, winter radishes and Cremona mustard, was typical—original but neither far-fetched nor overwrought. I also tasted the latest version of a Taillevent classic, tarragon-flavored lobster sausage, currently served with a light star anise emulsion rather than the cream sauce of yore. It was spring, so the food struck a light, Mediterranean note; in fall, it turns towards the north. At dinner later the same week, golden frogs legs arrived on a marvelously smooth, risottolike bed of plump grains of herbed *epautre*, or spelt. That was followed by memorable baby lamb from the Pyrenees, the loin and the chops uniformly pink from the center right out to the edges, the meat packed with lamby flavor, tender but firm-textured. The delicious innards were served on a skewer. "My kind of food," Vrinat said. "Simple. You can see what you're eating." When the cheese came—no showy trolley, just two wicker trays—it was Vrinat's kind of food, too, perfectly ripe specimens of well-known varieties, except for *olivet cendre*, a soft cheese with a spicy aroma from the village where his father lived during the war. The rest of that night's diners—an elderly French couple celebrating their 59th wedding anniversary where they had celebrated 30 others, a group of Japanese businessmen, five jolly Americans from San Francisco, a table of Portuguese—seemed as delighted as I.

In fact, it is Vrinat's taste, his perfectionism, his refusal to settle for second-best that propels Taillevent. "Taillevent is my mistress," Vrinat told me with a rueful smile. Unlike most of today's most renowned restaurateurs, he is a front-of-the-house man, a manager rather than a cook, but no chef works harder. At 69, he arrives at his office at 7:45 a.m. every day, weekends included, to deal with mail and requests for reservations, which he personally controls. He takes great pride in the fact that Taillevent is the least expensive of Paris's ten three-stars, and that it has always made a profit even though, unlike others, he has no backing from a hotel group or a Champagne house in meeting his payroll (22 employees in the kitchen, 21 in the dining room, to look after about 70 clients at lunch and 70 more at dinner). Taillevent serves a four-course menu at lunch for $85, not including wines, and seven-course degustation menus for $160 and $220, again not including wines. The average tab per person at lunch is $145, the average tab at dinner is $230, including both service and wine. Business is brisk; weeknight reservations must be made six to eight weeks in advance, and Friday-night bookings a full three months ahead.

Vrinat glides around the floor five days a week, lunch and dinner, greeting guests, taking orders and inspecting plates. Slight, balding, elegantly tailored and imperturbable, he never intrudes or raises his voice. Often, though, he allows a feline little smile to play across his face, by way of letting people know they should enjoy themselves. His place is "a restaurant, not a cathedral," he says. He likes to hear laughter there, not whispers.

The same relaxed but exacting approach is taken by the second in command in the two dining rooms, Jean-Marie Ancher, who started at Taillevent three decades ago at 16 and has never worked anywhere else, and by Marco Pelletier, the 30-year-old sommelier, Canadian-born and largely self-taught. Captains and waiters wear business suits, not dinner jackets or uniforms, further enhancing the informal atmosphere. Although he has been redecorating the restaurant almost continuously since he took over, Vrinat never achieved the precise look he wanted until last year, when a softer, predominantly beige color scheme was introduced, the handsome oak paneling and Classical pilasters were lightened and a pair of 17th-century carved wooden geese from China, which the boss found in a Paris antique shop, were given a place of honor on the low divider between the dining rooms. To the dismay of his wife, Sabine, Vrinat drives a 16-year-old car, but he is an insatiable art collector. He is also obsessed with light, which he considers 80 percent of a restaurant's décor, and in the latest refit he replaced traditional chandeliers with squarish, startlingly modern custom-made brass fixtures. They automatically adjust to match the light outside—brighter on a sunny afternoon, dimmer on a wintry night.

After maybe 25 meals at Taillevent, stretching back 40 years—Taillevent is not an every-month sort of place—two incidents stick in my mind. One demonstrated Vrinat's utter lack of pretense. Some time ago, I was eating lunch with an acquaintance who considered himself the day's, perhaps the year's, most important customer. When Vrinat excused himself to move on to another table, my companion protested, and Vrinat responded firmly if courteously that he wanted to talk to some of his first-time customers. After lunch, he told me, "This may be the only three-star meal some of them will ever eat, and I can't let them go back to Omaha or Clermont-Ferrand and tell their friends that the *patron* only talks to the big shots." The other episode showed Vrinat's uncanny instinct for divining a client's wishes. "What for dessert, then?" he asked me at the end of our recent lunch. "Guess," I parried. *"Baba au rhum,"* he replied at once, unerringly picking the one dessert among the 11 on the menu that I coveted most. When I asked him how he knew, he eyed my ample figure and said, "Oh, you look like a *baba* man."

Taillevent's menu is fastidiously laid out on a stiff ecru card, 26 by 19 inches, folded once, with the first courses (usually eight), fish dishes (six) and meats (eight) on the front, the desserts on the back. A selection of 300 or so wines is listed inside, predominantly carefully aged Bordeaux and Burgundy (Château Pétrus 1985 costs $1,925) but also including less grand French bottlings, among them a Bergerac, a Petit Chablis and a Bordeaux Supérieur for $34 each. A dozen wines from other European countries and from the New World are also offered, including a trio from California.

But that's only the beginning. The full wine list encompasses 2,500 labels, and Vrinat bought 45,000 bottles of the great 1998 Burgundy vintage alone. It is an old house tradition, inspired by Raymond Baudoin, the legendary founder of the *Revue des Vins de France*, one of Andre Vrinat's great supporters in the early days. But things might have been different for the Vrinat family, and its scion might now be buying California wines for an American restaurant. Henri Soule, who came to the United States just before the war and ran the celebrated Pavillon in Manhattan for many years, tried to persuade the elder Vrinat to come with him. But his wife had died when their children were very young, and his mother, who looked after them, was unwilling to make the trip. "If he had gone, I'd be an American," Jean-Claude Vrinat said. As things turned out, Taillevent's first customer was Ridgeway Knight, an American ambassador, and he has been followed by thousands of other Yanks (although at a time when the dollar was all-powerful, Vrinat imposed a temporary quota on Americans to avoid them inundating his restaurant).

Vrinat retains an abiding fondness for the United States. He does not visit it often, but in 2002, Taillevent's 50th anniversary party was held at the Gramercy Tavern in New York, owned by Danny Meyer, for whom Vrinat has served as a mentor and a role model. I even spotted him at lunchtime once (in a sports shirt!) at Blue Smoke, Meyer's barbecue joint. Elegant he may be, a snob he most decidedly is not, this Mr. Taillevent.

Paris, November 1, 2005

Visiting an Old Friend, Finding
a New Radiance

Nothing is harder in the gastronomy game than reinventing a restaurant. Nothing is more necessary.

Décor gets tatty, chefs die or retire, cooking styles change. Even at the elite establishments awarded three stars by the *Guide Michelin*, the hyperconservative guardian of French culinary tradition, standards can sag and ratings can suffer. Restaurants that had three stars for years—Baumanière, Lasserre and Meneau, to name three—now have only two.

But change too much too fast, and you risk losing what made you great in the first place.

Which makes what has happened here in Roanne all the more remarkable. Troisgros, the restaurant that put this provincial city on the global map of gourmandise more than three decades ago, has in the last few years radically changed the way it looks and the way some of its food tastes, without sacrificing the familial warmth and the clean, fresh, unaffected approach to cooking that first won it renown.

More than 40 years ago, Christian Millau, the food critic, hailed the cooking of the brothers Jean and Pierre Troisgros as "simple and pure and good." This year's edition of the *Gault Millau* guide, which he helped to establish, restores its top rating, 19 out of 20, to the restaurant, now run by Pierre's son Michel. It had slipped to 18. "It's necessary to rediscover Troisgros," the guide says, rattling off the names of some of Michel's new creations, but noting that the restaurant still lives by "the truth of the market," as it always has.

Before his devastatingly premature death at the age of 56 in 1983,

Jean told me that "cooking is three-quarters shopping." Today, there may be star anise in the strawberry napoleon, ginger and cumin and slices of jalapeño in the aubergine in lime jelly, *harissa* on the saddle of lamb and explosive Japanese spices in the bouillon used to poach the plaice, but the focus remains squarely upon the basic materials and not upon the flavorings added by the chef.

There is no cause to protest that the internationalization of the menu is a sin against the culinary gods. French chefs borrowed from the cuisines of their country's overseas possessions, like Martinique and Pondicherry, as early as the 19th century. Escoffier has a recipe for shrimp curry. The borrowings were limited to a few dishes, as are those on exhibit in Roanne today.

Yes, Troisgros today owes a great deal to Tokyo, where Michel cooks for several days every year and owns boutiques in several Odakyu department stores. He admires traditional Japanese chefs, he said, because "they spend a whole lifetime mastering a complex art and arrive at an extreme simplicity."

But it owes just as much to Jean and Pierre Troisgros, including many of the classic dishes that they developed, and to California. Michel worked at Chez Panisse in Berkeley in the winter of 1978, as part of a tour of the world's great kitchens, including Girardet in Switzerland, Comme Chez Soi in Brussels, the Hotel Connaught in London, Michel Guérard in southwest France and Taillevent in Paris. Who else but a soul mate of Alice Waters would specify on his menu the breed of pig from which his succulent pork chops come (Black Bottom), as well as the place where the pigs are raised (St.-Yrieix in Limousin)?

La Maison Troisgros is indisputably Michel's show now. Pierre, who rather resembles Oliver Hardy, is as round as a medicine ball at 73. Ever jolly, he chats a lot with clients and chums, often in the restaurant's garden, which is shaded by box and bamboo planted in giant terra-cotta pots. He stays out of the kitchen most of the time. But when Michel is away, he said, "I help out a bit, so there will be a Troisgros in the kitchen, as always."

One of the things he talks most about is his pride in his family, starting with Michel, a short, dark, lively man of 40 with beetling brows, and continuing through Michel's siblings—Claude, his older brother, who runs the classiest restaurant in Rio de Janeiro, and Marie, who owns Gravelier, an elegant place in Bordeaux, with her husband.

Michel's wife, Marie-Pierre, has had as large a role as her husband in reshaping the family's main place of business, which today bears no resemblance whatever to the simple inn that Michel's grandfather Jean-Baptiste bought in 1930. With the help of gifted young architects and designers, she changed the look of its reception rooms, its dining rooms and its bedrooms, propelling them all into the 21st century.

To tell the painful truth, most French three-stars are remarkably ugly. Luxurious, of course, but filled with awful furniture, banal fabrics and third-rate paintings. Gold-plated faucets are a specialty. Troisgros was never that bad. At the beginning, it was too plain to be offensive. A modernization program in the '70s produced a gleaming, efficient kitchen with refrigerators innovatively tucked beneath the work counters and a welcome view of the garden for the chefs. But it also produced a jazzed-up dining room that was too cold, too calculated, too chromium.

Upstairs and down, the old has been swept away in favor of a sober and elegant modernism. Pattern has been banished, except for a few bold stripes; intense reds, maroons, mustards and olives lend warmth to floors and furniture. Every detail is minutely considered and, of course, luxurious, but not by dint of swag and gilt; here the technique is discreet understatement, and the vocabulary is leather, bronze, rare woods, fine linen and beveled glass.

Again, the influence of Japan is inescapable. The team in the dining room includes not only several grizzled, good-humored men who have worked here for years, but young women wearing stunning black pinaforelike smocks designed by Yohji Yamamoto. "Roanne has moved to the suburbs of Kyoto," one of the old-timers joked, clearly delighted by the transformation.

Troisgros has always catered to, and depended upon, a local as well as a national and international clientele. Unlike other celebrated restaurants like Bernard Loiseau's at Saulieu, George Blanc's at Vonnas and Paul Bocuse's near Lyon, Troisgros lies well off the autoroute linking Paris and Provence.

But it lies at the center of a food-loving region where most people, as Michel Troisgros put it, "would rather go out to dinner than take a trip to the Caribbean." One day last July, amid tables of traveling businessmen and vacationing Germans and Americans, there were a couple of big groups of locals in shirtsleeves and simple cotton-print dresses, laughing and gossiping their way through some celebration or other as the good Beaujolais flowed on.

"The spirit here is young," Michel said. "The style is today, not Louis XII, but this is still a family place, with a family-style welcome. And we're the only three-star in France with a public bar, where you can walk in off the street and have a drink."

It must have been 1966 or possibly 1967 when I first ate chez Troisgros. I was driving through the Beaujolais hills when a heavy snow started falling, and I lost my way for a while. By the time I regained my bearings I found myself a few miles from Roanne, which, the Michelin guide informed me, had a pretty fair restaurant—one with two stars, hence "worth a detour."

Naturally, I detoured.

Roanne struck me then, and still does, as an underwhelming place. A city of about 45,000, an hour northwest of Lyon, it makes textiles, like Lyon. It also makes tanks, like Lima, Ohio. But it was predestined to have a great restaurant, with the beef of Charolais to the north, the wines of Beaujolais to the east, the cheeses of the Auvergne to the southwest and the salmon from the Allier and the Loire, which flows right through town.

The restaurant that fulfilled Roanne's destiny, which I located after several false starts, was a decidedly funny-looking place, painted salmon pink, across from the railroad station. (At one time, I later discovered, it had styled itself the "Hôtel Moderne, face à la gare.") The dining room was more subdued, with a small bar tucked into one corner and a lot of rather plain wooden furniture, but everyone was having a fine old time, especially a sturdy, elderly gent with tinted glasses who seemed to know everyone there. That turned out to be Jean-Baptiste Troisgros, the strict but merry paterfamilias.

When I asked for the wine list, I heard Jean-Baptiste murmur to one of his cronies, "Let's see whether the rookie knows anything." I ordered a '71 Bonnes-Mares, which was pure luck. Bonnes-Mares proved to be one of Jean-Baptiste's favorite Burgundies, and that bottle served as my passport into the family circle; after dinner I found myself talking shop with Jean and Pierre. But first, I got down to business.

I ate my way through the house specialties: *pâté de grives*, made from thrushes; a scallop of salmon with sorrel sauce, invented here and copied everywhere, but not with such a perfect juxtaposition of slightly sweet fish and slightly sour herb; a thick little fillet steak topped with a medallion of bone marrow and a sauce made from Fleurie, one of the best Beaujolais; and a potato gratin, mystifyingly described on the menu as "Forezienne" in style. Only this year did I learn that the Forez is the fertile plain south of Roanne.

After the spuds came the cheeses, and after them, ice creams, sorbets, fresh and stewed fruits, fruit sauces and other temptations, which you could combine as you liked, called *"le grand dessert."* It, too, has been very widely imitated.

Remarkably, every item on that list remains on today's menu at La Maison Troisgros, with the single exception of the pâté, which decades ago was a specialty of the chef Fernand Point. None of them tastes the least tired. If you order the salmon it comes on a plate that informs you that the dish was developed in 1960. The pâté? I couldn't get anyone to tell me whether it has disappeared because thrushes are scarce or because it is now considered ecologically insensitive to sacrifice songbirds to the whims of gastronomes.

After my first visit to Troisgros, I went back as often as I could. Pierre began greeting my arrival by scat-singing a personalized version of the "Marseillaise"—not "ba-bum-ba-bum" but "pa-pomme-pa-pomme"—*pomme* being the French word for "apple," of course. Jean took me on his early-morning rounds of area farmers, from whom he bought fruits and vegetables and small game birds that they had shot.

He also introduced me to single-vintage Cognacs, which he much preferred to the big commercial blends, and when we finished sampling several from his immense collection, very late at night, he would often suggest that we conclude with *"un Beaujolais Américain"*—a cold Coca-Cola.

Having won its first Michelin star in 1955 and its second in 1965, Troisgros gained its third in 1968. But the family never put its nose in the air, and never outgrew its regional identity. When Gerard Cortembert, the chef at Le Cep, a much-admired village restaurant in Fleurie in the Beaujolais, died suddenly at 40 one day in 1990, my wife, Betsey, and I happened to be at Troisgros, and Pierre dispatched us to take his condolences at once to Chantal Chagny, the restaurant's owner.

Jean and Pierre occasionally tolerated my klutzy presence in the kitchen, cleaning and peeling and chopping. I remember a staff lunch of chicken legs, roasted to a golden turn with plenty of garlic, and a late supper of scrambled eggs with sea-urchin roe, whose creamy magnificence nearly made me swoon.

The brothers were lionized for a time, at home and abroad, as champions of the almost universally misunderstood nouvelle cuisine, which was all about lighter sauces and letting the natural flavors of foods come through, and never about raspberry vinegar and kiwis or reducing calorie counts. Curnonsky, the self-styled prince of gourmets who reigned over French gastronomy between World Wars I and II, said it perfectly: "Food should taste like what it is."

That was also the philosophy of Fernand Point, who helped revolutionize French cooking at La Pyramide, his restaurant at Vienne, south of Lyon, and trained a whole generation of French chefs, including Paul Bocuse, Alain Chapel, Louis Outhier and the Troisgros brothers. They slaved in the master's kitchen and filled their free time with pranks. Once they painted the postman's bicycle pink while he enjoyed a glass too many as Point's guest. Another time they disassembled the grandstand for Vienne's Bastille Day parade and put it back together backward, so the spectators faced away from the marchers.

You can almost sense the great man's ghost looking over Michel Troisgros's shoulder in certain dishes, like a translucent *raviolo* of sugar peas, in which almonds enhance the sweetness of the peas, or an exquisite tenderloin of lamb, unexpectedly enlivened with a shower of grated orange zest, or a simple roasted cherry tomato, perfectly peeled and bursting with candy-sweet flavor.

As always, cheeses come in profusion, highlighted for me on our last visit by one I had not known, called Brebis du Lavort, a rich sheep's-milk delicacy from Puy-de-Dôme, in the Auvergne. It is shaped like a *Kugelhopf*, the Alsatian cake. Desserts flavored with jasmine tea and mandarin orange followed, then heaps of tart, juicy red currants and peaches poached with verbena, and miniature pastries, including a jewel-like blueberry tart, and homemade chocolates and five kinds of macaroons, until even a single-minded trencherman like me could go no further.

—*Roanne, France, September 12, 2001*

● ●

RACK OF LAMB WITH CLOVES
(Adapted from Troisgros)
Time: 1 hour 15 minutes

    2 racks of lamb, each with 6 ribs, about 1½ pounds each
    Olive oil
    20 cloves
    Sea salt and freshly ground black pepper
    2 shallots, peeled and minced
    1 tablespoon unsalted butter
    1 tablespoon red wine vinegar
    2 tablespoons sauvignon blanc or other dry white wine
    1 tablespoon Worcestershire sauce
    1 bouquet garni (fresh bay leaf, thyme and parsley tied in
       cheesecloth)
    1 teaspoon fresh lemon juice, or more as needed

1. Preheat oven to 425 degrees. Using a flexible, sharp knife, trim most of the fat from the racks of lamb. Coarsely chop the fat,

and place in a small roasting pan. Rub with olive oil, and roast until the fat is crisp and has released its liquid, about 15 minutes; do not turn off oven. While fat is roasting, use the tip of a knife to lightly incise two shallow, parallel cuts about 1 inch apart across the chops. Cut five crosswise incisions, about 1 inch apart, to make a grid pattern. Insert cloves where lines intersect. Season racks with salt and pepper to taste, and set aside.

2. Sauté shallots in butter until translucent. Remove roasting pan from oven, and discard crisp fat. Add shallots, vinegar, white wine, Worcestershire sauce and ½ cup water. Stir well to deglaze. Transfer sauce to a small saucepan, and add bouquet garni. Place over medium-low heat. Simmer 20 minutes, adding water if necessary to keep about ½ cup of liquid in pan. Remove from heat, and season to taste with olive oil, lemon juice and salt and pepper. Strain sauce and keep warm.

3. Lightly rub a large roasting pan with olive oil. Add lamb racks and roast 15 minutes. Remove from oven and set aside.

4. Preheat a broiler. Broil the lamb racks just until well-browned, turning once, about 1½ minutes on each side. To serve, cut each rack into chops, and place two chops on each of six serving plates. Circle the chops with sauce, sprinkle with salt, and serve.

Yield: 6 servings

SALMON WITH SORREL SAUCE
(Adapted from Troisgros)
Time: 30 minutes

1⅓ pounds center-cut salmon fillet, skinned and boned
2 shallots, peeled and minced
½ cup fish stock or bottled clam juice
1 cup Sancerre or other dry white wine
1 tablespoon vermouth

1¼ cups heavy cream

3 ounces fresh sorrel leaves, trimmed of tough veins

1 teaspoon fresh lemon juice, or more if desired

Salt and freshly ground black pepper

1 tablespoon butter

1. Cut salmon into four pieces of equal size, then cut each quarter into thirds, for a total of 12 slices. Place each piece between wax paper, and flatten gently with a mallet just until they are of even thickness. Set aside.

2. In a medium saucepan, combine shallots, fish stock, white wine and vermouth. Place over medium heat, and simmer until reduced to a glaze on bottom of pan. Add cream, and continue to simmer until sauce thickens, about 5 minutes. Tear sorrel leaves into large pieces, and add to pan. Add lemon juice and salt and pepper to taste. Remove from heat and keep warm.

3. In a nonstick sauté pan, melt butter over medium heat. Season the skinned (less presentable) sides of the salmon with salt and pepper to taste, and place in pan seasoned side up. Sear about 25 seconds, turn and sear again about 15 seconds; fillets should be rare in center.

4. To serve, spread sorrel sauce equally among four large, warm plates. Place three overlapping slices on each plate. Serve immediately.

Yield: 4 servings

• • • • • • • • • • • • • • • • •

Finding Perfection in a Lumpy Little Round

It was more than 35 years ago, alas, when I first visited La Pyramide in Vienne, south of Lyon, the great restaurant where Fernand Point trained so many of today's three-star French chefs. I was in the formative years of my career as an eater, still relatively slim, as yet unacquainted with 12-course tasting menus and uninstructed in the catechism of gourmandise.

But I was eager to learn, and M. Point's widow, Mado, proved an enthusiastic guide, leading me from trout braised in port through the famous *marjolaine* cake. Along the way, she introduced me to Condrieu and Côte Rôtie, her husband's wines of choice, and poured, with my coffee, a glass of crystalline eau-de-vie from a bottle that had somehow got a pear inside it.

The whole experience remains fixed in my memory, including the masses of orange gladioli in one corner, the biggest flower arrangement I had ever encountered, and the dogs under several tables, the first I had ever seen in a proper restaurant. Nothing so impressed me that day, however, as the cheese Mme. Point chose: a disk three inches in diameter and an inch thick, white with a slight blush of beige.

"St.-Marcellin," she announced. "It was M. Point's favorite. You won't need anything else."

Roaming later through the hallways of that august establishment, I examined the dozens of framed menus posted on the walls, mementos of great and not-so-great occasions when a head of state or a local alderman or a gourmet club had visited. In almost every instance, M. Point had served one and only one cheese: St.-Marcellin.

From that day to this, it has been my favorite, too—as good a reason for visiting the gastronomically rich area centered on Lyon as the region's celebrated restaurants, like Bocuse and Troisgros, Pic and Blanc and Chapel.

For it is no great traveler, this firm little package with (at its best) such unctuous insides. I have eaten pretty fair Roquefort in Hong Kong and delicious vacherin in Italy and more than acceptable Cheddar in the United States, to name three other obvious candidates for the title of the World's Greatest Cheese. But precious few prime St.-Marcellins are to be found more than a hundred miles or so from their birthplace in southeast France.

There are exceptions, of course, but not very many. Patrick Rance, the monocled Englishman who was to cheese as Izaak Walton was to fishing, had this to say: "What reaches most corners of the outside world is a stodgy, white, pasteurized misrepresentation of the real thing." Unfortunately, that includes most—but thankfully not all—of the St.-Marcellins you are likely to find in the United States.

St.-Marcellin is a village of 6,500 people in the valley of the rushing River Isère, which tumbles down from the Alps past Grenoble to the Rhône. To get there, you turn off the A7 motorway at Tournon and head east through pear, apricot and peach orchards that were brightened by glorious fields of sunflowers on the July day when my wife, Betsey, and I made the trip. (The Isère Valley also produces the eau-de-vie *de poire* that Mme. Point used to serve.)

The mountains, whose north face is covered with snow even in midsummer, loom picturesquely above St.-Marcellin. With streets and squares shaded by plane trees and cedars, the village itself has a certain bucolic charm, especially on market days, when merchants set up their stalls around an old bandstand with ornate stained-glass panels bearing the names of Wagner, Rameau and Rossini. We did a little business with Marie-Claire Reveillac, a plump, smiling woman who comes into town three times a week to sell the St.-Marcellins that she makes on her farm near the neighboring hamlet of St.-Vérand.

When I asked her how long she had been making cheese, she replied, "All my life," which may be why she does it the old-fashioned way, using a little goat's milk along with the more usual cow's milk. Laid out on her table were disks of various ages—some made a day or two before, some aged a week or two, some aged so long that they had the consistency of a hockey puck.

For less than $2, we bought a couple from the middle of the range. It would be gratifying to report that they were memorable, but they weren't; they were decent, but nothing special. They lacked the finishing touch.

Like children, St.-Marcellins need a careful upbringing to show their stuff. That process is best carried out by what the French call an *affineur*, or "maturer," or, sometimes, an *éleveur*, which means much the same thing. Like artisanal cheeses themselves, traditional *affineurs* are a threatened species; there are probably not more than a couple of dozen left in all of France. Those who survive buy directly from the cheese maker or from a regional co-operative and bring their cheeses to perfect ripeness in their own cellars, which are often made of limestone.

In the case of St.-Marcellins, the proper amount of aging, which varies from cheese to cheese, produces a supple exterior crust and a slightly runny, magnificently rich interior—not as strongly flavored as Maroilles, the sweaty-socks cheese, or even Livarot, the most pungent of the fine Normandy cheeses, but voluptuous and by no means bland. The texture and the ivory color remind me of Devon cream.

At its very best, St.-Marcellin has a mild smell, with no trace of ammonia or putrescence in the aroma, and a fine, slightly nutty, distinctly lactic taste that builds up to a little bite at the end. *"Il pique la langue"*—it stings the tongue—I once heard a happy client cry in a bistro in Lyon.

According to local legend, the future King Louis XI, then a young man, was out hunting one day in 1445 when he got lost and encountered a giant bear. He shouted for help, and two woodcutters came to his rescue, taking him to their cabin and feeding him bread and a local cheese. It was love at first bite. St.-Marcellin was on Louis's table in the Louvre Palace by 1461, warranted by the king, and for 500 years now it has been known as a king among cheeses.

That much history I knew. At the Cheese Museum here, we learned that St.-Marcellins are first mentioned in manuscripts written in 1251. At that time they were made exclusively from goat's milk, and so they were until a law passed in 1936 authorized the addition of cow's milk. From 1980 on, the cheeses have been made exclusively from cow's milk, mostly from a brown-and-white breed called Montbé-liard (although a few stubborn peasants like Mme. Reveillac pay little heed to regulations).

More than 700 farmers in the two hilly departments that lie between Grenoble and Valence, the Drôme and the Isère, produce milk for St.-Marcellin. Many of them are clustered around villages just up-river from here, like Izeron, Têche, Vinay and Rovon. Vinay is particularly charming, with old stone-and-timber houses; it calls itself "the walnut capital," and people there and elsewhere in the Isère Valley eat walnuts with their St.-Marcellin.

Cheese is made on 15 farms and in 12 small-scale factories—35 million St.-Marcellins a year, consuming roughly 15 million gallons of raw milk.

St.-Marcellin is a source of fierce local pride. A dozen years ago, after a copious lunch cooked by the modest, extravagantly talented Jacques Pic at his plain little restaurant in Valence, I complimented the maître d'hôtel on one of the dishes—quail, as I recall—and Betsey, a cheese maven from way back, complimented him on the St.-Marcellin. We were already in the car, ready to head south, when Suzanne, M. Pic's hospitable wife, ran out and handed Betsey a small foil-wrapped package.

"St.-Marcellin," she said breathlessly. *"Pour votre pique-nique."*

The manufacturing process is simple: the milk is heated, rennet is added and the curd is poured into round molds pierced by holes that allow the whey to drain off. It is fed to pigs. Unmolded, the disks are salted on each side and placed on racks to mature.

Enter the *affineur*. Combining experience, a watchful eye and a sensitive nose, he or she knows what to buy and when to send the cheeses to market. The best St.-Marcellins go on sale in summer and early fall, flavored by the tender young grasses the cows nibble in spring. Eat one in its prime and you will exclaim, as did the French actor Sacha Guitry, who was once an habitué of La Pyramide, "St.-Marcellin, I understand now why they canonized you."

There are plenty of good *affineurs* in the region, and some farther afield. The two best in Paris, in my view, are Roger Alleosse at 13, rue Poncelet, near the Arc de Triomphe in the 17th Arrondissement, and Marie-Anne Cantin, at 12, rue du Champs de Mars, across the Seine in the Seventh. The crowds of customers that often spill out into the street at these two shops are testimony enough to their proprietors' skills. Both of them make a specialty of St.-Marcellin.

Jean d'Alos in Bordeaux is equally gifted, as is Philippe Olivier in Boulogne-sur-Mer on the English Channel. His cheeses grace the tables of many of the best restaurants in London and the English countryside, and they are also served at Buckingham Palace.

But the champion *affineur* of St.-Marcellin, without doubt, is Renée Richard, a vibrant blonde who runs a stall in the Lyon central market with her daughter, also named Renée. At the grand gastronomic temples of the region, at Jean-Paul Lacombe's wonderful Léon de Lyon and at most of the workingmen's *bouchons* like Chez Georges and Chez Hugon, you will be served St.-Marcellins wrapped in her trademark red-and-white paper. Even Mme. Richard's Lyon rivals, such as the excellent Alain Martinet, whose yellow-and-black-wrapped cheeses are a little sourer and a little less sharp, might grant her primacy.

Few people can resist her brassy, wise-cracking charm any more than her cheeses, and few want to. In his book *The French at Table* (William Morrow, 1985), the American writer Rudolph Chelminski tellingly describes her as "the Wife of Bath incarnate."

Unhappily, there is no American Renée Richard. Most St.-Marcellins that reach these shores are made from pasteurized milk; federal regulations forbid the importation of raw milk ("*lait cru*") cheeses less than 60 days old, and St.-Marcellins are pretty far gone by then. Ed Edelman, the owner of the Ideal Cheese Shop in Manhattan, has stopped selling the pasteurized version, which he dismisses as "glorified cream cheese," but he and a few other zealous cheese merchants around the country occasionally manage to stock the real thing.

"Most of what we can get is not worth having," said Max Mc-Calman, the cheese director at Terrance Brennan's two New York restaurants, Picholine and Artisanal, and the co-author, with David Gibbons, of *The Cheese Plate* (Clarkson Potter, 2002).

"It's been a while since I've tasted a raw milk St.-Marcellin, but I can certainly remember that it was one of the best things I've ever had in my mouth. It's a cheese of the future for us, I would hope, and in the meantime, it's a good excuse to go to Lyon."

—St.-Marcellin, France, September 5, 2001

The Bouchons of Lyon

L yon is France's gastronomic capital—a preeminence that almost certainly stems from its privileged geography. Alpine streams to the east supply the city with pike, trout and crayfish. The Dombes plateau, to the northeast, abounds in game, and the plain of Bresse, beyond that, produces France's finest chickens (which, with their red combs, white plumage and blue feet, are also its most patriotic). Due north lie the vineyards of Beaujolais, which yield fruity, inexpensive red wines that are best drunk young, while just a few miles farther, the Mâconnais region turns out fresh, lively white wines—most notably Pouilly-Fuissé. The unremarkable village of Charolles, to the northwest, gives its name to the best French beef cattle—the white Charolais, raised in the pastures surrounding the town. Superb cheeses are close at hand, too: Fourme d'Ambert, Cantal, and St.-Nectaire from the Auvergne, southwest of Lyon; St.-Marcellin, rumored to have been King Louis XI's favorite, from the Isère to the southeast. The Rhône Valley, south of the city, produces great wines (Condrieu, Côte Rôtie, Hermitage) and fruit (raspberries, cherries, peaches, pears), and in the days before railroads and superhighways, the Rhône itself provided a convenient route north for good things from Provence and Italy—which may be why macaroni and cheese became a popular dish in Lyon and why so many Lyonnais seem to have black hair and olive skin.

Cooks in and around Lyon learned long ago how to burnish these choice raw materials, and their descendants have obviously not forgotten the skill. At the moment, the *Guide Michelin* scatters a total of 13 stars around the city and its immediate vicinity, with many more within 50 miles or so. However, good eating in Lyon is by no means necessarily Michelin-starred, a fact vividly illustrated by the city's unique *bouchons*—the tiny, animated, artless places that keep the basic culinary traditions of Lyon alive.

Bouchons are bistros of a sort, but with even more limited menus. Their décor tends to be modest to the point of austerity. Some have paper tablecloths, and some don't change the cutlery between courses—but the food and ambience of any good *bouchon* will warm the coldest heart. The majority of these establishments are family-run, and most of the chefs are women—the spiritual descendants of Mère Brazier, Mère Fillioux, Tante Paulette and other female master chefs who contributed so much to the glory of Lyonnais gastronomy earlier this century. *Bouchon* prices are always reasonable: Ample menus for $25 or so (including service, but not wine) are common.

Unless they get off the autoroute for a Michelin-starred meal, travelers tend to rush past Lyon on their way between Paris and the South of France. This is nothing new. On his famous journey in 1838, Stendhal skipped Lyon entirely—and in 1882, Henry James, en route from Orange to Mâcon, contented himself with some soup at the train station. "By no means an ideal bouillon," he reported, though he did admit to finding it "much better than any I could have obtained at an English railway-station." If only he'd found a *bouchon*, James could probably have tasted a *quenelle de brochet*—a succulent pike dumpling, perhaps with crayfish sauce. He could also have sampled one of Lyon's many memorable tripe dishes, typical in their transformation of unpromising ingredients—especially *gras-double à la lyonnaise*, in which the linings of ox stomachs are cooked with parsley and onions, and *tablier de sapeur*, which is *gras-double* breaded and fried. This latter dish takes its name from the original *tabliers de sapeur*, the leather aprons (which these edible *tabliers* are said to resemble in shape) that French firemen once wore. The food served in *bouchons* is almost always based on humble ingredients. While local temples of gastronomy may feature foie gras, lobster, truffles, morels and vegetables snatched prematurely from the cradle, *bouchons* are more apt to make do with cocks' combs, calves' feet, pike, cardoons, lentils and Swiss chard.

The first *bouchons* were 19th-century Lyonnais equivalents of our truck stops—taverns where grooms and coachmen paused for a glass and a bite after brushing down their horses. Since *bouchon* means "cork," I had always assumed these places took their name from the many bottles that were uncorked inside. One Lyon Internet site seems to give that derivation an official seal of approval: In earlier times, it notes, most inns insisted that customers eat as well as drink, and the rare establishments willing to serve drinks without food displayed corks outside. At least one present-day *bouchon*, Au Petit Bouchon (popularly known as Chez Georges), still shows a popping cork on its sign. But something about this explanation always bothered me: To begin with, *bouchons* are at least as famous for their food as for their drink. And corks don't figure much in *bouchon* tradition anyway— since the wines that *bouchons* serve are usually decanted from the cask into corkless, heavy-bottomed bottles (the famous pots invariably filled with Beaujolais or modest Côtes-du-Rhône). Upon inquiring further into the matter, I discovered that *bouchon* can also mean the handful of straw used for rubbing down horses and that a more likely explanation is that taverns with facilities for horses hung bundles of straw over their doors as insignia, the way bakeries hung out pretzels.

That Lyon's *bouchons* have survived in an era that worships the big and the bold is a miracle of sorts—but in fact they have more than survived. Though mostly tucked into side streets and known mainly to their regular customers, they have positively flourished. I wonder if this is not largely because Lyon tends to throw away less of the past than most cities do. It has, to be sure, its modern buildings—perhaps most notably, Jean Nouvel's brilliant, barrel-shaped reconstruction of the city's opera house. But its pre-18th-century arcades, called *traboules*, and its lack of Parisian hustle and bustle create a pleasantly dated atmosphere. As the writer Bill Bryson observed not long ago, it is "as if the Lyonnais found the 1950s to their liking, and decided to stay there."

Today, most of the best *bouchons* are clustered near Lyon's City Hall, in the middle of the Presqu'Île, the three-mile-long peninsula, washed on one side by the Rhône and on the other by the Saône, that extends through the middle of the city. One classic here is Café des Fédérations, which the Lyonnais affectionately refer to as Les Fédés. Long, skinny sausages hang like stalactites from the ceiling of the establishment, while Raymond Fulchiron, the droll, dapper boss, and his cheeky waitresses keep up a steady line of chatter with the regulars as they serve prodigal plates of food—things like assorted charcuterie; salads of curly endive, eggs and chunks of salty bacon (the famous *frisée aux lardons*); servings of the custardy little chicken liver mousse known as *gâteau de foies blonds de volaille*; and three-inch disks of St.-Marcellin—a creamy and slightly tangy cow's-milk cheese with a brownish rind that is the quintessential *bouchon fromage*. Though hardly required, it is considered quite acceptable for each diner to eat an entire St.-Marcellin at a single sitting—which calls for minimal sacrifice. (Les Fédés is an exception, but at many Lyon *bouchons* the St.-Marcellin appears swathed in a white wrapper identifying it as having been ripened by Renée Richard, the best cheesemonger in the city.)

During the G-7 international economic summit in Lyon the summer before last, my wife and I decided that we needed something more nourishing than windy speeches about trade and slipped away for lunch at Chez Hugon, the domain of Arlette and Henri Hugon. A few tables, an old bar, a kitchen the size of a broom closet—that's all the place is. But Arlette, blond and outgoing, will offer you a perfect *bavette* (a delicious, albeit fibrous, skirt steak) with shallots, an exemplary *blanquette de veau* (veal stew), a juicy chicken with vinegar—or, in summer, her simply magnificent stuffed tomatoes.

Because the streets were closed off for the conference, we were alone in the restaurant except for a handful of tradesmen. One fixed gutters, I remember—and all took their duty to knife, fork and wineglass very seriously indeed. Between bites of Arlette's glorious *boudin aux pommes*—blood sausage with starking apples that become golden and unctuous after having cooked over a low flame for an hour and a half—we laughed constantly. I don't know if it was the jokes or the peppery Côtes-du-Rhône that Henri kept flowing, or both.

One of my favorite *bouchons*, on the rue du Garet, is Chez

Georges—a jolly, cluttered little place where about 25 customers can sit elbow-to-elbow to devour classic Lyonnais cold hors d'oeuvres on the order of *museau de boeuf,* a salad of pressed calf's muzzle; cold chicken liver salad; or pink, unsmoked *cervelas* sausages served with lentils dressed with a tart vinaigrette—followed by gratinéed tripe or by andouillettes (sausages here made from both tripe and veal intestines), their edges charred by the grill, served with a creamy mustard sauce. In winter, at lunchtime only, a sublime pot-au-feu is sometimes offered—and for dessert, all year round, there is a moist, sweet apple tart, worthy of three stars. Michel Deschamps, the burly proprietor, works the front of the house in a blue apron, spreading joy. (One hot day, guessing that we were American, he thoughtfully brought ice to the table for our water.) "A *bouchon,*" Deschamps says, "needs a soul." The chef is his wife, France—a sinewy, peppy little woman who looks as if she grew up in small-town Ohio. In fact, she comes from Normandy, proving, I suppose, that you don't have to be born with Beaujolais in your veins to cook in the Lyonnais style.

La Meunière, not far from Chez Georges, is a picture-postcard *bouchon,* with chipped paint, hanging lamps with white glass shades, faded oilcloth on the walls and—down the center of the room—a long buffet filled with more than a dozen salads. Proprietor Maurice Débrosse, who used to be Paul Bocuse's maître d'hôtel, suggested I try the lentils with a spoonful of *cervelle de canut,* which literally means "silk weaver's brain"—an herbed cream cheese that was once a favorite dish of the silk weavers who helped make Lyon rich. (The delicacy is called a "brain" either as a commentary on the reputed intelligence of workers in the silk trade or because it was thought to look like brains when squeezed through a pastry bag.) Débrosse was dead right about that, and about every other thing that he recommended—including a beef fricassee with pearl onions, a cheesy potato gratin, a parade of sinful desserts both typically Lyonnais (crème caramel) and less so (a cold soufflé, flavored with Chartreuse, more Bocuse than *bouchon,* and a cherry *clafoutis*—a specialty of the Limousin region, far to the west), and eventually a brilliant eau-de-vie *de poire* from the Distillerie de Malleval, in the Ardèche. The sweetness of the place is exemplified by the welcome I saw extended one day to an old woman, obviously not rich, who came in alone, a bit unsteady on her pins, ate like a bird and drank only a glass or two of wine. The waiters, smiling and solicitous, danced attendance upon her as if she were a duchess or a princess.

Lyon's Michelin-starred chefs, including Paul Bocuse, tend to hang out at a *bouchon* called Val d'Isère, across the Rhône, right by the back door of the city's bountiful central market. They gather there for coffee every morning, alternately paying court to Bocuse and needling him. Sometimes they eat a *mâchon*, the Lyonnais workingman's breakfast of pâtés, terrines and various cold meats washed down with Beaujolais instead of coffee. Val d'Isère also serves a tasty pig's foot, stuffed with ham and parsley, as well as sausage cooked in Beaujolais.

For me, though, nothing in this part of Lyon matches À Ma Vigne, a cubbyhole that's lovingly tended by Joséphine Giraud and her son Patrick. The place has dim watercolors on the walls and only three tables in its front room. Joséphine and her sister Francine cook tripe with the best of them, but almost everyone orders three other dishes in succession: *moules maison* (mussels cooked in white wine), the best steak and fries in town (the former awash in a *beurre noisette* the color of hazelnuts, the latter satisfyingly crunchy), and an exquisite lemon tart, its filling made with exactly four ingredients: lemons, sugar, eggs and butter. The Girauds opened on January 1, 1960, and have changed nothing since. I hope they never do—and since this is Lyon, they probably never will.

—*Lyon, France, December 1997*

A Prime Kettle of Fish

I t is made from bony, spotty, spiny little fish, each one uglier than the last, creatures that cooks in many places disdain as trash. It was originally a product of peasant thriftiness, created by fishermen as a cheap way to feed themselves and their families with the fish their customers would not buy. But one man's trash is another man's treasure, and the fish have become so expensive that today a carefully fashioned bouillabaisse can cost $40 or more.

All along the corniche that follows the coast south from Marseille, and tucked into the *calanques* or coves beyond that, you come across small, little-heralded restaurants, some of them not much more than shacks, few of them paid great heed by gastronomic guides. At such spots, like Le Rhul and Chez Aldo, Chez Fonfon and Le Lunch, they take their bouillabaisse seriously. So, too, on the Riviera, at glossy Bacon in ritzy Cap d'Antibes and fashionable Tétou, smack on the sands in Golfe-Juan.

I have tasted no more sumptuous rendition than the one I devoured on Bastille Day at L'Épuisette, a spare, good-looking one-star establishment in a weathered wooden building hunkered down on the rocks near the tiny fishing village of Vallon des Auffes. The excellence of the bouillabaisse was only enhanced by the view across the pale green waves to the Château d'If, made world famous by Alexandre Dumas père in *The Count of Monte Cristo.*

Nothing that you can put in a bowl or on a plate catches the magic of a summer's day on this bewitching coast quite as perfectly as bouillabaisse. Every spoonful evokes the fresh sea breezes, the clean, salt-seasoned air and the brilliant light that so captivated Cézanne when he came to the neighboring village of L'Estaque to paint.

Marseille, the venerable, polyglot, slightly louche Mediterranean port city where bouillabaisse was invented, is currently in the midst of a major revival, sparked in significant part by the new TGV Mediterranée, an ultra-high-speed train that links the city with Paris in only three hours.

The Marseillais have their roots everywhere, in Algeria and Armenia, Vietnam and Italy, Greece and Lebanon. The city's ethnic wards have produced, in addition to some particularly cunning criminals, luminaries like Zinedine Zidane, Europe's premier soccer star, and Serge Tchuruk, chairman of Alcatel, the big French telephone combine. Almost 1.5 million people live here, making this France's second city.

Wherever their parents or grandparents came from, they take superior seafood as their birthright. For them, as Daniel Young writes in his authoritative new book, *Made in Marseille* (HarperCollins, 2002): "Bouillabaisse is not just a fish soup. It is a way of life."

There is plenty of ill-made bouillabaisse, of course, even here. Frozen fish, all too often the wrong fish, go into it, and you can get a serving for $10 or $15. But that's like using canned clams in clam chowder.

But the real thing—the rust-brown, tomato- and fennel-based, saffron-infused bouillon, enriched by dollops of a fiercely garlicky mayonnaise called rouille, followed by a plate of fish that have been cooked in the bouillon—is well worth the hunt.

In her hymn to Marseille, *A Considerable Town* (Alfred Knopf, 1978), M. F. K. Fisher confessed to being haunted by the place and asserted that "freshly caught fish, scaly or in the shell, have a different flavor and texture and smell there than in any other port in the world." Which may be why, with only a few exceptions, the farther you go from Marseille, the harder it is to find anything that approaches the true taste and aroma of the planet's very finest kettle of fish.

Norman Douglas, the English novelist and epicure, who spent a career celebrating the joys of Capri and other parts of southern Italy, where the fish are not exactly second-rate, attributed the primacy of

Marseille's bouillabaisse to its cooks as well as its raw materials. It is delicious, he once declared, "because it's cooked by the French, who, if they cared to try, could produce an excellent and nutritious substitute out of cigar stumps and empty matchboxes."

Controversy clings to bouillabaisse like barnacles to a ship. Is it a soup? Perhaps not, because the broth and the solids are eaten separately. Is it a stew? Surely not, because a stew by definition is cooked very slowly, and bouillabaisse must be boiled furiously to achieve an amalgamation of olive oil with water and wine. It is best described as a fish boil, which is what its name seems to imply. *Bouillir* means "to boil" in French, and *peis* means "fish" in Provençal, but inevitably that etymology is challenged, too.

Although it was once a one-pot meal, cooked in a cauldron over a wood fire on the beach, bouillabaisse is usually prepared today in two stages for greater richness. First, a stock is made using tiny fish or fish heads (often including the bulbous head of a monkfish), vegetables and seasonings. After the stock has been strained and well laced with saffron, it is used to poach larger fish and sliced potatoes.

But exactly what fish? You will not be astonished to hear that learned authorities disagree. Even the authoritative Bouillabaisse Charter of Marseille, signed by 11 restaurateurs in 1979, does little to clear up the confusion. The French version of the document specifies that at least four fish from a list of eight must be used if the bouillabaisse is to be considered authentic, and it includes monkfish, which the English version omits. The English version lists only six fish, and it includes skate, which the French version omits.

Sometimes a small crab or two or a spiny lobster goes into the pot, and to the immense irritation of purists restaurants more interested in ostentation than culinary tradition sometimes toss in a baby lobster. In days past, a *cigale de mer*—literally, a sea cricket, which looks like a stubby, snub-nosed lobster—was often used, but those are harder and harder to obtain.

Oily fish like mackerel and sardines are seldom encountered; their flavor is far too intense. I have, however, eaten bouillabaisse that included species on neither official list, including *sar*, a silvery member of the bream family, with black stripes across its body; *pageot*, another bream, with silver-pink skin marked with pale blue dots, and even *loup*, the regal (and dauntingly expensive) Mediterranean bass. Rules are made to be broken, here as elsewhere.

Be that as it may, nobody in the South of France would dare attempt a bouillabaisse without *rascasse* (scorpion fish, a cosmetically challenged denizen of the coastal rocks) or its cousin *chapon*; *galinette* (gurnard, another notably unpretty rockfish); conger eel, for body, and *vive* (weever), a small, elongated fish with poisonous spines that provides a certain mellowness of flavor. Nor would many choose to omit onions, garlic or orange peel from the list of seasonings, and many include a dash of Pernod for aroma and a Scotch bonnet pepper for bite.

Fresh *rascasse*, gurnard and weever are almost impossible to find in American shops and markets, or for that matter in those of northern Europe, a circumstance that gives rise to yet another controversy. Can an acceptable version of bouillabaisse be fabricated hundreds or even thousands of miles from its Mediterranean homeland?

No, says the great British food writer Elizabeth David; it is "useless" even to try. Clifford A. Wright, the scholarly American authority on the food of the Mediterranean, begs to disagree. "I have never been attracted to this kind of food snobbery," he writes. "It can be done. I have done it."

A. J. Liebling, who liked a good fight as much as a good feed, jumped into this argument in 1962 in the pages of *The New Yorker*. Noting that his first bouillabaisse, eaten in New York in 1918, had for him overshadowed the end of the First World War that same year, he said the waiter who served it to him had described the dish as a poor substitute for the real thing. "It lacks *la rascasse*," the waiter said. "It is like a watch without a mainspring. The *rascasse* does not exist except in the Mediterranean." Liebling then goes to comically extravagant length to demonstrate that on the contrary, the *rascasse* or its kissing cousins do live in American waters. He sprays ichthyological Latin across 11 pages without ever quite claiming to have tasted an American *rascasse* or a bouillabaisse made with one.

Mr. Young is with Mr. Wright. After much experimentation, he suggests the use of monkfish and John Dory, two of the fish on the official list that are fairly readily available in the United States, plus American substitutes like red mullet, red snapper, halibut and porgy. But he acknowledges that the result is only an approximation.

At least it's a closer approximation than the one turned up by the food historian Alan Davidson in a book called *An Odd Volume of Cookery*, published in Boston in 1949. Its authors, Louise Lane Morrisey and Marion Lane Sweeney, offer a helpful, fish-free recipe for bouillabaisse that begins, "Put one can tomato soup and one can pea soup in top of a double boiler and heat."

Tradition dictates that bouillabaisse be served as well as cooked in two stages: first the broth with croutons rubbed with garlic and topped with rouille, followed by the fish, which must be shown whole on a platter to the diner, according to regional etiquette, then filleted and returned.

Tradition is honored at L'Épuisette, except that both rouille and the paler, less peppery aioli, another garlic mayonnaise, are offered with the croutons that go into the liquid. When the rouille is stirred in, it creates a seductive brick-red streak. On the day of our visit, five fish and a quantity of sliced boiled potatoes, moistened with more cooking liquid, were presented after I had polished off two bowls of bouillon.

The fish were all that could be asked for—tender, juicy and infused with the complex flavors of the broth: *rascasse* and *chapon*, monkfish tail and conger, and most delectable of all, a subtly flavored weever.

Only one restaurant in the atmospheric sailboat-filled Vieux Port at the heart of Marseille has in recent years served a bouillabaisse that did justice to the spankingly fresh fish sold every morning along the Quai des Belges, which closes one end of the port. That one, Le Miramar, benefited from the shopping prowess of its owners, Pierre and

Jean-Michel Minguella, but they have just sold it, so beware. In any event, the décor is pure 1960s kitsch, complete with photos of semi-forgotten film stars, and dishes other than bouillabaisse can be quite catastrophic. The chef likes to douse some of his fish—I kid you not—with mandarin orange liqueur or with Bailey's Irish Cream.

Michelin gives a star to Le Miramar in the current guide, which will no doubt be withdrawn because of the change in ownership, and another to Michel, on the corniche. For me, Michel, also known as the Brasserie des Catalans, is more Disneyland than Marseille, with fish displayed in a beached dory and a waiter dressed up as Popeye, although the bouillabaisse is worthy enough.

So best head elsewhere—to the little places farther down the corniche, or farther afield to Tétou or Bacon. I particularly like the latter, where the owners, the Sordello brothers, still do the buying, with Adrien heading for Cannes every morning and Étienne heading for Antibes. Last summer, my wife, Betsey, and I shared a bouillabaisse there with our old friend Jovan Trboyevic, the retired proprietor of several of Chicago's notable restaurants.

Like most, the bouillabaisse at Bacon has its minor idiosyncrasies. Whole garlic cloves come to the table, to be rubbed on the croutons at the client's discretion, and the potatoes are served whole, not sliced. The day of our visit, the spread included *rascasse*, weever, monkfish, John Dory and red mullet, all delicious, though not, if memory serves, quite as thoroughly imbued with the essence of the broth as this summer's superlative fish at L'Épuisette.

Splashing happily through my meal, I thoroughly stained the beautiful white tablecloth. Étienne Sordello, a cheerful man in a short-sleeved blue shirt, commented drily when he stopped by, "I see you like rouille."

We drank a Bandol rosé, from the Domaine de Pibarnon, near Toulon; people at other tables were drinking other classic accompaniments to the dish: white wines like Bellet from the hills near Nice and Cassis from a town near Marseille. After such a feast, Bacon's celebrated homemade mille-feuille seemed a bridge too far, so I settled for a passion fruit sorbet.

Not everyone in Marseille likes bouillabaisse, as Guillaume Sourrieu recognizes. Mr. Sourrieu, the wizard who presides over the stoves
at L'Épuisette, serves not only the classics, including grilled fish as
well as bouillabaisse, but also creative dishes that show the influence
of Spain, Italy, Asia and especially North Africa.

More adventurous than I, Betsey was rewarded with a delightfully original tagine of sole, a delicate Moroccan stew cooked under a conical ceramic cover that included, in addition to the fish,
poached quail's eggs, small potatoes, asparagus and baby purple
artichokes.

The chef of the hour in Marseille, Lionel Lévy, a 29-year-old disciple of
Alain Ducasse, serves no bouillabaisse at all at his restaurant, Une Table,
au Sud. When I asked him why, he replied, "It doesn't attract me." But
then, he was born in Toulouse, in southwest France, far from the sea.

What he does serve is choice, and he serves it in a second-floor dining room overlooking the Vieux Port. (The Samaritaine Café, the prime
people-watching and pastis-sipping spot in Marseille, is downstairs.)

On a bright, breezy day, Mr. Lévy produced for our table an astonishingly fresh gazpacho, accompanied by anchovy beignets; Nice-
style stuffed vegetables—round zucchini, zucchini flowers and
artichokes—that lifted that grandmotherly dish to new heights
through the use of shredded oxtail in the stuffing; and langoustines
of perfect tenderness.

Nominated this year by the *Gault Millau* guide as one of the "greats
of tomorrow," Mr. Lévy also likes to mix sweet and savory in a salmon
crumble with ginger and lime, for instance, and a tomato stuffed with
fruits and nuts for dessert.

No high jinks like that for Aimé Bergero, the single-minded former diver who presides at Tiboulen de Maïre, a simple little pavilion
with dry-stone walls that stands in a savage landscape at the point
where the coastline turns east. Short, stocky and full of beans at 65, he
spends his days in his motorboat, touring Marseille's fishing villages,
buying the best line-caught fish he can find.

They never touch ice and are never gutted. Back at the restaurant, they are rolled in *fleur de sel de Guérande*, a moist, gray sea salt from Brittany, and without further ado plopped onto a formidably hot lava-rock grill. The crackles and pops of the fish skin are audible in the dining room.

For starters there are mussels, or fish soup ("No saffron," Mr. Bergero told us; "too expensive"). When the fish emerges from the kitchen, it is presented whole for your admiration, then deftly filleted by Mr. B, who works his plain tile-floored, whitewashed room in blue jeans. A succulent tomato slice, grilled with herbs, is the sole side dish and a lemon the sole flavoring agent. Salt and pepper stand on the sideboard but stay there, and all requests for olive oil are rebuffed.

More rigor: If the mistral blows too hard for small boats to venture out of port, Tiboulen de Maïre does not open until the wind subsides. And when all of the morning's fish is gone, the restaurant closes for the day.

Moistened only by its natural juices and those oozing from the tomato, our magnificent three-pound *daurade* (a golden bream) made us understand why Mr. Lévy had urged us to drive down to Tiboulen de Maïre.

Mr. Bergero knows, as well as anyone in Marseille, the essential point about fish: where it is caught, how it is caught and when it is caught matters at least as much as how it is cooked in determining how it will taste.

Marseille, France, August 7, 2002

● ●

FISH STOCK FOR BOUILLABAISSE
(Adapted from Made in Marseille*)*
Time: 1 hour and 15 minutes

    ¼ cup olive oil
    2 large onions, peeled and minced
    2 leeks (white part only), minced

4 cloves garlic, peeled and crushed

3 pounds small to medium fish heads (gills removed) and bones

6 to 8 ripe plum tomatoes, quartered

Peel of 1 orange, cut in strips

1 celery stalk, cut in pieces

2 sprigs fresh thyme

3 bay leaves

¼ to ½ teaspoon cayenne pepper

2 teaspoons pastis (Ricard or Pernod)

Salt and freshly ground black pepper

4 quarts boiling water

1. Place a large heavy-bottomed stockpot over medium heat, and heat olive oil. Add onions and leeks. Sauté gently until softened but not colored, about 10 minutes. Add garlic, and continue to cook until onions and leeks are very soft and breaking apart, another 5 to 10 minutes. Put 4 quarts water in a large pot, and bring to a boil.

2. Meanwhile, add fish to onion mixture, raise heat to high, and stir vigorously until pieces begin to fall apart, 7 to 10 minutes. Add tomatoes, orange peel, celery, thyme, bay leaves, cayenne and pastis. Season with salt and pepper to taste. Reduce heat to medium, and sauté for 10 minutes.

3. Add boiling water; simmer 25 minutes.

4. Working in small batches, pass mixture through a food mill or strainer. Press fish scraps and vegetables through with the aid of the fish broth to ease flow. Allow to cool. Store refrigerated or frozen.

Yield: 4 quarts

BOUILLABAISSE

(Adapted from Made in Marseille)

Time: 40 minutes, plus 3 hours for refrigerating fish

3½ to 4 pounds mixed fish fillets (John Dory, red mullet, red
   snapper, porgy, pompano, striped bass, monkfish, grouper,
   hake), cut into 3-inch chunks

1 tablespoon pastis (Ricard or Pernod)

1½ to 2 teaspoons saffron threads, crumbled

¾ cup olive oil

Salt and freshly ground black pepper

4 quarts Fish Stock for Bouillabaisse (see recipe on page 244), plus
   a few tablespoons for rouille

2 pounds (about 3 large) potatoes, peeled and cut into ½-inch
   slices

Cayenne pepper

4 to 5 cloves peeled garlic

1 small hunk country bread, crust removed

1 baguette or loaf of country bread, cut into slices and dried in
   oven

1. In a large mixing bowl, combine fish, pastis, two pinches of saffron and ½ cup olive oil. Season lightly with salt and pepper,
   and mix well without breaking up fish. Cover, and refrigerate for
   at least 3 hours.

2. In a large heavy-bottomed stockpot, combine fish stock and
   remaining saffron. Place over high heat, and bring to a rapid
   boil. Add potatoes, and cook for 7 minutes. Add largest, firmest
   pieces of fish from the bowl, and cook for 2 minutes. Add remaining pieces of fish, and continue to boil until potatoes are
   tender, about 10 more minutes. Season with salt, pepper and cayenne to taste.

3. Prepare the rouille: Crush 2 to 3 cloves garlic, and use a mortar
   and pestle to mash with a pinch of cayenne pepper. Dunk hunk

of bread into 2 to 3 tablespoons hot fish stock, squeeze out liquid, and add to mortar. Mash well.

4. Take two to three slices potato from Bouillabaisse, and mash with pestle into a thick paste. Gradually add remaining ¼ cup olive oil, drop by drop, mashing mixture in a circular motion until thick and smooth. (If mixture breaks up, add a teaspoon or two of hot fish stock or a little more soup-soaked bread.) Season with salt and pepper to taste.

5. To serve, remove fish and potatoes from soup, and arrange on a large serving platter. Ladle some soup over fish, and keep warm. Rub slices of bread with 2 cloves garlic, and place in a dish on the table along with bowl of rouille. Have diners dab croutons with rouille and place them in soup plates. Ladle soup over croutons, and place a serving of fish and potatoes into each plate.

Yield: 8 to 10 servings

In a Glass, a Swashbuckler
Called Armagnac

To tell the truth, I don't remember when I had my first swig of Armagnac, but I know when I really fell for the stuff. It was a rainy day in the fall of 1971, or maybe 1972, at a restaurant in Villenueve-de-Marsan, a little crossroads town about halfway between Bordeaux and the Spanish border. The food was excellent (two stars in the Michelin guide, as I recall) and the wine copious. But it was the encyclopedic Armagnac list that bowled me over.

I was a semiretired war correspondent at the time, a two-fisted eater yet to learn the more recherché points of food and drink. I knew I was in the Armagnac-producing region, but I had no idea I was at the very heart of it, at the nexus, at the epicenter. It turned out that this place, called Darroze, was to Armagnac exactly as the Second Avenue Deli is to corned beef.

I was too green to choose intelligently among the 50-plus offerings, and too thirsty not to ask for help. So the kindly patron, Jean Darroze, picked an Armagnac for me that I found fascinating—bold, yet full of velvety finesse. When I said something subtle and worldly like *"Zut alors!"* he smiled, suggested I stay the night and asked me to his cellar.

To Ali Baba's cave, you might well say. I eyed, sniffed and tasted Armagnacs both young and very old, some dating back 100 years. Mr. Darroze showed me how to shake the bottle and watch the foam that formed; if it lasted too long, that was a sure sign, he said, that the booze had been doctored. "Notice how the aroma lingers in the glass even after the liquid is gone," Mr. Darroze said after we had sampled one bottle. *"C'est un vrai!* It's a real one!"

Today, the Darroze clan is the first family of Armagnac. One of Jean Darroze's sons, Francis, an international rugby star in his youth, spent three decades building up unrivaled stocks of the best his region has to offer. Armagnacs bearing a plain tan Darroze label slowly found their way onto the drinks trolleys of the best restaurants in Europe, and a few in the United States.

Francis retired recently, and his son Marc, 33, took over the family business. One of Francis's brothers, Claude, owns a classic restaurant in Langon, south of Bordeaux, offering a vast array of wines and Armagnacs, and his daughter, Hélène, owns a chic, innovative place on the Left Bank in Paris. Both have stars in the current Michelin guide.

Hooked by "le Roi Jean," as his friends called the patriarch, I have been happily tasting Armagnacs ever since. Almost without exception, I have found, the best ones come from the westernmost of the three Armagnac districts, known as Bas-Armagnac (the other two are called Haut-Armagnac and Ténarèze). The best of the best come mostly from a sandy area only 10 miles from east to west and 20 miles from north to south—from villages with evocative names like Labastide and Arthez, Hontanx and Le Houga, scattered along the border between the two most important Armagnac-producing *départements*, Gers and Landes.

Although Armagnac antedates Cognac by more than 200 years, having been introduced in the 16th century, it has had to play Avis to Cognac's Hertz for generations. The Cognac region, north of Bordeaux, is five times the size of the Armagnac region. Worldwide, Cognac sales are 25 times as large as those of Armagnac; in the United States, the ratio is 120 to 1. But in France competition is keener, with Cognac outselling its rival only three to one.

There are fundamental differences between the ways the two brandies are produced. For Cognac, wine is distilled twice, but for Armagnac, it is distilled only once, and at relatively low temperatures, which helps foster robustness of flavor. Cognac is aged in white oak, Armagnac in black oak with more pronounced tannins.

As a result, Armagnac is racier, rounder and fruitier than its cousin from the north, with an earthier, markedly more pungent aroma. Much of the best of it is sold unblended—the product of a single artisanal distiller in a single year, or vintage. Vintage Cognac is rare; skillful blends are the norm, usually produced by large *négociants*, or shippers. Armagnac, therefore, has more *"goût de terroir,"* as the French say. It is more rustic, and thus more identifiable with a single piece of land.

If a sip of Cognac transports the drinker to the lounge of a London club, a sip of Armagnac evokes the swashbuckling aura of D'Artagnan and his fellow Musketeers, who, like foie gras, rugby and bullfights, hold a central place in the culture of this part of France, which is known as Gascony.

This is a profoundly rural area, isolated from the main highways and rail lines of France. Its people cling to the old ways, and its undulating landscape has been little touched by the modern world.

As Montesquieu said of his beloved estate, not far north of this area, "Here nature is in its nightgown, just getting out of bed."

But as we drove west from Condom to Villeneuve-de-Marsan this summer, my wife, Betsey, and I passed fewer fields planted with vines than on past visits. More plots were planted with golden sun-flowers, destined for the oil mill, and tall green corn, destined to fatten ducks and geese.

According to some estimates, as little as 15,000 acres are now de-voted to growing the grapes used in distilling Armagnac. Thousands of acres, we were told by knowledgeable people, have been ripped out by small farmers in need of more reliable cash crops.

"People make Cognac for profit, but they make Armagnac for love," said Michel Guérard, the noted chef, as we sat in the garden of his Michelin three-star restaurant, Les Prés d'Eugénie at Eugénie-les-Bains, just outside the Armagnac zone. "Like Champagne, Cognac is a corporate drink, with tremendous marketing resources behind it. There have been several efforts to assemble big combines in Armag-nac, but no luck. Gascons just aren't joiners.

"More and more, sadly, Armagnac has become an esoteric drink, a drink for connoisseurs who have the patience to smell out good producers."

In fact, crisis grips the region. Sales of Armagnac are falling steadily.

"With the market in turmoil, Armagnac is becoming a depressing subject for many farmers to talk about," writes Charles Neal, a California importer of premium wines and spirits, in his excellent, privately printed 1999 study, *Armagnac: The Definitive Guide to France's Premier Brandy.* (Wine Appreciation Guild, 1999) "The financial compensations for products of the vine are extremely unpredictable."

The independent producers and their unblended, carefully aged spirits have been hardest hit; Armagnacs less than five years old now account for 85 percent of worldwide sales. The consumer, Mr. Neal asserts, "wants something that doesn't exhibit tremendous personality," so much Armagnac is reduced to 80 proof with water, rather than letting time and natural evaporation do their work, and sugar and other substances are added to "round off" the flavor.

But adulteration has undermined authenticity while helping sales only slightly. Social and political trends have hurt, as well.

"For me, Armagnac is the bijou of brandies," said Michel Trama, who stocks a dozen Armagnacs, including a half-dozen of the very best, at his restaurant, L'Aubergade, in Puymirol, east of the Armagnac region. "Historically, it's our regional drink. But not many people order it here anymore. If they're driving, they're afraid of the cops. And if they're not, they may order a whiskey after dinner, because it's chic.

"I sell a Cognac once a night, an Armagnac twice. It's depressing, but it's true."

A few independents have managed to swim against the tide, finding means to distribute high-quality Armagnac reasonably widely and to earn consistent if modest profits.

Among these are the Domaine de Jouanda at Arthez, owned by the de Poyferré family, which once owned part of Château Léoville-Poyferré, a second growth in the commune of St.-Julien in the Medoc; the Domaine d'Ognoas, also at Arthez, owned by the Landes government, where distillation is done in a magnificent copper still, made in 1804; and the Château de Lacquy, in the hamlet of that name, which has been in the de Boisseson family since 1711.

Annual output is small—at the Domaine d'Ognoas, only about 30 barrels of amber liquid, with aromas of vanilla, prune, cinnamon and licorice.

One domaine is linked to another by roads no wider than the driveways in American suburbs, often shaded by plane trees, with their distinctive dappled, two-tone bark. Some villages have unusual pyramid-capped church towers; others have squares surrounded by medieval stone arcades.

We stopped in Labastide, a charming village built in 1291, for coffee with two of the more colorful figures in the Armagnac trade, Marguerite Lafitte and her daughter, Martine. In the jolliest way possible, they teased us with tales of inexplicable Anglo-Saxon behavior— for example, how Armagnac samples sent to the United States were held up on one occasion by customs but cleared the next time when the container was marked, "Holy Water from Lourdes."

Naturally, Armagnac from the family's Domaine Boingnères was served with the coffee, though it was still early afternoon. One of the most intriguing was a rich, refined 1975 made wholly from colombard grapes, which Martine described as the grape of the future for Armagnac. It is more widely used for wines; *ugni blanc, folle blanche* and *bacco* are the more usual Armagnac grapes.

Bacco is the subject of considerable controversy. It is a hybrid, a cross between *folle blanche* and an American vinifera grape called noah, developed by and named for a local schoolteacher in the 1930s. European Community officials, hostile to hybrid grapes, are trying to outlaw its use; some producers argue heatedly that *bacco* alone can give Armagnac the full-blown character they seek. Others have torn out all their vines, as the Lafites did in 1991.

Although *négociants*, who buy and usually blend spirits produced by others, are less important here than in Cognac, there are several of consequence, including Samalens and Trépout. Some, like Janneau and Sempé, have undergone wrenching changes of ownership. But none can match Darroze, mostly because of the unusual way the firm does business.

Darroze does no distilling. It does no blending. Its trade consists of buying individual barrels from the finest artisan distillers when they become available, sometimes a barrel at a time, sometimes more—as in 1976, when Francis bought the entire stock, about 300 barrels, of the Domaine de St.-Aubin at Le Houga. That was the coup that made him famous.

Once the casks were kept in Francis Darroze's garage. Now 600 of them from 30 domaines, each chalked with the producer's name, lie on two levels in a modern *chai*, the older ones downstairs, where the atmosphere is humid, the younger ones upstairs, where it is drier.

As the Armagnacs are coaxed toward their prime, which he defines as roughly 25 years after distillation, Marc Darroze bottles that for which he receives orders, and no more. The producer's name goes on the label together with the vintage, as well as the firm's name. On a separate back label the date of bottling appears—a vital detail because spirits do not improve once they leave wood and enter glass.

"We get good stock," said Marc Darroze, who spent part of his apprenticeship in Sonoma County, Calif., "because we respect the little farmers who make it. We use their name, we never blend their stuff with someone else's, we use no water or additives. That's all very important to these guys."

Using up-to-date office systems, Mr. Darroze has brought the firm into the new century, strengthening sales in Britain, the United States and, recently, Russia. Two days a month, he drives into the backwoods, looking, as he said, "for barns with dark roofs," caused by the mold that grows as Armagnac evaporates. Sometimes he finds a widow who sells him a few barrels.

We tasted some old bottles together, including a 1965 from Eauze, which hinted delightfully of cacao and tobacco. That Armagnac, he said, "was the work of my father, and now I work for my son"—Clément, then just 20 months old.

—*Labastide d'Armagnac, France, September 18, 2002*

ITALY

The Crossroads Cooking of Trieste

In Italian gastronomy, as in Italian art, a few miles make all the difference. Trieste is only about an hour's drive east of Venice. But it is six miles from the Slovenian border and was once a place where Europe's three great civilizations—Latin, Germanic and Slavic—intersected. Stroll up the Corso Italia into the modern business center, and you'll hear people switching from Slovenian to Italian to German and back. Likewise, menus list goulash and *crauti* (sauerkraut) along with pasta and the same sweet, fresh fish that constitute the mainstay of the Venetian diet.

Roman in ancient times, the city belonged to Austria and then Austria-Hungary for more than 500 years. It was the Austro-Hungarian empress Maria Theresa who made Trieste the chief port of a domain that, by the middle of the 19th century, stretched from the Balkans north to Poland, from Romania in the east to northern Italy in the west. Coffee, black pepper, nutmeg, saffron, dates and other exotica from Africa and Asia flowed across Trieste's quays, along with outbound goods like central European paprika and caraway—and all these were taken up by local cooks. Strudels, baked but also boiled like pasta, entered the city's repertoire, as did gnocchi, most often stuffed with fruit and eaten as dessert. Italian food became an unmistakable element in the city's culinary mix, even though Italy did not take possession of Trieste (and the Istrian peninsula below it) until just after World War I.

Then, in 1946, Winston Churchill broadcast to the world the fate that had befallen Trieste: in an electrifying speech at Westminster College in Missouri, he said that an iron curtain had descended across Europe "from Stettin in the Baltic to Trieste in the Adriatic." Eight years later, Communist Yugoslavia relinquished its claims to Trieste in exchange for retaining most of Istria. Nevertheless, the cold war slowly cast the grand old city into the penumbra of obscurity. Once so cosmopolitan and influential, Trieste found itself at the far edge of the Western world, on a highway to nowhere.

While Venice and Florence and Rome were overrun by visitors, few foreigners ventured to Trieste. Those who did sensed a pall of melancholy shrouding the city—as much a part of its atmosphere as the bora, the fierce wind that periodically rakes its streets. Young people fled, and Trieste, like cold-war Berlin, became a town of old people living their lives in limbo.

When at last the cold war ended, Trieste again became a vital link between eastern Europe and western Europe, and fate eventually furnished a new leader in the person of Riccardo Illy—whose grandfather founded illycaffè, the famous coffee company, there in 1933. As mayor, Illy cleaned the handsome Hapsburg buildings in the city center, opened them to public use for concerts and meetings and created pedestrian precincts to revive street life. Along the way, he helped convince the people of Trieste that they had, in the words of his proud father, Ernesto, "a future and not just a past."

Today, now that the vast empire once served by Trieste's bustling port has gone, the city makes its living more from science than from shipping, with a major university and a series of research institutes scattered around town, dealing in theoretical physics, neurology, genetic engineering and space optics, among other things. Luckily—as is nearly always true—cultural traditions and landmarks have persisted long after the disappearance of the geopolitical circumstances that shaped them. Near the water are squares reminiscent of Prague's, as well as the Serbian Orthodox church of San Spiridione, whose soaring, powder blue dome would look right at home in Belgrade or St. Petersburg. The monumental piazza Unità d'Italia is wide open to the Adriatic, as if to symbolize not just Trieste's embrace of the sea but also its welcome to all comers—for the city's tolerance is proverbial: in addition to the Latins and Slavs and Germans who make up its core population, other peoples have arrived over the centuries from many parts of the globe, from Morocco and Egypt to Britain and France, to find both work and the freedom to live in peace. Today, nationalities are jumbled together in and around Trieste like boulders in a moraine. "But here," a Triestine of my acquaintance told me, "we have Bosnians and Serbs, Croats and Kosovars, and they don't slit each other's throats."

Such long-standing openmindedness has fostered a cuisine that reflects Trieste's vibrant past, and you'll taste it in kitchens both within the city and in the countryside nearby. Trieste itself has innumerable buffets, which are local institutions, often specializing in boiled meats, that bring together elements of the trattoria, the bar and the charcuterie. Then there are the cafes, which can stand comparison, in their number, their décor and the quality of their coffee, with those of Turin, Venice and Vienna. And, of course, there are any number of restaurants serving food influenced by Venice, Slovenia, Austria and Hungary.

Even at a tiny, working-class buffet like L'Approdo, near the piazza Goldoni, the variety of snacks is astonishing—salt cod and fritto misto from the steam table, a dozen hot and cold salads and a half-dozen meats sliced to order from the bone, including prosciutto di San Daniele from nearby Udine province, one of Italy's two great hams (the other is the prosciutto from Parma). The most famous of the buffets, Buffet da Pepi, serves boiled pork with strong horseradish (*cren* in the local lingo), hot sausages and *brovada*, which are autumn turnips soaked for 30 days in wine lees, then shredded and cooked. Antico Buffet Benedetto, not far from the train station, specializes in panini, elegant open-faced sandwiches. Some of these have typically Italian toppings, like salami or cheese, but others bear the unmistakable stamp of Mitteleuropa, like herring or *liptauer*, the Hungarian blend of cheese and paprika. Many buffets serve German beer on draft.

The cafe tradition in Trieste dates to the time of Maria Theresa, when Triestines began importing, roasting and drinking coffee. They have never lost the habit, perhaps partly because illy—which is generally (and to my mind justly) considered the best espresso in Italy and therefore the world—is roasted here and only here. In their literary associations, the cafes rival those of Paris. James Joyce, who lived in Trieste for the better part of 14 years, finished *Dubliners* and started *Ulysses* in Trieste cafes. Rilke, Freud and Italo Svevo also spent long hours at cafe tables.

The exquisite Pasticceria Caffè Pirona has a picture of a young James Joyce on one wall, looking tortured but natty in a straw boater and bow tie. It still sells Joyce's favorite confection, a horseshoe-shaped pastry called *presnitz*, full of walnuts, candied orange peel and raisins. Caffè illy offers not only superb coffee and chic, minimalist décor by the London-based architect Claudio Silvestrin, but also fine local wines and delicious small plates of food (pastas, ham smoked over cherrywood and sliced by hand, coffee-flavored bavarian cream). In the throbbing, more modern part of town stand a pair of local institutions. Tiled and spotless, Cremcaffè has a long chrome bar where up to 5,000 cups of coffee a day are served to clients standing two deep. In hot weather, people order tiny glasses of cold, unsweetened coffee, undiluted by ice cubes, with whipped cream on the side. Antico Caffè San Marco is the local showplace of Art Nouveau (called *stile* Liberty here); a richly paneled, L-shaped room with marble-topped tables, it is filled with chess players, newspaper readers and weltschmerz.

For a taste of the past that won't provoke a lament for the present, Suban, a mainstay of Trieste restaurants since 1865, is the place to go. Suban serves delicious grilled meats and dessert crepes (*palačinke*) straight from Vienna. But the don't-miss-it dish there is a

definitive version of the city's favorite soup: *jota*, a burly amalgam of
sauerkraut, pancetta, potatoes, beans and cumin seeds. A real bora
buster, that.

Trattoria da Giovanni is one of those restaurants someone has to
tell you about; there's no sign outside, and it's not in the guidebooks.
(My wife, Betsey, and I found it through Manhattan restaurateur
Lidia Bastianich, who was born in Istria, spent some of her girlhood
in Trieste and visits the city often.) But it is a great lunchtime favorite,
a plain, décor-deprived little room, jam-packed with men in suits and
little old ladies and utility workmen in fluorescent coveralls. Regional
wines are served from the barrels behind the bar, including an exceptionally fruity, tangy tocai vaguely reminiscent of ginger ale. The
food, cooked in a broom closet kitchen by two motherly sisters, is
notably light but full flavored—pasta with a graceful tomato and calamari sauce, spicy and tasting vividly of the sea; herby *polpettone*, or
meatloaf, so loose textured that only the chef's willpower seemed to
be holding it together; and a near-weightless *frittata* with beans, broccoli and carrots. I theorized that it must be a lot like what a good
Trieste home cook would prepare, and the businessman at the next
table said I was right.

There is plenty of good fish in Trieste itself, notably at Al Bragozzo
and at Al Bagatto, which produces a knockout fritto misto, completely greaseless, featuring minuscule shrimp and squid. But you
would make a mistake if you didn't head for Trattoria Risorta, in
Muggia, a little town with a Venetian-style campanile, across an in-
let from the city itself. Triestines say that the fish on their side of the
Adriatic tastes better than the fish on the Venice side because the sea
bottom near Trieste is rocky rather than sandy. I'm ready to believe
it after spending a long evening at this unpretentious trattoria, sampling Dante Bertoldini's pure-tasting sea bass (*branzino*) with chanterelles and his rich shellfish ragout, which includes plump, firm
crustaceans called *gamberi*. Seven inches long, they resemble langoustines. In the summertime, if you sit on the terrace by the sea,
you'll be checked out by a multitude of envious neighborhood cats.
No matter what the season, you will bask in the warm attention and

profit from the expertise of Signor Bertoldini, a tall transplanted Venetian.

At Savron, a small tavern near the hillside hamlet of Opicina, on the Slovenian border, the kitchen led us back to the days of empire. Michele Labbate, the dapper owner, whose dining room walls are hung with decorative plates and hunting trophies, plied us with beer from Villach, in Austria, and a menu listing dishes like thinly sliced veal with caper sauce, which shared a plate with a similarly thin slice of roast pork with anchovy sauce (a little too salty); bread dumplings (*Semmel-knödel*) with goulash; boar sausages; roast pheasant; and gnocchi stuffed with apricots and served with cinnamon and brown butter (a little too sweet). A zucchini-and-ricotta-stuffed strudel made for a light and savory first course at lunch. I couldn't help wondering what a Florentine or a Neapolitan (or an Italian-American) would make of it.

Another day, we visited Devetak, a trattoria (or *gostilna*, in Slovenian) 20 miles north of Trieste near Savogna, on a country road not far from Slovenia. We arrived in a somber mood, having just passed the immense World War I ossuary at Redipuglia, where 100,000 Italian soldiers, killed in months of now largely forgotten fighting along the Isonzo River, are buried. But the Devetaks cheered us immediately with wines from Agostino Devetak's amazingly diverse cellar and the inspired cooking of his wife, Gabriella Cottali.

It was hard to imagine a more heartfelt hospitality: the trattoria was being redecorated, so the Devetaks gave us dinner at their own table. Gabriella, dark-eyed and dimpled, brought out homemade bread and honest, rustic food with tongue-gnarling names and crystalline flavors—*frico* (fritters made with montasio cheese), *zlicniki* (goat cheese with olive oil and nuts), *mlinci* (oven-dried handmade pasta, sauced with butter, herbs and wild fennel), what she called "our old Sunday dish" (a juicy, meltingly tender shoulder of veal) and, for dessert, *struc-coletti* (walnut strudels). "It's just home cooking," said Cottali. "Maybe you won't like it." She needn't have worried.

—*Trieste, Italy, April 2002*

The Fresh Fish of Venice

L ook at this," said Cesare Benelli, brandishing a plastic bag with a slab of fish the color of raspberry Jell-O inside. "Mummified tuna. Nothing to do with our native fish. It's caught in Indonesia, treated with sulfites, then vacuum packed and shipped to Italy. It has no taste at all, but people buy it, because it's cheaper."

A silver-haired, Hollywood-handsome chef who owns Al Covo, one of the city's best restaurants, Mr. Benelli champions authentic regional ingredients, especially fish and shellfish from the Venetian lagoon and the inshore waters of the Adriatic. A few years ago, with like-minded restaurateurs, he organized an alliance dedicated to the preservation of local culinary traditions.

He had asked me to meet him underneath the 19th-century neo-Gothic arches of the Pescheria, the open-air fish market near the Rialto Bridge, to see for myself what he and his friends—the proprietors of holes-in-the-wall like Alle Testiere, as well as famous establishments like Da Fiore—are up against. And what visitors to this jewel-like city face as well if they wander heedlessly into one of the Serenissima's countless tourist-trap restaurants.

Tourists have been feasting on seafood here for generations, going all the way back to the participants in the 18th-century Grand Tour, and unscrupulous restaurateurs have been fleecing customers for just as long.

Yet at their best, the city's fish and shellfish are sublime—small, delicately textured and incomparably sweet, especially those from the outer lagoon's shallow, brackish waters, which are rich in plankton, fish eggs and other foods, and regularly scrubbed by saltwater tides.

260

The best is now increasingly scarce and costly, frighteningly so. Inevitably, inferior substitutes abound—farmed fish, foreign fish, frozen fish. I saw a farmed Dutch turbot on sale for $29.50, and a wild local turbot, of the succulent variety the Venetians call *chiodato* or "nailed," because of its bony, nailheadlike protrusions, priced at $59.50.

Mr. Benelli also pointed out defrosted octopus, farmed bay scallops from Scotland and worst of all, a shell game played with clams.

Vongole veraci ("*caparossoli*" in Venetian dialect) are cute little characters with two valves, indispensable to a proper dish of pasta with clams.

But the local population has been hard hit by pollution, much of it from factories and oceangoing ships, so Manila clams, seeded in the lagoon some years ago, are rapidly supplanting them. Coarser in texture, less subtle in flavor, with rounder shells, they cost a third as much and reproduce three times as quickly. It takes a discerning eye to tell one from the other in the market.

Pollution is only part of the problem. Overfishing has taken a toll, as well, although large sections of the region's fisheries are closed at different times for a month or two each summer, to allow stocks to regenerate. This is known as the *fermo pesca*. Fish farming and improved transportation have created fresh competition.

Now a new threat looms. Always precariously poised between land and sea—Ruskin famously warned that it had as much chance of surviving as "a lump of sugar in hot tea"—Venice is increasingly plagued by spells of *acqua alta*, the extrahigh tides that flood the city's streets and squares.

The sea level around Venice has risen by about four inches in the last century, which many Italian scientists attribute to global warming and the gradual melting of the polar icecap. The city has settled about five inches in the same period, partly because of the increased use of underground fresh water in the nearby industrial port of Marghera.

Scientists expect further rises in the sea level. So after decades of study, the government has begun to build a multibillion-dollar system of 79 movable barriers to seal off the lagoon at times when surge tides threaten the city. This will be necessary only occasionally,

engineers who planned the defenses insist, and the periods of clo-
sure at the three lagoon inlets will be brief.

Some environmentalists disagree, convinced the closures will be
longer, and they worry that the fragile ecology of the lagoon will be
changed forever.

For their part, chefs and fishmongers fret that the project will dis-
rupt the prime fishing grounds for the boats based at Chioggia and
Caorle. Those are located around the inlets where the salty water of
the Adriatic meets the less saline water of the lagoon, precisely where
the barriers are supposed to be built.

"It's a war, finding fresh, local fish," Mr. Benelli said. "Only 53,000
of us are left here, and I worry that we're losing our identity as Venetians. Much more than our fish—our collective memories, our dialect,
our culture, our flavors and our tastes."

Once upon a time, hand-lettered signs saying "*nostrano*," or "ours,"
meaning "local," guided customers to the choicest fish. Now such
signs may appear on boxes of crabs from Spain or John Dory from
Morocco—but not, of course, at the stalls of respected dealers like
Luca D'Este and Marco Bergamasco.

Their fish tend to be more expensive, but they are carefully labeled
with the Latin name, the exact sea zone they came from, as defined by
the United Nations Food and Agriculture Organization, and the name
of the fishing boat.

For the Venetians, water is the giver of life. Long ago, initially out of
sheer necessity, they became a species of sea creature themselves.

The Pescheria is small, but the range of fish is absolutely spell-
binding. What most Americans might call shrimp go by many names
in Venice, including minuscule creatures called *schie*, still wriggling
in their boxes at the market, which turn from gray to brown when
cooked, and larger, fatter, standard-issue pink *gamberi*.

Scampi are not shrimp at all, no matter what Italian-American
restaurants may insist, nor are the bigger, brinier *mazzancolle*; both
are saltwater crayfish, with claws. Weird-looking crustaceans with

squinty eyes on their tails, called *canoce* or *mantis* shrimp or (incorrectly) *cigale*, are caught at night when they emerge from their muddy burrows; they have a nutty, lobstery taste.

Gourmands that they are, Venetians differentiate between two types of *triglie* (red mullet), one from waters with sandy bottoms, the other from waters with more rocks. They prefer *seppioline*, or baby cuttlefish, born in the lagoon, not in the open sea. Among crabs, they have one word for males, another for females. We poor Anglophones have to make do with "she-crabs."

At Al Covo, Mr. Benelli and his peppy, throaty wife, Diane, who grew up in Lubbock, Tex., serve a lot of their fish raw—the famous local sea bass, *branzino*, seasoned with coarse salt and spider-crab roe; jumbo sea scallops in their shells; and small *scampi*, unbelievably creamy and ethereally sweet. The raw langoustines that Joël Robuchon serves in Paris and David Pasternack's raw fluke at Esca in Manhattan are perhaps better seasoned, at least to my taste, but there is no doubt that Al Covo's raw materials take first prize.

"When fish is this fresh and this good," Mr. Benelli told us during dinner, "it becomes the protagonist. The less the chef does to it, the better it will be."

With that philosophy in mind, he serves crabmeat cool, mixed with its coral and parsley, on a bed of microscopic leaves—"24-hour lettuces," as he calls them—allowing the captivating, low-key notes of the spider crab's flavor to be appreciated to the full, without distraction from the drums and trumpets of strident sauces.

Razor clams, no bigger than a pinkie, are flipped, flipped and flipped again on a flat grill, to keep them moist. And rosy *gamberetti* are combined with white polenta and fruity, exceptionally peppery olive oil to produce an elegantly restrained version of Charleston's creamy shrimp and grits.

The day after our most recent visit to the Benellis, my wife, Betsey, and I managed to squeeze three small meals into a single day, and each of those also exemplified, in its way, the Venetian gift for inspired simplicity.

At lunch at the sumptuous Hotel Cipriani, I asked whether I could have turbot, my favorite fish, but without all the elaborate furbelows proposed by the menu. But of course, sir; out came several fish scaloppine, sautéed no more than a moment or two, their lusciousness nicely cut by the bitterness of grilled radicchio.

At Alle Testiere that evening, we had time only for a few *cicheti*, or snacks, with our preprandial slurps of white wine. There are only 10 tables, mostly for two, jammed into its single tiny room, and we had to make way for serious diners to follow, but Luca Di Vita, one of the partners, ferried plates to our table so speedily that we managed to taste several delicious tidbits, including gnocchi with *tenderissimo* baby squid, octopus salad enlivened with apple and clams with ginger (a throwback to the days when Venice traded with the Orient, like the more familiar sweet-and-sour *pesce en saor*).

Mascaron, a bare-bones, cash-only *osteria* with paper napkins, thronged even in low season, served us a raft of vegetable antipasti and well-grilled sole and *orata* (the gold-spotted bream that was sacred to Aphrodite). But the highlights were the Rabelaisian humor of Gigi Vianello, one of the proprietors, and the steaming, copious plates of spaghetti with clams. No sauce, no garlic, just tiny *vongole veraci*, oil and gobs of parsley atop perfectly chewy pasta. Four ingredients that produce pure bliss.

Neighbors still gather at the bar of Da Fiore, which is surely Venice's best restaurant, for a glass of prosecco or tocai. It began life as a *bacaro*, or tavern; now its dining room is a study in sophistication, with silk wallcoverings and high-backed wicker chairs.

The urbane Maurizio Martin, whose wife, Mara, does the cooking, brought us a parade of dishes of such bright, transparent flavor that our usual lunchtime badinage subsided into a series of happy monosyllables, mainly "mmm." We started with *baccalà mantecato*, a rich, milky, whipped fish purée made not with salt cod, as elsewhere in Italy, but with the dried cod preferred by Venetians.

Nothing flashy, perfectly executed, a classic. I could say nothing less about the *scampi* risotto that followed, with shellfish and *carnaroli* rice both hitting the magic mark of tenderness shy of mushiness.

"Devastatingly good," said Betsey, a devastating critic of second-rate risotto, mine and most of Manhattan's included.

For some reason I had never ordered eel (locally known as *bisato*) on any of my 15 or 20 visits to Venice, even though it is a local favorite, eaten by tradition on Christmas Eve. So I hastened to do so at Da Fiore, and it was so sensationally unctuous that I neglected to ask how it was cooked; I suspect that it was skinned, boned, butterflied and baked or grilled over bay leaves, which is the textbook preparation.

We had more classics at Graspo de Ua, brought back to life after a long slumber by Lucio Zanon, once a Harry's Bar stalwart—fried fresh sardines, one of the "blue" or oily fish the Venetians love, and a risotto made with cuttlefish and their "ink," appropriately robust and slightly chalky. And at Fiaschetteria Toscana (confusingly, neither Tuscan nor a wine bar) we gorged on *moeche*, deep-fried soft-shell male crabs no bigger than a half-dollar.

After all of this, we should have been sated. But for two years I had carried around a ragged piece of paper on which my pal Burton Anderson, nonpareil wine writer and ferreter-out of undiscovered but excellent restaurants, had jotted two mysterious words: "Laguna" and "Cavallino."

A few inquiries and a ride on a crowded ferry took us to Punta Sabbioni, a hamlet on a sand spit just northeast of the Lido, part of a chain that separates the lagoon from the Adriatic. A car was waiting to shuttle us to the Trattoria Laguna in nearby Cavallino, sent by Olindo Balarin, its proprietor.

An unassuming place facing the lagoon near a trailer park frequented by German sun seekers, ignored by the Michelin guide, the Laguna has a real country atmosphere, with wood fires on crisp days, copper pots hanging from the ceiling and baskets of chestnuts still in their prickly husks.

The loquacious Mr. Balarin educated us about the special virtues of fish from the *valle*, a kind of underwater trench between two small streams that flow into the lagoon.

We passed the time until the food started arriving with squash chips and doughy home-baked rolls rather like savory hot cross buns. Before we finished three hours later, we sampled (just for starters) ice-cold raw shellfish; *orata* smoked over laurel wood, sliced and sprinkled with 40-year-old balsamic vinegar; a dazzling duo of scallops the size of pencil erasers, called *canestrelli*; and reddish little razor clams from the Adriatic. These were grilled and served on an arugula salad dressed with seafood juices and oil from Puglia.

It was all exquisite, and so were the *telline*, microscopic mollusks with purple-tipped white shells, new to me, that looked like angels' wings when open. When he was a child, Mr. Balarin said, he found them by the thousands on the beach; now rare, they are delectable with a squirt of lemon.

There was more, much too much more, including bites of two seafood pastas. Happily, we paced ourselves, because the pièce de résistance was Trattoria Laguna's star turn—a whole *orata*, slow-roasted in the oven in a salt crust.

Mr. Balarin broke the crust (with a hatchet!) and deftly boned the fish, depositing neat fillets, soft, sweet and shimmering with moisture, on our plates. This time, he chose a milder Ligurian olive oil as the flavoring agent.

"It is natural for fish," our teacher said, "to be in salt."

—*Venice, March 3, 2004*

Grappa, Fiery Friend of Peasants, Now Glows with a Quieter Flame

Through uncounted decades, grappa was little more than a cheap, portable form of central heating for peasants in northern Italy.

A shot (or two, or three) after dinner helped ward off the damp, misty cold that often settles over the Alpine foothills and the flatlands just beneath them. And a shot in the breakfast espresso—yielding a *corretto*, or "corrected coffee"—got the motor started in the morning gloom.

Grappa is made by distilling debris left in the press after grapes have yielded up their precious juice. The debris is called pomace and consists of skins, seeds and dry pulp. A fiery, rustic, usually colorless alcohol, grappa (the name derives from the Italian word for grape stalk) has an oily, earthy taste with something of the barnyard about it, and a marked alcoholic kick.

Even at its best, grappa is not subtle. The French writer J. K. Huysmans said, with some justice, that if Cognac's music resembled a violin's and gin and whiskey "raised the roof of the mouth with the blare of their cornets and trombones," grappa's "deafening din" suggested the growl of the tuba.

But properly distilled and served cool (not cold), it has a beguilingly smoky taste, with hints of stone fruits like cherry and plum. Especially if made from the pomace of dessert wines, it can display a slight sweetness.

Grappa used to be made mostly by traveling distillers or by big industrial outfits like Stock, the Trieste brandy manufacturer. Too often it was a cheap, ill-made product, an Italian version of white lightning.

Fancier Italians, and most foreigners, disdained it.

But that was before the Noninos of Percoto came to prominence. Here in their native town, a furniture-making center about 75 miles northeast of Venice and only 10 miles from the Slovenian border, they tamed grappa, taught it table manners and gave it mass appeal, not only in Italy but overseas, too.

The United States has become the second-largest export market, trailing only Germany. At Felidia in New York, Obelisk in Washington, Spiaggia in Chicago, Valentino in Los Angeles and dozens of other fine restaurants across the country, grappas are prominently displayed and eagerly consumed after dinner instead of Cognac or some other diges-tif. Tony May, the owner of San Domenico in Manhattan, said he had sold $50,000 worth this year, not to Italian visitors, but to Americans "who come to Italian restaurants determined to laugh like Italians, eat like Italians and drink like Italians."

You might say, with a bit of poetic license, that grappa runs in Benito Nonino's veins. For several generations, stretching back into the 19th century, his family has been distilling in Friuli, the northeastern cor-ner of Italy. A questing, hawk-nosed man, he and his handsome, extro-verted wife, Giannola, longed, as he often says, "to turn grappa from a Cinderella into a queen."

Together, the two of them did it. Instead of a single still, they in-stalled a whole battery of discontinuous copper stills, which allowed them to interrupt the process in the middle of the run, when the spirit was at its peak, and discard the rest—a process known as "top-ping and tailing." The pomace could thus be processed faster, while it was fresher, which muted the barnyard taste. While continuous stills are cheaper, they boil the pomace nonstop.

Unlike Cognac and Armagnac, which are made by distilling acidic wines few would care to drink, the best grappa is a byproduct of the best wines. The Noninos contracted for pomace from the stars of

Friulian winemaking, including Mario Schiopetto, Josko Gravner, Livio Felluga and Gianfranco Gallo.

But raw ingredients and technique would not have been enough. The Noninos had another idea: instead of lumping all the pomace together, the residue of common grapes mixed with that from the more noble varieties, they would distill each separately, starting with picolit, a variety that produces a sweet, delicate dessert wine. The result was a delicious, highly perfumed grappa.

The Noninos made their first batch in 1973 and bottled it in individually blown flasks with silver-plated caps. The labels, handwritten by Giannola, a budding marketing genius, were tied onto the bottles with red yarn.

If the idea was to call attention to the product and to themselves, it worked. Others soon copied them, but the Noninos demonstrated a rare gift for self-promotion. In their ads, they used a sunny family photograph of Benito, now 63, Giannola, 59, and their three stunning daughters—Cristina, 34, Antonella, 31, and Elisabetta, 29—which soon became familiar all over Italy. They commissioned special bottles from great glass makers like Baccarat, Riedel and Venini, and even established an annual literary prize. Most important, they worked tirelessly to ensure that the best Italian restaurants stocked their products.

"The picolit is still our best grappa," Mr. Nonino said with an eloquent shrug. "I know it, the customers know it. I'm satisfied. You can ask for one miracle in life and get it, but to ask for two is ridiculous."

Nardini, a big semi-industrial concern based in Bassano del Grappa, northwest of Venice, was the first to begin commercial production, in the 18th century. Now, more than 1,000 Italian vintners, including many of the very best, like Bruno Ceretto in Piedmont, Silvio Jermann in Friuli and Antonio Mastroberardino near Naples, either produce their own grappa or have a distiller produce it from their pomace and then send it to market under their own labels.

Although their products do not quite fill the mouth in the same way as the best of the Italian grappas do, American distillers like Clear Creek in Oregon and Germain-Robin in California have leaped aboard the grappa express, as have winemakers like Araujo in the Napa Valley. The French make a grappalike drink that they call *marc*, with special success in the Burgundy and Champagne regions, and the Spanish also produce a version of their own, called *aguardiente*.

But Nonino remains the marquee name, and this year, the Noninos will sell almost 1.3 million bottles of grappa. Giannola and Benito Nonino retain a remarkable zest for life and for work. One evening last fall, when my wife, Betsey, and I were visiting Percoto, he said his farewells after a long day at the office, jumped onto his bike and pedaled away, whistling "Sentimental Journey."

With the exception of a few grappas that are aged in wood, giving them an amber hue, one looks just like another. So how do I distinguish my colorless liquid from yours? Like vodka distillers, grappa makers quickly found an answer in packaging. In addition to Nonino's flasks, you now find grappa in colored bottles and hand-painted bottles, in containers shaped like a bunch of grapes or a perfume flacon, even in bottles topped with miniature Alpine fedoras.

Some people think that things have got out of hand, like George Lang, the New York author and restaurateur, who remarked tartly not long ago, "I'm afraid that grappa making has turned into glass blowing."

But it would be a mistake to conclude that clever packaging is always a ruse to conceal an inferior product. A case in point is Jacopo Poli, who makes grappas with finesse and packages them in elegant, long-necked bottles. I especially like his Amoroso di Torcolato, which has an appealing floral bouquet. Should you ever find yourself in Bassano, you can taste it at his little grappa museum, filled with portraits of Louis Pasteur and Leonardo da Vinci and Catherine de' Medici, shelves of ancient tomes on distilling technique and old alembics, or stills.

"Distillation, daughter of alchemy, was born in remote antiquity," a placard announces gravely.

Bassano itself is a pretty, welcoming place, tucked beneath a pre-

Alp called Monte Grappa. Some of the fiercest battles of World War I took place there, and it is now crowned with an ossuary holding the remains of 25,000 Italian and Austro-Hungarian soldiers. The neighborhood is dotted with Palladian villas, including Maser, where Veronese painted a delightful set of frescoes, and Palladio is also said to have designed the often-rebuilt covered wooden bridge that crosses the sparkling little River Brenta in the center of Bassano.

The Nardini company operates a smoky, atmospheric grappa bar at one end of the bridge, and one of the best artisan distillers in Italy, Vittorio Capovilla, a muscular man with an evangelical spirit, can be found at the end of a dusty lane just outside the village of Rosa, a half-hour's drive from Bassano. Armed with the latest in German technology, he makes not only grappa but also *uva*, which is distilled from the grapes themselves rather than from pomace, and which he considers much easier to digest. The seeds in the pomace used for grappa, he told me, contain essential oils that "stun the gastric juices," causing trouble.

Mr. Capovilla's masterpieces, however, are distillates made from cultivated fruits like Gravenstein apples and Saturno pears, as well as rare wild fruits like sour mountain cherries and honey pears that he finds on his hikes in the hills. His products bear comparison to the best in Europe, but they are all but impossible to find; he has yet to master the ropes of commerce.

And then there is Romano Levi, the one and only, the living national treasure, the uncrowned king of Piedmontese distilling. A minute, Hobbit-like figure in a Greek sailor's cap, he works in a ramshackle old structure in the village of Neive, tending a Rube Goldberg assemblage of antique copper boilers and tubes. It is the size of a one-car garage, this world-famous grappa factory, and every bit as cluttered.

But it works. The grappa is superb, if a bit aggressive.

Mr. Levi is a recycler. To fire his still this year, he uses bricks pressed from the residue of last year's distillation. After they have burned, he returns the ashes to the wine producer who originally supplied the pomace, to use as fertilizer in the vineyard. He calls this the Piedmont life cycle.

He is also an inspired improviser. He offers visitors tastes of his products not by pouring them into glasses from bottles or from a pipette, but by lowering a medicine jar on a string through the bunghole into a Slovenian oak cask, hauling some grappa out and handing it over. You drink from the jar.

"You have to go back to the Etruscans to find anything this rudimentary," said Burton Anderson, the wine writer, who was with us when we visited the operation. Black eyebrows arched, Mr. Levi professed not to understand how his gear operated; indeed, he told us, "I know nothing at all about grappa."

Maybe not, but he has the soul of a poet and an artist. Asked how long he had been in business, he replied that he used only one match a year, to fire up his alembic when it was time to begin distilling, and had used 53 matches so far. He makes 6,000 to 10,000 liters a year, using pomace from Angelo Gaja and other Piedmontese winemakers, and he writes all the labels himself—in colored inks on torn pieces of paper, or directly on the bottles with paint.

I am currently working on a bottle produced in 1988, decorated with pictures of flame-red hibiscus flowers. The label specifies that the liquid inside is 48 percent alcohol, and as ever there is a line of enigmatic verse.

"In a dream," it says, "I dreamt."

—Percoto, Italy, December 31, 1997

Finding Its Voice, Naples Sings an Aria

For decades on end, Naples was the city Italy forgot and everyone else avoided. Poor. Dirty. Hopelessly corrupt. A suburb of the third world, where a foreigner could have a purse or a wallet stolen in broadest daylight. It happened to me, right on the main drag.

But all that started to change in 1994, when the G-7 meeting of world leaders inspired a cleanup effort here. Like every mayor of every city that has played host to a summit conference in recent years, Mayor Antonio Bassolino promised that the self-improvement campaign would continue after the big shots had left town. Unlike most of them, he kept his word.

At the time, I wrote that Naples looked "like Eliza Doolittle scrubbed and dressed in silks." It still does. Crime lingers on in all its forms, but it is down sharply, and prudent visitors need not worry. Neapolitans are as extravagantly, unreservedly theatrical as ever, hugging and kissing in the narrow streets, dodging mopeds, gabbing on cell phones, laughing, crying, gesticulating *molto con brio*. This remains a city of Pagliaccis.

And a city of eaters. With the lightest touch imaginable, good Neapolitan cooks transform the bounty of the achingly beautiful Bay of Naples, the vegetables grown in the rich, fertile soil of Vesuvius and the fruits of the sun-blessed Sorrento peninsula into simple but splendid meals.

Some of the most knowledgeable local trenchermen make a point of eating often at Masaniello, a low-key, brick-walled restaurant built beneath the vaults of a 500-year-old stable. Any sensible person would go back again and again just for one of the simplest dishes: cherry tomatoes picked at the moment of ultimate ripeness and concentrated flavor from the slopes of the volcano, cut in half, sauteed for a minute or two until they begin to break down, then tossed quickly with pasta and Tuscan olive oil.

Food fit for the gods, but no better than two Neapolitan classics that may well follow, an exquisite mixed fry of fish and a boozy *baba*.

Slowly, the word is seeping out. New Neapolitan restaurants have opened in Rome and London. In the United States, where "red sauce" has long been a term of derision among foodies, there is fresh interest in the food of southern Italy, the Mezzogiorno. Arthur Schwartz's treatise, *Naples at Table* (HarperCollins), was published in 1998; Rao's, a venerable Neapolitan-style spot in East Harlem, has become so chic that it's opening a Midtown branch; and Tony May, Naples-born but hitherto a champion of northern Italian food at San Domenico, has put the kind of dishes he ate in his childhood on the menu at Gemelli, his World Trade Center outpost.

The relatively few Americans who come here (not counting the military types based in Naples and the tourists who use it as a jumping-off place for Pompeii, Capri and the Amalfi Coast) are discovering the joys of the Neapolitan table. They quickly learn a few hard lessons about the city's restaurants: the guidebooks are mostly wrong, plainer is better and you can't eat panoramas. They also learn about the demonic taxi drivers.

"*Solo un consigilio,*" mine said with a dismissive shrug when I lodged a protest as he sped through a red light. The light is only a suggestion. Naples is not Milan; getting around town is always an adventure.

But make no mistake. Along with the sight of Vesuvius silhouetted by the full moon and the inexhaustible exuberance of the Neapolitans themselves, along with the Farnese bull in the archaeological museum and the Titians and Brueghels in the Capodimonte Museum, which has been rebuilt with the guidance of German experts, eating can be one of the great joys of Naples.

●   ●   ●

Duck into the hole in the wall called the Osteria della Mattonella, on a back street in the Spanish Quarter, and you will see how much Neapolitans can do with humble ingredients. It's a tiny room, with space for 22 (small) people, tiled walls, oilcloth on the tables, pictures of the great comedian Toto on the wall. The sharp-featured host introduces himself as Peppino, brings wine in a colorful Vietri pitcher and feeds you.

To start, a strip of eggplant wrapped around mozzarella (made from a mixture of cow's and buffalo milk, Peppino said, because all-buffalo cheese gets too gummy) and then deep-fried. Then rigatoni with what the locals call *genovese*—essentially onion soup cooked down to a slightly syrupy consistency. And finally—as a separate course, mind you, not with the pasta—*polpette*, or meatballs, in a light tomato sauce that cooks for 12 hours. This is common folks' food, the beef for the meatballs having been "stretched" with a lot of bread soaked in cold water, then squeezed dry. The result is light, juicy and throughly elegant in its simplicity.

The night I was there, salt cod, plumped and rid of the slightest salty taste by a bath of running water, was offered as a fishy alternative, served in the same sauce. Again, poor people's fare; salt cod is far less expensive than the seductive fresh fish and shellfish on which you feast at Da Dora, a family trattoria on a dark alley off the Riviera di Chiaia.

Dora's *spaghetti con vongole* sets the standard for the whole town. It is made with dime-size clams, called *vongole verace*, colored a beautiful brown with cream stripes, plus olive oil, garlic and gobs of parsley. The pasta is dressed when it is blazingly hot, which helps it to drink in all the fruitiness of the oil, the brininess of the clams and the herby freshness of the parsley. *Ecco!* A cliché becomes a classic.

I kept ordering things, because I was alone and the plates headed elsewhere looked so good. Each dish was a study in glorious simplicity: a little heap of deep-fried calamari, flavored with a few drops of juice from a sweet-tart Sorrento lemon; four grilled *scampi*, their long, charred shells lending them an evocative seaside taste and aroma; a delicate little fish from Capri called, I think, a *pezzogna*, cooked in a spicy bouillon called *acqua pazza* (crazy water); and a plate of wild strawberries with perfect lemon sorbet. The waiter wrote out the name of the fish for me; it tasted like *orata* or another of the breams, but I can find no reference to it anywhere, not even in Alan David-son's encyclopedic *Mediterranean Seafood*.

But then Neapolitan cooking is full of unfamiliar ingredients. At the nearby Cantina di Triunfo, in a rustic setting that lurks behind a crumbling facade, I made the acquaintance of *friarelli*, a variety of broccoli rabe, spiced with red pepper, served at room temperature. The Cantina's food is cooked to old recipes, mostly regional. There is no menu; the half-dozen items on offer are described with both pas-sion and precision by Tina Concetta, an owner, as she makes the rounds of the eight tables.

I liked the short ribs of veal, a weakness of mine, but I loved a dish of *bucatini* pasta, dressed with a sauce of cherry tomatoes, eggplant, bell peppers and basil, whose ripe flavors blended into something rich, "meaty" and altogether new. And I was blown away by a little pastry barquette filled with superb whipped cream and unbelievable lemon marmalade—those Sorrento lemons again. The recipe, Ms. Concetta said, came from Procida, a tiny island not far from Ischia.

No wonder, I reflected, that the French consul brought François Mitterrand to this little place during the summit. For all I ate, plus more red wine than I could drink and a first-rate grappa, I paid $35.

My friend Faith Willinger, the Florence-based American food writer, took me to meet her friends Eugenio and Alfonso Mattozzi, father and son, at their restaurant, Europeo, a more bourgeois place near the university. There the ingredients were a little more expensive, but it was still the ingredients and not the legerdemain of the chef that jumped off the plate at you. (Although they shared a little trade secret with me: in winter, when the body needs more calories, they add some pork to the tomato sauce and cook it longer.)

We met an old ingredient in a new form: grilled red mullet the size of anchovies, crisp and eloquently gamy. New ingredients, too: a soup of mussels and zucchini flower buds, unopened and unstuffed, and a white (tomatoless) pizza with *ventresca*, a sort of belly fat smoked over pine boughs.

Ah, pizza. Invented by Neapolitans, they claim; certainly perfected by them. Forget the anchovies and pepperoni. The thing to order is a *margherita*, a small individual pie named after a 19th-century Italian queen; it is made with basil, tomatoes and cow's-milk mozzarella—green, red and white, the colors of the Italian flag.

If you want to look like a native, fold the pizza in two or four—*a libretto*, "like a book"—and eat it out of hand.

You can try one at Brandi, where it was invented; at Di Matteo, in the heart of Spaccanapoli, the old city, where President Clinton, no pizza neophyte, hung out during the summit; or at my favorite, Trianon, where the pies emerge from the cherrywood-fired oven with blistered brown bits around the edges.

Trianon is just across the street from Da Michele, which many locals consider the best in town. As a result, Da Michele is usually impossible to get into.

Pizza dough is put to countless uses in Naples. At Don Salvatore, a handsome ocher-and-white restaurant with vaulted ceilings, it comes as wedges of bread, topped with coarse salt and herbs, to eat with the house's flawless rendition of *insalata caprese*: tomatoes with the perfect Neapolitan balance between acid and sweetness, sliced mozzarella, basil, black pepper, a little dried wild oregano and extra virgin olive oil. It's a kind of deconstructed pizza *margherita*. On the hills above the city, at the Friggitoria Vomero, they make succulent fritters by deep frying little wads of dough.

At Mimi alla Ferrovia, a jolly place near the train station, where the waiters love to banter, laugh and swap jokes with their customers, they turn pizza dough into a savory escarole pie. They also wrap it around an *orata*, carving mock scales on the sides. The fish is steamed inside the crust, locking the juices and vapors in until it can be boned and served.

The escarole pie is part of Mimi's ample antipasto. An even larger one, plenty for a meal, is served at Al 53, a brasserielike establishment that I visited one Sunday noon, when most restaurants are closed. The waiter set a dozen little plates on the table—three vegetables in oil, three grilled or deep-fried (including oyster mushrooms), pieces of octopus with lemon juice, slices of two kinds of *frittatas*, two kinds of fritters (vegetable and cheese) and a baseball-size, slightly flattened, chewy, sour and slightly salty mozzarella, by all accounts the best in town.

That and a dense, aromatic coffee, served in an overgrown shot glass, more than satisfied me.

But miniature cannoli—crisp, about two inches long, and filled with light, fresh pastry cream, in sharp contrast to the gross, soggy things you usually see in the United States—came with the coffee. Naples is like that; little extras all the time. Since meals are so light, usually cream-free and often meat-free, people here always have room for snacks.

I mentioned the fritters up in middle-class Vomero; it also has the city's best ice cream shop, Otranto, where yes, again, the flavor to order is lemon—ice cream, not sorbet. For fancy pastries, Moccia is the place.

For gossip and espresso, it's Gambrinus, on the piazza del Plebiscito, a onetime parking lot that has been swept clear of cars by the mayor. So now you can study the Royal Palace as you sip, or watch the pretty girls and the handsome boys watching each other from their Vespas as they zip by.

—*Naples, Italy, December 8, 1999*

● ●

SPAGHETTI WITH CLAMS
(Adapted from Da Dora restaurant, Naples)
Time: 30 minutes

  ½ cup extra virgin olive oil
  4 cloves garlic, peeled
  3 cherry tomatoes

1½ pounds small clams, like Manila, mahogany or small cherry-
   stones
1 pound spaghetti
½ cup chopped Italian parsley

1. Bring a large pot of lightly salted water to a boil for pasta.
2. In a deep saucepan or casserole over medium-low heat, heat olive oil and add garlic. Sauté until light golden brown, 10 to 12
   minutes.
3. Add cherry tomatoes to pan with garlic, and cook 1 minute.
   Add clams, stir well and cover pot. Steam until clams have
   opened, about 5 minutes. Turn off heat, and keep pot covered.
4. Add spaghetti to boiling water, and cook until al dente, 7 to 8
   minutes. Drain well, and transfer pasta to a large skillet. Pour
   oil and liquid from pot of clams into skillet; keep clams in pot,
   holding them back with lid as you pour. Place skillet over high
   heat, and cook uncovered for about a minute, until liquid bubbles and spaghetti jumps in pan.
5. To serve, add parsley to skillet and mix well. Divide pasta among
   4 deep serving plates, and place equal portions of clams on all.
   Serve immediately.

Yield: 4 servings

FRITTATA WITH ONIONS
(Adapted from Al 53 restaurant, Naples)
Time: 30 minutes

3 medium yellow onions, trimmed and peeled
⅓ cup extra virgin olive oil
6 large eggs
¼ cup finely grated Parmigiano-Reggiano cheese
Salt and freshly ground black pepper

1. Halve onions lengthwise (root to top), and slice into very thin wedges. In a 12-inch nonstick skillet over medium-low heat, heat oil and add onions. Sauté until onions are very soft and golden yellow, 15 to 20 minutes; do not let onions brown.
2. While onions are cooking, combine eggs in a mixing bowl and whisk until blended and frothy. Add cheese, and season with salt and pepper to taste.
3. When onions are soft, pour egg mixture into pan and immediately stir once or twice to mix. Cover pan, and let mixture cook until browned on bottom and set in the middle, about 8 minutes. Check *frittata* by lifting one edge with a spatula and sliding spatula toward middle. When *frittata* is firm in center, flip it over and continue to cook until underside is lightly browned, about 2 minutes more. Transfer *frittata* to a warm serving plate, and cut into four wedges. Serve immediately.

Yield: 4 servings

From the Vines of Vesuvius, the Gift of Summer in Winter

The great Chilean poet Pablo Neruda called tomatoes "the stars of the earth," which "grant us the festival of ardent color and all-embracing freshness."

Well, not all of us. Not us Americans, most of the time. We are subjected to tomatoes bred for thick skins, picked when half-ripe, gassed, shipped hither and yon and chilled until they give up the ghost.

Except for the few precious weeks every summer when back-yards and farmers' markets yield up fat, juicy, vine-ripened fruit, Americans would have but little way of knowing that the tomato, as Marcella Hazan has written, is "one of agricultural man's greatest triumphs, one of the most glorious products he has ever grown."

Neapolitans know. For 10 months a year the sun shines bright in Naples and here on the Sorrento peninsula, which divides the Gulf of Naples from the Gulf of Salerno. The region's fertile soil, enriched for centuries by Mount Vesuvius, would make a pogo stick bear fruit. And Italian geneticists know enough not to monkey with perfection.

Today, Neapolitan tomatoes are acknowledged as the best in the world. They have thin skins, a vibrant red color, dense yet tender flesh and, most important, an ideal balance between acid and sweetness. They are never as one-dimensionally sugary as a jumbo home-grown beefsteak in summer and never as tart as a hothouse tomato in the dreary days of midwinter.

It is almost as hard to imagine Naples without tomato sauce as salt without pepper. Neapolitans use it on meat, fish, pasta and, of course, pizza. They make it with basil or oregano, celery or carrots, garlic or onions, with or without meat. They cook it not at all, for a few minutes or for hours. But they seldom eat two consecutive meals without it.

In season, they eat tomatoes raw, notably in the delectable *insalata caprese*, invented in the 1950s at the Trattoria da Vicenzo on the Isle of Capri—just sliced tomatoes, cow's-milk mozzarella, basil and a slim filament of olive oil. It quickly conquered the world.

For seven or eight months a year, the Neapolitans make their sauces with fresh tomatoes. The crop peaks on Ferragosto, the Feast of the Assumption, on Aug. 15. At the end of the harvest, many cut down whole plants, with quite a few tomatoes still on them, bundle them with string and hang them in courtyards, under the eaves, out of the winter winds. The tomatoes wrinkle a bit but last for weeks, perfect for cooking.

When those are gone, canned tomatoes come into use, typically those shaped like little flasks. The best variety originally came from a village near Pompeii named San Marzano sul Sarno.

These San Marzano tomatoes, which gave birth to the Italian canning industry in the 1800s, are now grown throughout Campania, as the region surrounding Naples is known.

No Neapolitan chef or pizza maker or housewife apologizes for using canned tomatoes when fresh ones are not available. Cookbooks in a dozen languages specify canned Italian tomatoes, meaning tomatoes from this region. As Mrs. Hazan and others readily concede, they are much the tastiest any cook anywhere will find in the 4 or 6 or 10 months when local tomatoes are out of season.

Sunshine in a can, sanity in a can, salvation in a can—they provide not only fresh taste but a magical moment of psychological relief in the long months when the days are shortest and the skies are dullest.

In October, I mounted a tomato-tasting expedition to these parts, along with Faith Willinger, the author of *Red, White and Green* (HarperCollins, 1996), a gold mine of lore and inside dope about Italian vegetables.

Because the commercial harvest had ended, we based ourselves at Don Alfonso 1890, the first restaurant south of Rome ever to win three stars in the Michelin guide (and one of only three in the entire country with three stars in the current edition). Alfonso Iaccarino, the chef, makes extensive use of tomatoes and other fruits, vegetables and herbs grown in the restaurant's kitchen garden, which he tends with his wife, Livia.

They call it their farm, but agricultural precipice would be more accurate. It is located at Punta Campanella, right at the tip of the peninsula, across the strait, called the Bocca Piccola, from Capri.

Ms. Iaccarino, chic in high-heeled white boots and zippy blue trousers, took us there, zigzagging down a cliff face, 500 feet above the water, in her little Fiat Panda. The road was no wider than a small-town sidewalk. I tried, with no luck, to concentrate on the million-dollar view of the island, floating like a gray iceberg in the azure sea.

There was no fence.

"Have you ever visited paradise before?" she asked me, as the road narrowed and the wheels crept toward the edge of the cliff. I wondered how long it would take the medics to find us if she miscalculated.

But I had to concede that it was a kind of paradise. Wild oregano, sage and rosemary grew out of cracks in the rock, the way they do in Dürer engravings. There were eggplants and squash, salad greens like rocket and peppers growing on nets; chickens that laid eggs with yolks that were almost red (the Italians call yolks "*rossi*"); and cows for both milk and fertilizer. Small olive trees lined each terrace, mixed with citrus trees.

"Our citrus are happy, because they spend their lives looking at Capri," Ms. Iaccarino said impishly. "Makes them taste better."

But the 12-acre Azienda Agricola Peracciole, to give the farm its formal name, is most of all a tomato ranch. Its soil is exceptionally fertile, and its location traps the sun year-round. The Iaccarinos and five workers pick tomatoes twice a day from late spring until mid-January, when Don Alfonso closes for six weeks. In Sant'Agata, there were fresh tomatoes on the table for Christmas and New Year feasts.

Ms. Iaccarino walked up and down the rows, basket in hand, plucking tomatoes from the vine only when they looked and felt perfectly ripe. She chose San Marzanos, which resemble our plum tomatoes; cherry tomatoes (*pomodorini vesuviani*); and big pink *cuore di bue* (or "ox hearts," after their shape)—all grown by organic methods, all washed by salt air, which makes it unnecessary to add much salt in the kitchen, Mr. Iaccarino said.

Less than an hour later, we were back at Don Alfonso, seated at a corner table, ready to eat an impromptu, almost all-tomato lunch. Before we tucked in, Mr. Iaccarino came over and said that the farm was the secret of the restaurant's success.

"My fate was to own my father's little hotel," he said. "But I loved to eat and drink. Livia and I went all over the world, eating in famous restaurants, and I asked myself what was missing for us to be like them. I decided that even though we had beautiful products in southern Italy, we weren't getting the best oil, best tomatoes and best ingredients."

Now they are, and Don Alfonso, a pink-and-green retreat shaded by plane trees, is full almost every night of the year that it is open.

We started with a perfect salad: mixed lettuces tasting of the minerals in the soil, a few home-cured capers, split cherry tomatoes and the house's own extra virgin olive oil. No vinegar, because the tomatoes and capers provided enough acid to balance the oil; no salt. The flavors were robust, yet the dish as a whole gave a sense of weightlessness.

Then came strips of San Marzano tomatoes, seeded but not peeled, cooked for a minute with some basil and spooned over spaghetti. A bit of garlic had been swirled in the pan and then discarded. Simple. Classic. No cheese was offered, nor did anyone brandish a pepper mill the size of a ham.

"This is the greatest dish on the face of the earth," said Ms. Willinger, who is not known for her ambiguous gastronomic judgments. "It's really nothing but pasta with wilted tomatoes and a little basil."

Last, the kitchen sent out another salad, this one composed of mozzarella made that morning, basil, incredibly aromatic dried wild oregano, oil from a bottle labeled with a vintage date and sliced *cuore di bue* tomatoes—sweeter than the others, but still balanced by acid.

What fascinated me was that each type of tomato had its own individual flavor and texture. I liked them all, the San Marzanos the best because their skins were so thin and their flesh soft without being mushy. Was the flavor so remarkably concentrated because it was so late in the season?

A concluding lemon sorbet of merciful lightness gave us a reasonable chance of eating a proper dinner. Naturally there were tomatoes on the dinner menu, too: in a savory jelly served with lobster, in a tomato and anchovy broth, in a sauce for baby gnocchi, another for *bucatini* and a third—a light but more lengthily cooked ragu—for a timbale of rice.

Lest someone feel deprived as the time came for the main course, there was veal tongue with tomato sauce and *pesce di scoglio*, or rockfish. With tomatoes.

"Making the year's supply of tomato sauce is the most important ritual in the Sicilian summer," Mary Taylor Simeti writes in *On Persephone's Island* (Vintage Books, 1995), "and each housewife believes in the efficacy of her method with a fervor equal to that with which she believes in the efficacy of her favorite saint."

Exactly the same thing could be said about Campania.

The whole staff at Don Alfonso used to help put up 2,000 glass jars of tomato sauce each year; I remember eating some of it, with a slight sting of chili, ladled over mozzarella and eggplant, when my wife, Betsey, and I dined there in 1994, before the restaurant became the toast of Italy. They sell that sauce at the restaurant and a few other places now, but not in the United States.

Still, there are plenty of canned Italian tomatoes on the American market, and everyone from Ms. Hazan to Lorenza de' Medici endorses their use for sauces when vine-ripened domestic tomatoes are unavailable. In fact, canned San Marzanos are better for that than some vine-ripened varieties on the United States market.

The best are packed in their own juices. Avoid those combined with a sauce or a puree, which is often of obviously inferior quality. Cirio—pronounced like the cereal—is one of the oldest and best names, founded in Turin in 1860. Others to look out for are La Valle, Tutto Rosso and Asti.

Cirio, which still runs a tomato research station in the northern suburbs of Naples, followed Italian emigrants wherever they went, establishing a firm identification between Italy and tomatoes around the world. In Italy, Cirio is the biggest seller and commands the highest prices. In the New York area, most of these brands are available for $2 to $4 for a 28-ounce can.

What's better about the top brands? Well, for one thing, they are made from the best fruit, processed in many cases within 30 minutes of reaching the factory. No greenish or yellowish tomatoes need apply, nor any tomato bits and pieces. Little or no citric acid, a preservative, is added, so the flavor remains pure.

There is a lot to like about canned San Marzanos. Their skins slip off easily. Just like fresh San Marzanos, they have an ideal equilibrium between acid and sweetness. And because they have less juice than most American tomatoes, they cook down more quickly, preserving more of the fresh, clear, summery tomato taste.

Buy tomatoes in glass, if you come across them; they are not at all common on the shelves of American shops. And if you buy cans, buy only a few at a time; the longer the tomatoes are in there, the tinnier they taste.

—*Sant'Agata Sui Due Golfi, Italy, January 5, 2000*

● ●

RICE SARTU IN AN EGGPLANT WRAP
(Adapted from Don Alfonso 1890)
Time: About 3 hours

1 cup plus 6 tablespoons extra virgin olive oil
½ cup finely chopped onion
½ cup finely chopped carrot

½ cup finely chopped celery

½ pound ground beef

1 cup dry white wine

1 28-ounce can San Marzano tomatoes

1 bay leaf

Salt and freshly ground black pepper

1½ cups *carnaroli* rice

1 small onion, peeled

¾ cup fresh or frozen peas

4 cups chicken broth

1 fresh roll, crust removed

½ cup milk

3 egg yolks

Nutmeg to taste

Flour for dusting

2 ounces chicken livers, cleaned

¼ pound fresh mozzarella, diced

⅓ cup freshly grated Parmesan

1 medium eggplant, sliced thin

¾ cup bread crumbs

1. In a medium saucepan, heat 4 tablespoons olive oil, and sauté chopped onion, carrot and celery until tender. Add half the beef, crumbling with a fork. Add ½ cup wine, and cook until it evaporates. Add tomatoes and their juice with bay leaf. Simmer 30 minutes. Pass through a food mill, season with salt and pepper and set aside.

2. In a heavy saucepan, place 4 tablespoons oil, rice and peeled onion. Heat, stirring, until rice begins to turn golden. Add peas. Combine remaining wine with broth, and add ½ cup to pan, stirring, until liquid is absorbed. Add liquid, ½ cup at a time, stirring as rice absorbs it. When risotto is slightly underdone, remove from heat, remove onion and place risotto in a large chilled bowl.

3. Tear roll into small bits, and soak in milk. Combine with

remaining beef; add 1 egg yolk, and salt, pepper and nutmeg to taste. Mix lightly. Form into about 12 nut-size balls. Dust with flour; lightly brown on all sides in skillet in 4 tablespoons oil. Set aside.

4. Heat 2 tablespoons oil in small skillet. Add chicken livers, and cook for about 5 minutes, turning, until done. Chop into small pieces, and add to risotto. Add remaining egg yolks and mozzarella and Parmesan. Mix well.

5. Heat remaining oil in large skillet, and sauté eggplant until brown, turning once.

6. Preheat oven to 350 degrees. Oil a 2-quart mold or soufflé dish; coat with crumbs. Line bottom and sides with eggplant. Spoon in ¾ of risotto, and pat up sides, leaving a hollow. Combine meatballs with 1 cup tomato sauce, and place in hollow. Cover with remaining risotto; sprinkle with crumbs.

7. Bake for 20 minutes, until rice and crumbs are crusty. Allow to cool and settle for 20 minutes before unmolding onto a platter. Serve with remaining tomato sauce.

Yield: 6 servings

Where the Buffaloes Roam,
Mozzarella Is Made

O n March 23, 1787, the great German poet, dramatist, scientist and aesthete, Johann Wolfgang von Goethe, headed southeast by carriage from Naples to the Gulf of Salerno.

"We drove by rough and muddy roads toward some beautifully shaped mountains," he wrote in his journal. "We crossed brooks and flooded places, where we looked into the savage, blood-red eyes of buffaloes. They looked like hippopotamuses."

Today, the roads are paved and the marshes have been drained. But the ruins of the noble Greek temples at Paestum, which thrilled Goethe to the tips of his toes, are still standing on the broad coastal plain, right beside the sea, and the descendants of his buffaloes roam nearby. They have gentle eyes with Betty Boop lashes, and they look nothing like hippopotamuses.

But they produce the ultrarich milk that goes into mozzarella, one of those regional delicacies that is imitated everywhere and duplicated nowhere. Cows' milk has about 3.5 percent butterfat, buffalo milk about 9 percent; not surprisingly, cows'-milk mozzarella, known as *fior di latte*, which can be made anywhere, is a lot leaner. It melts better (and hence is the perfect pizza cheese), but it never approaches the richness and subtlety that buffalo milk gives.

The production of mozzarella is confined by Italian law to buffalo milk, and thus to Salerno, the province south of Naples, and Caserta, the province to the north, the only two places in the country suited to the raising of buffaloes.

Regulations do not limit its consumption to this region, which is called Campania, but they might as well. Genuine mozzarella travels worse than a colic-plagued baby. Its characteristic taste, which is mild with salty, lactic and nutty overtones, and texture, which must be springy but not rubbery, begin to deteriorate soon after it reaches its peak on the second day after manufacture.

At its best, the cheese oozes whey when cut; a fine mozzarella is as juicy as one of Harry & David's pears. Chilling the cheese, unfortunately, kills it.

Some Italian buffalo-milk mozzarella makes it to New York. But it is mostly pasteurized—a no-no to connoisseurs—and sometimes over the hill by the time it reaches stores.

The only *mozzarella di bufala* made in the United States comes from a company called Italcheese in Norwalk, Calif., which is run by Virgilio Cicconi, an immigrant from Italy. But it is kneaded and shaped by machine, not by hand, which changes the texture, and it is available only on the West Coast, mostly in Southern California supermarkets.

In Naples, true buffalo-milk mozzarella is ubiquitous—on the antipasto table, in salads, as a filling in fritters, in the glorified toasted cheese sandwich known as *mozzarella in carrozza* (literally, "cheese in a carriage"). But it is rare north of Rome and scarce even there.

Which is why the world—well, the world of Italian cheese lovers, anyway, along with a few foreign interlopers—beats a path to Antonio Palmieri's door near this hamlet 25 miles southeast of Salerno.

Dickens wrote that people in this part of Italy didn't so much live their lives as enact them. He could have been talking about Mr. Palmieri. Slim, faultlessly tailored, with a dapper mustache, he looks more like a matinee idol than a farmer, but a farmer he is. He runs Caseificio Vannulo, the Vannulo dairy farm, which makes almost 900 pounds of mozzarella every day, entirely by hand, from the unpasteurized milk of its 350-buffalo herd, one of only three in Italy fed completely on organic forage. It may well be the best mozzarella anywhere.

You can see evidence of that in the dairy's parking lot, which is filled with cars of people from all over Italy who come to buy mozzarella.

Mr. Palmieri sells his entire output at the dairy, with a single exception: a small amount goes directly to the region's only Michelin three-star restaurant, Don Alfonso 1890. Because none of his output enter retail commerce, he does not need to put his cheese, with its preservative bath of milky water, into the sealed and dated plastic packages that the government requires as a protection against contamination and spoilage. Along with many traditional mozzarella makers, Mr. Palmieri thinks packaging harms the cheese.

Mozzare means "to lop off," and cutting or breaking a small piece of cheese from a larger one is a key step in the manufacturing process, which is carried out here by men in T-shirts, caps, trousers and rubber boots as white as the mozzarella they make.

The product begins life as a tofulike curd, to which boiling water is added. That makes the "dough" stringy, and as it is kneaded by one man and stirred with a pole by another, it quickly turns into something glossier and silkier. Excess water is scooped off, and when the consistency is right, one man holds up a football-size chunk of cheese and another breaks off a fistful, using his fingers like pincers.

The resulting cheeses—braids called *treccie*, rounds the size of baseballs or grapefruits, and little mouthfuls called *bocconcini*—are dropped into tubs of salted water, where they cure for several hours. As the mozzarella cools, the workers told me, its center gets rubbery.

Eight hours later, it starts to "relax," and by the second day the cheese reaches its apogee. By the fifth day, it will no longer be fit to eat fresh.

Mozzarella di bufala is a very old product, wrapped in tradition and superstition. Up until the 1960s, a farmhand would wear a buffalo skin when a baby buffalo died in hopes of assuaging the mother's grief and improving her milk.

It used to be said that buffaloes could not be milked by machine; the Palmieri operation disproved that. It used to be thought that buffaloes had to spend large parts of their lives wallowing in mud to protect their skin; half of the Palmieri animals now live mud-free lives.

But no one knows for sure where the buffaloes came from in the first place. Some local mozzarella mavens say the original herds were brought to Italy from India by way of Greece in the sixth century. Others say they came from Africa with layovers in the Arab world and then in Sicily. In any event, they differ markedly from American bison; they have no shaggy cowl, and their horns are straighter.

Because buffalo-milk mozzarella costs three times as much as *fior di latte*, many makers use a blend of 30 percent buffalo milk and 70 percent cows' milk. Some falsify their labels. But for the knowing eye, there is a dead giveaway. The genuine article is pearly white, because buffalo milk contains no carotene, the orange hydrocarbon found in carrots and other vegetables. Carotene in cows' milk makes *fior di latte* yellowish.

But does it all matter? Is there a real difference? I used to have my doubts. But they were erased by tasting the best of both cheeses at the source—*fior di latte* from Latticini Cordiale on the Sorrento peninsula one day, Caseificio Vannulo's mozzarella the next. I'm convinced now that it's no contest. It's the difference between a juicy vine-ripened tomato from your own garden and a rock-hard hothouse special.

Mozzarella at its best is one of the world's greatest cheeses, simultaneously sweet and pungent. *Fior di latte*, good as it can be, is never much more than a pizza topping.

—*Capaccio Scalo, Italy, December 15, 1999*

GERMANY AND
CENTRAL EUROPE

In Germany, Spring Wears White

On weekend mornings at this time of year, the traffic backs up alarmingly at the Beelitz exit on the Berlin-Leipzig autobahn. For about two months—from late April until June 24, the feast of St. John the Baptist—Berliners go bonkers over asparagus, especially the white asparagus grown in the sandy soil around this modest market town 30 miles southwest of the capital.

They call the annual season of madness *Spargelzeit*, or asparagus time. Along with the flowering of daffodils and lilacs, the appearance of the fat, juicy spears marks the end of the wet, cheerless Continental winter, and entire households jump into the family Volkswagen or Mercedes for a jaunt out into the countryside to sample the freshly cut asparagus. Some eat it on the spot, doused in butter or hollandaise sauce and eased down by a beer or a glass of white wine, on picnic tables set out by farmers, to the accompaniment of an oompah band. Others buy a few dozen stalks and take them home to cook.

How deeply has *Spargel* sunk into the German psyche? During

World War II, the poles that the Nazis set up in Normandy in a bid
to deter landings by Allied gliders were nicknamed "Rommel's asparagus."

American asparagus growers, in states like Washington, Michigan and California, have been hard hit by imports from Peru, which
ships the vegetable to the United States year-round. But in Europe, it
remains a local, seasonal delicacy, much like sweet corn in the Midwest. The 10-month wait for the moment when the stalks reappear
on market stalls—"like coronets among the cabbages," in the words
of the British food writer Nigel Slater—only enhances the pleasure of
the year's first succulent bite.

In town and country restaurants across Germany, chefs vie to
produce special asparagus menus. The least imaginative among them
will offer a half-dozen standard variations, perhaps including asparagus with ham, cream of asparagus soup, asparagus with scrambled
eggs, asparagus with cheese sauce, asparagus salad and asparagus
with Wiener schnitzel. I have even seen (but never tasted) asparagus
ice cream.

Lillian Langseth-Christensen, the longtime *Gourmet* contributor,
painted a word picture in 1988 that must have rung true for every
German who came across it. As she ate a plate of delicious early-season
asparagus with marinated salmon, she wrote, the seasons seemed to
change right in front of her eyes: "Birds began to sing in the chestnut
trees before the door, the sun shone warmly, and in rereading the asparagus menu, we knew there would be blissful days ahead."

On a recent sojourn in Berlin, my wife, Betsey, and I ate asparagus
at least once, sometimes twice, a day; Betsey is such an asparagus ma-
niac that on an earlier German trip I christened her "Spargel Plenty."

At Vau, Kolja Kleeberg's award-winning restaurant just off the
Gendarmenmarkt, we sampled two particularly light, vivacious asparagus creations—white asparagus and crayfish awash in an ethereal green asparagus emulsion, and white and green asparagus with
a scallop of fried chicken and a very lightly boiled egg. At First Floor
in the Palace Hotel, another top local table, we tried Matthias Buch-
holz's asparagus with lobster (very good) and with morels and bear

garlic, a first cousin of our Appalachian ramps (even better, in my view, combining prime seasonal ingredients to conjure up all of the loamy mystery of a forest in springtime).

"Spring is not spring without asparagus," Mr. Kleeberg remarked.

But to tell the truth, German white or, more precisely, ivory-colored asparagus best fulfills its destiny when least fiddled with. Give me a dozen smooth, carefully steamed spears, thick as George Foreman's thumb, not too squishy, with the merest hint of crispness remaining, heaped onto a platter, and I'm a happy man. Of course, a boat of hollandaise sauce on the side would be welcome, its lemony overtones an ideal foil for the vegetable. And perhaps a plate of salty ham, too, for further contrast.

As it happens, we ate just such a dish for lunch (minus the ham, plus a few chopped chives for color) at Lutter & Wegner, a cozy *Weinstube* that dates back to 1811. But the asparagus was not quite as fresh as the batch that we bought another day near Beelitz on an outing with our friends Christoph and Ragnhild Bertram, which she cooked in their Berlin apartment only three hours after it had been cut. Stringless, tender, with luscious texture and an intensely vegetal, slightly nutty flavor, this was ur-*Spargel*.

With it came melted butter (for more abstemious souls) and hollandaise (for me, please), as well as boiled potatoes and ham. Some ham! Mr. Bertram had made a special trip to Fleischerei Obitz, Berlin's leading butcher, to lay in a supply of the hand-sliced artisanal ham that is smoked over beechwood on small farms in Holstein, his native province north of Hamburg. Its pungent aroma filled the room, and its salty-sweet flavor knocked the socks completely off any Black Forest ham I have ever tasted.

Mrs. Bertram served this ample repast on striking, dead-simple white porcelain plates, which showed off the food to great advantage. Given their timeless elegance, we were not terribly surprised to learn that they had been designed by Germany's eminent neo-Classical architect, Karl Friederich Schinkel. His parents received them in 1934, Mr. Bertram said, as a wedding present.

With asparagus, freshness is paramount, as Betsey and I learned five years ago when we stopped at a roadside inn called Vogelherd near Dessau in eastern Germany. There the proprietor grew his own in the surrounding fields, harvesting it each morning before dawn to make absolutely sure that the sun did not compromise its whiteness.

Germans devour 72,000 tons of white asparagus a year, and they argue endlessly about what region produces the best. Sandy soil similar to that in Brandenburg, the state that encircles Berlin, is also found in Baden-Württemberg in southwestern Germany, notably near the town of Bruchsal, north of Karlsruhe. Standing in KaDeWe, Berlin's premier department store, admiring asparagus piled high like kindling, I was advised by the matron standing beside me to choose the spears marked "Bruchsal." "It's the best in the world," she said with the assurance of a woman who has tasted it all.

Beelitz may have an Asparagus Apotheke, or drugstore; a Spargel Museum full of silver asparagus holders and majolica asparagus plates; a road called the Spargelstrasse; and a Spargel Queen, who wears a crown made of white asparagus spears. But it has plenty of competition, and not just from other towns in Germany.

The French prize the asparagus of Argenteuil, in the outer suburbs of Paris, and Villelaure in Provence. Italians covet the prize asparagus grown near Bassano del Grappa, in the northeastern corner of the country. In Britain, partisans debate the virtues of asparagus from Sussex, from St. Enodoc in Cornwall and from the Vale of Evesham, where a pub called the Round of Gras serves two and a half tons each year.

"So what?" Germans ask. They have Helmut Zipner. Known here as the Spargel-Tarzan, he is credited with having peeled a ton of asparagus in 16 hours.

Asparagus, a member of the lily family, has been around since Roman times. Cato the Elder gave instructions for its cultivation around 200 B.C., Caesar and Pliny praised it and in A.D. 304 Diocletian issued an edict against corrupt practices in the sale of asparagus—i.e., price gouging.

Introduced into Germany from France in the 16th century, asparagus arrived in Beelitz in 1861 and quickly established itself as the prime cash crop, with 1,500 acres under cultivation by 1937. World War II and the advent of Communism—this entire area was in East Germany—caused production to dwindle to almost nothing. But a marriage of German capital and Polish labor has produced a remarkable renaissance, and by 2010 asparagus fields are expected to cover 2,500 acres.

At the Syring Family Farm in Zauchwitz, east of Beelitz, where an inflated, 20-foot-tall plastic Herr Spargel greets hundreds of visitors a day, men from Poland do the digging and cutting of the asparagus, and women from Poland feed it into a machine that washes it and cuts off the woody ends. They then sort it by hand and load it into plastic boxes for sale at the farm, in Berlin wholesale markets and to elite restaurants and hotels like The Four Seasons.

Their foreman, Jurek Wojciakowski, also Polish, said they make about 750 euros a month each, about $900, which is three times the going rate back in Poland.

Standard green asparagus with violet tips are grown and eaten here, but like most people in Continental Europe, Germans consider white asparagus, with its subtle, delicate flavor, much the more-refined product. To keep it white, the spears must be protected from chlorophyll-producing sunlight, which would turn it green. The minute the furled tips threaten to poke through opaque plastic covers covering the long mounds in which the vegetable grows, workers lift the covers and harvest the asparagus.

"You try to spot the soil breaking," said Thomas Syring, the 24-year-old son of the farm's owners. "If you wait until the head comes through, it's too late."

Mr. Syring and his family produce close to 250 tons of asparagus on 75 acres in a good year—one with a mild spring and plenty of rain. (Asparagus is 90 percent water.) If it gets too hot under the covers, he explained, the vegetables' tips unfurl like flowers, spoiling them; the heat is controlled by reversing the plastic, so that its white, reflective side faces the sun, rather than its black, absorptive side.

The choicest spears are smooth and straight, with white tips (purple ones mean that the sun has had an effect). Biggest, in this case, is not best. Bernd Trittel, a jovial leather-vested salesman from Potsdam who had set up his small stall in the main square in Beelitz on the Saturday we were there, said the tenderest, most expensive spears run a bit less than an inch in diameter.

"Germans are perfectionists," Mr. Trittel said. "They know what they want and know what it is worth."

—*Beelitz, Germany, May 19, 2004*

The Miracle of Rye

In Germany, I sometimes think, they don't care which side their bread is buttered on, or whether it's buttered at all, as long as it's made from rye.

Rye began life as a weed that invaded and contaminated wheat fields, but it has proved itself a most useful citizen of the vegetable kingdom.

But rye has qualities that wheat does not: It can be grown in poorer soils, with less sun and at higher altitudes than wheat, and it can tolerate damp and drought. It is made to order, in other words, for northern and eastern Europe, where it has been widely grown since the Middle Ages, and for parts of Canada.

Rye flour makes bread that lasts longer and, for those who love it, tastes infinitely better. True devotees will eat nothing else; the Russian food writer Yuri Chernichenko says that "white bread is cotton wool."

Russia, Poland and the Scandinavian countries all love rye bread, and emigrants from those countries, along with Germans, brought rye bread with them to the United States. For generations, ham on rye was the proletarian sandwich of choice in the Midwest, corned beef or pastrami on rye in New York.

Now, after a decade of obsession with French and Italian styles, Manhattan bakers are beginning to rediscover classic rye breads.

But the Germans have always had an unequaled passion for traditional ryes, whether tan, brown or almost black. Most have a malty, slightly sour taste. The best are moist when fresh. When you bite into a dense, delectable slice, you have a sense that you are eating something primeval, something undying, something expressive of its origins, like honest wine.

Germans make more kinds of bread than anyone else, some 300 varieties, a vast majority containing rye flour, said Heinrich June- mann, the head of the Berlin bakers' guild. They also eat far more bread than anyone else—185 pounds a year, on average, for every man, woman and child—and in the bleak, hungry years after World War II, when little other food was available, that amount was 310 pounds a year.

"Misery time," Mr. Junemann said, "is bread time."

In this country, people invest bread with a spiritual significance. Consider these words, painted on a wall outside Mr. Junemann's of- fice: "Holy and eternal is bread. It keeps you from hunger and misery. The Creator himself gave it to us. He who dishonors bread dishonors life itself."

Bread matches people, in a way. It's as hard to imagine a French- man, full of Latin flair, choosing pumpernickel every day as it is to imagine a stolid German with a baguette or a *ficelle* on his table each morning.

I have heard it said (only by gastronomic philistines, of course) that rye bread is for peasants, white bread for the more discrimi- nating.

Maybe that was true 200 years ago, though I doubt it. For me, rye bread was part of the sacred Midwestern German-American trinity that I grew up with: sauerkraut, dill pickles and chewy rye with cara- way seeds.

Rye bread can make a meal fit for a kaiser, as it does at the Hotel Adlon, the sumptuous new establishment near the Brandenburg Gate, where the breakfast buffet includes up to 15 breads from three local bakers, plus house-baked walnut bread, to say nothing of Dan- ish pastry from Lenôtre in Paris and bagels, donuts and muffins from Starbucks—for homesick Yanks, no doubt.

It can make a philosopher happy, too, as I discovered a decade ago when, thanks to an introduction from a mutual friend, I ate lunch with the late Isaiah Berlin at the Garrick Club in London. Ar- riving at the table, the Russian-born scholar asked whether I liked bread. When I replied that I did, he said the club's bread was wretched, reached into the ample recesses of his black suit coat and produced two great chunks of rye, one dark, one light, both wrapped in wrinkled brown paper bags. It was the best thing we ate that day, and it went very nicely, thank you, with one of the club's elegant clarets.

Germans eat rye bread for breakfast, with cheese, ham, salami and other cold cuts. In the old days, after a cooked meal at midday, they ate rye bread for supper, too, with cheese, ham, salami and other cold cuts. Some still do, but the big meal is often eaten at night now, with a snack for lunch.

German picnic kits are simple, too—just a board and a knife, to cut the rye bread, cheese, ham, salami and other cold cuts.

At KaDeWe, a Berlin department store whose food hall tries to stock everything good from everywhere, and comes close to succeeding, the German bread department sells more than 100 types of rye. Thick-crusted, 11-pound oval loaves from Pomerania, near the Polish border, are neatly arranged next to onion bread and olive bread and pumpkin-seed rye and miniloaves just two inches across, studded with salt and caraway. There is bread baked in KaDeWe's own ovens and by small bakeries scattered across Berlin. Bread from Hamburg, from Bamberg, from Nuremberg.

The one from Bamberg, in the Main Valley east of Frankfurt, is something special—a big, round, spicy sour bread, made from mixed rye and wheat flour by the Schuler bakery there. People come from all over Berlin for it.

"We generate traffic for the whole store," said Norbert Konnecke, the food hall's manager. "We have 200,000 people living in our general area, and nothing pulls them in, week after week, like our German rye breads."

Surely there is no bakery anywhere whose display cases can match KaDeWe's for sheer prodigality. Today, the cornucopia of fresh, fragrant loaves seems a metaphor for German affluence. But in fact, the tradition of offering ryes from all over Germany arose in harder times, during the cold war, when West Berlin was isolated, travel was hard and people longed for a taste of home.

"We get deliveries three times a day," said Karin Kummerer, the trim, efficient woman who oversees the operation. "Even in the afternoon, a lot of the bread is still warm. People like that—it reassures them. They're health-conscious these days, as well, so they sometimes ask you whether the bread has any chemicals it. It doesn't, I tell them, none at all."

The store sells 400 to 2,500 loaves of rye a day, with Saturday the biggest day. Most customers buy two to four half-loaves; "it would look stingy," one explained to me, "not to offer a choice at breakfast." Given the pains that are taken, the price does not seem excessive: about $2.50 for a standard, Berlin-style 2.2-pound rye loaf, called *Graubrot* (gray bread).

Although the rules are not as unbending as those embedded in ancient laws that govern the brewing of beer in Germany, the baking of bread in this country is a serious, meticulous business. This is not Rye Bread 101.

To begin with, it is illegal to use bleached flour, which is widely used in the United States. Traditional German bread has only six basic ingredients: rye flour, wheat flour, baker's yeast, water, salt and a sour starter similar to that used in making sourdough bread. No milk, sugar, fat, additives or preservatives, though the bread lasts up to eight days.

Breads containing only rye flour are seldom made, said Marcus Bertram, KaDeWe's master baker. The taste, he said, "is just too strong for most people." The texture, he was too polite to add, is ingotlike. So wheat flour, which has more gluten, is added to lighten and refine the loaf.

What differentiates one rye from another is mainly the proportion of rye flour to wheat flour in the dough. Under the German system, it is white bread if it contains 90 to 100 percent wheat flour, and white-mixed bread if it contains 49.9 to 90 percent wheat flour; it is rye bread if it contains 90 to 100 percent rye flour, and rye-mixed bread if it contains 50 to 89.9 percent rye flour.

The Germans are nothing if not systematic.

There are other variants, as well. These are some of them:

- The bread can be baked in modern ovens in large batches or in old-fashioned stone-hearth ovens in small batches. The latter produces a rougher crust, often almost half an inch thick, and a more darkly flavored crumb.
- Some ryes are made from whole-grain or roughly crushed rye rather than milled rye flour, which gives them a considerably coarser texture.
- Seeds may be used, or not, and the variety available is large— not only caraway, but also linseed, pumpkin, sunflower and poppy seeds. Olives, carrots, oats, walnuts, hazelnuts, raisins, onions and even ham may also be added.
- Size and shape—oval, round, rectangular—also affects flavor.

Unless it is cool, the bread is handed to the customer in an open-ended paper bag. And except for behemoths like the 11-pounder from Pomerania, it is never sliced in the store. That is the responsibility of the consumer.

"There used to be a test for young German women," Mr. Junemann said, looking over the glasses perched on the end of his nose, blue eyes dancing. "If they couldn't cut a loaf of bread evenly, they couldn't get married."

—Berlin, July 15, 1998

Where Paprika Is Measured in Pounds, Not Pinches

Driving south from Budapest across the Alfold, the Great Hungarian Plain, you pass men walking behind horses, guiding plows through earth the color of Hershey bars. The willows are wearing gauzy-green spring outfits, and the forsythia is blooming. It is March, planting season in paprika country.

By tradition, seeds go into the ground or into hothouse beds on or shortly after St. Gregory's Day, which is March 12. And this is a region where tradition continues to be served, although some of the horses have been replaced by tractors. My wife, Betsey, and I saw hundreds of long, low plastic tunnels full of tiny, pampered pepper plants. Come Sept. 8, the Nativity of the Holy Virgin, the paprika peppers will be ripe, ready to pick by hand (tradition served once again).

Some will be threaded into garlands, like the chili *ristras* of Mexico, and hung on the eaves of houses or elsewhere to dry; more will go into commercial ovens for the same purpose. After a month, those on the strings will clack like castanets in the wind, and their color will have turned a deep, lustrous scarlet.

Eventually, the dry pods will be ground into the familiar brick-red powder.

"The garlands are not just there for tourists," Dr. Gyorgy Somogyi, a botanist who works for the State Paprika Research and Development Department, told me. "It's the same as with flue-cured tobacco. Air-drying is slower but definitely better. Peppers are still 50 percent sugar when they're harvested. Air-drying them gives the sugar a chance to turn slowly into complicated flavors, instead of turning into caramel."

Paprika doesn't amount to much in the American kitchen. Most of us use it to brighten up pale, monochromatic foods like cottage cheese, yogurt and deviled eggs. That, and maybe to spice a goulash every two or three years. Too often, what we buy in the first place is coarse, second-rate stuff from Hungary or elsewhere, lacking in depth and piquancy, and almost always we leave it in an opened container to dry out in the deep recesses of the spice cabinet.

But for the Hungarians, paprika is a way of life, a source of flavor as indispensable to their cuisine as lemongrass is to the Thais and basil is to the Neapolitans. One of the greatest Hungarians, Dr. Albert Szent-Györgyi, won the Nobel Prize for discovering that paprika is a prime source of vitamin C, which he named ascorbic acid. That explains the lustrous skin of Hungarian women, his countrymen will tell you, and the very long lives of a people whose diet is loaded with animal fats, starch and sour cream.

Each Hungarian consumes a pound of the stuff a year.

A thousand richly savory, richly reassuring Hungarian recipes begin with onions sizzling in fat, followed into the pan by several teaspoons of paprika. Paprika goes into the fisherman's soup and *gulyas* (goulash) soup the Hungarians love, giving them both tang and body. It is the essential ingredient in paprika chicken, a dish that conquered the world after Escoffier served it in Monte Carlo in 1879. It goes into the famous Hungarian salami, giving it its distinctive rosy color.

Talk about comfort food. I can't imagine anything more comforting than the *szekelygulyas*, an inspired blend of sauerkraut and goulash, rich in paprika, that they serve at Kehli, a red-tablecloth tavern near the Danube in Budapest. But maybe that's just my Mittel-European roots showing.

"Onions, paprika, garlic, lard," murmured Gyorgy Laszlo, the executive chef at the Hotel InterContinental in Budapest. "The holy quartet. I even use them in omelettes at breakfast."

* * *

For generations, Hungarian paprika was considered the world's best, far superior to Spanish, Californian or Mexican. But the Communists gummed up the works. Today Hungary controls only about 6 percent of the world market, down from 25 percent in the 1950s, and its paprika no longer automatically commands a premium price.

Things are starting to change. Small, private mills are opening, like the Rubin company here. It was started six years ago in a garage—shades of Hewlett-Packard!—by four partners, each from a different profession. They have long since given up their day jobs, and their new plant grinds paprika using traditional methods six months a year, three shifts a day.

Old plants are hustling to keep up. The Szegedi Paprika Company, the successor to a former state monopoly, was recently taken over by the company that makes Pick salami. Behind massive steel doors inside the old factory, with its crumbling, gloomy stairwells, a modern facility has been installed, all gleaming stainless steel and immaculate white tile. It could be an emergency-room operating theater.

"The Communists concentrated everything in a few big factories, and they emphasized mass production," said Eszter Salamon, a Szeged lawyer who is organizing a farmers' co-op in a bid to restore standards and improve farmers' incomes. "Price mattered to them, not quality. So there was no incentive for the farmers to take the pains needed to grow great peppers.

"The factories have been privatized, and attitudes are slowly changing. The mill owners still want to buy cheaply, but there are seven or eight of them here now, instead of one. Eventually, we hope, competition will improve quality, and our farmers will be paid more if they grow the best they can."

Paprika is planted in more than 13,000 Hungarian acres, and most of the 4,000 families that till them are smallholders, as always.

The narrow, cone-shaped pods from which paprika is made grow on shrubs about two feet tall, turning from yellow-green to red when ripe. They are thick-skinned and leathery, utterly unsuitable for eating raw. The plant is a member of the Capsicum genus, Capsicum annuum, var. longum. A cousin of tobacco, tomatoes and potatoes, it is, like them, a native of the Americas.

(The nomenclature is a nightmare. In the rest of the world, the word "paprika" means only the powder; in Hungary, it is also the word for all of the numerous fleshy varieties of peppers, including the green bell pepper.)

How paprika got to Hungary is the stuff of myth, legend and controversy, but it seems likely that Columbus or one of his sailors brought the first seeds across the Atlantic. From Spain the trail led to Italy, Turkey and Bulgaria. Either the Ottomans or the Bulgarians apparently introduced the plant to Hungary.

"Amid this welter of conflicting evidence," wrote the Hungarian-born restaurateur George Lang in his exhaustive study, *The Cuisine of Hungary* (Atheneum, 1982), "we are sure of only one thing: before Columbus, paprika was unknown in Europe. For all intents and purposes, therefore, let us consider paprika a delightful fringe benefit of Columbus's discovery of America."

However it got here, it found a home in the flatlands around the towns of Szeged, on the Tisza River, and Kalocsa, on the Danube, both close to the Yugoslav border. These towns have more sunlight than any others in Hungary, about 200 days a year, with plenty of rain in May and June, plenty of hot weather in July and August. The Tisza, a lazy, meandering river like the Mississippi, is just as prone to flooding—some sections of Szeged have been under water this spring. The flood waters enrich the soil.

Paprika is paprika, you might think. But no. It is almost as complex as the Hungarian language, which is related only to Finnish and Basque, as far as anyone knows, and sounds like something falling down stairs.

According to Dr. Somogyi, the botanist, the best paprika comes from plants that are started indoors, then bedded out in April or May. With that head start, he said, they ripen earlier, in August, when the sun is hot.

"That gives them 30 percent more pigment and flavor than the later harvest," Dr. Somogyi explained. "With paprika, the redder the better."

But most emphatically not the redder the hotter. Hungarian paprika is made in a number of styles, ranging from *eros* (fiery) through *feledes* (semisweet) to *edesnemes* (premium sweet), which is most commonly used in cooking. If Hungarians want their food spicy, they often add dried, crumbled cherry peppers.

At the city museum in Szeged, which has a collection of paprika memorabilia, they show a film in which old women complain about having to douse their hands in water to stop the stinging from handling hot peppers. Until 1859, it was worse: the seeds and veins of the peppers, which contain the heat-producing substance called capsaicin, had to be removed by hand. But in that year the Palffy brothers invented a machine to do it. And starting with the early-20th-century work of a scientist named Ferenc Horváth, the Hungarian breeders have gradually bred the hot out.

As things now stand, there is no premium-grade Hungarian paprika available on the American market. Several Hungarian brands, including Budapest's Best and Pride of Szeged, are sold in fine-food shops and some supermarkets, and they are superior to most of the products sold under familiar brand names or house labels. But they don't have the deep, round flavor, with more than a hint of the taste of fresh peppers, that you find in Hungary.

"What you find here," Mr. Lang said recently, "is midlevel commercial quality—acceptable, but nothing to write an ode about. As with wine, as with other things, the best comes from small growers and small mills, which produce small quantities of the finished product, mostly consumed at home."

Most paprika, even in Hungary, is ground from the stems as well as the shells of the peppers. That's one shortcut that lowers the quality, and we saw it everywhere. Another, equally undesirable, is using metal grinders instead of old-fashioned millstones.

Bitterness is a constant danger with paprika, induced by too much heat. In the milling process, a certain number of seeds are crushed along with the pods. They yield oil, which keeps the temperature down and keeps the color bright. Water is added, bit by bit, to do the same. The miller must walk a line between slight caramelization, which produces a malty aroma and a certain sweetness, and over-heating, which produces an acrid, unpleasant aroma and flavor.

A hint of that aroma clings to the paprika factories, especially when grinding is under way. Both Betsey and I, unused to it, found ourselves coughing and sneezing repeatedly, and the sharp smell clung to our clothes and our hair for several hours after we had left the premises.

The battle against bitterness must continue in the kitchen. Mr. Laszlo, the InterContinental chef, said he always adds a little water to the pot when he adds the paprika. Kalman Kalla, the executive chef at Gundel, the capital's leading restaurant, said he sometimes puts the paprika in only after the meat has begun cooking, if he wants to preserve the paprika's color and bite.

The spice starts to deteriorate almost as soon as it has been ground. Lajos Lakatos, one of the top officials of Kalocsa Paprika, the biggest Hungarian producer, demonstrated that for us. At his sprawling factory in Kalocsa, a charming old town with a cluster of pastel-colored Baroque buildings at its center, a table was filled with dozens of saucers, each containing a sample of a different grade of paprika. They had been sitting out overnight.

When he gently scraped away the paprika on the surface, it was obvious that it had begun oxidizing. The paprika beneath was ruddy red. What had been exposed to the air was tan.

There are no dates on paprika packages, but here are a few rules to follow in buying and handling it in the United States. Buy it in small quantities. Buy it in tins, if possible, rather than glass (light is also an enemy). Close the tin tightly after use, and store it in the refrigerator.

Hungarians, as must be evident by now, love their food; Joseph Wechsberg, the much-traveled gastronome, envied them. Born in

Czechoslovakia, raised in Vienna, both close by, he once said that "to be a Hungarian is a permanent delight." But they are picky, picky, picky about their paprika. They have a saying, Mr. Lakatos confessed to us: "One paprika for the mother-in-law, another for the mother, a third for the wife."

Mr. Kalla and Mr. Laszlo both said they preferred paprika from Kalocsa, and Mr. Lakatos, eager to press a competitive point, said he thought the alkaline soil around Kalocsa helped grow better peppers. Mr. Lakatos also mentioned that Kalocsa peppers grew up, while Szeged peppers grew down. But he conceded that the differences were hard to distinguish, all other factors being roughly equal.

"Tasting blind, I can tell Hungarian from American," he said, "but not Kalocsa from Szeged."

—*Szeged, Hungary, April 28, 1999*

• •

SZEKELYGULYAS (SAUERKRAUT GOULASH)
(Adapted from the Kehli tavern, Budapest)
Time: 2 hours 45 minutes

2 tablespoons vegetable oil
⅓ cup finely chopped onion
¼ cup sweet Hungarian paprika
Pinch of hot Hungarian paprika, or cayenne
1½ pounds boneless pork shoulder, cut into ½-inch cubes
1 clove garlic, peeled and minced
½ teaspoon caraway seeds
½ teaspoon minced fresh dill
½ Italian frying pepper, finely chopped
½ ripe tomato, finely chopped
3 pounds packaged (refrigerated, not canned) sauerkraut, rinsed
    and well drained
1½ cups sour cream

1½ cups heavy cream
1½ tablespoons all-purpose flour

1. Heat the oil in a 4- to 6-quart saucepan or casserole over medium heat. Add onion and sauté until translucent, about 3 minutes. Remove pan from heat, and add 2 tablespoons water and the sweet paprika and hot paprika. Place pan over low heat, and sauté 3 minutes. Add pork, garlic, caraway seeds, dill and 2 more tablespoons water. Cover, and cook until pork is tender, about 1 hour, stirring occasionally and adding a tablespoon or two of water if it seems too dry.
2. Add chopped pepper and tomato to pan. Cover, and cook over low heat for 10 minutes. Uncover and cook, stirring occasionally, until most of the liquid has evaporated. Add sauerkraut and toss gently to combine. Cover and cook over low heat, stirring occasionally, for an additional hour.
3. Combine sour cream and heavy cream and mix well. Transfer half the mixture to a serving bowl, and refrigerate until needed. Add flour to the remainder, and stir until smooth. Add to pan. Cover and continue to cook, stirring occasionally, for 15 to 20 minutes. Garnish with a dollop of the reserved sour cream mixture, and pass the remainder separately.

Yield: 6 servings

Where Poseidon Sets
a Bountiful Table

When I was asked this summer to lecture on a cruise along the Dalmatian Coast, I accepted in a matter of minutes, having heard tales for years about its craggy beauty and captivating old cities, but I never dreamed that I would eat and drink well.

I guess I should have known better. Two of the most estimable fish restaurants in the United States, Uglesich's in New Orleans and Tadich's in San Francisco, now run by the Buich family, have Dalmatia in their DNA. I recall now that Dr. Ernesto Illy, the coffee king, once told me over dinner in Trieste, his base of operations, that the fish and shellfish on the Croatian side of the Adriatic Sea, where the bottom is mainly rocky, were better than those on the Italian side, where it tends to be muddier.

Many Italians would no doubt disagree. Yet restaurateurs in Venice and in Puglia confess that some of the best fish that Italian boats bring into local ports are caught off Croatia, especially *scampi* (or langoustines) and *branzino* (or sea bass), but also sea scallops and monkfish. "The quality of their fish is really astonishing," said Cesare Benelli, the exacting owner of Al Covo, one of Venice's finest seafood trattorias.

My wife, Betsey, and I couldn't agree more after sampling Dalmatian fish and shellfish, less thoroughly than we would have liked but adequately enough to judge how pristine, clear of taste and skillfully cooked it can be. As in Venice, which ruled much of the region for centuries, plenty of pasty risotto and overcooked squid is on offer in

Croatia. In Dubrovnik an entire street, Prijeko, is lined with restaurants whose staff members stand outside, noisily touting their indifferent food. Again as in Venice, the best dishes are the simplest; ventures into creativity and complexity often end in fiascoes.

But restaurants like Proto—a few steps off Dubrovnik's pedestrian-only main drag, whose limestone paving blocks have been polished to a high gloss by hundreds of thousands of feet—buy the best and know just what to do with it. We were stunned by the sweet, magically tender shrimp, cooked on a wooden skewer, and the ruddy *scampi*, which were so plump they could almost have passed for baby lobsters.

They were rockets of flavor intensity that scored direct hits with us both. The young waiter told us why: "They were alive when they came in this morning, and they're barely cooked—two or three minutes on the grill, depending on size."

Our lunch at Proto was one of those meals where everything worked perfectly. Our table, covered with a sea-blue cloth, was shielded from the fierce midday sun by an awning and cooled by a fresh breeze. I am not much of a fish salad fan, but my starter was exemplary—a mixture of delicately flavored baby octopus, succulent little mussels, chopped red onion, ripe tomatoes, fleshy black olives and round, wonderfully juicy Mediterranean capers. Betsey's shrimp came with a mound of saffron rice, every grain distinct and slightly crunchy, and a salad of tart rocket dressed with oil from Korcula.

The espresso, with a perfect head of *crema*, would have pleased Dr. Illy, and it went very nicely, I thought, with a slug of slivovitz, the local plum eau-de-vie. Well, not exactly local; I thought I detected a note of regret in the waiter's voice as he took the order, and then I realized that slivovitz is Serbian, not Croatian. The last time I had been in these parts, the rival countries were both part of Yugoslavia.

After decades of rule by Marshal Tito and his Communist brethren and years of internecine warfare, all Croatia is springing back to life. In Dalmatia, encompassing the strip of land along the Adriatic Coast and the 1,000-odd offshore islands, fruit, vegetables and fish are piled high in outdoor markets. The tall, handsome Dalmatians are stylishly turned out. And the tourists, absent for so long, are beginning to return.

Croatia may still be terra incognita to most Americans, but not to Europeans, who have watched a strapping Croatian tennis player, Goran Ivanišević, win the Wimbledon singles title in 2001, and the Croatian soccer team battle mighty France to a draw in the European championships this year.

Lured by the unpolluted, too-blue-to-be-true waters, the coruscating light and the scent of lemon trees and cypresses, celebrities, including Sean Connery, Andre Agassi and Gwyneth Paltrow, have discovered the island of Hvar, which is carpeted with wild lavender; the island of Korcula, a miniature Venice where Marco Polo may or may not have been born; and of course this ancient, golden city, of which George Bernard Shaw once said, "Those who seek paradise on earth should come to Dubrovnik."

The London newspapers have taken to describing the Dalmatian coast as "the new Côte d'Azur" and Dubrovnik as "the new St.-Tropez." To an American eye it looks much more like Maine—with rather more hours of sunshine, of course, and a lot more Romanesque and Gothic and Renaissance architecture, but precisely the same sort of pine-clad mountains and islands.

A big group from the cruise ship assembled for dinner one night at Proto's sister restaurant, Atlas Club Nautika. They put us at a long table on a terrace overlooking the sea, with a moonlit view of the Bokar fortress, one of the 15th-century bastions in the old city's massive, remarkably intact encircling walls. The langoustines were luscious again, if slightly smaller, and the proprietor brought out a silver tray with an array of glistening fish, dominated by a huge bream.

Too huge, in my view, to grill whole, but he insisted that it was the best and freshest fish in the house, so we took it. Skillful though the kitchen was, subtly seasoning the bream in Dalmatian fashion with rosemary and anointing it with extra virgin olive oil, some sections of the big fellow inevitably came off the flames a little dry.

But the oysters and mussels from farms near the village of Mali Ston at the base of the long, majestic Peljesac peninsula, northwest of

Dubrovnik, seldom disappoint. Nor does Croatian street food, some of it familiar in neighboring countries in southeast Europe, like *burek*, a flaky pastry filled with cheese, delicious when fresh and hot, a gooey mess when not. Little grills set up in alleys and on street corners dispense *raznjici*, which are small kebabs, and thumb-size, skinless sausages called *cevapcici*, made from pork, lamb or veal, or a blend, and bright with paprika, onions and garlic.

Italy has left its mark, as well, with a spicy fish stew called *brodet*, not unlike the famous *brodetto* of Ancona, the risottos of Venice, the pizzas of Naples and especially *prsut* (the word is pronounced pur-SHOOT, which gives you some idea what it is: a local variety of prosciutto). *Prsut* is a smoked ham that is home-cured in the bora, a dry winter wind that blows from the mountains through passes down to the sea.

And as Rebecca West remarks in her monumental travel book, *Black Lamb and Grey Falcon*, first published in 1941, people in this part of the Balkan peninsula "cook lamb and suckling-pig as well as anywhere in the world," especially in the hills behind the coast, where sage, thyme and basil grow in lush, perfumed profusion.

What to drink with all this? Croatian wine, once celebrated, is staging a comeback, too, with a Dalmatian-American named Mike Grgich leading the charge. He immigrated to the United States in 1958, he likes to say, "to escape the Communists and find freedom." Settling in the Napa Valley, he made the 1973 Chateau Montelena that famously outshone white Burgundies at a Paris tasting, then founded Grgich Hills Cellar in Rutherford, where he continues to produce top-rated reds and whites.

In 1996 he revisited his homeland, readopted his Dalmatian name, Miljenko Grgic, and founded a winery called Vina Grgic, near Trstenik on the rocky Pelješac peninsula. It is the first air-conditioned winery in Croatia and the first to use French barrels. Semiretired, he spends two months a year in Croatia, producing two wines we drank with great pleasure: Posip, a crisp, chalky, flowery white made from the same grape as Hungary's furmint, and Plavac Mali, a dense, chewy red, full of pepper and blackberry notes, which is a cousin of California's zinfandel.

Although the Vina Grgic wines are costly, Croatia is proud of them. We found them featured on the lists at both of the top Dubrovnik restaurants, and you can drink Grgic Posip with the local oysters at Villa Koruna in Mali Ston. Most days Grgic wines appear at other ambitious restaurants, like Adio Mare, on Korcula, known for its grilled, freshly caught octopus; Macondo, in an alley near the central square in Hvar, with a dandy seafood pâté; and Boban, in Split, a modern city that grew up in and around the palace that the Roman Emperor Diocletian built in the third century A.D.

It may be true, as Ms. West wrote, that "this coast feeds people with other things than food," like glorious art and history. But the food's not so bad, either.

—*Dubrovnik, Croatia, September 15, 2004*

SCANDINAVIA

Where Danish Means Lunch

L eave it to the Danes, those past masters of form and color, to turn sandwiches into still lifes.

At Ida Davidsen's snug little basement restaurant, a couple of blocks from Amalienborg, the royal palace, they build small works of art out of fish, meat, cheese, eggs and vegetables, flavored with dill or lemony mayonnaise or mustard made with beer and brandy. Some are based on humble ingredients like sardines, potatoes or salami. Others use caviar, lobster or prime beef.

It is hard to imagine anything less like a New Yorker's jaw-stretching corned beef on rye or a ballpark frank than a meticulously made *smørrebrød*, or open-faced sandwich, with its components chosen not only for the way their tastes complement one another but also for the picture they present.

Between 300 and 400 sandwiches a day emerge from the kitchen. Not one of them is ugly or sloppy. Not one is gloppy or greasy. This is Denmark, the homeland of Georg Jensen and Arne

Jacobsen, where careful craftsmanship is the norm and not the exception.

Some smørrebrød are complex. An extravaganza featuring Danish (pork) liver pâté begins with a buttered slice of rye bread. Two slices of pâté go atop that, and they in turn are topped with three slices of tomato, arranged diagonally. A ribbon of pale green cucumber salad, made with vinegar, crosses the tomatoes, next to a ribbon of crunchy fried onions.

"Red and green, sweet and tart, soft and crisp," Ms. Davidsen said. "Here you have contrasts in color, flavor and texture in a single sandwich."

Other sandwiches are simpler—a mound of maybe three dozen tiny pink shrimp, for example, piled with precision on a buttered slice of white sourdough bread. A turn or two of the pepper mill provides all the seasoning that is needed. But there is art even here; the shrimp are peeled each morning, and they are stacked so the head of each faces in the same direction.

Ms. Davidsen is the guardian angel of Danish smørrebrød. She is the great-granddaughter of Oskar Davidsen, a wine merchant who began serving innovative sandwiches in 1888 in his shop on the outskirts of Copenhagen. By 1900, Oskar Davidsen was offering 178 varieties of smørrebrød almost every day, most of them available on any of four kinds of bread. The menu was a yard and a half long.

Ms. Davidsen's grandfather, Vagn Aage Davidsen, began the practice of creating new sandwiches and naming them for well-known figures. The Hans Christian Andersen, one of his creations (and one of the gems on today's menu), uses ingredients mentioned in Andersen tales—bacon, liver pâté, tomatoes, jellied consommé with port and coarsely grated horseradish. It adds up to a kind of supercharged BLT.

Many of Ms. Davidsen's creations center around products smoked by her husband, Adam Siesbye, at their country house, including duck (served with a mayonnaise-bound beet, cabbage and leek salad on rye), salmon, tuna and even pastrami (eaten with sauerkraut, pickles and that boozy mustard).

When my wife, Betsey, and I ate our way through a fair portion of the current repertory on two visits this summer, we were particularly taken with the smoked tuna, sliced translucently thin and served with a poached egg, spinach and lemon zest—a fabulous combination. Another winner was a tangle that Ms. Davidsen calls the Fireman's Nightcap: smoked potatoes, bacon and chicken salad on rye, showered with crisp-fried carrot matchsticks.

Smørrebrød dates from the 1600s, when farm families took baskets filled with bread, butter, sausage and smoked fish into the fields. There they made their own open-faced sandwiches. As Denmark slowly became more urban, sandwich making moved to the kitchen, and preparations became more elaborate. But the renowned Danish pork products—bacon, ham and salami—remained prime ingredients, along with preserved anchovies, herring, eel and salmon.

For a time, a couple of decades ago, the national taste for *smørrebrød* seemed to be dying. But today many Danes eat *smørrebrød* for lunch several times a week, either at restaurants or at their workplaces, buying sandwiches at carryouts or bringing them from home in specially fitted lunchboxes. They are sold on trains and ferries. And at home, *smørrebrød* are often served when friends are invited by for the evening, especially in the summer.

"For us," Ms. Davidsen remarked, "*smørrebrød* can provide a vehicle for leftovers, the way pasta sometimes does for the Italians and crepes sometimes do for the French. You look in the refrigerator, and there's a cooked pork chop. You slice it up, sauté some onions, boil an apple with sugar and lemon, slice that, and put everything together with bread, butter and a bit of leftover gravy. A delicious lunch."

The word *"smørrebrød"* is derived from the Danish words for bread and butter, and those are the two essential ingredients of every Danish sandwich. The Danes bake excellent bread as well as their much better-known breakfast pastries, and their butter is so good that it is widely sold across northern Europe.

Custom decrees that the butter should be spread smoothly and evenly, right to the edge of the bread.

Custom decrees, furthermore, that *smørrebrød* should be eaten in a fixed order, like the dishes in a Swedish smorgasbord. Pickled herring comes first, often topped with onions or dill or capers or all three. At Slotskaelderen Hos Gitte Kik, another of Copenhagen's top *smørrebrød* restaurants, across the street from Parliament, Lene Just offered us our choice of seven or eight kinds of herring. Only when we picked one did she place several pieces on a piece of pumpernickel; if made in advance, she explained, the sandwich would get too soggy.

After that, a fish- or shellfish-based sandwich—perhaps crayfish tails with dill mayonnaise, if they are in season, or fried plaice, the mild-tasting Baltic flatfish adored by the Scandinavians, with rémoulade sauce. And after that, something meaty, like sliced tongue with Russian salad. That makes three, which is what most men eat for lunch; the average for women is two.

Ms. Just, whose restaurant has been in business since 1797, sized me up and suggested a fourth, "to round things off." With only the feeblest protest, I succumbed, and she brought over a little number with the subtlety of a sledgehammer: slices of strong, mature cheese, reminiscent of Limburger, arrayed with onion rings and a strip of beef aspic on a slice of sourdough bread spread with pork dripping. A tot of rum had been poured over the ensemble.

Betsey took a bite, muttered, "This thing needs a Listerine chaser," and reached for another taste.

But back to *smørrebrød* ritual. The prescribed accompaniment to a meal of Danish sandwiches is a large glass of Danish beer and a small glass of Danish aquavit, which is always taken neat and ice cold. And thereby hangs a cautionary tale.

I was visiting Denmark for the first time, overseen by my parents, sometime in the 1960s. We went to the Søpavillonen (Sea Pavilion), an elaborate *smørrebrød* temple operated by Ida Davidsen's parents. I ate and ate, drank and drank, tossing back aquavit as if it were iced tea. My parents seemed impressed by my capacity until I fell down a flight of stairs as we were leaving, landing with a thud at my mother's feet. She was not amused.

That restaurant closed in 1974 (not, as far as I know, because of my antics). By that time, Ms. Davidsen had spent four years, "when Hollywood was Hollywood," working in California at Kenneth Hansen's Scandia, then the leading Nordic restaurant in the United States, making *smørrebrød* for Danny Kaye, Elizabeth Taylor and friends.

Now it was her turn to hoist the family's banner, and she and her husband opened their little place on Store Kongensgade here. With two children to raise—Oskar, now 35, and Mia, now 33, both of whom work with her—Ms. Davidsen decided to open only five days a week, and only for lunch, although she serves "lunch" from 9 a.m. on, and there are usually passengers from the Norwegian ships that dock nearby waiting outside for a pick-me-up when she unlocks her door.

I was surprised, the first time I went there a couple of decades ago, that the restaurant wasn't airier. Why, I asked her, did she choose a space with small windows and low ceilings?

"We have bright, beautiful summers," she told us, "but the winters are long and dark. We get up in the dark, and we get home from the office in the dark, so you use bright colors, you light a lot of candles and you try to make rooms *hygge*, meaning cozy."

If the gloom is particularly Stygian, you could do much worse than pay a lunchtime call on Ms. Davidsen. She is at work most business days in her clogs, chef's whites and a towering toque, with her red plastic eyeglasses on a pearl chain around her neck. Blond, round-faced and rosy-cheeked, seldom without a smile on her face, she is the personification of sunshine.

By noon most days, every seat is filled. Local businessmen, shoppers and tourists vie for places, and foreigners get an exceptionally warm greeting. Either Ida (she pronounces her name EE-da, not EYE-da) or Oskar explains the composition of the sandwiches displayed in glass cases to each customer, and those who find the nomenclature hard to manage can order by pointing.

The lunchtime feasts need not be expensive, even if there is a dollop of caviar or a smidgen of smoked salmon on one of your *smørrebrød*. Our parade of delicacies, irrigated by Carlsberg and aquavit (in more judicious quantities this time), cost $78.

Some of the very best *smørrebrød* depend on ingredients with short seasons. So be sure to inquire about the availability of crayfish, lobster and the sweet little fjord shrimp. And if you are lucky enough to find yourself in Copenhagen in late April or in May, when the first delectable new potatoes are dug, do not fail to order a sliced potato sandwich with apples, thyme and onions.

Sound strange? Well, it's Ida Davidsen's favorite *smørrebrød*, and the favorite of many other Danes, too. Competition among restaurants to serve it is so fierce that the year's first sack of spuds can fetch as much as $65 a pound.

—*Copenhagen, October 23, 2002*

Herring, the Fish That Roared

Capt. Bo Christianson, the skipper of the *Ron*, a sturdy 115-foot trawler out of Fiskebäck, a small port on Sweden's west coast, warned me to be careful. The deck was covered with slippery silver scales. Then he lifted a hatch so I could see the night's catch in the hold below: tens of thousands of beautiful fish, 8 to 10 inches long, with bluish backs, iridescent sides and gold eyes, kept fresh in a bath of refrigerated seawater.

Herring. Clupea harengus.

Men like Captain Christianson have put to sea for centuries in search of herring; Scandinavian burial mounds dating from Neolithic times contain herring bones. Humble though it may be, and about as glamorous as a galosh, it is a fish that has shaped the political and social history of Europe like no other, with the possible exception of cod. The Hanseatic League, the medieval economic guild, came into being because the Germans had the salt that the Scandinavians coveted as a preservative for their herrings, and British and Dutch sea power was built on the back of the herring trade.

Herrings remain a staple in the diets of northern Europeans—not only the Scandinavians but also the Dutch, British, Germans and others.

The French grill them and serve them with mustard sauce. The British cool-smoke them, turning them into breakfast kippers. The Germans fillet them, cure them and wrap them around onions or pickles to make *rollmops*.

We Americans are not great herring eaters, although we speak of misleading data as "red herrings" (because smoked herrings were once used by poachers to throw dogs off a fox's scent). And we sing of "darling Clementine," who shod her feet, size 9, with "herring boxes without topses."

Smoked, salted or pickled in countless ways, flavored with mustard or curry, tomatoes or dill, Scandinavian herrings have manifold virtues. They keep well, in some cases without refrigeration. They are packed with proteins and healthy oils. They are cheap, versatile and delectable.

At least to me they are, although I admit that every time I tell certain of my friends I'm bound for Sweden, they make sour faces and mutter, "Yuck, herring." I guess they think herrings are slimy or smelly or something. Well, they aren't, not in the hands of a capable cook. Pickled herrings are plump, firm and rich, suffused with the sweetness of the sugar and the contrasting tartness of the vinegar in their brine. Believe me, they beat a shrimp cocktail every time for jolting a jaded palate.

Swedes don't eat as much herring as they once did; there are too many options that didn't exist a century ago. For many people, for example, cereal and yogurt have supplanted herring at breakfast. But herrings are still deeply rooted in national tradition.

"The first new potato of the year is still an excuse for eating herring," said Ulrika Bengtsson, who once cooked for the Swedish consul general in New York and now runs a restaurant on the Upper East Side specializing in *husmanskost*, or Swedish home cooking. "So is Easter, and so is midsummer, and the midwinter holiday that we call Lucia, and Christmas, of course."

Herrings are, in fact, accorded special status in the Swedish language. A sole or a plaice or a turbot is a plain old "*fisk*," or fish. But a herring, as Bertil Adolfsson, chairman of the Swedish West Coast Fisherman's Organization, told me emphatically, "is something special: it's a *sill*, not a fish." A *sill*, that is, if it comes from the Skagerrak or the Kattegat or the North Sea; if it comes from the less salty Baltic Sea, off the east coast of Sweden, it will be smaller and less oily, and it will be called a *strömming*.

•　•　•

Since time immemorial, herrings have moved in vast shoals, migrating every year from one area to another in seemingly fixed patterns, then mysteriously failing to show up, leaving fishing fleets with nothing to catch. It happened at Marstrand in Sweden a century ago, after many decades when you could scoop the fish from the harbor with buckets; at Scheveningen in the Netherlands in the 1950s; and at Siglufjördur and all over Iceland in 1968. Overfishing was certainly a significant factor.

But for the moment, regulations imposed by the European Community and by Baltic governments appear to have improved the situation. Boats from the Swedish west coast are limited this year to 34,917 metric tons from local waters (the Skagerrak and the Kattegat) and 47,102 metric tons from the Baltic. They were also barred from fishing between June 22 and Aug. 5.

The week I visited him, Captain Christianson, a fifth-generation fisherman, sailed on Sunday and dropped his net about 9 o'clock that night as the fish rose toward the surface. He lifted it five hours later, then dropped it again for a shorter trawl. By 9 o'clock Monday morning, he was tied up at the Paul Mattson processing plant here in Ellos, 40 miles north of Göteborg on a stretch of granitic, heavily indented coastline much like Maine's.

Grabbing a nine-inch-wide rubber hose awaiting him on the dock, he plunged it into the hold, switched on the pumps and soon 30 tons of herring, plus the chilled seawater keeping the fish cold, were headed into the plant. There, gleaming stainless-steel machinery sorts the fish according to size, culling imperfect ones and sending them to a fish-meal factory. Those that survive go onto six filleting lines. A few fillets are shipped fresh, either directly to Göteborg, to be sold in the city's famous fish market, known as the Fish Church because of its odd Gothic design, or elsewhere. But most go into plastic barrels filled with pickling brine.

That, I had thought, would be it, but no. After they have been filled, the barrels are shuttled to storerooms tunneled into a cliff behind the plant. At any given time, 15,000 of them are stored there, at 32 to 35 degrees Fahrenheit. They stay for up to a year, maturing like casks of wine or brandy. The length of time and the makeup of the brine in each lot is specified by the customer.

About 60 percent of Mattson's output goes abroad, mainly to Germany, and the rest goes to processors in Sweden, like Abba, whose products are widely sold in the United States, or to markets or restaurants. They add sauces or flavorings.

The permutations are endless. At Melanders Fisk, a leading fishmonger in Stockholm, I counted eight varieties, all house-made— marinated herring (with sour cream), spiced herring, herring in mustard sauce, herring with garlic, herring in curry sauce, herring in tomato sauce, glassblowers' herring and *matjes* herring. *Matjes* means "maiden," and *matjes* herring is made from female fish that have not spawned. Glassblowers' herring is made by pouring pickling liquid into a glass jar filled with layers of salt herring, sliced onions, carrots, horseradish root and ginger, and seasoned with allspice, bay leaves and mustard seed.

In the canned and bottled fish section of a typical supermarket in southern Sweden, I counted no less than 24 varieties of herring, many available in several different brands.

I've met plenty of herring I didn't like. I find the odor of *surströmming*, fermented Baltic herring, unspeakably foul. *Sotare*, or chimney sweeps, which are herrings grilled until soot-black, don't do a whole lot for me, either.

But bockling, or hot-smoked herrings, are a joy, the flesh moist and delicate. And there will always be a place on my table for Janssons Frestelse, or Jansson's Temptation, named for a cleric, opposed on principle to pleasure, who couldn't resist it. It's a simple dish, essentially scalloped potatoes cooked with sliced onions and anchovies. But there's a catch. The anchovies the Swedes use aren't anchovies at all but tiny herrings pickled with sugar and sandalwood. Standard anchovies are too salty.

The various smoked and pickled herrings claim pride of place on the smorgasbord, the traditional Swedish buffet, occupying one end of the table and eaten first. Modern life has been hard on the smorgasbord, which at its most lavish can hold 60 or more items. The resplendent buffet at the Operkälleren in Stockholm, initiated in the 1960s by the great restaurateur Tore Wretman, is no more, but Ulriksdals Wärdshus, north of town, still sets a sumptuous table.

Much more commonly encountered these days is the herring plate as a first course—tidbits of three to six herring preparations, almost always accompanied by crisp bread or a brown bread flavored with molasses or malt. A boiled potato usually comes along for the ride, and often a slice or two of Västerbotten cheese as well.

Västerbotten is a potent item, too little known outside Sweden, with the texture of Cheddar and the bite of Parmesan. Made in 40-pound wheels in the remote province northeast of Stockholm for which it is named, it is aged for 11 months. The best comes from the village of Burträsk.

But cheese with fish? It works; perhaps the sharpness of the cheese provides a counterpoint to the richness of the herring.

Two presentations seemed exceptional to my wife, Betsey, and me as we nibbled herring all across Sweden last summer. One was the fat, luscious *matjes* filet at Norrlands Bar and Grill, one of Stockholm's hip new restaurants. It came to the table warm, showered with chives and chopped red onion. A kettle of brown butter for dipping came with it. Casual Norrlands may be, but not with food and drink; the mandatory aquavit was served in wittily anthropomorphic mini-carafes called grandmas.

The other winner was offered by Leif Mannerström at Sjömagasinet, a seafood Valhalla in Göteborg, housed in an old Swedish East India Company warehouse. At Christmas, he told me, he lays out a hearthside feast including 16 kinds of herring and serves 10,000 people in 22 days.

We settled for less, but it was still remarkable. The herrings came in handsome black iron pots cradled in ice, and the spread included not only pickled herring in horseradish and sour cream but also mild fried *strömming*. Both were new to us, and delicious. The mustard sauce was better than most, brightened by masses of chopped dill. There were two kinds of Västerbotten, with cumin and without. And the bottle of aquavit—O. P. Anderson, Göteborg's favorite—had its own icy place of honor.

Aquavit, if you haven't had the pleasure, is a caraway-flavored spirit, colorless but lethal. For foreigners, it is often the prelude to a three-hour nap. For Swedes, it is always an invitation to song, much of it ribald. Not surprisingly, the favorite is "Helan Går"—roughly "Bottoms Up!"

—Ellos, Sweden, October 30, 2002

ASIA AND AUSTRALIA

ASIA

Devouring Singapore's Endless Supper

"Food is the purest democracy we have," K. F. Seetoh said as we dug into breakfast bowls of bak kut teh, a peppery, restorative Teochew soup of pork ribs, mushrooms and kidneys. "Singaporeans recognize no difference between bone china and melamine."

Slurp, slurp. Yum, yum. The clear, aromatic broth, full of tender, close-grained pork, perked up by herbs and whole garlic cloves, was cooked in a hole-in-the-wall next to a busy expressway and eaten at a sidewalk table. Cabdrivers, teachers and a few junior executives slurped around us. Bak kut teh is the city's preferred hangover remedy, and Ng Ah Sio makes the best, which is why Mr. Seetoh took me there.

This was the start of 16 hours of almost continuous talking and eating, with the rollicking Mr. Seetoh—"K. F. stands for King of Food," he joked—as my guide and noshing companion. Racing around this island city-state in his Mitsubishi van, with two brief pauses to shower and change clothes (eating in Singapore can be messy), we would make 18 stops before midnight.

"Don't eat, just taste," he kept saying. I tried, but I failed. More gourmand than gourmet, I finished much of what was put before me at a dizzying array of food stalls, storefronts and hawker centers, which are so called because they were built by the government of Prime Minister Lee Kuan Yew to get open-air food-sellers, or hawkers, off the sidewalks and indoors.

Fish balls followed *chwee kueh, soto ayam* followed *roti prata,* and *rojak* followed chicken rice, in a multicultural parade of gastronomic hits that issued, in most cases, from kitchens no longer than walk-in closets. With so little overhead to defray, gluttony was cheap: $2 a plate on average.

Singapore is one of the most food-mad cities in an ever more food-mad world, with more than 6,500 restaurants and 11,500 food stalls jammed into its 250 square miles. They offer Cantonese, Teochew, Hokkien, Hakka and Hainanese dishes—all with roots in China—plus curries from south India, tikkas from north India, Malay and Indonesian and Thai specialties, and adaptations and mixtures of all of them.

It adds up to a feast fit for the gods, but for the ordinary visitor, even one who has been here often, it can seem more like culinary chaos. Which is where Mr. Seetoh, 40, steps into the picture. Once by his own description "a useless street kid," he skipped university, learned photography in the army.

But food was his passion, and in 1998, he and Lim Moh Cher, an equally enthusiastic eater, started a guide to street food.

They called it Makansutra, from the Malay word for "eat" and the Sanskrit word for a set of rules or maxims. It has grown into a small empire, including a Web site and television programs as well as an amazingly comprehensive guidebook, whose current, 456-page edition contains detailed information about thousands of eating places.

Now Singapore's unchallenged makan guru, instantly recognizable in his trademark sunglasses and his crumpled cap, Mr. Seetoh is greeted by one and all as he chugs by on the yellow Vespa or the

Canondale mountain bike he uses—when he isn't lugging an elderly visiting makan maven around town.

I think the knock on Singapore is way overdone. Sure, it's squeaky clean and modern, but come on: Does anyone actually prefer the beggars, rubbish and shantytowns that deface many large Asian cities? Not the poor souls who live in them. It's plenty tough on miscreants, but hardly deserving of William Gibson's woundingly dismissive tag line, "Disneyland with the Death Penalty."

Under Goh Chok Tong, Lee Kwan Yew's successor, individualism has gained a little more breathing room. The longstanding and much-ridiculed ban on chewing gum has just been relaxed. Censorship guidelines are currently under high-level review. Nightclubs, once invisible, now throb into the wee hours. And the louchest of Maugham's or Conrad's characters would feel right at home in the seedy bars and brothels off Geylang Road, east of the city center.

Having spent many years bulldozing old buildings, Singapore is now busy saving others and putting them to new uses. One of these, a grandiose neo-Palladian pile close to the Padang, the city's central green, was once the General Post Office; now it is the Fullerton, a luxury hotel with one of the city's best upmarket dining rooms, Jade. Having spent years in headlong pursuit of Mammon, Singapore is now busy chasing culture, as exemplified by the new $343 million Esplanade arts center, known colloquially as the Durian because its spiky profile resembles that of a local fruit.

"We are witnessing many changes," said Tommy Koh, the country's dynamic former ambassador to the United States and the United Nations, who helped to bring many of the new developments about.

—*Singapore, September 10, 2003*

Looking Up an Old Love on the Streets of Vietnam

She used to walk past my little villa in Saigon, not far from the American embassy, her conical straw hat on the back of her head, white pajamas flapping as she loped down the street, soup makings dangling from the wooden yoke across her frail shoulders. She came early every morning, repeating the monosyllable with an inimitable inflection.

"Pho," she called, her voice gentle and plaintive. *"Pho."*

That was 35 years ago, and I took it for granted that the delectable, aromatic noodle soup she sold, crowned with a lush tangle of green herbs, had originated many generations ago in the fertile Mekong Delta. Wrong on both counts, as I discovered when I finally returned not long ago to this ancient land that struggled so fiercely for freedom. *Pho* was developed by cooks in Hanoi, not in the South, and not until after the French arrived late in the 19th century, importing their love of beef to a pork-eating culture.

The name might have given me a clue. *"Pho"* is pronounced almost exactly like *"feu,"* the French word for "fire," as in pot-au-feu. Did Vietnamese cooks learn its secrets while toiling in the kitchens of colonial masters? Some think so; others think it evolved from Chinese models, like the Vietnamese language and the people themselves.

Today it is a national passion, beloved across the country in hamlets as in cities. It is almost as widely available in the United States, where few big cities lack a *pho* shop, and some, like Washington, have dozens.

In Hanoi, *pho* is a cult. It is served in alleyways and on street corners all over town, usually on low plastic tables, surrounded by even lower plastic stools, only about 12 inches high, that always make me feel like a circus elephant trying to balance on a ball. These are set on the sidewalk, in the gutter and even in the roadway; the Vietnamese give special meaning to the phrase "street food."

Here the soothing broth is paler than in the United States or in Ho Chi Minh City (Saigon's official name, HCMC for short). The rice noodles are more delicately translucent, and fewer embellishments are added than in the more indulgent South. The result is light and thrillingly restorative. On a good day, I think I could eat three bowls and leave under my own power.

My wife, Betsey, and I stopped in at Mai Anh, one of a string of open-air *pho* shops on Le Van Huu Street, which runs along the southern edge of Hanoi's bustling French Quarter. Stock made by simmering oxtails and marrow bones for 24 hours, along with onions, star anise, ginger and cinnamon bark, was bubbling away in a cauldron perched on a charcoal stove. Bowls of various meats—cooked chicken, giblets, paper-thin raw sirloin, pig hearts—awaited our inspection. We chose beef.

If you choose chicken, you will be eating *pho ga*; if you choose beef, you will be eating *pho bo*. I don't imagine for a minute that you'll choose pig hearts.

The *pho* meister dunks a sieve full of flat, precooked noodles into a pot of boiling water (so they do not cool the soup), drains them and slides them into a bowl. Thinly sliced onions and chopped coriander leaves go in next, along with shavings of ginger. Then the blood-red beef, and last a few ladles of hot stock, which cooks the meat in a few seconds while giving off a fragrant, enveloping cloud of steam.

On the table are spring onions, red chili sauce and vinegar with garlic slices to enrich your meal-in-a-bowl, plus several lime wedges. A southerner would feel deprived without some bean sprouts, and without a plate heaped high with herbs—*rau que*, or Asian basil; earthy *ngo gai*, or sawleaf herb; and once in a great while *rau ram*, or

Vietnamese coriander. But the northerners are ascetics compared with their southern cousins. Still influenced by the puritanical Confucianism of their Chinese neighbors, they prefer their flavors pure, unadorned and crystal-clear.

As you will find when you dig in—chopsticks in one hand, plastic spoon in the other—no sacrifice of heartiness or complexity is entailed. Mix and slurp, sniff and gulp to your heart's content, for less than $1.

For some reason the snarl of the motorbikes as they stream past, all but nipping at your ankles, is no distraction. Maybe because it's so much fun to watch your fellow eaters, especially if some are novices. We saw an eager if inept German woman get through her soup by coiling her noodles around her chopsticks with her free hand.

The Vietnamese wax poetic about *pho*, assigning it a central and unifying place in their culture. Duong Thu Huong, a novelist, rhapsodized about walking the streets, inhaling the soup's subtle perfume as it rises from the stockpots. Huu Ngoc, a social historian, sees it as a symbol of the national fight for self-determination: even in the darkest times, when the wars against the French and Americans were going badly, the Vietnamese were always free to express themselves by making and eating *pho*, their own culinary creation.

"It was complete, nutritious, infinitely delicious and yet so easy to digest," he recalled a few years ago, "that we could eat it morning and night, day after day." And so the northerners do, looking down upon the southerners, who eat their *pho* mainly at breakfast and occasionally at lunch.

For the Vietnamese, even those who left the country long ago, *pho* tends to stir memories, the way a madeleine did for Proust. I, too, was ambushed by the past. A bowl of *bun bo Hue*, the imperial capital's spicier version of *pho*, made with round noodles, beef, pork, lemongrass and whole chilies, carried me back to the turbulent days of the Buddhist uprising of 1966, when John D. Negroponte, now the United States representative at the United Nations, was in charge of the American consulate in Hue, on the very street where I was eating.

Our friend Mai Pham, who was born in Saigon, runs a hugely successful Vietnamese restaurant, Lemon Grass, in Sacramento. She also writes cookbooks, most recently *Pleasures of the Vietnamese Table* (HarperCollins, 2001), and she has developed a refrigerated *pho* stock base, marketed to restaurants and institutions by StockPot, a subsidiary of the Campbell Soup Company.

Why, I asked her recently, does *pho* fascinate you so much?

"It's so beefy!" she exclaimed with a smile and without hesitation. "For me, it's the ultimate comfort food. You smell the soup's perfume, and it's so beefy!"

Her husband, Greg Drescher, director of education at the Napa Valley campus of the Culinary Institute of America, chimed in. Perhaps for the Vietnamese, for most of whom beef remains a great luxury, he said, but not for Americans, for whom it is one of life's commonplaces.

What attracts me is the hypnotic mixture of flavors in the broth, especially those imparted by spices like star anise and ginger. Preliminary charring of the onions and ginger adds a smoky undertone. In the South, the mingling of sweet, sour and salty tastes is further augmented by a few dashes of *nuoc mam*, the fermented fish sauce that plays the same role in Vietnam that soy plays in much of Asia. The clearest and most pungent comes from Phu Quoc island, off the south coast.

No one has ever accused me of being a minimalist; when I'm lucky enough to land within range of an In-N-Out burger joint, for example, I order my double double with the works. So it's no surprise that I load up my *pho* with a couple of squeezes of lime juice, a scattering of bean sprouts (if they're sufficiently crunchy), a disk or two of hot green chili and a variety of herb leaves, pulled carefully from their stems.

That's the Saigon style: a bowl of soup and a salad, all in one.

Saigon, or HCMC, to be proper about it, has a range of soup shops, from tiny ones in the Hanoi style to a few *pho* factories like Pho 2000, near the Ben Thanh market, which Bill Clinton put on the map by eating there. Occasionally, a gifted, energetic cook will make *pho* at home—a major task, given the time needed to make the broth—and one of the best bowls we ate was served to us at home by Nguyen Huu Hoang Trang, a veteran of restaurant kitchens.

So fine was her touch that every one of the key ingredients, from cinnamon to anise to ginger to onions, was individually discernible in the perfumed steam that rose from the soup, and in the flavor, too.

You could miss my favorite breakfast place in downtown Saigon if you got there at the wrong time of day, which is anytime after about 11 in the morning. There is no sign, and most of the furnishings disappear after the close of business.

Run by a tiny, wizened man whom people call Chu Sau, which means Sixth Uncle, it consists of a few battered Formica tables in a gloomy alley covered with a corrugated tin roof, plus several of those diabolically low tables and chairs, murder for my aging knees, on the sidewalk. The address is 39 Mac Thi Buoi, two long blocks from the Caravelle Hotel, toward the river.

Chu Sau's limpid *pho* comes with a bowl of notably crisp mung bean sprouts, hoisin sauce (best avoided, I think, because it muddies the soup's flavor) and an unusually bright orange chili sauce, as well as Asian basil and fuzzy-leafed mint. What set it apart, for me, was the mellowness of the amber-hued broth, in which the taste of cinnamon was pronounced. It glittered in the mouth, the way homemade bouillon does and beef stock made from a cube doesn't.

The noodles were perfectly al dente, if you will permit a solecism, and I enjoyed them so much that I didn't even give myself a demerit when I splashed chili sauce all over my white polo shirt.

Pho Dau, located in a courtyard off Nam Ky Khoi Nghia Boulevard, which leads to the airport, is an entirely different kettle of soup. During the war, it was a hangout for South Vietnamese generals; now it is a haunt of the new, privileged capitalists, whose Mercedes SUVs and $6,000 Honda motorbikes are parked out front. Bits of beef cartilage and tendon enrich its broth, as do quantities of coriander.

With our *pho*, we drank glasses of fabulously smooth *ca phe sua da*, which is Vietnamese filter coffee, served iced with condensed milk.

As we watched the well-dressed customers eating *pho* for breakfast, we talked about how odd soup seems to us Americans as a daily curtain-raiser. But it isn't that strange, really: the Japanese eat miso; the Chinese eat congee, a soupy porridge; the French (particularly Parisians) eat onion soup after a night on the town; and the Hungarians eat sauerkraut-and-sausage soup to ease a hangover.

Pho Hoa, an open-front restaurant on Pasteur Street, is less grubby and more cosmopolitan than most noodle shops, with comfortable tables and chairs. I learned some more lessons there, even though it came late on our soup schedule. Lesson 1: The richness that characterizes well-made *pho* broth comes not from fat, which must be skimmed from the broth, but from marrow. Lesson 2: You can order not only rare beef (*tai*) in your *pho*, but also well-done beef (*chin*) and fatty beef (*gau*).

My teachers were the affable gent at the next table, Lam-Hoang Nguyen, a visiting Vietnamese restaurateur from Thunder Bay, Ontario, on Lake Superior, and his wife, Kim-Ha Lai.

"When we come back," he confided after a while, "we always go right into the street. The street is where you find the quality in Saigon—not in hotels."

That's good advice, not only in HCMC, and not only when you want a bowl of *pho*. Vietnam is full of quick, fresh, readily available nibbles, and many people eat four or five minimeals every day.

In the main Saigon market, Ben Thanh, where you can buy a suitcase, look live snakes in the eye, shop for spices and snack the day away, we discovered *bun thit nuong*—an irresistible combination of vermicelli threads tossed in scallion oil, topped with lettuce, strips of barbecued pork, cucumber and carrot slices and peanuts and dressed with *nuoc cham*, a luscious sauce made from *nuoc mam* diluted with water, sugar, lime juice and chilies. Sweet and tart, bland and spicy, soft and crunchy, ample but light, it made a luscious hot-weather lunch early one afternoon.

No wonder Mr. Drescher always makes a point of heading for

the market to eat *bun thit* as soon as he steps off the plane from California.

One evening at Anh Thi, one of several Saigon crepe shops in narrow Dinh Cong Trang Street, we watched orange tongues of flame dart from underneath charcoal braziers to lick at the dusk. The crepes are called *banh xeo*, the word *"xeo"* an onomatopoeic rendering of the sound of batter hitting the pan.

The cooks sit on low benches in front of batteries of braziers topped with 12-inch pans; they control the speed of cooking by shifting pans from one fire to another. The crepes are yet another example of the Vietnamese genius for combining inexpensive ingredients to produce lively but never overpowering tastes and intriguing textures. In this case the secrets are a light, bright crepe batter made with rice powder, coconut milk, local curry powder and turmeric; a filling of shrimp, bean sprouts and unsmoked bacon; and, as is so often the case here, a wrap and a dip.

You tear off a piece of crepe, wrap it in a mustard-green leaf with an aroma so sharp that it made me sneeze, add a chili and some mint and dip the whole package in peppery, faintly sweet, faintly fishy *nuoc cham*. The special crepe, with an extralarge portion of shrimp, costs all of $1.35.

"Delicious, nutritious and cheap," Betsey said. "I think that's a pretty tough combination to beat."

At Lac Thien in Hue, whose proprietors are deaf-mutes, we sampled the local version of crepes, known as *banh khoai*, or "happy pancakes," served at steel-topped tables. These are smaller, about six inches in diameter, sweeter and eggier. They are served not with mustard greens but with coriander and mint, and not with *nuoc cham* but with a fermented soybean sauce.

Cha Ca La Vong in Hanoi, owned by the same family for generations, serves stunning freshwater fish, cubed and braised with turmeric. Dill, spring onions, peanuts and chilies are at hand to enliven flavor.

Splendid stuff. But except for *pho*, no street food we ate could touch the phenomenal fare at Bun Cha Hang Manh in Hanoi's Old Quarter, a four-story warren of tiny rooms and cracked floors. Crouching women cook everything on tiny propane stoves in the open-air entrance hall. "Everything" consists of two items, both of which are the best of their kind available, in Hanoi or anywhere else, for that matter.

One of them is *bun cha*, Vietnam's apotheosis of the pig. It consists of charcoal-grilled strips of belly pork and pork patties the size of a silver dollar. These arrive at a table laden with a plate of rice noodles, a plate of red and green lettuce and herbs of every description, a little bowl of finely chopped young garlic and a bigger bowl of *nuoc cham*, with slices of tenderizing papaya bobbing gaily in it. For hotheads, there are incendiary bird chilies.

Hang Manh's second dish is spring rolls (*nem ran* in the North and *cha gio* in the South)—great fat ones, as thick as your thumb, packed with crab, ground pork, wood-ear mushrooms, onions and bean threads. I noticed right away that the frying oil was changed every few minutes, and of course the rolls emerged from it crackling, light and greaseless.

"These rolls make the rest of what we've had here taste like so many Rice Krispies," Betsey announced.

We went twice, at 11:30 a.m. both times, to avoid the throngs that pack this humble restaurant, while ignoring others serving similar specialties. We ate until we could eat no more. I wonder: Can there be any better $3 lunch for two, anywhere in the world?

—Hanoi, Vietnam, August 13, 2003

At Ease in Vietnam, Asia's New Culinary Star

I t is enough to daunt all but the most gluttonous of gastronomes.

Right by the door stand piles of rice from several different provinces, some with large grains, some with small grains, some darker, some lighter, each with a wholly different aroma. Down the aisle are banks of vividly green herbs and vegetables, with their hyper-intense Asian scents and tastes, stunningly fresh despite the lack of refrigeration because they arrive direct from their growers in the middle of the night.

Many of the vegetables are Asian natives—bumpy bitter melons, lotus stems, long beans, banana flowers, luffa squashes and pungent Chinese celery. But others are European transplants—delicacies like baby cress, escarole, miniature artichokes and exquisite asparagus (which the Vietnamese called "French bamboo" when French colonial officials first imported it).

Over there is a cauliflower the size of a basketball. Over here are mounds of delectable, unfamiliar fruit—enormous knobby durians, which smell like rotting cheese but taste like rich custard, and spiny little soursops, which yield a sweet-and-tart juice that makes an unforgettable sorbet, and horrid lipstick-pink dragon fruit. Breadfruit. Jackfruit. Custard apples. Tamarind pods.

On the other side of a partition are caged chickens and other fowl, squawking noisily, and all kinds of sea creatures—iced squid, crabs tied with red ropes, clams the size of silver dollars with ridged shells, carp swimming in basins and tiger prawns that look as ferocious as their namesakes, all overseen by a raucous corps of vendors in rubber boots.

This is the tumultuous Ben Thanh market, which faces Quach Thi Trang Square in the heart of Ho Chi Minh City. A shedlike building with four entrances, it attests to this country's peacetime bounty. Visit it, look around, join the chattering, jostling crowd, listen to the noodle vendor's spiel, grab a snack. That will put you in the right frame of mind for the splendid meals that await you in a galaxy of attractively designed, mostly new restaurants near the big hotels here.

Restaurant cooking of real excellence has evolved in the last 10 years, and particularly in the last three, with bright young chefs innovating and adapting like their brethren in other major Asian capitals. French and Chinese and Indian influences remain, of course, the legacy of a long and clamorous history, but something new and manifestly Vietnamese is emerging.

Spring rolls and salad rolls on white tablecloths, you ask? Absolutely, and in Ho Chi Minh City's better places they might be filled with squid or grilled fish or chicken instead of crab or shrimp and pork. Chefs have no qualms about serving the traditional alongside the inventive: a plate of fat, rosy shrimp with satisfyingly sour tamarind pulp, for instance, together with a plate of tiny quail glazed with star anise and grilled with garlic and paprika.

My wife, Betsey, and I ate those two dishes, among others, at Nam Phan, a luxurious villa decorated with antique ceramics and scrolls. On our table, a single orchid floated in a silver and black lacquer box.

Nothing so deluxe could ever have been found in Ho Chi Minh City's former incarnation, wartime Saigon, where I was based for almost three years as a correspondent. It would have been easier to unearth a truffle. The ingredients weren't available (too many roadblocks), nor were the cooks (in the army). So we hung out in a series of joints that flourished in a world of low expectations and minimal competition.

On my return this year, I couldn't find any of them. Every one has been swallowed up by the 35 years that have passed since I left, but I remember them—a street-corner Basque place called Aterbea, with a jai alai mural, where I ate *boudin noir*, sautéed apples and mashed potatoes for lunch, because it was good and because the wizened

waiters assured me it was what the Foreign Legionnaires had ordered, and Amiral, where the resourceful Morley Safer gave a jolly
dinner party the same night that Truman Capote gave his storied
Black and White Ball in New York.

Also Cheap Charlie's, where my colleague Charley Mohr (no rela-
tion) taught me to pick up peanuts with chopsticks in a grueling session the night after I arrived; the Arc en Ciel in Cholon, where the
taxi dancers were more interesting than the food; Les Affreux, the
Ghastly Ones, a kind of bistro-in-a-bunker run by Corsicans displaced
from Algeria; and the Guillaume Tell, down by the river, whose proprietor used to drill holes in the bottoms of fancy bottles of wine and
refill them with plonk.

But back to Nam Phan, which is the latest venture of Hoang Khai, a
young entrepreneur who has quickly assembled a group of a dozen
Khai Silk shops, as notable for their décor (a goldfish pond, complete
with humpbacked footbridge, graces the interior of one of them) as
for the chic clothes they sell. His restaurant, like his silk business, is
aimed not only at well-off travelers and expatriates but also at the
growing coterie of high-living Vietnamese. With dinner checks aver-
aging $100 or so a couple, without wine, it is the town's costliest place
to eat.

The villa housing Nam Phan stands at the center of a walled garden on the busy corner of Le Thanh Ton and Hai Ba Trung, two of
the city's main streets. Inside, though, all is quiet. The high-ceilinged
rooms are painted in grays, taupes and whites, and furnished with a
spare, modern refinement rare in Vietnam; no 1930s nostalgia, no
Indochine *tristesse* here. A series of glassed, backlighted niches, each
holding a vase with a single flower, dominates one wall.

"Ravishing," said Betsey, who is not easily swept off her feet.

I would say the same about the food, especially the salads. One was
made from grilled dried beef and the tender leaves and crunchy stems
of water spinach, a relative of the morning glory. It was light and re-

freshing, just the thing on a warm day. Another, more elaborate and more assertive but equally appealing, included lotus stems, bits of pork and tiny shrimp, fried shallots, chilies, mint, *rau ram*, or Vietnamese coriander, and fish sauce. Tangy, fishy, sweet all at once, it had the layers of flavor the Vietnamese love.

Chicken and seafood were ground together to make the unusual, ethereal spring rolls, which were served, sparkling on the plate, in bite-size pieces.

But nothing, for me, matched the shrimp with tamarind sauce. The pulp inside the tamarind pods, which look like giant brown beans, had been sweetened just enough to balance its sourness, and gobs of black pepper added a contrasting punch. The combination was fabulous. I thought of semisweet chocolate, but Betsey put the matter much more aptly. "Spice candy," she said.

The plates and cutlery were good-looking and the service was charming. The only jarring note, at least to us, was the flag that we could see out the window—a yellow star on a red field. Just then, it was hard to believe we were in a Communist nation.

Two of the other choice spots in town, Mandarin and Hoi An, are located around the corner from each other. Both are owned by another Vietnamese businessman, Pham Quang Minh, and ably managed by an Australian, Frank Jones, a former actor.

Hoi An specializes in the cooking of the central coast town of that name, a photogenic little port whose food and architecture were influenced by the Chinese, Japanese, Dutch and Portuguese merchants who settled there in the 16th, 17th and 18th centuries. The restaurant is a facsimile of an old dining house, with ideograms on the walls and carved shutters dividing the rooms. Bonsai trees and shrubs decorate various corners. The chairs are ironwood.

In a typical example of central Vietnamese delicacy, the flavor palette in Hoi An's spring rolls is limited to shrimp and pork paste, black sesame seeds and Chinese coriander, and the paper in which they are wrapped, made from rice and cassava flour, is more brittle than most. The salad rolls, which are just as elegant, arrive with a miniature pagoda carved from a carrot.

Shrimp grilled in a banana leaf, another specialty, emerge rich and buttery. Dipped in a concoct-it-yourself sauce of lime juice and salt, they spoil you forever for shrimp cocktails. Sumptuous, chili-laced beef and onions, served inside a coconut, is vaguely South Indian in style; could that be the influence of the Portuguese?

Though the rice noodles are not authentic (only those made with water from a particular Hoi An well get the nod from the purists), the *ca lau* here is luscious all the same: thin slices of baconlike pork, butterflied shrimp and crushed bits of crunchy sesame cake are piled onto the broad noodles, and a bowl of clear, fragrant marrow-bone broth is served on the side. The dish reminded me again of the Vietnamese genius for making a lot from a little.

We went to Mandarin at the suggestion of Loren Jenkins, a colleague of many years' standing who is now the foreign editor for National Public Radio. "As good a Vietnamese meal as I've ever had," he announced when we ran into him in Hue, and he was not that far off.

Mandarin brims with class. A pianist, a cellist and a violinist play downstairs in the four-story, skylighted building; dinner is served on big, handsome blue-and-white plates; and shellfish, the house specialty, are delivered directly from Nha Trang on the South China Sea several times a week. Premium ingredients like abalone and shark's fin dot the menu, at a price.

Throwing self-control to the winds, and fortified by a couple of bottles of well-chilled Alsatian riesling from Gustav Lorentz, we managed to work our way through creamy, juicy bay scallops grilled in their shells and dressed with chopped scallions, peanuts and herbs; a tuna salad, served in a green mango, to be spread on rice crackers with a chili sauce—that familiar Vietnamese blend of spicy, fishy, salty, sour and caramelized tastes again, with so much ginger that it left a stinging sensation on the lips; a few pickles and other tidbits; and then a pair of gargantuan crabs steamed in beer.

The crabs left a lasting impression, to say the least. They had thick shells and big claws, like stone crabs, and they gave up firm, moist, glacier-white lumps of meat, as big as cherries, as sweet as you could ask.

En garde, Baltimore!

I must admit I wondered what I was getting us into when we walked into Blue Ginger, a place with Italianate arches and a tile floor. A "traditional" Vietnamese band was having a go at "My Bonnie Lies Over the Ocean."

But the menu held out promise, and the kitchen made good on it. Beef rolls flavored with turmeric and lemongrass, among other spices, wrapped in peppery *la lot* leaves and grilled over charcoal, got us off to a good start. Long, thin purple eggplants, roasted to a smoky, melting succulence, combined beautifully with crumbly, spicy pork. Fried chicken—we called it Eastern fried chicken—was suffused with the heady taste of lemongrass.

A tureen of sweet-and-sour soup was dazzling in its complexity, a far cry from the derisory brew served under that heading in tens of thousands of Chinese restaurants around the world. Among its ingredients were fiery bird's-eye chilies, coriander, Thai basil, lime juice, fish sauce, tomatoes, onions, star fruit and tiny, tender clams closely resembling Neapolitan *vongole*.

The stylish Temple Club, one of the older upscale restaurants in town, is an immensely cheerful place, where the merest acknowledgment of waiters and busboys produces faces creased with smiles. The hallway is lined with ceramic elephants, lighted by oil lamps, and more lanterns burn inside, casting dancing, romantic shadows onto the bare brick walls.

First things first: the martinis were world-class. We hugely enjoyed the black-lipped clams, steamed with a chili-laced broth in a clay pot; the maître d'hôtel said they had come from Vungtau, at the mouth of the Saigon River. Duck breast, flavored with ginger, grilled over charcoal, was served rare; in southeastern France, it would have been called *magret*, and it could have been no better. All Vietnamese fowl are free-range birds, and they taste it.

Camargue is another matter altogether, a thatched, two-story open-air pavilion where the European accents are in the foreground. Seated upstairs, we dined by candlelight with palm fronds dangling near us, overhead circular fans beavering away and billiard balls clicking downstairs. Feeling as louche as Bogart, we started with foie gras (cool, firm, brightened by a Sauternes jelly and altogether respectable, if not quite up to the standard of Chez L'Ami Louis) and *vitello tonnato*, as good a dish as we tasted in all of Vietnam during a 10-day stay.

Large prawns, listed on the menu as *gambas*, grilled and set on edge around a heap of remarkable, tarragon-infused ratatouille, not only tasted fresh from the sea, they had the supple texture that disappears in a split-second when our own gulf shrimp are flash-frozen. One flaw: A lemon butter sauce, which might have been fine in Lyons, seemed far too heavy in the tropics.

But other things were just as they should have been: quick, competent service from nattily uniformed waiters, crusty minibaguettes and the best wine list in town, with plenty of classified-growth clarets (a rarity in Vietnam) and a crisp, racy Pouilly-Fumé from Henri Bourgeois, a top-flight grower.

Betsey and I were constantly reminded of New Orleans as we moved through the languid streets that for me will always constitute Saigon. It was all there: the humidity lying over the city like damp cotton, the slow-moving river lined with decaying warehouses, the oleander blossoms, the scent of jasmine in the air.

And like New Orleans, Ho Chi Minh City is blessed not only with terrific big-time restaurants but also with worthwhile smaller ones tucked into nooks and crannies.

Got a lunch date? On Nguyen Thiep, a narrow street a couple of blocks from the Caravelle Hotel in the center of town, you will find three worthy choices.

Lemon Grass, a long room with minimally adorned white stucco walls, does a mean green mango salad, with slices of the fruit mixed with chopped peanuts, shallots and fish sauce, and herb-scented grilled chicken kebabs. (Green mango is not unripe, by the way; it is a special variety, bred to be green.) Whole crab in pepper sauce is terrific; the leathery fish cakes are not.

Globo, a bohemian bar and restaurant done up in black and white, with zebra-striped fans and Tunisian folk art, is a hangout for expats from all over, and Augustin, a bistro you might think had been transported intact from 1930s Paris, with a clientele that might very well have made the trip with it. You will recognize a lot of old friends on the menu—*salade niçoise, entrecôte bordelaise*, profiteroles—and they are all well executed.

Cup of coffee? Brodard, established in 1932, will serve you a fine one, with a perfect head of *crema*, with a slice of house-made chocolate cake if you want. Drink a Pernod if you are in the mood, or a delicious *citron pressé* (freshly made lemonade, best with soda water). Or order one of the juiciest *steak frites* in the city.

The place to go for a Vietnamese iced coffee, made by the drip-drip-drip of water through an individual aluminum filter, flavored with condensed milk, is Givral, catercorner from the Caravelle. Now as always, it is a headquarters for young, giggling schoolgirls, a few of whom, thank goodness, still wear the long and graceful *ao dais*.

If old-fashioned cafes turn you off, head for the I-Box, not far away, a youthful spot with a wildly funky décor.

Ice cream? The best you will find is at Kem Bac Dang, which has several locations around the city. Try the longan, kiwi, coconut or coffee, or spoil yourself with a luscious soursop milkshake.

They used to call Saigon the Paris of the Orient because of its lovely, tree-lined boulevards. The way things are going, with eating out here becoming the kind of preoccupation it already is in Hong Kong, Bangkok and Singapore, they may one day call Ho Chi Minh City the Paris of the Orient because of the quality of its restaurants.

—Ho Chi Minh City, Vietnam, August 27, 2003

A Trip to the Heart of Dim Sum

Eleven o'clock Sunday morning, in the 25th-floor kitchen of the Mandarin Oriental Hotel's Cantonese restaurant, Man Wah. Kong Tseuk Tong, 47, dressed in the white tunic and checked trousers worn by chefs around the world, stands at an immaculate stainless-steel counter, ready to work his magic. His assistants wait at a respectful distance.

Like a cabinetmaker or a glassblower, he is a skilled craftsman, the product of years of exacting training. Dim sum is his craft, and in Hong Kong Sunday lunch is showtime for the dim sum master. It is then that families rich and poor—children, grannies and all—gather to drink tea, discuss the week's events and eat the savories made by Mr. Kong and others like him.

Of course, North Americans and Europeans also like dim sum, which literally means "touch of the heart." Australians like it, too, although they call it *yum cha*, which means "drink tea." Restaurants like Yank Sing in San Francisco and Sun Sui Wah in Vancouver and especially Lai Wah Heen in Toronto (where in season you will find delicately sweet pea-sprout dumplings) serve dim sum worthy of any gourmand's palate.

But Hong Kong, which has about 10,000 places to eat, probably more per capita than any other city, is utterly obsessed with dim sum, and no place else comes close to offering dim sum of equal excellence and variety. This is dim sum nirvana.

Some people eat it every day. If few can afford to eat the meticulously handcrafted creations of Mr. Kong, and in a setting as ritzy as the Mandarin, nobody need go without. There is a dim sum parlor to fit every pocketbook, and at the biggest, noisiest and most frenetic of them people wait in line for up to an hour for their dose of *char siu bao* (fluffy white buns stuffed with barbecued pork) and *har gau* (translucent little purse-shaped dumplings filled with chopped shrimp and bamboo shoots).

"There are hundreds of kinds of dim sum, and new ones are developed every week," said Henry Ho, the Man Wah's courtly manager, who started there as a busboy in 1969. "Ours are a bit fresher than most, made to order from the best ingredients we can find, but the same rules apply here that apply everywhere else: take *char siu bao* and *har gau* off the menu this Sunday, and next Sunday you won't have any customers."

The best chefs apply special touches to the classics. I watched Mr. Kong, a stocky, powerfully built man with corded forearms and asbestos hands, apply his.

First he mixed rice flour, a bit of potato starch and boiling water in a small metal bowl—"Must be boiling," he explained, "or the pastry won't be clear." He turned out the resulting dough on the counter, kneaded it for a minute or so and added a bit of carrot juice before plopping the dough back into the bowl. "Carrot juice?" I asked. "Wait and see," he answered.

Next he nipped out a bit of dough, flattened it into a circle with a single blow from the side of his cleaver, and dropped a tiny lump of premixed filling (shrimp, bamboo shoots, pork fat and coriander leaves, all chopped finely) into its center. Holding the nascent dumpling in his left hand and pushing up its sides until he had a cup shape, he repeatedly pinched the top with his right to close it, moving so fast that I could scarcely follow what he was doing. A final shaping on a wooden board, and he was nearly done.

But not quite. He cooked a mixture of flour and beet juice on a propane stove, made a tiny pastry tube from kitchen parchment and used it to apply two red dots to the golden dumpling. Then he set the finished item in front of me. "Goldfish *har gao*," he said, laughing. Of course. With red eyes.

The whole process had taken about four minutes, and it took four more to steam the "fish," along with three others, in a bamboo basket.

When it came to the table, it looked astonishingly realistic, its tail and fins wobbling slightly when the steamer was opened, as if it were swimming languidly in a pond. The bright green of the coriander and the pink of the shrimp were on display beneath the thin pastry "skin," exactly as Mr. Kong had promised.

My wife, Betsey, and I sampled several other dim sum specialties at the Man Wah, including *siu mai* (a pork dumpling), topped unusually with a quarter-size slice of abalone and crab roe; a miraculously crisp deep-fried mango and seafood roll; and an ethereal coconut tart. There were 28 choices on the menu, which changes every three months, and that only scratches the surface of Mr. Kong's repertory. He told me he can make 15 kinds of pastry, European as well as Asian, and like many dim sum chefs he is adept at baking, pan-frying, deep-frying and steaming both sweet and savory dishes.

Man Wah's choice of teas was equally impressive, including oolongs like Ti Kwan Yin, a fruity green brew from Fujian Province, on the southeast coast; flower-flavored teas like rose, chrysanthemum and jasmine, which is the most popular; mild, yellowish Silver Needle, a "white" tea made from unopened buds; and my favorite, *pu-erh*, a potent, earthy fermented tea from Yunnan Province, not far from the Burmese border. All are served with sober ceremony.

Such refinement is a long way from the origins of dim sum. The Cantonese teahouses of centuries ago were boisterous places, where a man came to eat, argue and sometimes bet that his caged bird could outsing the one owned by the nobody at the next table. Like pubs in England and cafes in France, they flourished in part because only the very wealthy had houses or apartments big enough to receive friends.

Originally, the morsels on a Hong Kong dim sum menu were almost all Cantonese in origin. But as John J. Clancey, an American former priest who has lived in Hong Kong for many years and is married to a Chinese woman, explained to me over drinks one evening, the Cantonese are great assimilators. Salty Hunan ham, served with honey inside a hinge of soft white bread, is often encountered in local teahouses these days. Pot stickers, a dim sum standby, originated in Beijing, in the far-off North. Soup dumplings, like the impeccably juicy ones served at Xiao Nan Guo on Des Voeux Road in Hong Kong, migrated south from Shanghai.

And custard tarts, like the marvelous version served at Victoria City Seafood in central Hong Kong (more about it later), combine flaky European pastry with a smooth and creamy Chinese filling.

But the Cantonese are also keen businesspeople, and sometimes they cut corners, even in the most traditional of places, like the Luk Yu Teahouse. Wealthy men, leaving their Rolls-Royces and BMWs in Stanley Street in the care of their drivers, idle there for hours every morning. One of the teak booths is often occupied by a chic woman who consumes newspapers and cigarettes just as avidly as tea and dim sum.

The ceiling fans, the brass spittoons and the grumpy waitresses with tin trays slung around their necks have changed little in 50 years.

I joined William Mark Yiu-Tong at Luk Yu at 8 o'clock one morning, and I got an earful. A noted dim sum connoisseur, he drew diagrams of proper dim sum techniques on the tablecloth with a chopstick dipped in soy sauce, and he complained.

Complained that once-mandatory three-year apprenticeships are disappearing, that chefs are no longer willing to come to work at 3 or 4 a.m. to prepare dim sum for breakfast, that craftsmanship is giving way to machines and that "half the dim sum in Hong Kong is made across the border in Shenzhen," an hour away, and hauled in by refrigerated trucks.

"The quick-buck mentality," he said, tugging his Charlie Chan goatee and adjusting his red cardigan. "These are delicacies. They must be delicate."

Relenting a bit, Mr. Mark, who goes to the Luk Yu six mornings a week, praised the house's spring rolls—"obviously handmade and hand-filled," he said, "because the pastry is slightly uneven." They shattered satisfyingly when cut in two. But he was less generous about the *har gau*, although the skin was nicely translucent: "They've used sodium bicarbonate on the shrimp as a tenderizer," he said, "and look here, there are only nine pleats, when there should be at least 10."

Because I was sitting with Mr. Mark, I was shielded from the Luk Yu's notorious indifference (some would call it hostility) to foreigners. Immediately after World War II, the owners put up a sign saying, "We are licensed to serve Chinese only," which was patently untrue. But then even the Chinese can have bad moments in Stanley Street. Harry Lam, a local millionaire, was gunned down last Nov. 30 by a hit man, apparently from the mainland, as he finished his tea.

Dim sum is not expensive. At the plainer places, simple dishes like steamed chicken feet, popular with the locals but not, I confess, with me, cost only $2. Even in the dining rooms of the grand hotels, like the Mandarin, the Kowloon Shangri-La and the Peninsula, which serve dim sum only at lunchtime and in some cases only on week-ends, a portion of something comparatively recherché like bird's-nest dumplings or marinated goose costs only $8.50.

For the basic no-frills experience, the help of a Cantonese speaker is required, because no English is spoken in most of the bare-bones spots. We were lucky to have the company of Susan Macnaughton, a Scottish lawyer, and her Hong Kong-born assistant, Katherine Che-ung, on our visit to Chiu Chow Garden, a great barn of a place, with geese hanging behind a plate glass window, near the main Wing On department store.

Ms. Cheung showed us how to say "thank you" over the din caused by clashing plates and bellowing waitresses: simply tap two fingers on the table. I have heard a half-dozen explanations of this gesture, mostly relating it in some obscure way to the old custom of kowtow-ing to the emperor. She ordered lovely daffodil tea, and taught us how to slide the lid of the pot to the side when we wanted a refill. And she helped us to suss out what was being offered on each of the carts careering noisily around the room, identified (but not for us) by white plastic signs on the front.

Our visit came right before the Chinese New Year—red banners and lanterns wishing everyone good luck in the Year of the Goat were up all over town—and one of the things we ate were turnip squares, traditionally associated with the holidays because they could be made from staples when the shops were closed. Actually, they contain no turnips, but rather shredded daikon radish combined with cured pork, dried shrimp and chopped coriander, shaped into a flat cake, steamed and fried. Slightly sweet, slightly bitter, they are addictive. I could have eaten a dozen.

But there were other carts to pillage—shark's fin dumpling ("only one fishy bite in there," Ms. Cheung said; "it costs too much"), crunchy taro puffs, a meatball subtly flavored with dried citrus peel and an absolutely fabulous, if daunting-sounding, dish of beef lungs, tripe and liver, steamed in a broth rich with star anise. Fabulous for an innards lover like me, that is, but not for the women. Ms. Macnaughton announced that she had a culinary rule, "nothing above the neck or below the waist," and the others passed, too.

Even Ms. Cheung could not completely solve the day's mystery. It centered on a scrumptious bunch of greens that a waitress plunged into the vat of boiling stock on her cart, trimmed with scissors and dressed with a light, gingery sauce. The sign identified it only as "green vegetable"; it was obviously a member of the cabbage family, but there are 200 Chinese brassicas, many with no English names. Questions were asked, heads were scratched, a name was finally proffered—*wong tai choy*, literally "king vegetable." No help.

We found dim sum everywhere, even Oz dim sum, at a place called Oscar's Australian, which we didn't try. Also a couple of dozen first-rate vegetarian dim sum at a sweet little place with marble-top tables near the Happy Valley racetrack called, with negligible originality, Dim Sum. For us, Dim Sum's best dim sum weren't vegetarian at all. No, we voted for the good old pot stickers, made here with bits of pork, chives and carrots, unusually spicy for Hong Kong, crisp and caramelized on the outside, served with a zippy vinegar-based sauce. Two less familiar offerings were our runners-up—*cha siu so*, pork in pastry cases, almost as eggy as challah, studded with sunflower seeds, was one; shrimp dumplings with sweet chili sauce the other.

Maxim's Palace, in the City Hall, with windows looking across the harbor to the ships docked at the Kowloon piers, is just as big as Chiu Chow Gardens (more than 100 tables), but much snappier. Head waitresses in yellow jackets and long black skirts split to the thigh patrolled the room beneath three enormous crystal chandeliers. They (and most of their customers) chattered constantly into their cell phones. Starched white cloths covered the tables and, wonder of Chinese wonders, there was a no-smoking section.

Here, too, service was from carts, but communication was much easier. Succulent, chewy bits of veal in a sauce liberally laced with black pepper reminded Betsey of the *grillades* served with grits in New Orleans. I liked the crisp scallion pancakes. We both scarfed down the spring rolls, filled with shredded chicken, which looked as if they had been made from antique vellum, and something we had not encountered before—*cheung fun*, which are rolls of steamed rice paste, about six inches long, filled in this case with shrimp and yellow Chinese chives, but sometimes with barbecued pork or with beef. As with many dim sum, the taste of the rolls had an agreeable suggestion of sweetness.

The tea, boiling hot and almost too astringent, played a key balancing role, cutting through the richness of many of the things we ate.

Victoria City Seafood, atop the Citic Tower a block or so away, serves what many, including the writer Nina Simonds, consider Hong Kong's premier dim sum. Who am I to argue, after the lunchtime banquet they served the two of us?

It included steamed crab coral dumplings, chock full of rich, smoky, highly perfumed juice and the intense flavor of mud crab; small, roundish Shanghai minced meat pies, pavéed with sesame seeds as a ring is pavéed with diamonds, giving them a fine crunch; vegetable dumplings, as sheer as a stocking, filled with Chinese parsley, perilla and carrots; and a miniature packet of glutinous rice with bites of chicken, ham and wood-ear mushrooms, all wrapped in a lotus leaf.

We drank wine, not tea, which was a sacrilege, I suppose, but the temptation was great. A reserve wine vault was filled with magnums and jeroboams of first-growth claret, and I couldn't resist a fine Cold-stream Hills pinot noir from Australia.

When the unctuous mango pudding with coconut sauce came out, I surrendered. Even my mother's banana pudding, one of my favorite childhood sweets, couldn't hold a candle to it. But then she had no mangoes.

—Hong Kong, March 19, 2003

Shanghai, a Far East Feast

Made for trade, the modern city of Shanghai came into being in the second half of the 19th century as a commercial link with the West. British, French, German and American traders settled there, eventually followed by White Russian refugees. They built a metropolis with Asia's first telephones, running water and electric power, a city of drugs, warlords, brothels and legendary riches. And like all expatriates everywhere, they brought their tastes in food with them. To this day, the Shanghainese have an appetite for croissants and French pastry and for Russian borscht (*luo song tang*, or Russian soup, on menus), although many may well not know their precise origins.

After 1949, the old hedonistic culture was gradually submerged in Communist conformity, with gray tunics and shabby state shops supplanting the chic boutiques and throbbing dance halls that gave Shanghai its reputation as "the whore of the Orient." By all accounts, food, and especially restaurant food, took a backseat to ideology.

"Ten years ago, a good restaurant was one that paid you," said Don St. Pierre Jr., managing partner of ASC, China's leading wine importer, with only modest hyperbole. "Now we're on the verge of being a world-class restaurant town." Richard Bisset, another old China hand, said that 17 years ago, when he came to Shanghai, "the Western food here ranged from Kobe beef to prawn thermidor. Full stop."

Today, Shanghai is again one of the most galvanic cities anywhere, with foreigners once more pouring in to seek their fortunes and the port seemingly on its way to becoming the world's busiest. It makes an old-timer like me long to be young again and live there to share in its drama. For 13 straight years, it has maintained a double-digit growth rate, as the largely vacant landscape on the eastern side of the Huangpu River has been magically transformed into the steel-and-glass financial center called Pudong. With more than 2,000 flamboyant skyscrapers, Shanghai is now a vertical village rather than the low-lying city of the 1930s, much of it built by Jewish merchants of Iraqi or Syrian origin like the Sassoons and Kadoories. The only echo of the Sassoons today is a Vidal Sassoon (no kin) hairdressing salon. But the Kadoories, who control the Hong Kong-based Peninsula chain, are building a luxurious hotel on the Bund, the boulevard along the river.

The slightly pompous colonial buildings lining the Bund already house some of the toniest of the city's new generation of international restaurants, including the Michael Graves–designed Jean-Georges. Renowned chefs and obscure entrepreneurs from Britain, Singapore, Australia, the United States and elsewhere have flocked to Shanghai on the heels of the bankers and brokers, eager to serve you Italian, Japanese, Thai, German or Mexican food.

Foods from afar compete with heaping helpings of first-rate Chinese dishes, from Guangzhou, Sichuan, Hunan and of course Shanghai. Local river prawns, slow-cooked pork rump, hairy crabs (in season) and above all *xiao long bao*, the soup dumplings beloved in the United States, are all on offer in classic form.

The culinary renaissance is one reason, in fact, for Shanghai's re-emergence as a prime tourist destination, along with the city's refreshing green "lungs"—the many new parks and the thousands of plane trees in the former French Concession—its matchless new art museum, its Art Deco villas and office buildings and the endless joie de vivre of its people. Gloomy, unsmiling and reluctant to make eye contact when my wife, Betsey, and I last visited the city a decade ago, they laugh and joke today, free at last to indulge in those old Shanghai pastimes, making money and spending it with abandon.

On the second morning of our most recent stay in Shanghai, we ran into Jean-Georges Vongerichten and his right-hand man, Daniel Del Vecchio, at the Westin Hotel's startlingly polycultural breakfast buffet. That happy accident led to a sampling of Shanghainese food at its most down-to-earth at breakfast-time the next day.

Near the corner of Changle Lu and Xiang Yang Bei Lu, not far from the museum, where banners were incongruously heralding an exhibition about Versailles and Louis XIV, we each polished off a half-dozen steamed, pork-filled soup dumplings, the size of a silver dollar, with perilously fragile skins, without spilling too much of the scalding liquid on our shirts. Unlike most of the other stalls, the place where we ate these actually had a few tables and stools, and even a sign outside. Its name: Maxim's.

Thicker-skinned dumplings, *sheng jian bao*, fried cheek-to-cheek in shallow iron pans and then steamed, were dusted with chives and black sesame seeds. We followed instructions to dip them in the exceptional black Zhenjiang vinegar. Eye-poppingly good they were, too, although Jereme (pronounced Jeremy) Leung, a member of our noshing group, speculated slyly that the frying oil had not been changed in years.

There were crepes at other stalls—delicate *cong you bing*, or scallion pancakes, and *ji dan bing*, a kind of breakfast burrito. To make that, a short-order wizard spread batter on a drum-shaped grill with what looked like a painter's spatula, broke an egg on top, added a dab of fermented soybean sauce and threw in some chives, coriander and mustard-plant leaves. The whole process took just a minute. Then he slapped either a salty cruller called *you tiao* or a piece of crisply fried bean curd skin across the finished product and rolled it up like a scroll. Mr. Vongerichten, in seventh heaven, pronounced it "the best breakfast in the world."

By that time, I felt fat as a Strasbourg goose, but my eating buddies insisted that we stop at a 24-hour noodle shop on Shandong Zhonglu, behind the Westin, to watch a particularly deft cook do his stuff. "No need to eat," said Mr. Leung, a Hong Kong-born Chinese. "Just watch." Sure. We watched, all right, as a huge ball of dough was kneaded and rolled and tossed and hacked into ragged little squares that reminded Mr. Vongerichten, an Alsatian, of spaetzle, and twisted and stretched and flipped and folded into long, supple noodles. But of course I had to sample a bowl of beef noodle soup, lightly curry-flavored, before we left, and of course that spoiled my lunch.

Bao Luo, in the French Concession, is all you might expect a Chinese restaurant to be—big, raucous, smoke-filled, dingy despite the marble on the walls—and more. It's open until 6 in the morning, and it often features a parade of fashionistas in thigh-high white boots around midnight. Its menu provides a primer of home-style Shanghainese cooking, however bizarre the English translations (for example, "lima bean curd with crisp hell"). Cold dishes first—amazingly tender, custardlike tofu, a reproach to the flannel-like stuff often served outside China, topped with coriander and chili oil; *ma lan tou*, made from the crunchy stems of the boltonia flower (a member of the aster family that I grow, but don't eat, at my farm in Pennsylvania); "drunken" chicken, marinated in rice wine; and *kaofu*, bran cubes flavored by five-spice soy sauce. This is no cuisine for the squeamish.

Warm plates filled the table as six of us struggled to keep up. *Ti pang*, the fabulously fatty Shanghainese pork shank, was luscious as foie gras. (One of our six, Tina Kanagaratnam, a Singapore-born food writer, told me, "Shanghai girls say that if you don't eat the fat you won't have good skin.") Crystal river prawns, bathed in egg whites before stir-frying, and *yu xiang qiezi bao*, spicy caramelized eggplant, were among my favorites. Patrick Cranley, Ms. Kanagaratnam's husband, a fluent Mandarin speaker from Baltimore, noted that this was originally a Sichuan dish, long ago adopted by Shanghai as its own. "Something in the Shanghainese character," he said, "helps them to absorb, adapt and flourish."

Having emerged intact from Shanghainese culinary primary school, we moved directly to postgraduate studies at an unprepossessing four-table hole-in-the-wall called Chun, a block from the Jin Jiang Hotel, where Chou En-lai and Richard M. Nixon issued their momentous communiqué in 1972. Susan Shirk, the State Department's top China expert in the Clinton administration, recommended it, and Dingli Shen, the Shanghai-born, Princeton-educated executive dean of the Institute of International Studies at Fudan University, joined us there. He had never been before, he said, but by the time we finished a lunchtime feast, which cost less than $8 a head, under the naked, unforgiving fluorescent bulbs, he assured us that he had never eaten better in his native city.

That didn't surprise us a bit. Not after Lan-Lan, the round-faced, T-shirt-clad 47-year-old proprietor, who resisted all attempts to discover her formal name, had brought out her wares: among other treats, more heavenly tofu, served with salted duck egg yolk and clam strips; thin-shelled river shrimp, roe still attached, steamed with ginger; whole pomfret braised in soy (with plenty of Shanghai's beloved sugar added) and the pièce de résistance, giant snails whose meat had been removed, then chopped, mixed with pork and spices and reinserted into the shells. I don't know which was better, the fragrant juices we sucked out of the shells or the meat we pried out with toothpicks.

"To be born in Shanghai is a great privilege," Dr. Shen mused. "You get better education, better economic opportunity, better health care, better everything than elsewhere in China." To which I added, "And some of the world's best food."

Soup dumplings are the province of specialists armed with minuscule rolling pins. The most famous of all are made at the three-story Nan Xiang restaurant, adjacent to the ancient Yu Garden, whose teahouse served as the inspiration for millions of pieces of "willow pattern" china. All the world adores Nan Xiang, so reserve a day ahead, or resign yourself to a long wait.

Try in any case to wangle a seat on the third floor, the only place where the most scrumptious dumplings are served—those whose filling includes crab roe as well as the usual crabmeat, pork and scallions. Two things set great dumplings apart from ordinary ones: the quality of the "soup," or broth, which at Nan Xiang has the mellow richness of the best veal stock, and the texture of the dumpling skins, which at Nan Xiang are translucently, meltingly thin. Wobbling winningly in their steamer, these tidbits are rivaled in Shanghai only by those at Din Tai Fung, a branch of a legendary Taipei dumpling house, which also has an outlet in Arcadia, Calif., near Los Angeles.

In the rush to modernize, much of picturesque old Shanghai has been bulldozed, though not the junk shops of Fangbang Lu, where

Betsey bought a crystal ball, perhaps in hopes of divining the future of this remarkable city, where Communism and capitalism thrive alongside each other against all the odds. In Xintiandi, near there, renovated and reconstructed *shikumen* (stone-gated) houses have been grouped into a shopping, strolling and dining complex. Wildly popular with Chinese as well as with foreign visitors, it is Shanghai's first big stab at the adaptive reuse of old buildings.

They sometimes call Shanghai "Shang-buy," and in Xintiandi you can buy minimalist handbags and sleek silk pajamas with jade buttons at Annabel Lee, velvet blazers and feathered hats at Xavier and modern design from Scandinavia, Thailand, Italy and even China at Simply Life. You can drink coffee, nibble glorious pastries and buy handmade chocolates at Visage. You can have a drink at TMSK, sitting on crystal stools at a crystal bar, or at nearby Zin (short for Zinfandel), a nifty wine bar.

Xin Ji Shi is the serious-chow champ of Xintiandi, whose name means "new heaven and earth." It may well serve the best *hong shao rou*, or red-cooked pork, in town, made from cubed pork belly bathed in a sauce made from star anise, sugar and Shanghai soy sauce, which is considered China's finest. The décor may be upscale, nouvelle Shanghai, all burnished wood and smoky glass panels, but the cooking is traditional. Our meal at Xin Ji Shi was also memorable for a basket brimming with big, rosy prawns, roast chicken and dried chilies and for a bottle of 1993 Corton brought by Mr. St. Pierre, much less so for an eel dish totally overwhelmed by a sweet, sludgy sauce.

Hong Kong, in the form of the handsome glass-and-granite Crystal Jade dim sum emporium, is just a few steps away from Xin Ji Shi. All the southern Chinese favorites—including *char siu bao* (barbecued pork buns), shrimp-filled *har gow* and egg tarts, among many others—are prepared to order and served at once, not rolled through the dining room on carts. But this is Shanghai, so there are also more northern delights like crispy wontons with hot chili sauce and, of course, soup dumplings. All are light and delicate, altogether first rate.

You can eat modern Sichuan food at South Beauty's four locations and carefully made vegetarian dishes at Vegetarian Lifestyle's three.

But if pressed for time, I would make a beeline for Guyi, which wins as many points for its chic décor, featuring photos of the Shanghai that was, and its smiling (indeed giggling) service from young women as for its delicious Hunanese food. Not every dish is a flamethrower, which is as things should be. Among the high spots of a meal that balanced texture, color and intensity of flavor with unusual finesse: a great heap of green beans flavored by smoky Hunan ham; a short-rib hot pot with ginger, garlic and chilies; and fried prawns on a skewer.

Unless you like to drink at altitude or crave a steak (in which case head for the upper floors of the Grand Hyatt Hotel, housed in the 54th to 87th floors of the Jin Mao Tower building), there's no real need to visit Pudong. Stay on the western side of the river and do your gawking and talking there.

For location, location, etc., you can't match Michelle Garnaut's groundbreaking M on the Bund, opened in 1999. With a heart-stopping view of Pudong's sci-fi skyline right there in front of you, as bold as a billboard, and the Bund's brightly illuminated buildings curving away to your left and right, M's seventh-floor terrace is as fine a perch as Shanghai affords. On balmy nights, moneyed visitors and local movers and shakers still throng it, with their champagne flutes or superbly made dry martinis in hand.

Ms. Garnaut, an Australian longtime resident in China, serves mostly old-fashioned European food, some of it made from prime local ingredients—opulent Chinese foie gras; crisp-skinned roast suckling pig; and (during their brief season) sensationally sweet peaches from Nanhui, like the ones often depicted on *famille-rose* porcelain.

"We're proud not to be on the cutting edge," she told me. Fair enough. But the jelly with the foie gras was much too sweet for us, the salt-baked lamb was too salty and the kitchen seemed to lack the consistency that characterizes some competitors, notably the big, buzzy restaurants at Three on the Bund, a converted bank building.

The dining room of one of them, Laris, is drenched in white— white marble, white tablecloths, white orchids. "The food and clients provide the color here," said the man at its helm, David Laris, formerly chef at Mezzo in London. As befits someone of Greek ancestry, he serves great fish, including raw oysters from three continents, scallops with basil and Kalamata olives and a fabulously earthy cauliflower and caviar soup, not unlike the brew served by Jean Joho in Chicago.

For those who require turf with their surf, there's also a delicious cross-cultural pairing of five-spiced venison with Vietnamese banana leaf salad. And for the sweet of tooth, Mr. Laris makes a remarkable *panna cotta* flavored with pandanus leaves, which lend a subtle, vanilla-like taste.

Jean-Georges gave us a nearly flawless meal. After a single Kumamoto oyster with a coronet of Champagne jelly and raw tuna with a dab of mayonnaise made with Thai chili paste, the *chef de cuisine*, Eric Johnson, sent out an exquisite dish of cubed raw kingfish with Taiwanese mangoes (imported under a new trade agreement) and a chili-lemon granita. Peppery, sweet and acidic, yellow, orange and red, in one bite.

Dish after dish of similar excellence followed, as lunch stretched toward the cocktail hour while boats of every kind chugged along the river outside the restaurant's windows—more foie gras, with star anise flowers; peaches and endive hearts with pistachios and goat cheese dressing; crab dumplings with black pepper oil and tiny local peas; sweet scallops from Dalian, a port in north China, seared and paired with clams in a tomato jus; stunningly fresh steamed snapper on a basil purée, topped with cucumber strips for crunch; and Jason Casey's irresistible desserts, which coaxed every nuance of flavor from lush tropical fruits.

The service in the elegant copper-and-blue dining room was silent and skillful, which is more than one can say about the Whampoa Club, in the same building, where the gifted 34-year-old Mr. Leung presides. His *Normandie*-like setting, with shantung silk, ostrich skin and hammered metal panels, is elegant enough. But the reception was disorganized, the waitresses' heels clattered intrusively on bare floors, and language skills were so rudimentary that we were utterly bewildered until a supervisor came to our assistance. This is perfectly acceptable at $10 a head, but not at $100.

Mr. Leung's modern take on Chinese regional food is delightful.

His caramelized minisquid reminded me why I was once addicted to Cracker Jacks. His "lion's head" pork meatballs came in a sumptuous winter-melon broth, with enoki mushrooms impishly used as "eyes." His king prawns dazzled in a mild wasabi sauce. His crisp, spicy eel strips and smoked fish showed the potential of river fish, treasured in Shanghai.

"We begin with traditional peasant-style recipes and try to update and refine them," he said. "Take the smoked fish. Usually, it's fried in the morning and left to cool all day. It often tastes stale, even rancid. We fry it to order and serve it warm, not at room temperature. But the prawns—those, I must confess, are pure Jereme."

—*Shanghai, China, October 9, 2005*

Following the Pepper Grinder
All the Way to Its Source

Of all the distinctively flavored seeds, barks, roots, fruits and leaves that we call spices, pepper is the most widely used, and for centuries it was the most valuable.

In ancient times, the demand for pepper was almost insatiable; spicing meat was the only practical way to preserve it, and pepper made salted meat palatable. In that era, the vines that yield the small, well-rounded black berries grew only here in the lush, lovely Cardamom Hills of southwest India. So many ships came to trade for them that Cochin (now called Kochi) on the Malabar Coast became one of the world's great ports.

Alaric the Visigoth demanded 3,000 pounds of pepper as part of the price for sparing Rome in the fifth century. In medieval Europe a small bag of black pepper could be exchanged for a sheep. In the 16th and 17th centuries, pepper was sold in Western capitals for 600 times what it cost in India.

The United States entered the pepper trade in 1797, when an intrepid New England schooner-ship captain named Jonathan Carnes completed a voyage from Salem, Mass., to Sumatra and back. Trading directly with the local inhabitants, he circumvented the monopoly on pepper then held by the Dutch. Elihu Yale, a Boston-born Englishman, built a fortune in the spice trade and contributed some of it to a Connecticut university that took his name.

Even today, pepper is the constant companion to salt on the dinner tables of the world, either in a shaker or (preferably, since it loses much of its savor once ground) in a mill. Besides enlivening the flavor of everything from melon to macaroni, it helps to promote digestion. Without salt life would be impossible. Without pepper, it would be impossibly dull.

India has recently ceded its place as the world's leading exporter to Vietnam, and Brazil, Indonesia and Malaysia are also major exporters. But most epicures consider Indian peppercorns the world's finest, particularly the extralarge ones named after Tellicherry, on the Arabian Sea.

The climate and terrain here are very nearly perfect for the cultivation of pepper. Both phases of the unusual twin monsoon in this part of India deliver copious rainfall, making irrigation unnecessary. The region's soils furnish ample nutrients for the pepper vines, supplemented by the small amounts of fertilizer applied to crops surrounding them. And the slope of the hills provides reliable drainage.

"But if Vietnam had started to produce high-quality pepper many centuries ago, instead of having begun only relatively recently," said Thomas Phillip, the managing director of Cochin Spices, a local processor, "it is quite likely that the Portuguese, the Dutch, the British and others would have gravitated there, not here. And India might well never have been colonized at all."

Here where it originated, and where it provided the spark in local cuisine before the Portuguese introduced chilies from the New World, pepper grows amid other valuable plants, including vanilla vines, a species of orchid; tea bushes, as carefully trimmed as a dandy's mustache, which tuft the hillsides; and nutmeg trees, which produce both nutmeg and mace. Cardamom, treasured by the Arabs as a flavoring for coffee, is yet another big cash crop.

But the visitor looks in vain for pepper plantations, whatever the guidebooks may say. There are none.

Instead, pepper vines are trained to climb coconut palms or betel trees in backyards, or silver oaks used as windbreaks on the tea plantations, or any other tree with a tall, straight trunk. They have dark green leaves, ribbed and leathery, and reach a height of 12 to 15 feet. Flowers bloom after the first monsoon rains in the fall, followed by six-inch spikes of berries.

• • •

A farmer named K. P. Mathew, who works eight acres near this trading village, led my wife, Betsey, and me along dusty trails through a forest of spice trees and bushes, across canals that are dry except in monsoon season. He told us he was adopting organic, sustainable methods, like many of his colleagues.

"I burn coconut husks, roots and branches to generate the smoke to dry cardamom," he said. "I generate gas for cooking and household heating from cow dung."

It was a memorable stroll on a fine, cool winter's morning in the subtropics. The mango trees were in flower, along with the pale blue ipomoea vines, and the air was filled not only with the sweet smells of blossoms but also with the songs of exotic (and exotically named) birds—the red-vented bulbul, the white-breasted green barbet and the rocket-tailed drongo—identified for us by T. P. Binu Kumar, a naturalist who came along on our walk.

A few of the berries, yellowish when they first emerge, then green, were starting to turn reddish, ready for harvest by agile men who climb up precarious one-legged ladders to strip the spikes from the vines.

After picking, the berries are laid out on rush or banana-leaf mats to dry in the sun for five or six days. Any flat surface will do, and does—a roof, a courtyard floor, or a roadside. The drying causes the berries to turn black, shrivel and become hard.

If white pepper is desired, for use in a sauce or something else that would be marred by black specks, the raw berries are first soaked in running water, which causes the outer skin to loosen enough so that it can be rubbed off. Subsequently dried, they turn a creamy white. Because much of pepper's bite comes from piperine, a chemical concentrated in the skin, white pepper is less pungent than black.

Green peppercorns also come from the same vine, Piper nigrum. But they are preserved in their green, unripe state, usually by pickling.

Many other seasonings are called "peppers" and deliver a burning sensation to the tongue and palate but are unrelated botanically to Piper nigrum. Among these are pink peppercorns (Schinus terebinthifolius), Sichuan pepper from China and *malagueta* peppers from Brazil and Africa. Nor are capsicums, including bell peppers and cayenne, from the same family.

Small farmers sell their pepper to high-country traders, who consolidate little lots into larger ones for sale to processors in the coastal cities. One such is Mr. Phillip's company, Cochin Spices, a subsidiary of Burns Philp, a big Australian company, and a corporate sibling of Tone Brothers, of Ankeny, Iowa, which sells Indian pepper under the Durkee and Spice Islands labels.

"For the little guy," Mr. Phillip told me, "the beauty is that pepper, unlike most crops, keeps more or less forever. You take it out every year, dry it to prevent mold and stick it back in the warehouse. You sell it when you need the money to get your daughter married or fix the roof or buy a car. It's better than cash in the bank, because the tax man won't see it."

(There are big farmers as well. Tata Tea, part of the immense Tata conglomerate, is probably the biggest; one year not long ago, or so the story goes, it made more profit on the pepper grown on shade trees on its properties than on coffee or tea.)

Cochin Spices ships peppercorns whole or grinds them to order for shipment in huge containers all over the world. Processing is relatively simple. A series of machines wash and dry the peppercorns, eliminating stems, sticks and stones and other foreign matter, as well as "light" or hollow berries and "pinheads," which are undeveloped buds. Classification by size comes next, and then, if the customer wishes, the pepper is steam-sterilized before passing through a dryer that reduces the moisture content from 30 percent to the legally mandated 10 or 11 percent.

I had expected an overpowering smell when I visited Mr. Phillip's plant. Sure enough, it was all but impossible to stay more than two or three minutes in the rooms where chili is processed without experiencing smarting eyes and a runny nose, but in the pepper-grinding room, all I felt was slightly stinging nostrils. Pepper proved to be more mannerly than chili.

In addition to the farmers who grow the pepper and the companies that process it, there is a third significant element in the pepper business here in the Indian state of Kerala—the Kochi International Pepper Exchange in the heart of Jew Town, an evocative old neighborhood in Fort Cochin, across the broad and bustling harbor from the deep-water port at Ernakulam.

A few traders still maintain offices in Jew Town, but the numbers have dwindled with the advent of secure telephone, telex and Internet communication. Although Aspinwall & Company, founded in 1867, still occupies its fine old yellow building, many of the shuttered houses with the Star of David worked into their grilles now house antique shops rather than burlap bags of spices.

Just enough warehouses remain on the congested streets to perfume the warm air with a gingery-peppery clove-and-cardamom amalgam of aromas.

Most of today's action takes place, however, in the bland-looking building of the Indian Pepper & Spice Trade Association. There, in an air-conditioned second-floor room, 40 or so brokers in pepper futures—some in Western sports shirts, others in the white Indian loincloths called dhotis, all in bare feet to protect the polished floor— put up a hellish if episodic din.

Between napping and gesturing like a company of Barrymores, they shout and curse into their telephones. They trade an average of 450 tons of Kerala-grown pepper a day, or rather, six-month future contracts covering that amount. The object is to bring some stability into what might otherwise be a cyclical and rather chaotic world market.

"April—8875," one trader bellowed in a lingua franca unfathomable to mere onlookers like me as CNBC's commodity statistics flashed across numerous overhead television screens.

Some traders are members of the exchange; others act as brokers for large firms, including American companies like Tone Brothers, the Harris Freeman Company of Anaheim, Calif., and McCormick & Company of Baltimore, as well as companies in London and Rotterdam. K. J. Samson, the pepper and spice association secretary, told me that nearly all the floor traders were Gujaratis, whose grandfathers came south from a populous state in northwest India decades ago.

How much longer that tradition or others will survive remains unclear. The old "outcry" system's days are numbered. Trading will move onto computer screens soon.

—Thekkady, India, October 29, 2003

In South India, No End of Spice, No End of Flavor

Kerala is a mere frond of a state, long and narrow, green and fertile—15,000 palm-sheltered square miles in southwest India, rimmed by mountains called the Western Ghats, washed by the Arabian Sea and laced by an idyllic tangle of lakes and streams known as the Backwaters.

Its people, known as Malayalees, call it "God's own country" or "the blessed land," not least because of its irresistible food.

For centuries, long before the steamship, long before the jet plane, venturesome traders rode the trade winds to Kerala. Romans, Phoenicians, Chinese, Arabs, Portuguese, Frenchmen, Dutchmen and Britons all came here, and so did Jewish merchants from Venice. St. Thomas the Apostle is said to have landed along this coast in A.D. 52, and Christopher Columbus was headed west in search of Kerala's fabled spices when he stumbled upon America.

Each group of outsiders brought along their own culinary traditions, and each adapted to their new circumstances. The Arabs contributed fennel and fenugreek. On their quest for black pepper, the Portuguese carried the cashews and chilies they had discovered in the New World, changing forever the way the subcontinent eats. The Jews clung to kosher dietary restrictions, but they added green chilies and coriander to their meals.

Blending all these influences with the abundant native spices and coconut has yielded a light, bright and vividly varied cuisine, little known to the rest of the world and totally different from the hearty tandooris and creamy curries of arid northern India.

373

Happily, the culinary pleasure here lasts from daybreak through dinner. Sit down at breakfast, and you may be served luscious mango preserves or the most delectable fresh pineapple juice imaginable, together with the savory rice-and-lentil sourdough dumplings known as *idlis* and a bracing tomato chutney or perhaps some lime pickle.

In modern Kerala, Hindus, Christians, Muslims and the few remaining Jews (most having left for Israel or other countries after World War II) all speak the same language, Malayalam, which has given the world the words "teak" and "atoll." Their profound commitment to religious tolerance is symbolized by a venerable custom, known as *pakarcha*, of sharing the celebratory dishes of one's own faith with friends of different religions. My wife, Betsey, and I began to absorb some of this rich cultural history early on the first morning of an extended stay in Kerala.

We were picked up at our hotel, the Brunton Boatyard in Fort Cochin, which faces a channel plied day and night by an endless parade of ferries, rice barges, fishing boats and oil tankers, for an eye-opening trip across the water to Ernakulam.

(Kochi, the hub of Kerala, used to be called Cochin. It has three parts. If the vast harbor here were San Francisco Bay, which it rather resembles, evocative old Fort Cochin would be where San Francisco is, with the hotel at the Presidio, and raucous, fast-growing Ernakulam would be in Berkeley's place. Between the two is Willingdon Island, a landfill dating from colonial days.)

With one hand on the wheel of his little Hyundai van, the other on the horn, our driver, V. J. Paul, managed to safely negotiate streets clogged with trucks, buses, trishaws, bicycles, discarded refrigerators and goats—especially goats.

We passed hibiscus tumbling out of walled gardens, countless signs advertising computer classes and women carrying water jugs on their heads, then crossed a brand-new harbor bridge. Eventually, Mr. Paul stopped at a trim little house, an island of calm in a maelstrom, and hopped out.

His wife, Nimmy, a cooking teacher, greeted Betsey by twining jasmine flowers in her hair and placing a dot of sandalwood paste on her forehead.

Small and slim, dressed in a traditional white Keralan sari with yellow and navy bands at the edges of the fabric, she began with a chicken *kuruma*, a Mappila (Keralan Muslim) adaptation of the classic Kashmiri korma, flavored with onions, green chili and a staggering quantity of coriander. It was thickened not with cream or yogurt but with coconut milk and cashew paste.

"My grinding stones have gone into the garden," Mrs. Paul told me as she made the paste. "We use food processors now."

Partly because so many Keralites have lived abroad (1.5 million of them are now in the Persian Gulf), where they have been exposed to the temptations of steaks, chops, sausages and kebabs, vegetarianism is on the wane here. The *Hindu*, a national newspaper, reported recently that people in Kochi "are on a meaty binge," and some of the local vegetarian restaurants have closed.

But Mrs. Paul continues to turn out Hindu-influenced vegetarian dishes for her family as well as her students. One of her classics is *avial*, a ragout of vegetables, in which she uses matchstick-size pieces of carrot, cucumber, green beans, drumstick (long, ridged pods from the moringa oleifera tree, rich in vitamin C, with a delicate flavor resembling that of asparagus), *kovakka* or little melon (a kind of gherkin) and *brinjal*, a longish eggplant.

First she boils the vegetables with green chilies. Then she adds a mixture with the texture of oatmeal, including turmeric, coconut, garlic and cumin, along with homemade cow's-milk curd and *kari* leaves (highly aromatic and widely used in Kerala, these are often confusingly called curry leaves in the West; they look like basil leaves and taste of citrus and bell peppers).

Sambar, a lentil and vegetable stew, makes use of two unusual spices. *Asafetida*, a resin taken from the rhizomes of giant fennel, is admired in Kerala for its earthy scent when fried in oil, and fenugreek seeds are liked for their bitter caramel flavor. Together with tamarind, a souring agent, chilies and coriander leaves, they give the stew intricate layers of flavor.

Stir-fries called *thorens* are noted regional specialties. Usually made with a single ingredient, like beets or spinach (or a fish), their appearance is heralded by the sound of mustard seeds popping in a skillet or wok and releasing their pungent aroma. Grated unsweetened coconut, a masala or spice mixture, chilies and the ubiquitous *kari* leaves complete the dish.

"*Thorens* are a daily item," Mrs. Paul commented as she glided around her clutterless kitchen, which has a red cement floor and a big overhead fan but no air-conditioning. "You must have a *thoren*."

Unlike many Indians, Malayalees eat beef, but they eat a lot more seafood—shrimp and crab and all sorts of ocean fish, notably *seer*, a mackerel with mild, firm flesh that looks like a miniature tuna.

Mrs. Paul showed us two fish preparations, the first of which, called *molee*, is a great favorite of the local Syrian Christians, as the descendants of early settlers from Baghdad and Nineveh call themselves. It is a must for wedding feasts and Christmas.

Molee is made by frying a brown masala in coconut oil with other ingredients, combining the resulting paste with the fish and simmering it all in thinned coconut milk.

Our second fishy treat was made from an heirloom Jewish recipe given to Mrs. Paul by an elderly woman in Kochi. Red and green chilies gave a jolt of heat to seared fillets, which had been fried until dark and crunchy, and coconut vinegar added a stab of acidity. That much we figured out for ourselves. But there was something else in there, something sweet, musky, mysterious. After we made several stabs in the dark, Mrs. Paul told us. It was cardamom.

The coconut palm, I quickly came to realize, is the mainstay of Malayalee life. Its leaves are used for thatch, its fiber for rope, its roots for firewood, its trunk for furniture. And in the Keralite kitchen, coconut flesh, oil, milk and vinegar are indispensable sources of both flavor and texture.

Kochi markets offer a limited choice. Some kinds of vegetables, especially gourds and squashes, are plentiful, and 27 varieties of bananas grow here, large and small, red and yellow. So do the succulent Alphonso mangoes. But the kaleidoscopic variety of Southeast Asian markets is lacking.

Kerala is a poor place, with an annual gross domestic product per person of about $1,000, poor even by Indian standards, as poor as Cambodia and the Sudan. But it is also a striking example, as Akash Kapur argued in *The Atlantic* in 1998, of poor people living well. The Malayalees' houses and clothing may be simple, but their life expectancy is 72 years, close to the American average; the infant mortality rate is low; and population is under control.

Most impressively, the school system is extensive, reaching into every village, and the literacy rate is a startling 90 percent, in the same high echelon as Singapore.

"Everybody reads," said Thomas Phillip, the urbane managing director of Cochin Spices Ltd. "Even the guy who digs ditches, who can't afford his own newspaper, goes to a tea shop every day and reads theirs."

Syrian Christians—instantly recognizable by their biblical surnames, like Phillip, Thomas, Andrew, Peter and Paul—have shaped much that is distinctive about life in Kerala. "Christianity," wrote Arundhati Roy in her whirling, dreamlike novel, *The God of Small Things* (Random House, 1997), "arrived in a boat and seeped into Kerala like tea from a teabag."

Accounting for only a quarter of Kerala's 33 million people, the Syrian Christians are an energetic and ambitious group, entrepreneurial, philanthropic and devoted to higher education. They have had a large impact as well on the world of cuisine. Mrs. K. M. Mathew, who died last summer, was Kerala's leading cookbook author, with 24 titles to her credit.

As I said, our Kochi base was the charming and cozy Brunton Boatyard, part of the remarkable Casino Group. We later stayed at two of its other hotels, Spice Village, in the mountains, and Coconut Lagoon, in the Backwaters. The group, owned by the six Dominic brothers, builds its hotels in vernacular styles, emphasizes environmental sensitivity and serves superb regional cooking.

"We're not in the marble palace business," Jose Dominic, the managing director, told me one day. "We think luxury lies in the quality of the client's experience instead of the quality of the décor. Kerala is a late entrant in the tourism sweepstakes, and if we do it right we have a chance to avoid the excess of Bali and Phuket."

At the Coconut Lagoon, the chef, Raju Pik, sets out a spectacular dinner buffet that includes, in addition to meat and fish curries and grills, a dozen or so vegetarian dishes, including a banana-flower *thoren*, each with its own taste, aroma, color and texture. Monochromatic mush won't do in Kerala, where I saw on a single block of a single street a cascade of magenta flowers, a purple umbrella, a baby-blue church, a yellow house next to a pink one and two red saris.

The Boatyard's main restaurant, called the History, tells Kerala's tale in a 20-page menu devised by Sunitha Divakaran, the first woman Malayalee executive chef. Among the many dishes that excited my admiration were crisply fried, subtly spiced bites of okra; *vinha d'alio*, a vinegary, chili-laden pork dish of Portuguese origin, the granddaddy of vindaloo curries; *chutullimeen*, a flattened fish marinated in green spices and pearl onions "from the Jewish recipe books of Fort Cochin"; juicy king prawns in the Arab style, marinated in yogurt and spices, pan-fried and served atop saffron rice; and *amaranth kootu*, a vegetarian curry made with spinachlike leaves.

We soaked up as much tradition eating at the History as we did on our sightseeing rounds of Fort Cochin the next day, featuring visits to the huge, cantilevered Chinese fishing nets along the foreshore, whose design dates from the time of Kublai Khan, and the Dutch-gabled St. Francis Church, where Vasco da Gama was buried in 1524. The church is filled with plaques paying wistful tribute to English clerics, teachers, doctors and lawyers who died while serving here, so far from home.

The chandelier-lit 16th-century synagogue in Jew Town, where only four families now worship, is even more poignant.

Yosef Hallegua, one of the last "white Jews of Cochin," talked sadly early this year about his dwindling little community. "It's a great pity the younger generation left," he told a writer for the *Financial Times*. "I went to Israel for one month, but it was not home. This is home, and naturally I am an Indian. Soon it will all end."

Another evening, we indulged ourselves in another local culinary tradition: the fish barbecue in the shady Fort Cochin garden restaurant of the Casino Hotel, yet another Dominic property, this one on Willingdon Island, halfway across the harbor.

We ate some prawns fried with chili and coriander seeds to start with, dipping them in a soothing mint sauce. It wasn't strictly Keralite, but it was strictly delicious, and it perfectly tamed the boisterous prawns.

Then a waiter wheeled over a cart laden with scrupulously fresh local fish and asked which we would like to taste. On offer were halibut, gray mullet, red snapper, gray snapper and black pomfret, all ocean fish, all caught by day boats, and pearl spot, a dainty, bony fish caught in the brackish Backwaters. Because I had eaten frozen and not-fresh-enough pomfret in Indian restaurants in Europe and the United States, I was eager to taste the real thing.

The rich, oily, deep-bodied black pomfret belongs to the same family as Florida's pompanos and amberjacks. Perfectly grilled over an open fire, with just enough spice added to make things interesting, but not so much as to obscure the sweet, fresh taste of the flesh, with a simple sauce of melted butter on the side, my fish was remarkable. Suddenly, I understood why Indians go to great lengths to get their hands on even an inferior specimen.

In her authoritative book, *Savoring the Spice Coast of India* (Harper-Collins, 2000), Maya Kaimal, the daughter of a Keralite father and an American mother, writes: "Some of the best food in Kerala is eaten for breakfast or as a snack. Pancakes, dumplings or noodles provide the starchy element for the lighter meals of the day."

What an understatement that proved to be! There are the breads eaten all across India, like flaky *paratha* and puffy *pooris*, plus a Mappila yeast bread called *kameer*. There are those spongy breakfast *idlis*, whose fermented batter gives them a slightly sour taste; a noodle dish called *upuma* and a whole range of yeasty rice pancakes called *appams*, some of which Mrs. Paul made for us. As the Indian food writer Madhur Jaffrey says, "If a French crepe were to marry an English muffin, they would probably become the proud parents of *appams*." Most are used to scoop up the stews and curries that Keralites love.

But to taste Kerala's quintessential fast food, you must visit a *dosa* shop, preferably the Pai Brothers' open-air, pink-walled, bare-bones stand in a garish alley off M. G. (for Mahatma Gandhi) Road in Ernakulam. Thirty-six types of sourdough crepes are listed on the blackboard. Number 21, say, has tomato, onion and masala (in this context, a spicy potato mixture); Number 13, roasted onions. Watch the dosa master spread the rice flour and lentil batter on a griddle with the back of his ladle, add the fillings and sprinkle it all lavishly with pepper.

While the *dosas* cook, take your place on a plastic chair at a plastic table, and after a while the *dosas* arrive on big, round tin trays called *thalis*, folded over like Spanish tortillas. We loved their eggy, slightly fermented, boldly spiced taste; we loved the jolly, talkative brothers who made them; and we loved the price, too: 50 rupees (about $1.10) for two big *dosas* and a Coke.

—*Kochi, India, October 22, 2003*

AUSTRALIA

Out West, Aussie Style

Western Australia sits way out there on the edge of things. It is a gigantic place, nearly four times the size of Texas, and mostly empty, with a smaller population than Nevada's. Its hospitable modern capital, Perth, where nearly three-quarters of its people live, is one of the most isolated cities on earth, separated by a vast continental desert from Sydney and more than 2,000 miles from any other major city.

The southwestern corner of the state, including Perth and the gorgeous Margaret River area, faces west across the Indian Ocean, enjoying a Mediterranean climate and its perquisites—superb locally produced wines, wonderful food and a relaxed way of life. Plus world-class museums, uncrowded white-sand beaches, soaring hardwood forests and abundant wildflowers in springtime (meaning September, of course).

Perth reminds me of San Diego. It revels in its location along a lakelike stretch of the meandering Swan River, overlooked by the

1,000-acre Kings Park, whose lush gardens provide a popular setting for picnics and weddings and games of many sorts in a city that loves living outdoors.

Take a stroll there, admire the city's shimmering postmodern skyscrapers, rising from the flatlands below like Houston's, and then follow my wife, Betsey, and me to the soft, rolling countryside of the Margaret River. It's August—what the locals call winter. Ha! People are surfing and swimming in the foamy green waves crashing ashore, the bolder ones without wet suits. Plum and peach trees are in bloom, and countless clumps of calla lilies, considered noxious weeds by the locals, poke through the soil. Mares and their foals, tails twitching, gauzily backlit by the setting sun, graze in an emerald pasture near groves of orange and tangerine trees.

All around stand the obsessively ordered rows of vines that will in due time yield the grapes from which the region's renowned wines are made. You can taste these in the excellent vineyard restaurants and buy them in the vineyard shops, called "cellar doors." This is the good life, as lived Australian style. It is what lures so many visitors from other parts of Australia and increasingly from other parts of the world.

Life is less cushy in the arid interior. Subduing a hostile environment bred a tough, resilient people there—"hardy and independent-minded, like the people who settled the American West," as former premier Richard Court told me. Independent to the point of cussedness, you might say; in 1933, two-thirds of the state's voters backed an effort to secede from Australia.

But today, for all its remoteness, Western Australia feels firmly tethered to the wider world. The yachting elite gathered in 1987 for the races for the America's Cup in the waters off Fremantle, Perth's port. Pop and classical music stars, from Sting to the London Philharmonic Orchestra, come to perform at the annual concerts at the Leeuwin Estate vineyards. Two Perth researchers won the Nobel Prize in Medicine in 2005 for discovering the cause of stomach ulcers.

Jet planes and television helped to break down the sense of insularity, of course, but the seemingly bottomless thirst of China and

Japan for raw materials and energy has helped even more. Every day, armadas of ships sail north, laden with iron ore, alumina and lique- fied natural gas extracted from the depths of Western Australia. In just the last quarter century, the state's resource output has increased 12-fold, to $28 billion a year from $2 billion; it now produces 7 percent of the world's natural gas, and the Pilbara region in the Northwest has become one of the world's leading iron ore producers.

Trade has made the state very wealthy, and has broadened its out- look.

"The resource industry brings a lot of transients to us, and they raise the level of sophistication," said Alan R. Dodge, the director of the excellent Art Gallery of Western Australia, who was born in Maine and trained in part under the late J. Carter Brown, longtime director of the National Gallery in Washington. Although Mr. Dodge described his mission as "bringing the art of the world to Western Australia" through exhibitions like "St. Petersburg 1900," up when we last visited, the museum has a compelling permanent collection of considerable interest to visitors, including hundreds of works of both traditional and contemporary indigenous (i.e., aboriginal) art.

A second gallery worth any visitor's time is the Western Australian Maritime Museum, a strikingly modern structure on Victoria Quay in Fremantle, a 20-minute drive from downtown Perth. The proudly preserved town itself rewards strollers, with a nice mix of Art Deco and Victorian buildings, many with lacy ironwork reminiscent of New Orleans. Some of them once housed the offices of trading com- panies.

But the museum, a model of its kind, is the big draw. With the chirpy humor so typical of Australia, the official brochure comments that "this gallery is about people mucking about in the water," and so it is. It houses a rowboat once used for whaling (made in Mystic, Conn.!), a sailboat once used for pearl diving, and *Australia II*, the first non-American boat to win the America's Cup, in 1983. It also tells the intriguing stories of immigration to, fishing near and shipping from Western Australia.

The Red Herring restaurant, cantilevered over the Swan River near its mouth, served us an admirable lunch after we tore ourselves away from the maritime museum, even though it was raining cats and dogs and the isinglass curtains had been rolled down. Brendan Martin's eclectic menu includes everything from freshly shucked Ceduna oysters from South Australia to Thai curried mussels and yabbies (freshwater crayfish) to prawns with chili sauce and *roti pratha*—a cook's tour of the Indian Ocean rim. We tried a bit of everything, all of it delicious, attempting with mixed success between bites to feed Joe, the sluggish pelican, who was perched on a piling outside.

Back in Perth, the surprising array of dining choices reflects, in many cases, the city's proximity to Asia. At Jackson's, perhaps the town's top table, with a formidable selection of Australian wines, prime Australian lamb speaks with a Levantine accent, flavored with *za'atar* (also known as Bible hyssop or Syrian oregano) and served with couscous. At Star Anise, a dimly illuminated spot with suede-cushioned walls, even the green-lip abalone with duck-egg noodles is eclipsed by the captivating licorice ice cream flanked by slabs of star-anise-flavored meringue—edible Stonehenge. At the posh Balthazar, you may find *hiramasa* kingfish in miso broth or calamari seared with *dukkah*, an Egyptian spice mixture. At the casual 44 King Street, it may be Vietnamese chicken salad or chicken and tofu *laksa*.

A drink, perhaps a fine sherry? For that, Must Wine Bar is a must. A French meal worthy of two Michelin stars? Head for Alain Fabrègues's delightful Loose Box in the hills east of town. Young talent? The town's favorite Young Turk is a young Turk named Ismail Tosun, who cooks irreproachable feta *burek*, *imam bayaldi* that transforms eggplant into the food of the gods, and subtle minced lamb *kofte* (sausages) at Eminem.

From my perspective, most Perth hotels are too big, too commercial and too boring. The new Outram, in a quiet residential neighborhood near Kings Park but only a short cab ride from downtown, solves that problem. It offers 18 compact, cleverly laid-out rooms with soaking showers and all the electronics you could want.

But the essence of Perth is not indoors. It's out there on the Swan River, sailing or water-skiing like a native, or simply riding the ferry to South Perth. In any event, you won't want to miss the haunting black swans. Dutch sailors rowing upriver from the coast in 1697 were the first Europeans to spot ancestors of today's birds.

Heading out of Perth for the first time in a number of years, Betsey and I grew apprehensive as we passed one new seaside subdivision after another: Florida, San Remo, Waikiki. But fortunately, the frantic development that has engulfed the capital's suburbs, as well as the little city of Mandurah, has not yet reached the Margaret River, which lies three hours or so to the south.

So for the moment at least, the Margaret River—the name refers flexibly to a body of water, a village and a region—retains its principal asset, its unspoiled, bucolic nature. With no scheduled air service, no superhighways and no big resort hotels, it has avoided the fate of the Napa Valley and other arcadian winegrowing areas whose very beauty has proved their undoing.

That night, our hostess, Vanya Cullen of Cullen Wines, one of the best women winemakers in the world, pointed to the dark, star-strewn sky and said, "Sometimes the stars are so bright that you can walk by their light."

Although it accounts for only a tiny percentage of national production, Western Australia produces some of the continent's choicest vintages. Wine lovers around the world thrill to Cullen's Diana Madeline red—a cabernet-merlot blend named after Vanya Cullen's late mother, who planted the family vineyard with her husband, a physician—and to Leeuwin Estate's Art Series chardonnay and riesling. But the region's wineries' global success has led to serious overplanting, and that has led to chronic oversupply. Some wineries have been sold and others are in trouble.

"Next thing you know," said Denis Horgan, the sardonic owner of Leeuwin, "they'll be giving away a bottle of wine with every tank of petrol you buy."

Unlike American wineries, their Australian counterparts feed their visitors handsomely. There is no question of fobbing clients off with a weary cheese plate, especially in the Margaret River, where most of the best restaurants are to be found at wineries like Xanadu and Vasse Felix, whose scallops and shredded pork in hot tamarind dressing goes perfectly with the house's semillon-sauvignon blanc blend.

Styles vary. Ms. Cullen's eating place, called Cullen Dining, is a simple operation, best known for an overflowing vineyard platter of homegrown vegetables, fruits, meats, cheeses and dips, with terrific Turkish bread, served in a shedlike structure. Or you can take your meal outside for a picnic alongside the grapevines. But at Leeuwin, a bit farther south, a full-fledged restaurant with a view of the elegantly landscaped grounds serves Heath Disher's cosmopolitan food— things like grilled Pemberton marrons (another freshwater crayfish), roasted spatchcock chicken with prune stuffing and beef cheeks cooked in shiraz with spaetzle. All paired, of course, with plenty of first-class wine.

Which sets you up perfectly to explore the captivating landscape. Even as early as August, color is everywhere: pink myrtle, purple hovea and especially the arresting golden flowers of the wattle tree, a member of the acacia family.

Near Cape Leeuwin, where the Southern Ocean meets the Indian Ocean, jarrah and karri trees grow to great heights in magnificent forests so dense that the sun often struggles to dapple even a few corners with light. Both are eucalypts, hardwoods of many uses, including, late in the 19th century, the paving of London streets. Some of the karris are 100 to 120 years old.

From coastal Caves Road one morning, we turned onto a spur that led out of the forests and down off the plateau. Suddenly, we caught sight of a swath of sea. As we reached a broad, clean beach, backed by limestone cliffs, we were alone. We could see the surf leaping above offshore rocks in the distance, then calming itself. By the time they reached us, the waters were transparent green, turquoise and blue.

A sign said the place was called Hamelin Bay. It might have added that it was a perfect, tranquil example of what makes the Margaret River so magical.

What I have given you so far is a Western Australia starter kit, enough (I hope) to steer at least a few people toward Perth and the Margaret River region.

But there is much, much more to see in this vast state, still largely undiscovered by foreigners. Head east from Perth on the Great Eastern Highway, which parallels the Trans-Australian Railway, and after about 375 miles you will find yourself in the twin gold-mining towns of Kalgoorlie-Boulder, which merged in 1989, on the edge of the arid, almost treeless Nullarbor Plain. With only 26,500 inhabitants between them, they constitute the largest urban area in inland Australia.

Nobody would live there if not for Paddy Hannan, an Irish prospector who discovered the goldfields in 1893. His statue stands outside the well-kept Kalgoorlie City Hall, built in 1908. The Exchange Hotel, a riot of gables and balconies, where he and his mates drowned their sorrows, helps to preserve the rough-and-tumble frontier atmosphere of the place. But Kalgoorlie and Boulder are no ghost towns; their mines produce 7 percent of the world's gold today.

The biggest of the mines is a monster—a terraced hole in the ground called the Super Pit, three-quarters of a mile wide, two miles long and 1,150 feet deep, out of which more than 1,000 tons of gold have been taken in the last century. Viewed from its rim, the giant trucks and earthmovers maneuvering at the bottom resemble child's toys.

Up the coast from Perth, two and a half hours' flying time but still well within Western Australia, lies the lonely but scenically spectacular region called the Kimberley, far closer to Indonesia than to Sydney. Broome, its delicious main town, retains some of its wooden sidewalks as well as vibrant Chinese, Japanese and Malay communities from its days as the world's mother-of-pearl capital. Now pearls, some of the earth's most coveted, are farmed in the region and sold for a princely sum by Broome jewelers. They are the town's living, along with Technicolor sunsets and a pristine beach.

"Cable Beach is one of the great walks, and sometimes you have it to yourself," said my Aussie friend Leo Schofield, an impresario and inveterate traveler. "Fourteen miles of dazzlingly white sand, three seashells, two people and one wave."

Lord McAlpine, a Tory grandee who raised money for Margaret Thatcher's campaigns, moved to Broome in 1982. Purchasing a pearling master's house built in 1910, he extended it, installed a pool, cultivated luxuriant gardens and filled them with rare birds, including electrifyingly colored eclectus parrots. After a decade he moved on (he now lives in a former monastery in the heel of the Italian boot), and McAlpine House, shaded by deep verandas, became a secluded eight-room boutique hotel.

From Broome, Land Rover safaris, air tours and cruises (including trips on the *True North*, which sails with a helicopter onboard) reach the wild country to the north. At the Purnululu National Park, the Bungle Bungles (yes, the Bungle Bungles)—orange-and-black-striped, beehive-shaped sandstone domes, encased in silica and algae—flare 600 to 900 feet above a grassy, wooded plain. Remarkable as they are, they were unknown to white Australians until as late as 1983, although familiar to aborigines.

Long to go native? Head for the aptly named Bush Camp Faraway Bay, perched on a cliff above a romantic, utterly untouched stretch of coastline, with a 180-degree view of the ocean from each of eight outback-style cabins, cooled by sea breezes. It is a place, as its promotional material says, "where time is measured in sunsets and tides."

—Perth, Australia, January 1, 2006

A Chinese Jewel in Melbourne, Striving Toward Perfection

The flower drum, so called because it is shaped like a Chinese flower vase, is one of the world's oldest musical instruments. It is depicted on shells from the Shang dynasty, which ended around 1050 B.C.

The Flower Drum, Melbourne's and maybe Australia's most famous restaurant, has not been around quite that long. It dates only from 1975, but 28 years is an eon in a country even more obsessed with the new, the innovative and the fashionable than the United States, and deeply skeptical of institutions like the Flower Drum that are universally described as "great."

Gilbert Lau, the attentive, impeccably attired host, is the soul of the place. Its founder and former owner, he still comes to work several days a week, greeting old friends, suggesting a menu, inspecting plates as they emerge from the kitchen. The Flower Drum is Mr. Lau's monument, and it may well be the best Chinese restaurant anywhere, as its partisans believe.

Whatever it takes to please his customers, old and new, Mr. Lau has been ready to do: traveling to Hong Kong three or four times a year in search of inspiration, often buying luxury ingredients there for his elaborate Chinese New Year dinners; working until 4 a.m. night after night to perfect a new tangerine-skin and preserved-plum sauce for duck; importing exotic dried mushrooms from Japan; stocking no fewer than 11 teas; clearing dishes when the waiters are busy; even donning a Santa Claus cap in the days before Christmas.

"I've always thought that people are entitled to the kind of food and service they expect, not some of the time but all of the time," he told me over lunch. "When I was a young waiter, I'd say to myself, 'That's not right.' I decided then that one day I'd serve the kind of dishes that I had grown up eating."

And so he does, dishes marked by balance, subtlety, transparency of flavor and a disarming simplicity.

The Flower Drum's menu is fundamentally Cantonese, but open to outside influences. It capitalizes on the enormous range of prime ingredients available here, especially sparklingly fresh fish from the pristine waters surrounding this island continent. Among the house favorites are fish without chips, Antipodean style: crisply fried whiting, a cold-water species with firm, flaky flesh, and crayfish (or spiny lobster) with butter sauce.

Dishes from other parts of China further enrich the repertory: fork-tender fillet of grain-fed beef with an electrifying Sichuan pepper sauce, gossamer Shanghai dumplings filled with chicken or crab and magnificently lacquered Peking duck, which few customers fail to order; the restaurant sells 40 to 50 ducks every day.

Nothing is overblown. Like the service, the cooking is fastidious, allowing the quality of the raw materials to shine through, in keeping with the Cantonese principles that Mr. Lau learned as a boy in his parents' restaurant in Taishan, a village about three hours' drive from Canton. He was born there in 1942, a Year of the Horse.

His was a far-flung family, and he is not its first member to live in Australia. His great-grandfather came here during the great gold rush of the 1840s and 1850s, walking for many days from the coast to the mines at Bendigo and finding work there as a cook and laundryman. Mr. Lau himself came to Australia for the first time in 1957 for a family reunion and then, as he said, "just gradually moved here."

There is no dearth of restaurant choice in Melbourne. Old standbys continue to excel, like the Richmond Hill Café and Larder, with a special glass-walled room for aging cheeses, overseen by Australia's *gros fromage*, Will Studd. Some middle-aged places are better than ever, including Geoff Lindsay's ever-inventive Pearl, where you can eat dishes like watermelon salad with tomato jelly and feta or wok-fried meat from pearl oysters, deliciously dressed with soy and ginger, all served by cheeky waiters. New spots open every week, like Dining Room 211, whose chef, Andrew McConnell, learned his lessons thoroughly at the helm of Shanghai's wonderful M on the Bund.

Yet it was the Flower Drum, not some blast of culinary fresh air, that won *Australian Gourmet Traveller's* coveted Restaurant of the Year award in 2003. And for 2004, the Good Food Guide, published by the *Melbourne Age*, gave three toques, its top rating, to the Flower Drum, as well as to Ezard at Adelphi and Ondine, a couple of sleek, new, heavily hyped entries that emphasize hip and happy 21st-century cuisine.

In a way, the second was the greater achievement because this year Mr. Lau ceded the restaurant to his employees, headed by Anthony Liu, the head chef, who came here from Hong Kong 21 years ago. I had heard rumors, before arriving in Melbourne, that the sale was prompted by a gambling debt (Mr. Lau has been known to have a flutter). Not so, he assured me.

"I was very tired," he said, making a gesture of resignation with his slim, expressive hands. "I had a long run, and my sons are not interested in the business. In the early years I worked all the time, never a day off. I settled in at 90 hours a week for a while, and then I cut that to lunch and dinner, six days a week.

"You know, that doesn't leave much time to do other things."

As we worked our way through several plates of food, including the whiting, served with a small dish of salt that had been toasted with herbs, and a couple of soupy, thin-walled dumplings filled with King Island crab, red vinegar and ginger, he laid out his philosophy of food for me.

"I don't try to save money on ingredients," Mr. Lau said. "We try to sell what came in today, what's superb. If they want chicken, I'll serve them the best chicken I can, but I want to go beyond that, into rare ingredients. Like farmed abalone. We do it with blue swimmer crab and turmeric. Wood pigeon. Fish you don't see much, like Murray River cod and three-inch John Dory.

"I try to be as authentic as possible, but I'm privileged. We have beautiful ingredients here, with beautiful flavors, and I've traveled for years, not just to China but all over Asia, Canada, the United States, Europe, visiting markets and eating in restaurants. It has knocked down a lot of barriers, and I've learned. Like adding a touch of sherry to the hoisin sauce, to make it a bit lighter."

The food kept coming. Smoky Wagyu beef arrived, as tender as veal, a single piece cooked slowly in a wok for 12 to 15 minutes, then thinly sliced. Mr. Lau served me, choosing this piece, rejecting that, and arranging my plate with infinite care. A lamb clay pot also appeared, a favorite of the boss's, starring a cheap cut of Australia's favorite meat, called the flap, made tender by long cooking in moist heat, with fermented bean curd that tasted vaguely like cheese, and spinach plunged into the broth for just a moment. Delicious. So delicious that customers from Hong Kong come in and order 20 pounds to go.

We finished with one of those "rare ingredients," juicy chunks of sweet, fresh Golden Circle pineapple from a plantation in Queensland. Most of the crop is canned.

Marked by a purple sign, the Flower Drum stands in an alley in an unfashionable part of Melbourne. Its neighbors are a polyglot assortment of restaurants, none distinguished: Nyonya, serving Malaysian food; the Korea Palace; and the Hofbrauhaus, an outpost of Teutonic gastronomy.

You walk into the door and find yourself in a tiny lobby, much like the one at the Tour d'Argent in Paris. A young woman checks your reservation, then ushers you into an elevator. The sense of occasion is palpable. (Even after so many years, dinner reservations are hard to come by. The restaurant accommodates 200 diners a day, 50 at lunch and 150 at dinner. Saturday nights are booked up three months in advance.)

Upstairs is a single large room, roomy yet somehow intimate, with well-spaced tables, dressed with starched white cloths. A tomato-red deep-pile carpet covers the floor, and three dozen blood-red roses fill a vase. Chinese objets d'art are carefully placed, a Ching monochrome here and a gilded screen there. It is a little faded-looking, comfortingly without style.

On a dinner visit with my wife, Betsey, Mr. Lau was off. But the service was flawless, directed by Kevin Wong, the new general manager, a man with the build of a linebacker who has been working at the restaurant for 27 years.

Several of the 30-odd waiters, those assigned to our table and those just passing by, stopped to engage us in small talk, "just like geishas," as Betsey said. I remembered Mr. Lau's comments: "Your boss is your customers. You look after them, they look after you. You have to talk with them. You have to deduce what their backgrounds are and what their boundaries may be."

Out in the kitchen, the 20-man brigade, including four at the woks, two at the deep fryer, two handling steaming and fish, one chopping and one checking the timing, was in equally good form. First dish out was a small crayfish, raw. The translucent meat had been excavated from the tail, then reassembled and displayed on the plate with the crayfish head. The colors were spectacular, pure white flesh adjoining orange head. The flavor was subtle and sweet, the texture rich and lustrous.

I know a thing or two (well, maybe not that many) about Australian wine, but the extravagant, world-spanning list at the Flower Drum had plenty to teach me. With a little prompting, I settled on an unusual blend, chardonnay (a Burgundian grape, of course) and roussanne, from the Rhône Valley, with the crayfish; it was called Nantua Les Deux and came from the Giaconda vineyard, in Butterworth, Victoria. Terra incognita to me, but very well made, with plenty of acidity to balance the sweetness of the shellfish. Then another new acquaintance, a gracefully balanced pinot noir from TarraWarra in the Yarra Valley, also in Victoria.

The stylish, fruity pinot went well with the other five-star dish of our dinner, a boned and roasted rack of lamb with herbs and scallions, the meat with a slightly sweet edge, which made it an ideal partner for the soft, yeasty bread that came along with it.

Everywhere I looked, we saw something on someone else's table that we wanted, but we ended with beefy noodle soup—"calms the stomach," Mr. Wong said—and dark, potent *pu-erh* tea from near Kunming, in southwest China, which strikes me as Asia's eloquent answer to European digestifs.

—Melbourne, Australia, December 24, 2003

INDEX